STO

ALLEN COUNTY PUBLIC LIBRARY

P9-ELH-212

Command	Type	Reference	Meaning
LINE	$\mathcal{FLAP}$	8.3	Skip a line in the printout
LIST	$\mathcal{FLAP}$	8.3	Begin listing assembled commands
LSR	mnem	9	Long shift of registers A and Q
MCDEF	$\mathcal{FLAP}$	6.2	Begin macro prototype definition
MCDUP	$\mathcal{FLAP}$	8.1	Duplicate the defined sequence within the macro
MCEND	$\mathcal{FLAP}$	6.2	End the macro prototype definition
MCNTRCT	$\mathcal{FLAP}$	8.3	Stop listing the steps within a macro call
MCSTOP	$\mathcal{FLAP}$	6.6	End sequence of nested macros
MCSYMB	$\mathcal{FLAP}$	8.6	Prefix assembler created symbols with *address*
MCEXPND	$\mathcal{FLAP}$	8.3	List all step within a macro call
MLR	mnem	12	Multiply (A) by (M) and place rounded result in A
MUL	mnem	12	Multiply (A) by (M) and place result in the combined registers, $A \cup Q$
NMM	mnem	24	Subtract M from (n) and place in n
NPM	mnem	24	Add M to (n) and place in n
NOOP	mnem	14	Do nothing—continue to next command at $I + 1$
NRSRV	$\mathcal{FLAP}$	5.3	Change the number of cells reserved for *label* from *address 1* to *address 2*
OPEN	$\mathcal{IOCS}$	9.7	Open *file* or *list* of files
ORG	$\mathcal{FLAP}$	5.3	Set the origin of the object program to *address*
ORTA	mnem	6	Perform logical *OR* to (M) and (A) and place in A
ORTM	mnem	6	Perform logical *OR* to (M) and (A) and place in M
PAGE	$\mathcal{FLAP}$	8.3	List next step of the assembled program on the next page
PAUSE	$\mathcal{FOREMAN}$	11.9	Stop and restart after operator presses button
POOL	$\mathcal{IOCS}$	9.5	Establish pool called *name* of *number* buffers each of *size* words
PRINT	$\mathcal{FOREMAN}$	11.4	There are *number* entries. For each transfer to the printer *words* words starting at *start* and advance to a new line if ENDLINE is present in entry
READ	mnem	31	Read information into memory
READ	$\mathcal{IOCS}$	10.1	Read *file*; go to proper exit when exception arises
REWIND	mnem	33	Rewind designated file
REWIND	$\mathcal{IOCS}$	10.9	Rewind *file*
RGN	$\mathcal{FLAP}$	5.3	Define region
ROLLBACK	$\mathcal{IOCS}$	10.8	Make a complete dump entry onto the rollback file
RSRV	$\mathcal{FLAP}$	5.3	Reserve a block called *label* of *address* cells
SAVE	$\mathcal{FLAP}$	7.3	Insert index and indicator saving sequence in object program
SBA	mnem	11	Subtract the absolute value of (M) from the accumulator
SET	$\mathcal{FLAP}$	8.2	Assign *address* to *label*
SKIPABLOCK	$\mathcal{IOCS}$	10.8	Skip a block on *file*; go to *exit* when *EoT* is met
SKIPFILE	$\mathcal{IOCS}$	10.8	Skip *number* files on *file*
SLr	mnem	7	Enter M zeros leftward into register r
SRr	mnem	7	Enter M zeros rightward into register r
STOP	mnem	14	Stop
SUB	mnem	11	Subtract the contents of M from the accumulator
TDN	mnem	30	Tally down index n; if it is zero continue to $I + 1$, otherwise jump to M
TUN	mnem	29	Tally up index n; if it is zero continue to $I + 1$, otherwise jump to M
UCJ	mnem	15	Jump to M
UJIT	mnem	40	Jump to M and ignore index tag
UNLIST	$\mathcal{FLAP}$	8.3	Stop listing the assembled commands
WRITE	mnem	32	Write information from memory
WRITE	$\mathcal{IOCS}$	10.1	Write file; go to proper exit when exception arises
XAN	mnem	22	Transfer accumulator to index n
XMN	mnem	21	Put (M) in index n

(continued inside back cover)

DEC 27 '65

COMPUTER SOFTWARE

Programming Systems
for Digital Computers

PRENTICE-HALL INTERNATIONAL, INC., *London*
PRENTICE-HALL OF AUSTRALIA, PTY., LTD., *Sydney*
PRENTICE-HALL OF CANADA, LTD., *Toronto*
PRENTICE-HALL OF INDIA (PRIVATE) LTD., *New Delhi*
PRENTICE-HALL OF JAPAN, INC., *Tokyo*

COMPUTER SOFTWARE

Programming Systems
for Digital Computers

IVAN FLORES

Computer Consultant

Associate Professor of Electrical Engineering
Stevens Institute of Technology

PRENTICE-HALL, INC., Englewood Cliffs, N.J.

© 1965 by
PRENTICE-HALL, INC.
Englewood Cliffs, N.J.

All rights reserved. No part of this book may
be reproduced in any form, by mimeograph or
any other means, without permission in writing
from the publisher.

Library of Congress Catalog Card Number 65-21800
Printed in the United States of America

C-16582

1332435

PREFACE

Here is an advanced programming book which builds software before your very eyes. The purpose of the book is threefold

- examine the various kinds of software
- note generally how they are used
- observe the design principles employed in current and future systems.

The approach assumes a basic knowledge of programming, equivalent to that presented in *Computer Programming*.† This knowledge is needed to understand how sequences required for software are built and how the book incorporates them in subroutines to make larger routines and, finally, to make a complete system.

The book provides basic information for a programmer entering the software field. It will broaden the horizons of the systems programmer who is knowledgeable about specific systems by presenting general principles applicable to all programming systems. A systems programmer often works on a specific aspect of a small portion of a programming system. A view of the whole forest makes us appreciate the trees more.

† Ivan Flores, *Computer Programming*. Englewood Cliffs, N.J.: Prentice-Hall, Inc., 1966.

The background required for the book is reviewed in the first three chapters to fill any gaps in the reader's experience and to assure uniform terminology. Programming experience on a real computer is helpful but not necessary.

The difficult question is whether to use the assembly language of an actual computer or to make one up. An actual language, though new to the reader, would be useful since he might encounter this language in an actual machine. However, it brings with it all the inconsistencies and poor judgment which occur in actual design. To assure a systematic and consistent set of mnemonics an assembly language was designed called FLAP, for FLores Assembly Program. The mnemonics are close to those used in real machines.

Occasional reference is required to a machine on which the FLAP mnemonics might be used. The acronym FLAPJAC is given this machine because it is an Automatic Computer which executes FLAP. (The J is for euphony.)

The text covers most programming systems except compilers. Assembly language is emphasized because that is the language in which most programming systems are built. Further, many running programs are constructed in assembly language and even compiled programs are debugged in assembly language. The study of compilers is omitted because the subject could not be adequately covered together with the other topics. It entails detailed considerations of language, semantics and syntax.

Problems accompany each chapter to improve the reader's understanding. A preliminary discussion of software and the general plan of the book are presented in Chapter 1 and hence omitted here.

The author acknowledges the thoughtful help extended him from many quarters. The manuscript was examined critically by Andre Godefroy, Burton Walder and Julian Reitman; Henry Lazowski of Univac helped with both ideas and published materials; Amy Mastrogiovanni of IBM helped unearth documents about the 7094 System. Two fine secretaries labored over the manuscript: Patricia Maestri and Doris Beeler.

I. F.

CONTENTS

COMPUTER SOFTWARE

Programming Systems
for Digital Computers

1

INTRODUCTION

1.1 SOFTWARE

Definitions

It is not an easy matter to delineate just what **software** is. The term is applied here to a program whose purpose is not to solve a given problem or to operate an accounting system but to facilitate the use of the computer in one of these applications. As such the program is usually quite large.

An alternative way to define software is by extension, by enumerating all the program types we wish to include. These types are named here and defined later:

- translator
- supervisor
- input-output control system
- monitor or foreman
- service systems
- loader

1

Originator

In general, software systems are made by the manufacturers of the computers. In the old days a customer would buy or lease a computer and then figure out how to apply it to a problem. He has begun to realize that software is one of the most important, if not the most important, constituent of a computer. He now demands good software with his computer purchase. The manufacturer must design the best operating systems to keep his computer running and competitive. A new set of systems is required for each new computer he produces even when the systems are compatible with other machines in the line. Each software system requires many man-years to design, create, and debug. It is the job of the system programmer employed by the manufacturer to make these programming systems.

Occasionally in a large installation, the software furnished by the manufacturer may be inadequate, inefficient or unreliable. If he can afford it, the user may design and produce his own software which can be aimed at his own special needs and problems. This is costly and usually done only by very large users.

A relatively new source of software is the specialized software design group. Programmers have gone into business producing software which seems to have definite advantages over that produced by the computer manufacturers. It is aimed at specific machines and must produce some gain to induce a customer to purchase such a system. It cannot be too expensive or it will be priced out of the field.

Where Is It?

It is rare today that we find an installation where the computer does not have some software in it at all times, keeping it running efficiently. The most constant resident in the computer memory is the *supervisor*, whose purpose is to sequence from one job to another and to keep the installation running smoothly, free of errors.

It is possible that a zealous program might clobber the supervisor making it unavailable. Therefore a copy of the supervisor is usually kept accessible to the computer so that the operator can resuscitate the supervisor when needed. Still another copy is usually kept in a safe in the installation in case the intermediate copy is somehow destroyed. A master master is available at the manufacturer who makes copies of it for the customer. Other software is usually found on a system library tape and copies can be entered into the memory by the supervisor as needed. The memory copy may be erased to free the memory for other uses.

Does Software Change?

One might expect that a programming system once fixed would remain so indefinitely. Not so—all big programming systems are subject to occasional change. It is hard, and sometimes impossible, to get them completely debugged. Users may report errors which the manufacturer corrects or they may suggest changes to improve the effectiveness of software. As the manufacturer issues such changes, they must be entered into the master by some sort of editing program which is also considered software.

The Systems Programmer

The objective of the problem programmer is to write programs to solve specific problems or create sets of programs to fulfill a specific EDP objective. He may write his programs in an assembly language but more often he uses a procedure-oriented language such as FORTRAN or COBOL. In either case he must have recourse to software to do the translation. Although he uses software extensively either directly or indirectly, he has little incentive to know its design. Actually when he becomes acquainted with the operation and structure of the translator, for instance, he can provide better and more efficiently translated source statements.

The system programmer deals mainly with assembly language, for compilers use languages oriented to mathematical or commercial procedures, not to the language manipulations required by software. He understands the programming concepts used by the problem programmer who employs them in structuring the software. He needs to know what each system does, how to use the systems and their principles of construction.

1.2 PLAN OF THE BOOK

Summary

The major portions of the book fall into the following categories:

- review of fundamentals
- programming concepts—summary
- introduction to software
- the assembler
- IOCS
- the foreman
- various service systems
- the supervisor
- the loader

Fundamentals

The chapter on fundamentals discusses the general plan of the computer and its subsystems. It introduces a specific set of commands using mnemonics called FLAP. These commands are comparable to a subset of those provided by the IBM 7090 but the mnemonics are different. The chapter also covers indexing and various methods of addressing.

Programming Concepts

This chapter reviews the principles of construction of subroutines and loops, and proposes linkage and calling sequence conventions used in the remainder of the book. Lists are very important to all branches of programming and especially software. A symbology is developed for presenting list concepts. A uniform data-organization terminology is developed and presented next. Buffering is unavoidable in large computers with simultaneous IO (Input-Output) device operation. Various systems are discussed leading up to the buffer pool, the most advanced concept required for a complete IOCS (Input-Output Control System). The principles of list structures discussed earlier are now put into use.

Assemblers

Three kinds of assemblers are discussed, ranging from the very simplest to the most complete; the latter includes pseudos, macros, and quasis. The mnemonics for these are presented, keeping as close to convention as possible. Many features are discussed and the emphasis is on how assemblers are designed and special features incorporated into them.

IOCS

Having covered the basic principles of assemblers, it is possible to examine IOCS design. A complete set of commands and subcommands with automatic buffering is described in detail. This provides a neat and clean way for the programmer to direct IO traffic. The role of the foreman implicit in the IOCS discussion is brought to light in Chapter 11. Herein are presented the emergency procedures for getting the computer out of difficulty and for managing terminations and initiations which are concommitant to simultaneous operation.

Others

The need and use of service systems are presented in Chapter 12 and then several are constructed relying on IOCS commands and subcommands to implement them. The picture is almost complete and the role of the supervisor and loader can be tackled and disposed of promptly.

1.3 TUTORIAL SYSTEM

Standard

The explanation of programming and programming systems is simplified if we have a standard command, command structure, and word length. We might take an actual computer and use the commands provided for it and its hardware structure. If the reader were not familiar with this computer, as a bonus at the end of the book, he would have a knowledge of it and probably be able to program in this assembly language.

The difficulty with this approach is that we would be stuck with the mnemonics of the particular system. This would mean perpetuating faults inherent in such a system. Although mnemonics are designed primarily for human use no human engineering has been employed in their design. No perfect set exists.

The difficulty with some mnemonics is that they suggest the wrong thing. Several computers use the mnemonic TRA to signify a jump. This originated from the designation *TRAnsfer of control*. When first encountered it suggests transfer. It is certainly unclear except by usage that this is not a transfer of information.

It would be presumptuous to say that the set of mnemonics presented here is near perfection. At least some of the faults evident in other mnemonics have been omitted!

Mnemonics and FLAP

Chapter 2 introduces mnemonics. Wherever common and accepted ones make sense they are incorporated. Alternates are proposed when they are more suggestive. After all, the purpose of a mnemonic is to arouse from the user's memory an association, preferably the right one.

Since mnemonics are the kernel of an assembly language, an acronym for FLAP—FLores Assembly Program—is applied to emphasize the resemblance between them and FAP (FORTRAN Assembly Program) associated with the IBM 7090 series. There are even other variations on FAP such as *BELFAP*.

An Automatic Computer to go with FLAP suggests the acronym FLAPJAC where the J is included for euphony (and cuteness—all acronyms are supposed to be cute).

FLAPJAC

The computer associated with FLAP has a 36 bit word because this is a convenient size for both alphabetic and numeric information; it also complies with the IBM 7090 characteristics. In addition, it has all the addressing and index capacity described in Chapter 2, which makes it quite versatile. Other features are presented as required.

Some of the addressing and indexing characteristics can be achieved through programming methods, but it is certainly simpler to apply them if they are assumed to be present in the hardware system.

Expanded FLAP

The FLAP system is expanded in Chapters 5, 6, and 7 to be consistent with current assembler design and to furnish other types of assembly commands to be used in exercises included in these chapters. Pseudos, macros, and quasis are described and developed in those chapters. Their format and nature are similar, where possible, to that found in most other assembly languages.

PROBLEMS

1.1 (a) What is software?
 (b) Where is it?
 (c) Who makes it?

1.2 What accounts for changes in software?

1.3 (a) Name the major software systems.
 (b) What are their functions?

2

FUNDAMENTALS

2.1 COMPUTER SUBSYSTEMS

Organization of the Computer

The organization of the computer is illustrated pictorially in Fig. 2.1.1. The major parts which comprise the computer system are referred to as **subsystems** because their role is major and they do a complete task independently of the other parts. Thus an input operation delegated to an input unit is done independently of any of the other computer subsystems. The minor parts which make up the subsystem are referred to as units, either functional, operational, or logical.

THE MEMORY SUBSYSTEM

The memory subsystem is central. It receives all information entering from the outside world and passes all information over to output. It holds information to be processed, receives processed information and holds program information for the control unit.

INPUT AND OUTPUT

Hereafter we refer to the combined input and output functions simply as **IO**. The input devices bring in information from intermediate media:

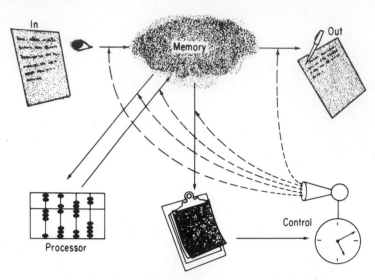

FIGURE 2.1.1. The subsystems which make up the computer system.

punchcards, magnetic tape, paper tape, CRAM, etc. The output devices transmit information and prepare new intermediate media as well as supply information to the high speed printer for immediate transcription.

PROCESSOR

The processor performs two major functions:

• arithmetic • editing

Arithmetic (addition, subtraction, multiplication, and division) is done with the assumption that the numbers involved are in the form peculiar to the command. Software problems are not generally arithmetical but are of a data handling nature, so a few arithmetic commands suffice.

Editing operations which the processor performs consist of:

• deleting
• appending
• formatting

CONTROL

The control sequences through the memory area, determining each task the computer is to execute. It then delegates this task to the required subsystem. It is responsible for delegation, timing and supervision.

Memory

The major functional units of the memory are interrelated as shown in Fig. 2.1.2. The **memory address register (MAR)** stores the address of the datum of interest. The **memory data register (MDR)** holds the datum to be recalled or receives the datum to be memorized. The **memory cells** are the actual storage elements. The **memory control unit (MCU)** supervises the activity and receives and produces control signals.

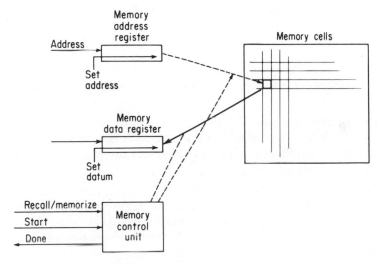

FIGURE 2.1.2. The memory subsystem.

The three functions of the memory are:

- storage   • recall   • memorization

STORAGE

The storage function maintains information for later recall even if the equipment has been turned off in the interim.

RECALL

When supplied with an address and asked to recall, the memory subsystem finds the datum associated with this address and enters it in the memory data register. An **address** distinguishes a particular physical cell in memory by a numeric or alphabetic designation; it is intransigent for the cell. The **content** of a cell is what is presently situated at that position in memory. Its identity is maintained until a new datum is entered there, destroying the old datum

To recall,

- an address is supplied to the memory address register
- the control unit is requested to recall
- a start signal is given

The MCU finds the cell from the address supplied and places the cell contents in the memory data register. It indicates that the datum is now available by issuing a *completion* signal.

MEMORIZE

To memorize information,

- an address is supplied the memory address register
- the datum to be placed at the address is entered into the MDR
- the control unit is requested to memorize
- a start signal is given

The control unit finds the cell and enters the datum from the memory data register into that cell. It then issues a completion signal.

Most memories are locked out when they are recalling or memorizing so that any request goes unanswered during that period and both registers are inaccessible.

Processor

The construction of the processor may be oversimplified to the point illustrated in Fig. 2.1.3. Notice that it then appears very much like the keyboard of a desk calculator. Three registers hold quantities for processing or which have been processed. In FLAPJAC the three registers are designated by the letters A, D and Q.

The processor control unit is notified of a function the processor is to perform and when it should start performing it. It issues a signal when the function is complete.

Besides particular functions which the processor performs we are interested in how information flows between the processor and other units. Data may be transferred into a register from memory, between registers of the processor, and from a register to memory.

IO

The impressive speed of the computer makes one realize how poorly the human is matched to it. It is impossible for the human to communicate directly to the computer without slowing it down tremendously except in the case of time-shared systems which are now being developed. To improve the match, information is accumulated by the human using some intermediate medium. It is then read into the computer at a much higher rate—one more matched to the computer's capability.

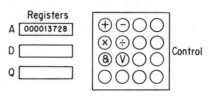

FIGURE 2.1.3. How the control subsystem views the processor.

Processed information for direct consumption can be produced by the computer on the high-speed printer which is capable of printing 300 to 2000 lines per minute with 120 to 160 characters per line. Information to be reentered into the computer can be placed on an intermediate medium.

Memory is central: information from input is entered into the memory and information for output is transmitted from the memory.

2.2   CONTROL AND COMMANDS

Program in Memory

Programming for anything but an internally programmed computer involves a different discipline and does not lend itself to the use of software. Hence it is mandatory that our program be stored in memory. A description of each task to be performed is found in a command word. A series of these words is stored, in general, in successive cells in memory. The control subsystem sequences through successive cells to get descriptions of the successive tasks it is to perform.

A complete task description can require a variable number of bits according to its extensiveness. The way in which these bits are formatted depends on the manufacturer and the computer. To facilitate our discussion, we assume that one command is stored in exactly one computer word. The control subsystem obtains and interprets successive command words.

Control Subsystem

Figure 2.2.1 illustrates pictorially the units and operations of the control subsystem.

The computer operation is divided into two cycles:

- fetch   • execute

During the **fetch** cycle the next command is obtained and brought to the control subsystem. During the **execute** cycle the command is interpreted and performed.

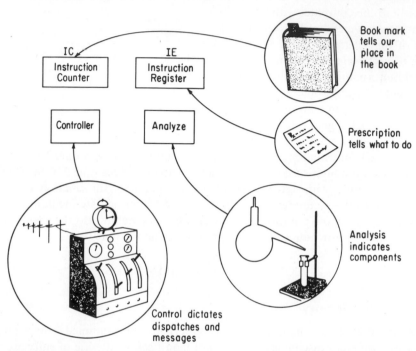

Book mark tells our place in the book

Prescription tells what to do

Analysis indicates components

Control dictates dispatches and messages

FIGURE 2.2.1. Tasks of the functional units of the control subsystem.

The control subsystem contains four functional units. The **instruction counter (IC)** stores the location of the command now being executed. The **instruction register (IR)** stores the command itself. The **analyzer** breaks down the command into its component parts. It produces control signals which operate switches to provide the proper information flow for the command. The **controller**, the control unit of the control subsystem, examines signals provided by the analyzer and then delegates subtasks to the subsystems in the proper sequence. It provides timing, supervises the activity, and delegates at the proper moment.

FETCH

The **fetch** cycle is outlined in Fig. 2.2.2. The address in the instruction counter is transferred to the memory address register, and the controller initiates a *recall* cycle. The memory produces a datum; this is the next instruction. The controller supervises its transfer to the instruction register.

EXECUTE

The command in the instruction register is interpreted by the analyzer and the relevant subtasks are delegated by the controller in the **execute** cycle. In so doing, a memory cycle is frequently required to *recall* or *memorize* a

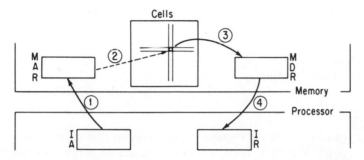

FIGURE 2.2.2. Operation of the memory and the control subsystem during the *fetch* cycle.

datum. The address of the cell concerned is included in the command word. This portion of the command word is supplied to the memory when its use is associated with the instruction.

Machine-Language Command

The command is the unit of work for the computer. The way the command word is broken up and what it contains is of vital importance to the program. The format of our command word is:

$$\text{task, tag} \qquad \text{address, number of characters} \qquad (2.2.1)$$

In presenting a command for description, we use small letters to distinguish a class of items. When discussing this class in the text, the class name is italicized.

A binary combination distinguishes each task and appears at *task* (2.2.1). **Tags** are bits for indicating when indexing is to be performed and with which index register, and the kind of addressing to be used. The address of the operand that takes part in this command appears at *address*. In the character-oriented machine, the number of characters associated with a given command must be set forth in the command word and appears at *number of characters*. Hereafter we disregard this qualifier and consider only fixed word length machines. The principles evolved apply equally to variable word length machines as long as an entry is made in the *number of characters* position.

Command Description

In what form can we describe what occurs in the execution of a command?

- verbal
- mnemonic
- arrow notation

VERBAL

Words can describe the transfer of information that takes place and how it is processed. However, brevity is not a feature of verbal description and we seek one which is more terse.

MNEMONIC

A set of three to six letters can suggest the processing carried on. Thus ADD indicates that addition is to be performed by the computer. It would be unwieldy, if not impossible, to provide a text containing only binary command codes or even decimal command codes. Hence we devise a cross between assembly language and machine language. It uses commands in the format:

$$\text{mnemonic, tag} \qquad \text{address} \qquad\qquad (2.2.2)$$

We can obtain the actual machine language command code by replacing *mnemonic* by its corresponding bit set, *tag* by its proper bit value, *address* by the bit equivalent of the decimal address and by properly formating all these bits into the command word. This simple job is done by a clerk or by the absolute assembler mentioned in Section 4.1. We handle these commands as though they were actually machine-language commands. We distinguish them in this text by Gothic type, *viz*, ADD.

ARROW NOTATION

Table 2.2.1 summarizes the arrow notation used in the text. Its meaning becomes evident with use.

TABLE 2.2.1   Symbols Used in Arrow Descriptions

Symbol	Meaning
A, D, Q	Register names
R, R′	One of register names A, D, or Q
M	Operand address
P	Immediate address
N	Index register
I	Current instruction address
( )	Contents of
[ ]	Address of
→	Enter into (information transfer)
⇒	Get next command from (jump to)

2.3   PROCESSOR COMMANDS

The Kinds of Commands

In this section we discuss commands which affect the processor. These commands fall into three classes:

- transfer
  - ∗ to   ∗ from   ∗ between
- arithmetic
- editing
  - ∗ shift   ∗ logic

Transfer commands move information which is handled by the processor. Arithmetic and editing commands do the actual processing.

TRANSFER

The transfer mnemonics are found on the first four lines of Table 2.3.1. In the entry transfer XMR, the character X indicates that a transfer is taking place, M indicates that the source is a memory cell, and R indicates that the destination is a register in the processor. An arrow notation shows that the contents of the memory cell with address M are copied into the register R.

To distinguish the memory cell in question, its address appears at *address*. Throughout the text where machine language commands are encountered, we use a three digit decimal number to designate one of a thousand cells which might be addressed.

TABLE 2.3.1   FLores Assembly Program (FLAP) Mnemonics

Line		Mnemonic	Operation	Mnemonic	Operation	Indexable
	Transfers					
1	To	XMR	$(M) \rightarrow R$			Yes
2	From	XRM	$(R) \rightarrow M$			Yes
3	Between	XRR′	$(R) \rightarrow R′$			No
4	Special	X0M	$0 \rightarrow M,$	X0R	$0 \rightarrow R$	Yes
	Logic					
5		ANDTA	$(A) \,\&\, (M) \rightarrow A$	ANDTM	$(A) \,\&\, (M) \rightarrow M$	Yes
6		ORTA	$(A) \lor (M) \rightarrow A$	ORTM	$(A) \lor (M) \rightarrow M$	Yes
	Shifts					
7	Out	SRR	$0 \xrightarrow{M} R$	SLR	$R \xleftarrow{M} 0$	No
8	Around	ERR	$(R) \xrightarrow{M} R$	ELR	$R \xleftarrow{M} (R)$	No
9	Long	LSR	$(A) \xrightarrow{M} Q;\ (Q) \xrightarrow{M} A$			No
	Arithmetic					
10		ADD	$(A) + (M) \rightarrow A$	ADA	$(A) + \lvert(M)\rvert \rightarrow A$	Yes
11		SUB	$(A) - (M) \rightarrow A$	SBA	$(A) - \lvert(M)\rvert \rightarrow A$	Yes
12		MLR	$(M) \times (D) \rightarrow A$	MUL	$(M) \times (D) \rightarrow A, Q$	Yes
13		DIV	$(A) \,/\, (M) \rightarrow Q$			No
	Decision and action					
	Unconditional					
14		NOOP	$\Rightarrow I + 1$ $\Rightarrow M$	STOP	$\neq$	No
15		UCJ	$\Rightarrow M$			Yes
	Decision					
16		CMP	$(A) > (M)\ 1 \rightarrow G$ $0 \rightarrow E, L$		$(A) = (M)\ 1 \rightarrow E$ $0 \rightarrow G, L$ $(A) < (M)\ 1 \rightarrow L$ $0 \rightarrow G, E$	Yes
	Conditional					
17		JOG	$G = 1 \Rightarrow M;\ G = 0 \Rightarrow I + 1$			Yes
18		JOE	$E = 1 \Rightarrow M;\ E = 0 \Rightarrow I + 1$			Yes

No.	Category	Mnemonic				Indexable
19		JOL	L = 1 ⇒ M; L = 0 ⇒ I + 1			Yes
20		CAS	(A) > (M) ⇒ I + 1	(A) = (M) ⇒ I + 2	(A) < (M) ⇒ I + 3	No
	Index manipulations					
21	Fill	XMN,n	$(M_M) \rightarrow n$	XNM	$(n) \rightarrow M_M$	No
22		XAN,n	$(A_M) \rightarrow n$	XNA	$(n) \rightarrow A_M$	No
23		XPN,n	M → n			No
24	Increment	NPP,n	(n) + M → n	NMP,n	(n) − M → n	No
25	Compare	CMPN,n	(n) > M 1 → G, 0 → E, L	(n) = M 1 → E, 0 → G, L	(n) < M 1 → L, 0 → E, G	No
26	Compare and jump	JNP,n	(n) ≥ 0 ⇒ M	(n) < 0 ⇒ I + 1		No
27		JNNZ,n	(n) ≠ 0 ⇒ M	(n) = 0 ⇒ I + 1		No
28		JNN,n	(n) < 0 ⇒ M	(n) ≥ 0 ⇒ I + 1		No
29	Increment, test, and jump	TUN,n	(n) + 1 → n	(n) < 0 ⇒ M	(n) ≥ 0 ⇒ I + 1	No
30		TDN,n	(n) − 1 → n	(n) > 0 ⇒ M	(n) ≤ 0 ⇒ I + 1	No
	IO					
31		READ	(Input) → M			Yes
32		WRITE	(M) → Output			Yes
33		REWIND	rewind device			No
34		JOIE	indication ⇒ M	no indication ⇒ I + 1		Yes
	Subroutine linkage					
35		JAS	I + 1 → M − 1 ⇒ M			Yes
36		JSR	I → RJR; ⇒ M			Yes
37		JRA	⇒ (RJR) + M			No
38		JSN,n	I → n; ⇒ M			No
	Others					
39		JOO	Overflow = 1 ⇒ M;	Overflow = 0 ⇒ I + 1		Yes
40		UJIT	⇒ M			No

The command to enter the contents of memory cell 365 into the A register has the mnemonic arrow interpretation:

$$\text{XMA} \quad 365 \quad (365) \rightarrow A \qquad (2.3.1)$$

Line 2 of Table 2.3.1 contains the mnemonic to memorize information from a processor register into a memory cell. It is used to store the contents of the Q register in memory cell 234 by:

$$\text{XQM} \quad 234 \quad (Q) \rightarrow 234 \qquad (2.3.2)$$

To pass information from one register in the processor to another we use the mnemonic XRR' in line 3 of Table 2.3.1. Here R is the source register and R' is the destination register. To duplicate the contents of the Q register in the D register we use:

$$\text{XQD} \quad (Q) \rightarrow D \qquad (2.3.3)$$

No address is required; if supplied it is ignored.

Two special commands are used to clear a memory cell or an arithmetic register by entering 0's into that cell or register. To clear memory cell 327 we use:

$$\text{X0M} \quad 327 \quad 0 \rightarrow 327 \qquad (2.3.4)$$

Logic

Logical commands are sometimes referred to as extract and deletion commands. The *AND* function is indicated in the arrow notation by &. When it is applied to two words the resulting word contains 1's only for bits where there are corresponding 1's in each word. When one of the bits in either word is 0, the corresponding bit in the resultant word is 0. This function extracts a desired portion of a word into the destination register.

The destination register for the resultant word can be specified as either the A register or the memory source cell if we specify either ANDTA or ANDTM, respectively. The following is the result of an application of the command ANDTA:

$$(M) = 123456789$$
$$(A) = 000011110$$
$$\text{Result} = 000056780 \qquad (2.3.5)$$

Notice the **1**'s in the A register (2.3.5) which appear in bold print. This indicates that they are not the four-bit code for the digit 1, but instead, four binary 1's.

OR

The logical *OR* function is performed in a similar way. A 1 appears in the resulting word if there is a 1 in the corresponding position in *either* operand word. A 0 appears there only if there is a 0 in the corresponding position in both words. In arrow notation, V indicates the logical *OR*. The result goes to the A register for O RTA and is returned to the memory source cell with O RTM.

Shifts

There are three kinds of shifts:

• end-around   • out   • long

END-AROUND

An end-around shift is indicated by a mnemonic beginning with E. The direction of a shift is distinguished by R for right and L for left. The register to be shifted occupies the last position. The contents of the indicated register are moved in the indicated direction and as characters are pushed out of one end of the register they reenter at the other end. Thus no information is lost; it is merely circularly permuted. The number of characters to be shifted is contained in the operand address of the command, as shown at line 8 of Table 2.3.1. To shift the Q register four places to the right we give the command:

$$ERQ \quad 004 \qquad (Q) \xrightarrow{4} Q \tag{2.3.6}$$

OUT

To discard information, a shift out is performed. For each character moved out in a direction indicated, one 0 is entered in the opposite end. Depending on the computer, this 0 may be four binary 0's, six binary 0's or a character code for *blank*.

The mnemonics for *shift out* start with S; the second letter indicates the direction of shift; the third indicates the register being shifted. To shift out the A register three positions to the left we give the command:

$$SLA \quad 003 \qquad A \xleftarrow{3} 0 \tag{2.3.7}$$

LONG

The long shift may be used to break up a word. It was traditionally used to reposition a double-word product after multiplication and therefore uses a double word register made by juxtaposing the A register on the left with the Q register on the right. For a *long shift right* characters shifted out of the A register on the right enter the Q register on the left; characters coming out of the Q register on the right enter the A register on the left. This is shown on line 9 of Table 2.3.1. To perform a long shift to the right of five places we request:

$$\text{LSR} \quad 005 \qquad (Q) \xrightarrow{5} A; \quad (A) \xrightarrow{5} Q \qquad\qquad (2.3.8)$$

ARITHMETIC

The arithmetic commands are found in lines 10 through 13 of Table 2.3.1. The A register, though not indicated, may actually participate in the command. For instance, in the ADD command the contents of the designated memory cell are passed over to the D register before addition starts. Within the processor the A and D registers are shifted through the adder and the final result is posted to the A register. The details of the other arithmetic commands are discussed elsewhere.†

The muLtiply-and-round command, MLR, will be used in the text and the exercises where multiplication is requested because it produces a single-word product rounded and ready for use.

2.4   REFLEXIVE ACTIONS

The kinds of reflexive actions discussed in this section are:

- unconditional actions
- conditional actions
- decisions
- combinations

A **reflexive action** affects the behavior of the computer with respect to the program rather than doing processing.

Unconditional

An unconditional reflexive action does not depend on the present state of the computer. Three of these actions are designated on lines 14 and 15 of Table 2.3.1. NOOP at step I signifies that no operation is to be performed; we do nothing more than get the next command from cell I + 1.

† cf. *Computer Programming*, Chapter 3.

The **unconditional jump**, UCJ, requests that the controller drop the present sequence of commands to obtain its next command from the location specified in the operand address M.

STOP interrupts the controller completely and requests operator intervention by lighting a signal lamp. In a system where software is present such a command is usually illegal. When the programmer wishes to indicate that his program is completed properly or that it must be terminated because of the detection of an error, he inserts a jump to a software system.

Comparison

Conditional actions are based on the finding of a previous command or the present state of registers in the computer. It is possible to do all programming making reflexive actions dependent only upon comparisons.

A comparison command, CMP, compares the size of two quantities, storing the order relation in three flip-flops contained in the controller and available for reference on other commands. These flip-flops, labeled G, E and L, indicate respectively that the first quantity is greater, equal or less than the second quantity. Only one of these flip-flops is set to 1; the other two are automatically reset to 0.

An order relation is built into the codes for digits as well as for letters. CMP requests the examination of the specified words as though they were straight binary numbers. If the words are really binary-coded decimal numbers or alphabetic information, the result recorded will still be correct if the character codes have the desired order relation. Thus, if the code for A is 010100 and the code for B is 010101, then the comparison order reveals that APPLE comes before BEETLE.

The accumulator contents (first) is compared to the contents of the command operand address (second) as shown in line 16 of Table 2.3.1.

Conditional Jumps

A **conditional jump** requests a jump to M if the flip-flop specified in the command is set; the next command in sequence, $I + 1$, is used otherwise. A variety of conditions can be used to determine whether a jump is performed. One popular condition is the sign of the contents of a given register. The ones we designate in this text depend only upon the result of the last performed comparison. Three such jumps are presented in lines 17 through 19 of Table 2.3.1. If a *jump on equal*, JOE, appears on step 35 specifying cell 279 in the operand position then we jump to cell 279 if the last comparison recorded showed equality; otherwise we get the next command from step 36:

$$035 \quad JOE \quad 279 \quad E = 1 \Rightarrow 279; \quad E = 0 \Rightarrow 036 \quad (2.4.1)$$

It is possible to combine the comparison with the action if the operand addresses can be implied. The *compare and skip* command, CAS, on line 20 of Table 2.3.1 is found on the IBM 709/90/94 and provides an implied action by skipping a number of steps based on the result of the comparison. It would seem that decision and action are achieved in a single command. However, UCJs must appear at I + 1 and I + 2 or else the action is defeated.

2.5 INDEXING

An index register is used to modify the operand address specified in the command, making indexing so useful in loops and array processing. The number of index registers present in today's computers varies from none in the very smallest computers to one hundred or so in large computers. To simplify specification FLAPJAC has nine index registers, one for each of the nine digits from 1 to 9. 0 specifies that no index register is used.

Indexable Commands

A command is **indexable** if an index may be specified to modify the operand address within a command. Such commands take the form:

$$\text{mnemonic, digit, tag} \qquad \text{address} \qquad (2.5.1)$$

Here *digit* is a decimal digit. Thus a nonzero digit specifies the index register corresponding to the digit; if it is zero or blank no index register is specified. The FLAP commands which are indexable are indicated in Table 2.3.1 where *Yes* appears in the right-hand column.

The effective address of the operand for an indexed command is given by:

$$\text{effective address} = address + (\text{index } digit) \qquad (2.5.2)$$

The contents of the index register specified by *digit* is added to *address*.

The ADD command is indexable. An ADD command specifying index 3 and operand address 245 actually adds the contents of cell 272 if index 3 contains 27. This is tersely indicated by:

$$\text{ADD,3} \quad 245 \equiv \text{ADD} \quad 272 \qquad \text{for } (N3) = 027 \qquad (2.5.3)$$

Index Manipulations

The power of the index register can only be exploited if we do other things with it besides using it to modify commands. The tasks that we examine are:

- transfers
- increments
- tests
- combinations

TRANSFERS

A transfer into an index register permits us to set it up for future use for the commands with which it is associated. Transfers out of an index register permit us to save index quantities for future use in other segments of the program.

INCREMENTS

The ability to add or subtract from an index quantity permits us to move up and down within a list that is being processed.

TESTS

Tests which depend upon the index register provide a means for determining when a list has been completely processed.

COMBINATIONS

When one command can replace two or more, the program can be written with less space and can be executed in a shorter time. Combination index commands fulfill several purposes.

Transfers

Transfers between a memory cell and an index register are done using the commands on line 21 of Table 2.3.1. *Digit* specifies the source or destination index register. It does not indicate that the command is *being indexed*. On the contrary, this command is not indexable.

The index register stores only the number of digits or characters required to specify an address. It would be wasteful for the index register to contain a full word. Hence a transfer to or from a memory cell involves only *a portion of the word* contained in that cell. The portion used depends upon the computer and the command word. For FLAPJAC the operand address appears as the three right-hand digits. Therefore these are the three digits in the memory cell that are affected by the transfer. For a transfer into a memory cell, the old contents are replaced by zeros in nonaddress positions. Thus, to store the contents of index 5 in cell 345 we use:

$$\text{XMN,5}\quad 345 \qquad \text{for (N5)} = 123, \qquad 000000123 \to 345 \qquad (2.5.4)$$

To fill an index from the A register or to transfer the contents of an index into the A register, the nonaddress portion of the A register is conserved. This allows us to change only the address portion of a word that is desirable for address alteration.

Since the index register and the address portion of a command are of comparable size it is possible to fill an index register directly from a command word. The operand address portion of the command, then, is the exact quantity to be entered into the index. This is an example of immediate addressing discussed in the next section.

To put 15 into index 3 we use the command:

$$\text{XPN,3}\quad 015 \qquad 15 \to \text{N3} \qquad\qquad (2.5.5)$$

There is no command to transfer the quantity from an index into the program!

Incrementation

The two commands on line 24 of Table 2.3.1 permit us to add or subtract quantities from index registers. The register to be incremented is specified by *digit* as before. The amount by which the register is incremented is given *immediately* in the address portion of the command. In other words, the quantity to be added or subtracted is that which is found in the address portion of the command.

To increase index 7 by 3 we give the command, *iNdex Plus Program*:

$$\text{NPP,7}\quad 003 \qquad \text{(N7)} + 3 \to \text{N7} \qquad\qquad (2.5.6)$$

Reflexive

Reflexive commands relating to index registers can be single or multiple in nature and are of the following type:

- test
- test and act
- increment, test and act

With more complexity, more is implied by the command.

TEST

The index comparison command CMPN tests the contents of index *digit* against the quantity contained in the address portion of the command. The result of the command sets one of the three flip-flops in the controller L, E, or G and resets the other two (as with CMP). To compare the contents of index 3 with 75 we give the command:

$$\text{CMPN,3} \quad 075 \qquad (N3): 75 \qquad\qquad (2.5.7)$$

TEST AND ACT

If the comperand for a test quantity is implied, action may also be specified in the command. The most likely quantity for testing is zero. The three commands on lines 26 through 28 of Table 2.3.1 permit us to test an index and jump if the accompanying condition is *not* met. The *jump index nonzero* command in cell 41 requires us to return to step 37 if index 3 does not contain 0; we continue to step 42 if the index register contains exactly 0:

$$041 \quad \text{JNNZ,3} \quad 037 \qquad (N3) \neq 0 \Rightarrow 37$$
$$(N3) = 0 \Rightarrow 42 \qquad\qquad (2.5.8)$$

INCREMENT TEST AND ACT

For incrementing by 1, a triple combination command may be used. This is useful when we process a listing contained in contiguous cells. The *Tally-Down iNdex* command (TDN) permits us to reduce a positive index toward 0, testing it to see if it is 0, jumping if it is not 0, and continuing to the next command when it is 0. The *Tally-Up iNdex* command (TUN) permits us to increase by 1 a negative index quantity in a similar fashion. These commands are on lines 29 and 30 of Table 2.3.1, and their uses are detailed in Section 3.2.

2.6 ADDRESSING

We shall discuss these kinds of addressing:

- implied
- immediate
- direct
- indirect
- relative
- indexed

Implied Addressing

Every transfer of information has a source and destination. Processing commands usually include a transfer. Therefore we expect that most commands refer to two registers or cells. If the command word has room for only a single address, how can we refer to both source and destination? The answer is that one or both of these is implied in the command. Thus the command XAM addresses the A register as the source of information by **implied addressing**. In fact, both source and destination may be implied; witness XQD.

Another way to imply the source or destination is through the index specification, *digit*. Thus the command XNM addresses by implication an index register; but the particular index register is specified by the digit which follows the command code.

Immediate Addressing

The computer normally deals with operands of a full word length so that such operands cannot be transmitted with the command. However, an operand of address length may be presented in the address portion of the **immediately addressed** command. Thus, index-associated commands often use immediate addressing to fill or increment an index.

Direct Addressing

The normal way to specify an operand is by **direct addressing** using the address of the operand in the command word.

Indirect Addressing

Suppose we know the address of a cell which contains the address of a desired operand. If we want the operand we go to the cell, get the address which is there, and use it to procure the operand. With **indirect addressing,** the address portion of the command contains the address *at which the operand address is stored.*

For direct addressing the operand is (M); for indirect addressing the operand is ((M)), where M is specified in the address portion of the command and ( ) means *the contents of.*

To indicate indirect addressing, the tag I follows the command mnemonic. Thus, if the ADD command indirectly addresses cell 237, and 237 contains the address 111, then this indirect command is equivalent to the directly addressed ADD command where the operand address is specified as 111. Thus we have:

$$\text{ADD,I} \quad 237 \equiv \text{ADD} \quad 111 \qquad \text{for } (237) = 111 \qquad (2.6.1)$$

The operand address in a command word may take us to a cell which contains an address of a cell which contains an address and so forth and so on. Finding the operand is like a treasure hunt: we move from one cell to the next looking for clues with the hope that a treasure is in the offing.

The treasure hunter can distinguish between a clue and the treasure by its specific nature. A data word does not have a specific nature to distinguish it from a clue (address). How then do we know that we are at the end of the trail?

When a cell is known to contain an address, it is only the address itself that is of use; other bits of the word are free to be used as tags. Just as a command word has a tag to indicate indirect addressing, so too the address word can contain a tag showing *further* indirect addressing. The command word tag, I, used in indirect addressing takes us to the first address. We examine the tag at this address. If it indicates direct addressing we know the next cell we reach contains the operand. If it is tagged as *indirect* we examine the next cell as an address. We continue this as long as *indirect* tags are present. The first direct tag indicates that the very next cell to be examined contains an operand.

Relative Addressing

For relative addressing we determine the effective address by adding the operand address to the contents of a base address register (BAR). Thus:

$$\text{effective address} = (\text{BAR}) + \text{M} \qquad (2.6.2)$$

One purpose of relative addressing is to increase the operand range of a command in a small, low-cost computer where the command word is small. If the address portion of a command is necessarily small because the command word is small, then the number of cells that this set of bits addresses is small compared with the full memory. Relative addressing ameliorates this difficulty. It is hardly used in larger machines except as below.

The address in the command could be interpreted relative to any register in the machine or even any cell. An effective register for relativizing is the instruction counter. This is most useful in jump commands when it is desired to indicate the next program step relative to the current step. For self-relative commands, the effective address is given by:

$$\text{effective address} = M + (IC) \tag{2.6.3}$$

The tag in the command word which indicates self-relative addressing is *. We have:

$$017 \quad \text{UCJ,}* \quad 4 \quad \Rightarrow 21 \tag{2.6.4}$$

The unconditional jump on step 17 is self-relative by an amount of 4. This is equivalent to a jump to step 21. Similarly,

$$071 \quad \text{JOL,}* \quad -3 \quad \begin{array}{l} L = 1 \Rightarrow 68 \\ L = 0 \Rightarrow 72 \end{array} \tag{2.6.5}$$

The above *jump on less* is self-relativized by -3; for *less* the jump takes us three steps backward from 71, landing us on 68.

Self-relative addressing is easily implemented in hardware. It is also available in assembly language (Chapter 5).

Summary

The kind of addressing for the command is conveyed to the controller by tags in the command word. It is possible to combine two or more modes of addressing. Thus we can have indexed indirect addressing. In that case, the effective address *of the next address* is obtained by adding the contents of the instruction register to the operand location. Further, any address participating in multiple indirect addressing can be indexed.

The tag conventions and the permissible combination of tags are presented in Table 2.6.1.

TABLE 2.6.1   Tags Associated with FLAP Addressing

Tag	Meaning
Blank	Implied, immediate, or direct addressing according to command specification
Number	Indexed by index register *number* or referring to index register *number* according to command
I	Indirect
R	Relative
C	Content
*	Self-relative
I, number	Indirect, indexed by *number*
R, number	Relative, indexed by *number*
*, number	Self-relative, indexed by *number*
R, I, number	Relative indirect, indexed by *number*

2.7 IO COMMANDS

IO commands may be classified into three different types.

- data-directed
- nondata
- inquiry

The **data-directed command** gives details about information being transferred between an IO device and the computer memory. A **nondata command** gives information about the handling of the intermediate medium or the

TABLE 2.7.1   Information Which Might Be Contained in an IO Command

Data directed

1. Unit
2. Memory source or destination
   a. start
   b. end
   c. number of locations
3. Document
   a. data-associated (e.g., forward/backward for magnetic tape)
   b. nondata-associated (e.g., line advance for printer)
4. Auxiliary data
5. Auxiliary process
6. Auxiliary control

Nondata request

1. Unit
2. Setup—choose unit, channel, function, etc.
3. Document
4. Auxiliary data
5. Auxiliary process
6. Auxiliary control

Inquiry

1. Unit
2. Nature of inquiry
3. Auxiliary control

device's reactions as it processes information or does an IO task. An **inquiry command** requests information about an IO operation just completed or in progress. Information contained in the command in each one of these categories is presented in Table 2.7.1.

The amount of information contained in a command and the particular command construction depend on at least three factors:

- the device being addressed by the command
- the characteristics of the computer
- the format of the command word

By "device" we mean the *particular* device so that a cardpunch made by IBM may differ in its characteristics from one made by Burroughs or Univac.

Data-Directed Commands

To show how IO commands are incorporated into software so that they may be used in exercises for the reader, some simple FLAP IO commands are presented here.

To bring information from an input device we use the READ command:

$$\text{READ} \quad \text{channel, unit, start, number} \qquad (2.7.1)$$

This requests that information be read from the device on *channel*, and with *unit* number, and placed in memory beginning with cell *start*, and copying a total of *number* words. Thus the command:

$$\text{READ} \quad \text{D, 3, 265, 10} \qquad (2.7.2)$$

requests that 10 words be read from unit D3 and entered at memory beginning at cell 265. How this information is formatted into the IO command word is unimportant to our discussion.

The WRITE command has exactly the same form:

$$\text{WRITE} \quad \text{channel, unit, start, number} \qquad (2.7.3)$$

It requests that *number* words beginning with *start* be written onto the device *channel, unit*.

Nondata Commands

Nondata commands are discussed as they arise. As an example of such a command, consider a request to rewind a given tape unit. This command need only contain the mnemonic REWIND and a device indication.

Test Commands

A test of an IO condition should reveal to the program the state of the IO device to enable the program a choice of activities. The activity choice is usually made by a conditional jump command. Therefore it is convenient to provide a conditional jump which is executed if a specified IO condition prevails. This is the JOIE, or *jump on IO equal*, command. The specification of the condition depends upon the command format and so forth. We distinguish the channel and unit and the conditions for which we examine. It may take another command to make this specification.

Combinations

Some machines incorporate two or even three different kinds of information in a single command. Thus the RCA 301 print command includes the data function and the line advance or nondata function. A data command may include an IO jump location so that if the device is busy the program jumps to another location to do a different portion of the program. We do not investigate combination commands.

PROBLEMS

2.1   Show pictorially the interaction of each subsystem of the computer and tell the purpose of each.

2.2   Show how the four functional units of the memory are associated. Describe the operation of each during the cycle of (a) recall and (b) memorize.

2.3   Describe the operation of the control subsystem. Distinguish carefully between the *fetch* and *execute* cycle.

2.4   With U, V, W, X, Y, and Z stored respectively at 500, 501, 502, 503, 504, and 505 code these operations:
(a) $U - W \rightarrow 506$
(b) $VX \rightarrow 507$
(c) $Y/Z \rightarrow 508$
(d) $(Y/Z)(U - W)/VX \rightarrow 509$
(e) $(UV - WX) \times (Y - Z) \rightarrow 510$
(f) $(UV + W)/(XY - Z) \rightarrow 511$
(g) $Z(UV - X) \times YW \rightarrow 512$
(h) $X(W(U + V) + Z) \rightarrow 513$
(i) Largest $(U, V, W, X, Y, Z) \rightarrow 514$

2.5   Which commands in Table 2.3.1 use implied addresses: (a) partially? (b) entirely?

2.6   With 024 in index 3, write a command using that index with effective address 789.

2.7   Write a set of commands to set the operand address of the command UCJ (which is at 337) to the quantity stored at 441. Why is the command XNM required in this sequence?

2.8   Write a set of commands to go to location 456 if $17 < (4) < 25$ and to 567 otherwise.

2.9   Write a routine to take the difference of two sets of 32 numbers. The minuends begin at cell 324; the subtrahends (to be subtracted) begin at cell 381; the differences are to be placed in cells starting at 443. The program goes $(324) - (381) \rightarrow 443$; $(325) - (382) \rightarrow 444$; etc.

2.10 Write an *add* command (a) to address relatively cell 789 when 345 is in the BAR; (b) indexed, to address relatively cell 789 with 345 in the BAR and 93 in index 4.

2.11 A chain of addresses, 345, 456, 567, takes us to *HARRY* who is in 678. We want to bring *HARRY* into the accumulator by indirection, first referring to cell 345. Write a command and show the contents of each intervening cell.

3

PROGRAMMING CONCEPTS

3.1 SUBROUTINES

Introduction

A **subroutine** is a command sequence to be *used* once or probably more at different points in the program. The subroutine may *appear* once or several times in the program. A **closed subroutine** is duplicated at each point in the program where it is required. This option would be of little use to the programmer except that he can have it duplicated automatically for him by the assembler as we see in Chapter 6.

The **open subroutine** *appears* only once in the program. It may be *used* at several points in the program and therein lies its attractiveness. If used frequently, it provides a considerable saving in space.

CONSIDERATIONS

Two important aspects of subroutines (abbreviated frequently as SRs) are:

- linkage
- calling sequence

The program and the SR are related to each other by the **SR linkage**. Each time the SR is used, the program gets to it using the linkage; each time the SR is completed, it returns to the proper position in the program using the linkage.

The **calling sequence** is one method by which data to be processed by the SR is provided to it and by which it returns results to the main program.

Linkage

The problem of linkage is shown in Fig. 3.1.1. It is easy for the main program at any point to specify a jump to the SR which then takes over and provides the processing sequence needed. At the end the SR must return control to the program somewhere near the point where it departed. The SR return is program-dependent; the return point must be provided somehow.

There are several methods for supplying the **return point**, the place at which the SR returns control to the main program:

- The main program may alter one or more of the steps of the commands of the SR.
- The program may make the return point available to the SR which then alters itself.
- The main program puts the return point in a special register.
- The program puts the return point in an index register.

The mechanism for linkage may be provided in one of two ways:

- entirely by program
- automatically by hardware

We concentrate on the hardware facilitation of linkage. When the hardware is lacking the specification for hardware, linkage can be implemented by an assembler which then replaces the linkage in the assembly program by the machine-language steps required for the computer.

Linkage Procedure

Alteration of the SR by the main program is performed by programming and is ignored here.

JUMP AND STORE

A computer with the command JAS as shown on line 35 of Table 2.3.1 stores the contents of the instruction counter *after incrementation* in the cell just previous to the one being jumped to. As an example of this we have:

$$42 \quad \text{JAS} \quad 225 \qquad 43 \rightarrow 224; \Rightarrow 225 \qquad (3.1.1)$$

The simplest way for the SR to make use of this command on its completion is to jump indirectly using the contents of the cell just previous to its start. For the foregoing SR we might find at the last step, at 244, the command:

$$244 \quad \text{UCJ,I} \quad 224 \qquad \Rightarrow (224) = 43 \qquad (3.1.2)$$

As you see, this returns us to the next step in the main program, namely 43. Figure 3.1.2 illustrates this. The main difficulty is that with this technique it is not easy to jump *past* the normal return point as required for most call sequences.

1332435

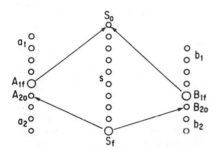

FIGURE 3.1.1. Two program segments, $a_1 a_2$ and $b_1 b_2$, each of which makes use of the subroutine, s.

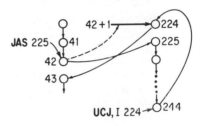

FIGURE 3.1.2. Subroutine linkage using the *jump and set* command, *JAS*.

JUMP SET RETURN ADDRESS

This method postulates two special commands. The first sets the departure point into a special register; the second uses the contents of this register in a jump command.

The JSR command, *jump set return jump register* (line 36, Table 2.3.1) sets the contents of the instruction counter into the special register before it makes a jump. As an example, we might have:

$$42 \quad \text{JSR} \quad 225 \qquad 42 \rightarrow \text{RJR}; \Rightarrow 225 \qquad (3.1.3)$$

For the SR to return, an unconditional jump referencing the return jump register is used, namely *jump to return address*, JRA. This command may offset the quantity in the return jump register by an amount specified in the operand address. Thus we might have:

$$244 \quad \text{JRA} \quad 003 \qquad \Rightarrow (\text{RJR}) + 3 = 42 + 3 = 45 \qquad (3.1.4)$$

This command permits jumping past the departure point from the main program. But it does not facilitate access to information in the calling sequence. Figure 3.1.3 illustrates this technique.

JUMP SET INDEX

The departure point from the main program is entered into an index by the JSN command, *jump set index* (line 38, Table 2.3.1). To leave the main program we might give the following command:

$$42 \quad \text{JSN,4} \quad 225 \qquad 42 \rightarrow (N4); \Rightarrow 225 \qquad\qquad (3.1.5)$$

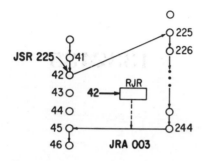

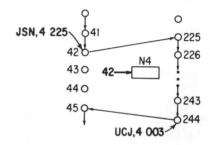

FIGURE 3.1.3. Subroutine linkage using the two commands: *jumps set return address, JSR* and *jump to return address, JRA.*

FIGURE 3.1.4. The main program return point is entered into an index as the jump is performed using *jump set index, JSN,* for subroutine linkage.

To return, an unconditional jump indexed by the register which was set as we left the main program can take us as many cells past the departure point as desired.

$$244 \quad \text{UCJ,4} \quad 003 \qquad \Rightarrow 003 + (N4) = 3 + 42 = 45 \qquad (3.1.6)$$

In the remainder of the text we use the JSN command for SR linkage, chiefly specifying index register 4 to store the departure point.

Figure 3.1.4 illustrates the technique.

Call Sequence

There are many ways in which information can be supplied to the subroutine. These are discussed at length elsewhere.† One of the most popular methods is the call sequence. This uses a few cells after the departure point in the main program to store data for the SR and for the SR to return results. This is especially convenient when the JSN command is used for jumping. Then the departure point is available in the index. Data is accessible as long as *its* position is known relative to the departure point. An item three

† cf. *Computer Programming*, Chapter 4.

cells away from the departure point is accessed with a command indexed by the linkage index and with operand address 3. For instance, this quantity may be entered into the accumulator with the command:

$$XMA,4 \quad 003 \qquad (003 + (N4)) \rightarrow A \qquad\qquad (3.1.7)$$

Return a result to the fifth cell in the call sequence using:

$$XAM,4 \quad 005 \qquad (A) \rightarrow 005 + N4 \qquad\qquad (3.1.8)$$

LISTS

The call sequence is especially powerful in handling lists when combined indirect addressing and indexing is available. When the subroutine is to process a list of items, the starting address of which is to be provided by the program, the SR design must specify an index to be used in traveling through the list. Suppose the SR design specifies index 5 and that the main program indicates the start of the list at cell 400. If the list address is put two steps past the departure point, we find there:

$$NOOP,5 \quad 400 \qquad\qquad (3.1.9)$$

The SR has control of index 5 as it passes through a list. If it is ready to use the seventh item of the list, it establishes 7 in index register 5. The seventh list item is added into the accumulator using the command:

$$ADD,I,4 \quad 002 \qquad (A) + ((002 + (N4)) + (N5)) \rightarrow A \qquad (3.1.10)$$

or

$$(A) + (400 + (N5)) \rightarrow A \qquad\qquad (3.1.11)$$

or

$$(A) + (400 + 7 = 407) \rightarrow A \qquad\qquad (3.1.12)$$

In (3.1.10) indirect addressing of the cell two steps past the departure point stored in index 4 is indicated by $(002 + (N4))$. The item in that cell is not tagged as indirectly addressed but it is indexed so we go to the seventh item in the list starting at cell 400.

3.2 LOOPS

About Loops

A **loop** is a set of commands which is repeatedly and consecutively executed on different sets of data. The form of the loop is displayed in

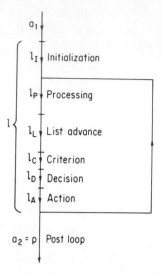

FIGURE 3.2.1. Analysis of the loop.

Fig. 3.2.1. It follows a section of the main program, a_1, and it is followed by another portion of the program, a_2. The loop itself is distinguished by l. The six divisions of the loop are:

l_I Initialization
l_P Processing
l_L List pointer advance
l_C Criterion calculation
l_D Decision
l_A Action

INITIALIZATION

Initialization, l_I, is not part of the loop proper because it is done only once and is not repeated. One or more of the following actions is performed:

- The computer hardware is cleared or set up as required by the loop which follows.
- Portions of the list are prepared or reset.
- The list pointer is reset.
- Program steps in loop sequences are reset.

PROCESSING

The processing sequence, l_P, does the repetitive work. In our discussion we replace a sequence of processing steps by a symbolic command multiple, PRO. A subset in the processing sequence is distinguished by a numerical suffix as PRO1.

LIST ADVANCE

We keep track of items being processed in one or more lists by advancing a pointer.

CRITERION

To know when we have finished processing our complete list, we examine the criterion. Often this criterion is immediately available but if it is not, if it is processing dependent, it may be calculated.

DECISION

The basis of a decision for terminating a loop is dependent upon the problem. It usually depends upon matching a criterion quantity just calculated or otherwise available with a test quantity.

The result of the decision section is used here to cause the computer to continue the loop or terminate the loop by jumping out.

Purpose of the Loop

Loops are used to handle lists of values. From a variable input list a single result may be prepared as when numbers on a list are added together.

From an input list, an output *list* of results may be prepared. A loop may produce a list of square roots corresponding to a list of numbers supplied to it.

The input to a loop may be a set of lists. A loop could be supplied with a pair of lists to form the difference of corresponding elements and to place it in a result list.

An iterative procedure is one by which we prepare increasingly better approximations to a desired result. Each new approximation is prepared by the loop. The criterion is the closeness of the approximation to the desired result. If it is not within the desired bound, the loop is repeated.

The iterative loop may be considered as a list-processing procedure. The input list is a list of intermediate or old results. The output list is a list of new results. Actually, the desired output is only the last result. Further, the lists are nonexistent at the start of the process except for the initial entry in the input list.

List Processing

The way a list is processed depends largely on the structure of the list. There are three considerations:

- *dimension*. A list of single entries is a one-dimensional list. A list of sublists or a set of lists is a two-dimensional object. Three or more dimensions are conceivable.
- *density*. Items in a list may be close to each other or may be separated by intervening spaces.
- *sequence*. A one-dimensional list may be examined from the bottom up or from the top down. A higher-dimensional list has many more alternatives.

The loop contains processing steps which are applied to each item in the list. Let us examine a list which starts at memory location t. It contains τ items. Each time we examine the list we refer to a new item.

A most effective way to point to a list item is to use an index register as shown in Fig. 3.2.2. The process command, for which we use the general mnemonic, PRO, would point if unindexed to the top of the list, cell t. The quantity in the index word register offsets the pointer. Thus we use the prototype command:

$$\text{PRO,N} \quad t \tag{3.2.1}$$

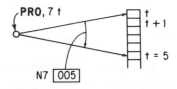

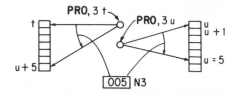

FIGURE 3.2.2. Use of an index for pointing to an item in a list.   FIGURE 3.2.3. One index may be used to point to corresponding items in several lists.

The effective address of this command is t plus the contents of the index register:

$$\text{EA} = (\text{N}) + t \tag{3.2.2}$$

To process the sixth item on the list at $t + 5$, the index register should contain the quantity 5.

Multiple Lists

The same technique can be used with several lists simultaneously. A quantity in an index register modifies in like manner all lists with which it is used. Consider now two lists, one starting at t and another at u. Figure 3.2.3 shows how the same index register can be used to offset by the same amount two different commands applying each to one of these two lists. Thus if we have 5 in index register 3, and we give the commands:

$$\text{PRO1,3} \quad t \tag{3.2.3}$$

$$\text{PRO2,3} \quad u \tag{3.2.4}$$

Then (3.2.3) uses the sixth item in the list beginning at t, and (3.2.4) uses the sixth item in the list beginning at u.

A pointer referencing an input list may simultaneously reference a list of results using the same technique to adjust its pointer. Thus, in taking a difference of two numbers, the minuend and subtrahend list pointers use an index; the difference list uses the same index. The difference then appears in the same place in the output list as do the two operands in their lists.

Part of the initialization process is to set the list pointer to the first item in the list. A command refers to a list item by using the list start address in the operand address location of the command. A zero is required in the associated index register in order to address the first item as we start down a list. This is accomplished with the XPN command. Register 3 is set to zero by:

$$\text{XPN,3} \quad 000 \qquad\qquad (3.2.5)$$

Advance and Termination

To advance an index one step, we add 1 to its contents using the *index plus program* command, NPP; the quantity to be added is in the operand address location.

$$\text{NPP,3} \quad 001 \qquad\qquad (3.2.6)$$

This command moves the pointer one location ahead when a processing command references index 3. To advance the index more than one position, the number of places appears in the operand address of the NPP.

TERMINATION BY COUNT

A loop is terminated when its lists are fully processed. Since the number of the last item processed is in the index after incrementation, it is a natural source for determining when the list has been processed. The index contents is compared to a criterion count by the *compare index*, CMPN. The comparand depends upon whether we examine the index *before* or *after* the pointer is advanced. After the last item is processed and *after* pointer advance, the index contains the number of items in a dense list. We test for completion of processing for a list of items using index 3 with:

$$\text{CMPN,3} \quad M \qquad\qquad (3.2.7)$$

Looping

CMPN sets one of the flip-flops L, E, or G and clears the other two. Any other loop criterion will also probably set one of these flip-flops. To act on a decision to continue processing, we return to the processing portion of the loop using a conditional jump. This is continued as long as a count is *less than* desired:

$$JOL \quad [PRO] \tag{3.2.8}$$

Combined Loop Conclusion

Conclusion of a loop by a count criterion includes three steps:

• pointer advance   • pointer test   • action

For *pointer advance* we increment the index by a specified quantity; for *pointer test* we compare the present pointer position with the desired position; *action* is accomplished with conditional jump back to a spot in the loop.

SINGLE COMMAND

A single command might do all three jobs. However, a quantity must be specified in connection with each task. The three quantities to be specified are:

• incrementation amount   • test quantity   • return step

To provide a single command in a single address system, two of these quantities must be specified by implied addressing. If we require incrementation by unity and the test quantity to be zero, then we need only specify the return step.

To use a test count of zero we process the lists backwards. This is usually possible when preparation of results is independent of the examination sequence.

TALLY-DOWN INDEX

The combined command, *tally-down index*, TDN, reduces the count in the specified index register by 1 and then compares this count with 0. As long as the count is greater than 0 we jump to the operand address; when it becomes 0 we take the next command in sequence. This command is used in a prototype processing string as shown in Fig. 3.2.4. The first command

Step	Command	Meaning	
1	XPN, 5 n	$n \rightarrow N5$	Load index 5 with n
2	PRO, 5 m − 1		Process next variable
3	TDN, 5 2	$(N5) - 1 \rightarrow N5$	Tally down index 5; jump
		$(N5) > 0 \Rightarrow 2$	to step 2 for index nonzero

FIGURE 3.2.4. Use of TDN in a protoype list processing sequence.

there fills the index with the number of items in the list. The next command processes the *last* item in the list. Finally, the last command increments, tests and does looping when the list has not been fully examined.

Several other ways to use combined commands within a loop are discussed elsewhere.†

3.3 OTHER LOOP CONSIDERATIONS

Termination Criterion

In determining whether a loop should be terminated, we have the following possibilities:

- count
- condition
- calculation
  * data dependency

We have examined the count as a criterion. When a condition in the form of a relation is satisfied, termination may be called for. The relations usually are those provided in the comparison command. The results of a calculation may be used, especially in iterative processing, to determine if the results are satisfactory.

To make a loop more flexible the criteria may be brought in with the data. Thus a loop may be constructed to add a set of numbers. The length of the list of numbers is supplied with the list as a datum. Only the maximum list length must be designed into the loop so that enough storage may be supplied.

Termination by Condition

Two conditions used for terminating a loop are:

- identity   • between

IDENTITY

We match a given item key with one in a list. When the given item and the list item key are equal, the item is found. We stop searching and leave the loop. Thus in a savings-account application we wish to find the account with the exact number of the activity item.

† cf. *Computer Programming*, Chapter 5.

The *identity* relation is suited to discrete items. The *between* relation handles continuous items. In examining a table of values for interpolation one finds the two table entries *between* which a desired entry belongs. *Between* can only be used if an order relation exists in the list examined.

If we are sure that the item searched for is in the list then only the required condition need be supplied. What happens if the item is missing from the list? If no other terminating criterion were provided processing would continue even after the list was exhausted. Therefore a count is often associated with a condition termination.

Calculation

An iterative calculation usually proceeds until its error can be reduced below a specified quantity. If we knew the exact error between the calculated quantity and the desired result, then simple subtraction should yield the exact result. Usually an *upper bound* for the error is provided in the iterative procedure. We know if the maximum deviation from the exact result is below this upper bound and, therefore, the actual deviation must also be below the upper bound.

The calculation of the upper bound of error may use calculations required to find the result. Thus, in an absolutely converging series, the size of the most recent term is an upper bound of error. However, a calculation completely separate from the result calculation may be used to determine the upper bound of error.

Data Dependency

The information supplied to the loop from one application to the next may vary if it is supplied with:

- new data
- new criteria
- both

A loop to add a set of numbers is supplied with the new set of numbers for which a total is desired. Thus, the list contents are different from one performance of the loop to the next.

Given a table it is desired to find a new entry in the table or to find the value of a dependent variable by interpolation. In either case it is the *new criterion* supplied to the loop which examines the same lists.

For variable loops one supplies not only a new list but also a new criterion. Thus a loop constructed to find a total of the list of numbers of variable length is supplied not only the list but also the length of the list.

Nested Loops

To include a loop *within* a loop is different from making a choice of several loops; it is also different from performing two loops in series, one after the other. For **nested loops**, part of the processing portion, l_{1P}, of loop l_1 contains within it another loop, l_2. Each time we pass through the **outer loop** l_1 we perform the **inner loop** l_2 a number of times determined by its criterion.

A single nesting of loops—one loop within another—can be used to do three kinds of processing:

- a list of sublists
- a list of variables, each processed by an iterative procedure
- an iterative procedure which contains in it another iterative procedure

As examples of these we have the following:

- finding a list of subtotals
- finding a list of square roots
- evaluating a series, each term of which requires the formation of a square root

Generally the inner loop is independent of the outer loop. Once the inner loop l_2 has been given control, only the steps in this segment of the program are executed until termination. Similarly, if the outer loop l_1 is in control, the steps in the inner loop are ignored until this portion gains control.

INTERDEPENDENCE

The outer loop may affect the performance of the inner loop in several ways.

- It may change the initialization of the inner loop so that a new sublist is processed.
- It may change actual commands in the inner loop.
- It may alter data or parameters referred to by the inner loop.

Similarly, it is possible for the inner loop to affect the outer loop.

MULTIPLY NESTED LOOPS

The inner loop of a nested pair may contain within it further nested loops like *boxes within boxes.*

Loops and Subroutines

The loop is closely related to the closed subroutine. It is a sequence of steps repeatedly applied but to different data. Only one sequence of steps appears in the program however. There is no reason why a loop cannot include reference to a subroutine. Another possibility is to have a subroutine which is a loop. The subroutine then processes a list or contains an iterative procedure.

This may be further extended: any nesting of loops within subroutines or subroutines within loops is acceptable as long as the machine hardware and the system software can handle it.

The possible exception which arises is the self-calling subroutine. A **recursive procedure** is one which specifies this in its own definition. This can be implemented by a subroutine which requests itself during the execution. This is difficult to implement without recourse to pushdown lists and list structures. Although a valuable theoretical procedure, it is not usually found in software systems.

3.4 DATA ORGANIZATION

Pieces of Data

The computer handles data and the application engineer speaks about data in quantities which depend upon the problem. It is important to have units of different sizes to conveniently discuss and manipulate data. The units of data manipulation should be clarified from the outset.

It would be ideal if the machine could handle information in chunks of the same size as required by the application. This is not usually possible and we categorize a data division accordingly.

Machine oriented data division partitions data into a size particularly suitable for manipulation by the machine. **Application oriented data division** breaks the data into a size convenient for human manipulation associated

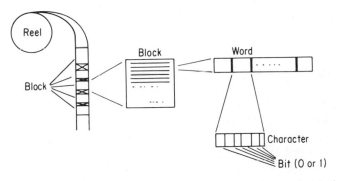

FIGURE 3.4.1. Machine-oriented data division hierarchy: reel, block, word and bit.

with the application under consideration. We distinguish four divisions in each category:

- machine-oriented
  * reel
  * block
  * word
  * bit

- application-oriented
  * file
  * record
  * field
  * character

These terms are explained below.

Machine Oriented

The interrelation of the four machine-oriented words is illustrated in Fig. 3.4.1.

REEL

The **reel** is the *maximum amount* of information which can be loaded on an IO device at one time. The definition is slanted toward the tape user where the reel is the object on which the tape is stored. But *reel* is presented here as a universal term also signifying the maximum number of cards received by the card reader, although this is more commonly called a **deck** or **stack**.

BLOCK

The **block** is the maximum amount of information transmitted from or to an IO device in a *single operation*. For the punchcard device, the block is often the card itself. This is true regardless of how full the card is. For the tape units, blocks may be of fixed or variable size.

WORD

The **word** is the unit of information transferred within the memory and processor and is usually fixed. Thus memory accessing and processing are specified in terms of words.

An important distinction from common usage is emphasized. Some machines such as the RCA 301 and the IBM 1401 are commonly regarded as variable word length machines. Actually the word size in both of these machines is exactly one character. A command specifies an operation and the number of characters to be processed. The number of characters processed can vary and is defined later as a *field*, since it is an application oriented unit. These computers should be referred to as variable field length computers.

BIT

Since the **bit** is the smallest amount of information, words are naturally rated in terms of bits.

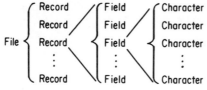

FIGURE 3.4.2. Application-oriented data division hierarchy: file, record, field and character.

Application Oriented

The application-oriented divisions are illustrated in Fig. 3.4.2. These terms are examined from the smallest unit upwards.

CHARACTER

The **character** is an application oriented unit because the character set defined depends upon the nature of the data furnished. The character is the smallest multibit data unit. In a scientific application, numbers made from digits are often sufficient. Digits can be units of four bits each. The EDP requires alphabetics and therefore at least a six bit character is mandatory.

The **field** is the smallest piece of information *distinguishable by the system*. By *system* we mean the data description and application interrelation. For a payroll system the sex of the employee can be distinguished by a single bit as either male or female. An employee's name may occupy several words. So far as the application is concerned, name and sex are both fields of equal status.

RECORD

A **record** is an assembly of fields pertinent to a *single individual or item*. A record is distinguished by the application of which it is part. Thus, for a checking account application, several checks may be drawn during a single day on the same account and each check comprises a record. It is an item with respect to the application even though the same individual may have several items or records in this particular run.

Further, a record is distinguished from records for the same individual in another file. Thus in a checking account application, each check is a record in the activity file and these items are different from the master record for that individual in the master file.

FILE

A **file** is an assemblage of records of the same type for a given job and a given run. Records of one type are classified in the same file. Thus in the checking account application, the check entries are part of the activity file; the record of an individual's account for the month is found under master file. The bank may have several computer applications so that the master file for one application is distinguished from that for another by the job to which it applies. Finally, the file for a given job must be distinguished timewise by the run on which it is used. Thus, the new master file produced today for an inventory application becomes the old master file for updating for tomorrow's application.

Information Division Overlap

We develop words here to describe the interrelation between machine-oriented and application-oriented data division.

REEL—FILE

The three relationships which may exist between a reel and a file are illustrated in Fig. 3.4.3. A **multifile reel** is a reel containing several files.

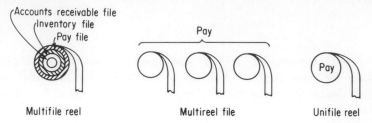

FIGURE 3.4.3. Reel-file interaction.

The one illustrated contains a pay file, an inventory file and an accounts receivable file. For a small company it is economical to keep several files on the same reel.

At the other extreme a large processing job may require several reels to hold a single file which is then called a **multireel file**.

When a reel holds exactly one file it is called, preferably, a **unifile reel** or, occasionally, a **unireel file**.

BLOCK—RECORD

As shown in Fig. 3.4.4, when records are very small compared to the block size, it is advisable that a single block carry information about several records. It is then called a **multirecord block**.

A record which contains a very large amount of information may require several blocks, called a **multiblock record**. When a single record conveniently fits into a single block, we have a **unirecord block** or, occasionally, a **uniblock record**.

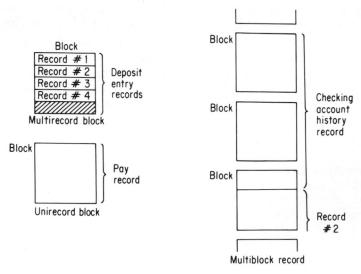

FIGURE 3.4.4. Block-record interaction.

As shown in Fig. 3.4.5, several small fields are fit into one word in a **multifield word**. Large **multiword fields** occupy several words. A word into which exactly one field fits is a **unifield word**.

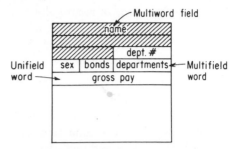

3.5   LISTS

FIGURE 3.4.5. Word-field interaction.

Characteristics

A **list** is a collection of records. We use the word *record* in a more general sense although it is perfectly proper to use it in the precise sense as in the previous section. The list record must be delineated either by having a fixed number of bits or with some characteristic beginning and end mark. A list may occupy a specific area of memory or may be diffuse throughout memory.

Each record in the list is identified by its **key**. Usually a record contains more than its key; the rest of the record is referred to as its **content**.

The list is distinguished by the properties of the records contained therein:

- format
  - * key length
  - * key location
  - * content format
- search and reference
- record alteration during processing

List properties, different from record properties, pertain to the following aspects of the list:

- construction
- search
- alteration

Alteration of the list (adding new records to the list or deleting old records from it) is different from the alteration of a record.

The kind of list proposed for a given application depends on its use statistics:

- frequency of record alteration
- percentage of records altered
- frequency of list alteration
- percentage of the list which is changed

Probably the most important aspect of the list is its organization. Three characteristics pertain directly to organization:

- list density
- order of records within the list
- type of list structure.

They are interrelated.

Order

Order in a list is relative to the key of the list records. Any one of several record fields can be used as a key for a given application. Having fixed upon a key we can then indicate whether a list is ordered. A list is said to be **ordered** if there is a monotonic relation among the keys of successive records.

We consider a list of records subscripted according to their positions in the list: M_i is the record in the ith position on the list. The list $\mathfrak{M}$ is an ordered set indicated as:

$$\mathfrak{M} = \{M_i\} \tag{3.5.1}$$

To indicate that records occupy contiguous cells or sets of cells we use a positional operator, $\prec$. Since consecutively subscripted records occupy successive positions, we have:

$$M_1 \prec M_2 \prec M_3 \tag{3.5.2}$$

In the following discussion we examine single word records. When records are *sets of words*, this phrase should be substituted.

A **dense** list is one in which consecutive records occupy consecutive cells (no intervening cells) as shown in Fig. 3.5.1. This is contrasted with a **loose** list where intervening cells may be empty as shown in Fig. 3.5.2. For the dense list, the relation between the keys of records and their positions in the list is:

$$M_{iK} \leq M_{jK} \supset i < j \ \& \ M_i \prec M_j \qquad (3.5.3)$$

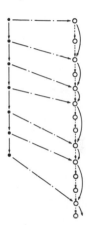

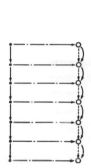

FIGURE 3.5.1. A dense list.   FIGURE 3.5.2. A loose list.

Records in a loose list must be distinguishable from nonrecords. The nonrecord item might contain blanks or z's or some other distinguishing feature in the key position.

For notational purposes, we use ° to indicate an empty item. A loose order list then meets the requirement:

$$i < j \supset M_{iK} \leq M_{jK} \vee M_i = {}^\circ \vee M_j = {}^\circ \qquad (3.5.4)$$

Here $\vee$ is the logical OR symbol.

Superdense List

It would seem impossible to pack more than one record per word but this is the object of the **superdense** list. A word in a superdense list may be replaced by a pointer to a sublist containing several items. This expedient improves the alterability of a long list.

To enter a new item into a dense list requires a hole in the list for the new item to go into. To make a hole, all the items either above or below the location where the hole is desired must be moved one position away. With a long list this is tedious. The superdense list allows us to remove an item and replace it by a pointer. The new item and the old item that was replaced by the pointer can then be placed in a sublist, the referent for the pointer. This is illustrated in Fig. 3.5.3. An example of entries on such a list appears in Fig. 3.5.4.

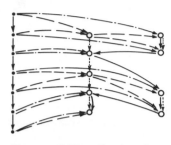

FIGURE 3.5.3. Graph of a superdense list.

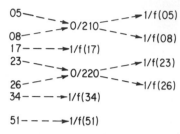

FIGURE 3.5.4. Example of a superdense list.

Superdense Loose Lists

To provide the maximum in alterability of a list, it should be possible to delete an item without having to close up ranks. This can be done if the deleted item is replaced by °. Items deleted make holes in the list and cause it to be loose; items appended cause sublists to be created and thus make the list superdense.

SUBLISTS WITH SUBLISTS

We extend the principle of sublists. When there is insufficient room in a sublist, why not substitute a pointer for a sublist item also? Now a search for an entry in the original list takes us to a sublist; a search in the sublist takes us to another pointer, this one to a subsublist where the item is finally found. Further extension of this principle is left to the reader.

Locatability

A list item is locatable in one of the following manners:

- serial
- directly
- neighborhood
- indirectly
- binary

All lists are **serially locatable**: an item in the list can be found by examination of all the records comprising the list.

A list contains **directly locatable** items if, given the key of the item desired, this key can be entered into a formula which provides the exact location of the desired item. Some tables are designed as directly locatable. Thus a table of squares might be constructed so that, knowing a number, one can immediately go to the entry in the table which contains its square. This being the case, the key need not be contained in the record.

If the key of the desired item can be entered into a formula which yields a cell address *near* the desired record then the record is **neighborhood locatable**. This technique enables us to localize a record in a long list. We can then make a short serial search of the neighborhood.

As in the superdense list, an item key may take us to a pointer which, in turn, takes us to the proper sublist. This is **indirect locatability**. An item may be singly or multiply indirectly locatable.

Binary search can be employed in an ordered list, preferably a dense one. Examination of the median record determines if the desired record lies in the upper or lower half of the file. Examining the median record of the indicated half of the file indicates which quarter of the file the desired record lies in. Continued partitioning localizes the record to a single item.

Ordering

To place a file in order in terms of a given key is called **sorting**. Many options exist on how to do the sorting and the one employed depends upon the list and record characteristics. These methods are discussed in detail elsewhere.†,‡

3.6 LINKED LIST

Concept

The record in the **linked list** consists of:

- an item
- the address of the next record

It is also referred to as a **threaded list**. Its power is the ease of alteration of the list. The disadvantage is that search of the list is usually only possible serially.

† cf. *Computer Programming*, Chapter 8.
‡ Ivan Flores, "Analysis of Internal Computer Sorting," *JACM*, VIII, No. 1 (1961), 41–80.

To simplify discussion we introduce the following two operators:

$\quad$ (i) means the contents of cell i. $\hfill$ (3.6.1)

$\quad$ α(i) means the address portion contained in cell i. $\hfill$ (3.6.2)

$\quad$ l(i) means the contents of the next cell in the chain. $\hfill$ (3.6.3)

It is clear that:

$$l(i) = (\alpha(i)) \qquad (3.6.4)$$

Notice that both the operators, α and l, apply to cell contents, (i).

If (i) represents the contents of this cell and $l(i)$ the contents of the next cell, we find the contents of the one thereafter by applying the operator l to $l(i)$. The number of times an operator is applied to the cell contents is indicated by a superscript so that we have:

$$ll(i) = l^2(i); \qquad ll^2(i) = l^3(i); \qquad \text{etc.} \qquad (3.6.5)$$

For the beginning of a list we may use a symbol, a name, or a cell number. For a list with name, L, we may also indicate its starting place by L. The next cell in the chain is therefore at $\alpha(L)$. There are at least two ways to indicate that we have reached the end of a chain. The first is to put the name of the list in the address portion of the last cell. Another method is to put a special symbol at this location. If t is the address of the last cell, we have for these two methods:

$$\alpha(t) = L \quad \text{or} \quad \alpha(t) = * \qquad (3.6.6)$$

We adopt the latter method and end a linked list with an asterisk. For a linked list of n items we have:

$$\alpha l^{n-1}(L) = * \qquad (3.6.7)$$

Deletion

We examine the two operations of list alteration with regard to the linked list. For an item at location j whose predecessor is at location i and whose successor is at location k we have:

$$\alpha(i) = j \qquad (3.6.8)$$

$$\alpha(j) = \alpha l(i) = k \qquad (3.6.9)$$

To delete the item at j, from the list we merely replace the address portion of the item in cell i by k, the address of the second removed item. This is indicated by:

$$k \rightarrow i_\alpha \qquad (3.6.10)$$

Where i_α refers to the address or link portion of the cell at i. We may also write:

$$\alpha l(i) \rightarrow i_\alpha \qquad (3.6.11)$$

The deletion activity is shown in Fig. 3.6.1.

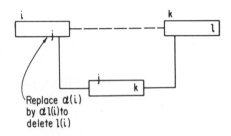

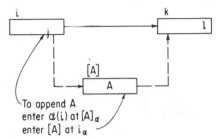

FIGURE 3.6.1. Deleting (j) from the linked list.

FIGURE 3.6.2. Inserting a new item, A, into a threaded list.

Insertion

Suppose a record A is to be inserted between the item at cell i and the item at cell j. At present i links to j:

$$\alpha(i) = j \qquad (3.6.12)$$

We want to link the item at i to the item A. The address of the item A is given by $[A]$. Further, we want to link the item at j to the item A. The latter is done if we enter j into the address portion of item A. This is indicated as:

$$j \rightarrow [A]_\alpha \qquad (3.6.13)$$

In addition, the address portion of cell i must be filled with the address of A:

$$[A] \rightarrow i_\alpha \qquad (3.6.14)$$

At the end of the insertion process we have:

$$\alpha(i) = [A] \qquad (3.6.15)$$
$$\alpha l(i) = \alpha A = j \qquad (3.6.16)$$

This process is illustrated in Fig. 3.6.2.

Space List

The need for a space list arises when there are frequent changes in the linked list. Cells deleted from the list must be returned to service somehow. Otherwise they will lie fallow and will not be available to the computer. The **space list** is a list of available cells from which are drawn cells for appending to a linked list and to which deleted cells are returned. The original list might be in order of position of the cells in memory. However, as deleted cells are returned, a loose structure results. Therefore, a good way to provide a space list is by making it a linked list too.

OUR SPACE LIST

Our space list is called S; S is also the address of the list pointer which is not available for appending to other linked lists. The address of the first available cell in the series is $\alpha(S)$. Other available cells are at $\alpha l(S)$, $\alpha l^2(S)$, etc., so long as the resulting address is not $*$. When the available space list is empty we have:

$$\alpha(S) = * \tag{3.6.17}$$

USE

A deleted cell could be returned to the available space list if we put it either at the beginning or at the end. In our list we enter the new cell at the top of the list so that the pointer points at the new cell which, in turn, points to the previous top of the list.

A cell is released for a new list when it is withdrawn from the top of the available space list. The pointer at S is revised so as to point to the next cell (or to contain $*$ if there are no more cells left).

Deleting with a Space List

To delete from a list the item at j whose address appears at i and to return this cell to the available space list, two tasks are required: deletion from L and appending to S.

Three subtasks are done to delete:

Enter the address of the item *past* the one we are deleting into the address portion of the item *preceding* the one we are deleting:

$$k = \alpha l(i) \rightarrow i_\alpha \tag{3.6.18}$$

- Enter the address of the deleted item into the space list pointer:

$$j \to S_\alpha \qquad (3.6.19)$$

- Enter the address of the previous first space list item into the new first space list item:

$$\alpha(S) = s \to j_\alpha \qquad (3.6.20)$$

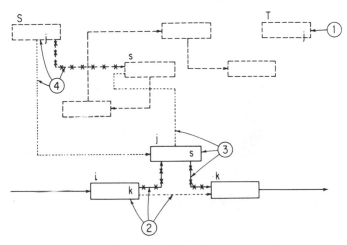

Change list

1. $\alpha(i) \to T; \quad j \to T$
2. $\alpha l(i) \to i; \quad k \to i$
3. $\alpha(S) \to \alpha(T); \quad s \to j$
4. $\alpha(T) \to S; \quad j \to S$

FIGURE 3.6.3. Deletion from the active list (below). Item added to the beginning of the space list (above). Changes are in dashed lines as per change list, left.

Execution of any one of these tasks obliterates some of the information required in the succeeding tasks. The problem is solved by a temporary storage cell, t. The location of the deleted cell is placed there:

$$\alpha(i) = j \to t_\alpha \qquad (3.6.21)$$

The rest of the deletion is provided by:

$$\alpha(j) \to i_\alpha; \qquad k \to i_\alpha \qquad (3.6.22)$$

$$\alpha(S) \to \alpha(t)_\alpha; \qquad s \to j_\alpha \qquad (3.6.23)$$

$$\alpha(t) \to S_\alpha; \qquad j \to S_\alpha \qquad (3.6.24)$$

The operation is illustrated in Fig. 3.6.3.

Appending

A word in t is to be inserted in a linked list L at a new location which is to follow the word stored at i. Presently the cell at i links to the cell at k:

$$\alpha(i) = k \qquad (3.6.25)$$

The next available cell from the space list is at s:

$$\alpha(S) = s \qquad (3.6.26)$$

The item from t is to be placed in the cell withdrawn from the space list which then becomes part of the list L.

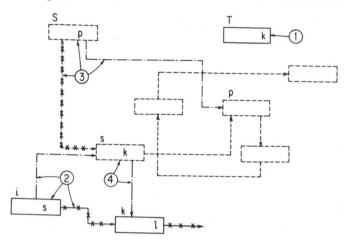

Change list
1. $\alpha(i) \rightarrow T$; $k \rightarrow T$
2. $\alpha(S) \rightarrow i$; $s \rightarrow i$
3. $\alpha l(i) \rightarrow S$; $s' \rightarrow S$
4. $\alpha(T) \rightarrow \alpha(i)$; $T \rightarrow s$

FIGURE 3.6.4. Appending to an actual list (below). The cell is provided in the space list (above). Changes are in dashed lines as per change list, left.

The following tasks must be done in some order:

$$\alpha l(S) \rightarrow S_\alpha; \qquad \alpha(s) \rightarrow S_\alpha \qquad (3.6.27)$$
$$\alpha(S) \rightarrow i_\alpha; \qquad s \rightarrow i_\alpha \qquad (3.6.28)$$
$$\alpha(i) \rightarrow s_\alpha; \qquad k \rightarrow s_\alpha \qquad (3.6.29)$$

It is left for the reader to determine an order in which these operations are performed and what temporary registers are required to do them. The operation is illustrated in Fig. 3.6.4.

3.7   BUFFERS

Need

It is important that IO operations proceed under their own steam: the less attention required by the computer, the more efficiency we can extract from a computer. This is aided by internal memory buffering. For small computers such as the IBM 1440 and the Univac 1005, simultaneous operation of IO units and the processor is not provided. Somewhat larger machines such as the RCA 301 and the IBM 1401/10 with overlap options provide for the simultaneous use of an IO device and processor. The very large machines such as the IBM 7090/94 and the Philco 2000, Model 212, provide multiple simultaneity.

MEMORY BUFFERING

For **memory buffering** a section of memory is used to store data brought by an input device or taken by an output device. When speaking symbolically of buffers we use boldface Greek letters; $\boldsymbol{\beta}$ is a generalized buffer symbol.

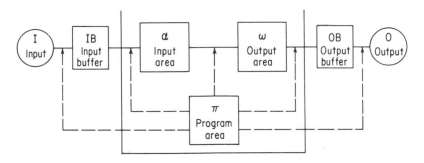

FIGURE 3.7.1. Memory and IO operator for the single record problem.

Single Buffers

One buffer is provided for each IO device for **single buffering**. **Filling** is the entering of information from an input device to an input buffer. **Emptying** is taking information from an output buffer through the output device to the output medium. Figure 3.7.1 shows processing using single buffering. Here the input buffer $\boldsymbol{\alpha}$ may be filled simultaneously with the emptying of the output buffer $\boldsymbol{\omega}$.

To process information the computer **takes** data from $\boldsymbol{\alpha}$—it uses information from an input buffer. The computer **puts** information into the output buffer $\boldsymbol{\omega}$. Information for *putting* may be copied from $\boldsymbol{\alpha}$ to $\boldsymbol{\omega}$ directly or it may be processed first and then entered into $\boldsymbol{\omega}$. After all information for output is *put* into $\boldsymbol{\omega}$, the computer releases the buffers for *filling* and *emptying*. It now waits until IO is done.

TRANSFER BUFFERING

Transfer buffering is illustrated in Fig. 3.7.2. Again $\boldsymbol{\alpha}$ is *filled* and $\boldsymbol{\omega}$ is *emptied* simultaneously. The input information from $\boldsymbol{\alpha}$ is transferred to a third buffer $\boldsymbol{\tau}$ for processing.

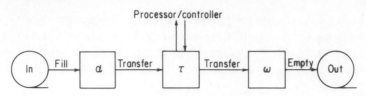

FIGURE 3.7.2. Transfer buffer.

Once τ is *full*, the computer can process the information by *taking* from τ and also by *putting* into τ. Since α is no longer needed, it may be *filling* during processing. When processing is complete, information from τ is *transferred* to ω and output initiated. When transfer time is short the use of a transfer buffer may increase simultaneity and reduce overall time. Otherwise it is no improvement over single buffering.

Swinging Buffers

Inefficiency of single buffering arises because the processor has to wait until *filling* and *emptying* are done. IO devices, in turn, have to wait until processing is complete. By providing each device with a buffer pair we expedite matters as shown in Fig. 3.7.3. At the moment, we are *filling* α_1 and *emptying* ω_1; α_2 was *filled* during a previous operation and is now being used by the processor to *take* information which it *puts* in ω_2. Nothing happens until:

- α_1 is *filled*
- ω_1 is *emptied*
- ω_2 is *put*

Now we interchange the identities between the input buffers and between the output buffers. The information in α_2 has been *taken* and it is available

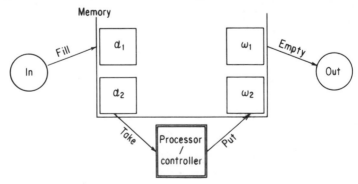

FIGURE 3.7.3. Swinging buffer.

to be *filled*. ω_2 has a record for output and is ready to be *emptied*. α_1 contains the last entered record which is now available to the computer. ω_1 is empty and is available for *putting* by the computer.

By this technique we are able to perform simultaneous operations which last for the longest of the three: *filling*; *emptying*; processing. Supplying more than two buffers to each device does not improve the activity.

ROTATING BUFFERS

Usually the processor need work with only one buffer. This suggests a rotating technique shown in Fig. 3.7.4. The figure shows three buffers labelled β_I, β_C, and β_O, whose function, respectively, is for input in-
formation, use by the processor
and output information. All three
operations transpire at once. When
all three are complete we are ready
to rotate the buffers. β_O is *empty*
now and is labelled β_I to receive a
new input block. β_C now has a pro-

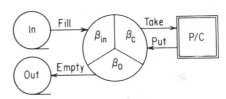

FIGURE 3.7.4. Rotating buffers.

cessed record and is ready for output. It is relabelled β_O. β_I now has a new input record and is ready for processing by the computer. Hence it is re-labelled β_C. The rotating refers to the circular fashion in which the buffers are relabelled.

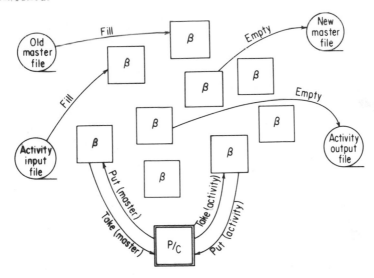

FIGURE 3.7.5. A pool of buffers.

Pool of Buffers

We have examined simple cases where only one input and one output device are concerned. Many IO devices may take part, especially in EDP applications. Sometimes several of the assigned devices are idle. If we provide buffers for the worst case, then during idle periods some of these buffers may become free to be used with active IO devices. This technique is used in the buffer pool illustrated in Fig. 3.7.5.

Several buffers are engaged in IO activity. Two more are being used by the computer for processing. The rest are available to be assigned to IO activity as the need arises. The only restriction is that one buffer per device must be reserved even for idle devices so that, should one suddenly be called into action, it has a buffer immediately without waiting for otherwise assigned buffers to be freed for this purpose.

3.8   BUFFER POOL MANAGEMENT

The buffer pool is an advanced technique for buffering used for the IOCS system discussed later in the text to make it efficient and extensive.

The Pool as a Link List

The buffer is a multiword item in a linked list. When the buffer pool is first made available for a problem, it is usually a set of contiguous blocks of words. These are associated together in a linked list as shown in Fig. 3.8.1. As buffers are withdrawn and returned to the pool, the list remains linked but the links may not be from one consecutive buffer to the next. The buffer pool serves the same purpose as the available space list discussed in Section 3.6.

Other linked lists provide waiting lists or queues for devices and for the processor. Buffers for these queues are taken from the pool as needed and returned to the pool when no longer needed.

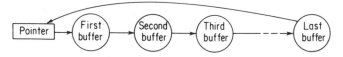

FIGURE 3.8.1. How the pointer and the buffers in the buffer pool form a linked list.

Buffers can be in any one of the following statuses:

- available
- filling
- full
- being taken
- taken
- being put
- put
- emptying
- empty

We might observe the following status changes in a buffer assigned to input. First, it is *available* since it is in the buffer pool; it is assigned to be

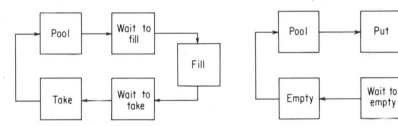

FIGURE 3.8.2. The chain of statuses that a buffer on input duty passes through.

FIGURE 3.8.3. The chain of statuses that a buffer on output duty passes through.

filled and the filling process starts. It is then *filled* and passed to the computer for *taking*. After the computer has *taken* information from the buffer it then becomes *available* and is returned to the pool. A similar progression is apparent for an output buffer.

Queues

On input duty a buffer really has several intermediate statuses. When it is assigned to be filled by an input device it is possible that the device is occupied filling another buffer. Since this buffer is assigned but not yet engaged in filling it is said to be in *wait to fill* status. If it is full even though it is ready to be *taken* by the computer, the computer may be otherwise occupied taking a different buffer. Therefore we distinguish a *wait to take* status. The status progression of an input buffer is shown in Fig. 3.8.2. Notice that *full* status is eliminated because this is identical with the *wait to take*.

A similar progression for status changes for an output buffer is shown in Fig. 3.8.3.

The **request queue** is that queue on which buffers are placed either to be *filled* or to be *emptied*. We have the following queues:

- pool
- request
- put
- take
- hold

The last, or *hold*, category is a special one for internal buffers described in Chapter 9 and just mentioned here in passing.

Queue Subroutines

Each of the queues mentioned before requires two subroutines, one to enter a buffer to the queue and another to remove the buffer from the queue.

To QUEUE

Queue handling subroutines are similar to the subroutines for appending to or deleting from a linked list. Besides these duties the subroutine also provides full information in the pointer block regarding the status of each queue. A **to queue** subroutine to enter a buffer onto a queue does these extra functions:

- accept buffer information: size, address, etc.
- start a new queue when none exists
- reset chain pointers
- update chain counts

FROM QUEUE

Besides the normal list-processing duties a **from queue** routine must do the following:

- obtain information about the *next* buffer: size, address, etc.
- reject request for buffer from empty queue
- reset pointers
- reset beginning and end of the queue
- update counts
- make counts and flags available to the user

A summary of queue subroutines is given in Table 3.8.1.

TABLE 3.8.1   Queue-Handling Routines

To routine	Queue	From routine
To pool	Pool	From pool
To take	Take	From take
To request	Request	From request
To hold	Hold	From hold

Queue Routines

Buffer manipulation requires that a buffer be withdrawn from one queue and entered onto another. A routine thus combines two subroutines. A summary of queue manipulating routines together with their constituent subroutines is found in Table 3.8.2.

TABLE 3.8.2   Buffer Maintenance Routines and Their Subroutines

Type	Release	Uses	
		From	To
In	From take	Take	Pool
	From fill	Fill	Take
	To fill	Pool	Fill
Out	To put	Pool	Put
	To empty	Put	Empty
	To pool	Empty	Pool

PROBLEMS

3.1   The square-root subroutine starts at 379, continuing to 395. It is called for at step 108. Show how to use JSN for linkage. What commands must SR contain and where?

3.2   Do problem 3.1, this time for a quadratic equation SR starting at 678 and ending at 697. A dummy may be stored at 698. The program has just reached step 125 when it requires a solution. Data and results follow directly in the calling sequence which contains, in order: A, B, C, X, and Y for the equation $Y = AX^2 + BX + C$. Show all steps of the main program and the SR which pertain to the linkage and calling sequence.

3.3   At step 144 the sum of squares of a number of variables is required. The calling sequence contains, in order: the number, N, of variables; the value for each of the N variables. The SR starts at 789. Describe:
(a) the linkage using JSN

(b) the return and its setup by the SR
(c) the calling sequence
(d) operand acquisition for the SR

3.4   For problem 3.3, the calling sequence now contains: the number of variables, and the starting cell of the variable list. Repeat (a), (b), and (c) above.
Show operand acquisition by direct indexed addressing with SR command
alteration; by indirect indexed addressing.

3.5   Repeat problem 3.2. This time we expect the quadratic routine to require a
square root at step 683. It uses the root SR at step 379 (see problem 3.1).
Propose a method of linking and communicating between the two SR's
and write the pertinent steps in each SR.

3.6   Find the sum of the squares of 35 values in cells starting at 408. Put the
answer at 407.

3.7   There are 27 items stored at cells starting with 301. Write a loop to find the
sum of every third item starting at 301; twice the square of every third item
starting at 302; the cube of every third item starting at 303. Combine these
tasks into a single loop repeated only nine times.

3.8   Find the largest of 66 items starting at cell 301, and put it in cell 300.

3.9   The Newton–Raphson method for finding the square root, Y, of X by itera-
tion requires an initial guess, Y_1 for Y. Given Y_i, the next approximation
for Y, Y_{i+1} is found using:

$$Y_{i+1} = Y_i + \frac{1}{2}\left(\frac{X}{Y_i} - Y_i\right)$$

Let us use half of X as a guess for Y:

$$Y_0 = \frac{X}{2}$$

Write a FLAP subroutine to find $\sqrt{X}$ where X appears in that order in the
calling sequence. Here T is the test quantity which permits us to stop when:

$$|Y_{i+1} = Y_i| \leq T$$

Place the routine at cell 700; use index 4 for linkage.

3.10   Write a FLAP subroutine to find the real roots of the quadratic equation
$AX^2 + BX + C = 0$. The calling sequence for the task is A, B, C, $R1$, and
$R2$, where $R1$ and $R2$ are the roots found by the SR. If there are no real
roots, place $99\ldots9$ at $[R1]$. Use the square root SR above. Place this SR
at 800 and use index 4 for linkage.

3.11   Given the rectangle in the figure and the constants P,
Q, and T in cells 901, 902, and 903, we wish to find a
value of X so that the area and perimeter of the rectangle are equal.

3.12   Give examples of the use of the eight data descriptions of data organization on page 147.

3.13   Consider a character-oriented machine. Each *character* in memory has a unique address. There are special field and record characters. How do the data descriptions of page 147 apply here?

3.14   Completely design a master recording for checking-account application to be updated daily and charged or credited monthly. Consider the bank's requirements for knowledge about: (1) activity; (2) minimum balance; (3) overdraft; (4) credit; (5) debit/credit sequence.

3.15   Write a subroutine to hunt for a key in the address portion of an unordered file of one-word items. The calling sequence contains: the number of items; the starting cell address; the key (filled with 0's on the left); the found item; the item address; an error return (SR jumps here if item is missing).

3.16   Write an SR as in problem 3.15 but for items of four words. The calling sequence provides four-word spaces for the found item.

3.17   Write an SR to find a one-word item, and replace it with the word in 999. Use the SR of problem 3.15.

3.18   Write an SR to find a four-word item, and replace all four words with (999). Use the SR of problem 3.16.

3.19   Write an SR,DELETE to delete an item from a linked list and return it to the available space list whose pointer is at the symbolic location, S. An address mask is stored at AMSK and DELETE-I should be used for temporary storage, T. *Hint:* When an item to be augmented is in the accumulator, XNA enters the index register contents into the *link* portion without affecting the rest of the word. The calling sequence is: address of the item *before* the deleted item—the one whose link is changed.

3.20   As in problem 3.19, write an SR,APPEND to append a new item to the list, getting a cell from the space list to do so. The calling sequence contains: address of item preceding desired item (the one to link to the desired item); the item to be appended (with junk in the link); an error return for an empty space list.

3.21   P is the symbolic address of the pointer of a push down list. Write an SR,PDIN to add an item to the list from a space list at S. The calling sequence contains: the item to be added; an exit for empty space list. Any SR's above may be used.

3.22   As in problem 3.21, write an SR, PDOUT, which copies the item from the PD list into call sequence and returns its cell to the space list. The calling sequence is: cell for next PD item; exit for empty PD list. Use any preceding SRs.

3.23 Write a FLAP SR, TOPOOL, to return a buffer to the pool. The call
      sequence contains in order:

1. The number of words in a full buffer (including all accounting words
   contained therein).
2. The absolute address of the buffer *preceding* the one to be deleted.
3. The address of the pool pointer.

The link portion of the buffer is M of the first word in the buffer. Assume
FLAPJAC, define all masks, and ignore accounting procedures.

4

SOFTWARE
INTRODUCED

4.1 TRANSLATORS

Introduction

Most programming today is in a language different from machine language. We say that the program is in **machine language** when it can be fed directly into the computer, where the loader places it in memory and it is ready to run. A **source language program** requires one or more stages of translation to produce the machine language program.

SOURCE LANGUAGES

The programmer usually writes in a **source language**. We distinguish several kinds of source languages according to their use.

ASSEMBLY LANGUAGE

Assembly language provides commands which are very close to machine-language commands, and it falls into the three categories which will be discussed. The mnemonic language introduced in Chapter 2, FLAP, is an assembly language. Other extant assembly languages for IBM machines include FAP and SOS; Univac® assembly languages include UTMOST and ALMOST.

POLS

The programmer is provided with languages which convey information in a manner similar to that in which he normally expresses himself in writing out his algebraic or business problem. These are called **procedure oriented languages**, abbreviated occasionally as **POL**s. They include FORTRAN, ALGOL, and COBOL. These are also called **compiler languages** after the programming system which translates them, the compiler.

PROBLEM ORIENTED

Problem oriented languages are aimed at stating a problem for which a general solution has already been programmed. The Report Generator Language enables us to state the design of a given report; the Sort Generator allows us to communicate the nature and format of records to be sorted.

SPECIAL

Special languages are structured for the statement of special kinds of problems. A System Simulator Language is designed to state the properties of a system which is being simulated on the computer. IPL-V (Information Processing Language Number Five) is designed to express problems which simulate human thinking.

Assembly Languages

We distinguish three kinds of assembly language:

- absolute assembly language   **AAL**
- symbolic assembly language   **SAL**
- macro assembly language   **MAL**

ABSOLUTE ASSEMBLY LANGUAGE

Early FLAP, introduced in Chapter 2, is an example of an **absolute assembly language**. It differs in only two ways from actual machine language:

- A mnemonic—a set of letters—is substituted for the binary command code.
- A letter or number code is used for a memory cell instead of the binary representation of this code.

AAL is a shorthand notation for machine language commands. These are translated to machine language by a clerk or by a very simple assembler. No storage allocation is done.

SYMBOLIC ASSEMBLY LANGUAGE

A **symbolic assembly language** is discussed in Chapter 5 and is exemplified by Middle FLAP. In this language, the location of data is denoted symbolically and need not be allocated by the programmer. The assembler does the full allocation of storage and keeps track of all memory cells. To talk to the assembler about the nature and format of data, pseudocommands are introduced in Chapter 5. The SAL can also deal with arrays and provide address modification by addition and subtraction.

MACRO ASSEMBLY LANGUAGE

Most notably, the **macro assembly language** permits the programmer to define and name a subroutine and then to call it forth any place in the program that he desires. This feature, among others, is discussed for Contemporary FLAP in Chapter 6. Conditional assembly, built-in macro sequences, and other extensions of FLAP are discussed in Chapters 7 and 8.

AL—POL Contrast

The absolute assembly language has the characteristic that each source language command is represented by exactly one machine language command. Symbolic assembly language introduces pseudos present in source language but absent from machine language. The macro assembly language introduces strings of commands in the macro definition which are entirely absent from the machine language translation. It also introduces single macro commands which are replaced in translation by a string of machine language commands. Despite these variations a pattern is evident: most assembly language translations present a one-to-one structure—one machine language command for one source language command. When the structure is violated, the sequence of machine language commands is evident in the source language problem statement.

For the procedure oriented language *one* source language statement is *usually* translated into *many* machine language statements. More important, the sequence of statements produced is a function of the POL compiler and the object machine, and is not at all evident in the source language statements.

The most important differences between the AL and POL are:

- A sequence of machine language steps is nowhere implied in the POL.
- The one-to-many characteristic is customary in the compiler whereas in the assembler it is an exception.

Mixed Characteristics

There is no incentive to incorporate AL characteristics in the POL. When POL characteristics are incorporated into assembly language, categorization becomes difficult.

Lists are handled in assembly language by:

- indexing
- operand address modification

Both of these features are built into the assembler. Index specification uses the command tag. Index manipulation is done just as in machine language. An array is defined by pseudos which reference it to an initial address such as DATA. Elements of the array are referenced by address modification so that the fourth element in the array called DATA is addressed by DATA + 3. This feature may also be used to count backwards from a given landmark; information can be addressed by a description such as DATA − 6.

Some assemblers permit arithmetic expressions to be used as operand addresses, where such expressions include multiplication ($*$) and division ($/$). They tolerate an expression such as:

$$3 * A + (B - 3)/2 \qquad (4.1.1)$$

A and B in (4.1.1) are values supplied to the assembler or with the data. In the first case the assembler must evaluate the arithmetic expression, but in the second case a string of machine language commands must be substituted in the object program to evaluate the expression. In any case the procedure is not one which falls under our definition of an assembler; this is definitely a POL characteristic.

Translator Names

Occasionally a company issues a translator which does not follow our name convention. A company may produce a simple assembler which it calls an *assembler* and a symbolic or macro assembler which it calls a *compiler*. This may be misleading.

On the other hand, some assemblers provide compiler features such as the use of arithmetic expression for operand address. But this is not present in our assembler nor is it discussed in the text since it is considered a compiler feature.

4.2   INTERPRETERS

The **interpreter** combines translation and execution. A sequence of commands is supplied in source language to the interpreter which examines each command, determines the SR to replace it and executes it if possible.

The source language for the interpreter may be one of several:

- an assembly language for *this* computer
- an assembly language for *another* computer
- a procedure oriented language
- a special language
- a combination

USES

The interpreter can do several very different tasks:

- translate and execute a source language program
- simulate the action of an alien computer
- simulate other systems
- aid in debugging

Operation

During operation of the simulator, the computer memory contains:

- Input
  * Problem program
  * Problem data
- Program
  * Interpreter supervisor
  * Interpreter analyzer and translator
  * Component subroutines

The supervisor sequences through the problem program keeping track of its place in the program. As each new command is encountered the translator–analyzer is brought in. It determines the task and turns over control to the proper subroutine to execute the task. When the subroutine is finished it turns over control to the supervisor which then procures another command.

INDIRECT

It is emphasized that the source language statements do not directly activate the computer. It is the interpreter program which analyzes the command to determine which subroutine should be called to perform it.

Problem Solver

In solving problems the interpreter does both translation and execution. Statements to solve the problem are written in a source language which is performed as it is presented to the interpreter.

The difficulty with this procedure is that execution is usually mandatory. With the assembler the programmer is free to ask for frequent translations of his program. When the assembler turns up an error, the programmer can change the source statements and reassemble. If he finds errors during execution he can reassemble and check his program before resubmitting it for execution. Since translation is going to be much shorter than combined translation and execution, there is much wasted motion in using an interpreter, hence, it has fallen into disfavor.

Computer Simulator

Specifications and program codes for a computer are often released before the computer becomes available. A simulator of a new computer on an old computer is quite valuable in three respects:

- checking format and legality of commands
- timing out the program
- checking the loops and subroutine structure

System Simulator

Special programs have been written to simulate both computer systems and systems of other kinds. These generally use interpreters. A special language is required to communicate to the interpreter the composition of the system and the way the components react. The simulator, using the interpreter, tells the programmer how the system as a whole reacts to various stimuli.

Debugging

Debugging aids are often actually interpreters. The programmer can insert special instructions in his source language program. These *jumps* turn over control to the debugging interpreter which extracts information from the computer proper and from neighboring commands in the machine language sequence. It summarizes this information and presents it to the programmer. It determines when control is to be returned to the main program and when required, does so. The machine language program continues as though the interpreter were not there until another debugging statement (jump) appears.

The debugging interpreter can be disconnected from the system by several expedients. One of these is to replace all jumps to the interpreter by NOOPs. The machine language program then becomes continuous, never referring to the interpreter.

4.3   OTHER SOFTWARE

What the Operator Sees

The programmer and operator can "talk" to the software. There is software in the computer at all times. When it is necessary to "speak" to it the message is entered via the **control input device**, a unit set aside for this purpose among other things.

Frequently we distinguish software conversation from data and program information by prefixing it with $.

We get the attention of a software system by calling it by name. We shout,

$SYSTEM to the supervisor
$LOAD to the loader
$FLAP to the FLAP assembler
$FORTRAN to the FORTRAN compiler
$IOCS to the IO Control System
and so forth.

Once we have the attention of the software system we direct it. We might ask the supervisor to make new system IO unit assignments prefixing this request with $ASSIGN. We tell the loader that the information which follows is data prefixing this with $DATA.

Supervisor as Coordinator

A portion of the supervisor is in the memory at all times (usually). It is available for use by other subsystems which may call upon it without intervention. For the operator to get the attention of the supervisor a $SYSTEM request is made. This must be recognized by all subsystems so that the supervisor can recoup control even from an operating program.

It is not necessary that one subsystem recognize another subsystem's name. This can be done in two steps using first $SYSTEM and then $SUBSYS (where $SUBSYS represents the name of any other subsystem such as $LOAD).

The supervisor gains control when a subsystem gets into trouble. An improperly mounted input tape might be an instance of this. The running program may return control to the supervisor by a built-in command. The supervisor determines if the system or program is in trouble and, if so, attempts to remedy it. If it is recovered from the situation it may turn over control to the original subsystem. If the program ends successfully, the supervisor may continue by examining further control information. If the supervisor cannot recover satisfactorily, it requests the help of the foreman in printing out a message to the operator.

The supervisor does other tasks such as facilitating conversation with the human, keeping track of IO assignments, and doing time and cost accounting.

Translator

Translators may be in the form of assemblers, compilers or interpreters. They can be called in when SYSTEM is in control. Thus to call in FLAP we use $FLAP.

Further instructions to the translator may be included on this calling card. For a compiler, the card may indicate whether assembly is required if compilation is successful. For an assembler, the card indicates whether execution is required should assembly be successful. The translator is told whether a printout and card punching are required, and so forth.

The translator is told that it has reviewed all the statements of the source program when it comes to END in source language. After translating the program, the translator remains in control and looks for new input information—another program for translation. Otherwise control information should follow telling the translator what to do next or to turn control over to the supervisor.

Loader

The loader is called in by $LOAD which may follow translation. In that case, the translated program is loaded if the translation is successful. An object language program to be loaded is preceded by $LOAD. The loader brings in and locates properly all segments of the program which follows. It must also bring in the subroutines and link them with the program. After so doing, it turns over control to the program. The loader determines the end of the program it is loading by observing a $DATA card.

Foreman

The foreman does all the IO device handling. It takes care of errors which arise in these devices and tries to extricate the computer. It handles, interrupts, and even takes care of interrupts which arise during interrupts. It is usually required by the supervisor, the translator and IOCS. Most programs also require it so that it is in memory most of the time.

IOCS

IOCS is a set of routines vastly simplifying the programmer's IO requests. With a single source statement he controls complicated buffering procedures and sets off whole chains of IO devices. IOCS uses the foreman extensively and is used by both the program and service systems. Usually neither the supervisor nor the translators need it.

PROBLEMS

4.1 Describe in your own words the distinguishing qualities of these languages: *machine, source, assembly, procedure oriented, and problem oriented.*

4.2 How do the three kinds of assembly languages differ: *absolute, symbolic,* and *macro*?

4.3 How do mixed assembler-compiler characteristics arise? Give examples from your experience.

4.4 What are *interpreters* used for?

4.5 Describe the data and program for the interpreter. How would you distinguish between the source program for the interpreter proper? Which should rightly be called the *program*?

4.6 What are the $ words used for? What is the purpose of the symbol "$"?

4.7 Discuss the use of the *supervisor, translator, loader, foreman,* and *IOCS.*

5

ASSEMBLY

5.1 THE ASSEMBLER

The Importance of the Assembler

It is estimated that over 99% of translation uses assemblers. Most domestic compilers produce an intermediate output which requires assembly. Further, most small machines such as the IBM 1401 and 1410 and the Burroughs 200 series have small memories and are less suitable for full compilation or even macro assembly. They rely heavily upon assemblers although they often call them Autocoders.

When you consider how much computer time is spent in translation (at least 20%?) and what part the assembler presently plays in translation (99%?) can you avoid the conclusion that it is vital?

Superiority of the Assembly Language

Mnemonics make it easy for the programmer to handle machine commands; symbolic addressing removes from the programmer's consideration the data assignment and accounting problem. Identifying data by symbols so that they may be referenced by name is a natural extension. The POL helps the person who has not been specifically trained in programming skills and whose primary interest is the solution of a program. But the POL does not displace the assembly language for several reasons:

- Most US compilers supplied by manufacturers perform an intermediate translation from source language into assembly language.
- Frequently, the trained programmer makes changes in the assembly language translation because of his familiarity with it.
- Although these changes do not necessarily constitute an ideal procedure, it is the practice of many installations and programmers and documentation is in assembly language.
- The assembly language is superior for some applications.
- It is more *efficient* in some sense.

Assembly language is used almost exclusively in the construction of software because the POL is not oriented to this purpose. Hence, assembly language produces more efficiently running software. This is important because software operations take up so much of the computer's running time.

The discussion about assemblers is based on the FLAP mnemonics presented earlier. The frills and extra commands incorporated into the language resemble, for the most part, the IBM assembly languages, FAP and SCAT. The implementation of the assembler is discussed generally, but specific examples are used which exist in real assemblers. The inner workings of specific assemblers are held by some manufacturers as proprietary. Therefore, it is difficult to obtain precise information about their internal construction.

Assembly Command Content

The FLAP assembly command includes a mnemonic, a symbolic address and tags to specify indexing, addressing mode, and other supplementary information which the object computer is capable of using.

Commands may include symbolic identification: a **label** allows the command to be referred to as an operand which is especially necessary in jump instructions. Unlabeled commands can be referenced to the most recent labeled command. Thus a command which is three positions ahead of the command labeled POLY is referred to as POLY + 3.

Finally, the programmer is aided because he is allowed to include notes and comments. Of course, these comments do not become part of the program, but they appear when the assembly translation is printed. They permit the programmer to check his translation, mark his place and provide a different programmer with a line-by-line commentary which he usually finds useful.

The FLAP command looks like this:

$$\text{label} \quad \text{command} \quad \text{address(es)} \quad \text{comment} \qquad (5.1.1)$$

separators or blanks

Command Types

There are five kinds of assembly commands:

- mnemonic
- pseudocommand (or simply pseudo)
- macrocommand (or simply macro)
- quasicommand (or simply quasi)
- conditional assembly commands

Mnemonics were discussed earlier. They are represented to the assembler as alphabetic combinations of two to six letters.

When the assembly programmer uses the command ADD, the assembler replaces it by a binary combination which is the machine language command for this computer. This may have the intermediate representation, 56, for instance. Then 56 could convey to the human that the computer operation code is either 0101, 0110, or 101110, depending upon whether it is to be interpreted as decimal or octal.

PSEUDO

Pseudo comes from the Greek root meaning false. Its purpose is to transmit information to the assembler rather than to be incorporated directly into the machine-language program. The nature of pseudos is detailed in Section 5.3. Let us pause for a simple example.

When several programs are assembled in succession, we distinguish between two adjacent programs with the END pseudo. It announces the *end* of one string of commands for assembly. Other pseudos are used to talk with the assembler about the kind and quantity of information that it must provide for, and so forth.

MACRO

Macros are replaced by a number of machine language commands as discussed in Chapter 6.

OTHERS

The quasi and conditional assembly are presented in Chapters 7 and 8.

Data Addressing

The programmer has at his disposal five forms of data addressing:

- absolute
- regional
- symbolic
- relative
- literal

ABSOLUTE

The programmer indicates the physical address in memory where his data is stored; *he* does the allocation function so far as this data address is concerned.

The machine address code for the location may not have the identical form as the programmer's designation. For instance, if there are 4096 cells in the machine's memory, each of the cells can be referenced using a four-digit decimal number less than 4095. The choice of numbers indicates that the actual machine designation is a twelve-bit binary number. Thus if the programmer refers to cell 500, the assembler translates this to the binary number 000111110100.

The resemblance between assembly and machine addressing is much greater in the system for the IBM 1401 where information is designated by two or three character combinations. Each character can be a letter, a numeral, or a symbol. The machine language address is found by a direct binary substitution.

REGIONAL

The programmer segments memory into a number of regions to which he may or may not assign absolute starting addresses. He then refers to a datum in this region by its position relative to the starting address.

For instance, in SOAP, an assembler for the IBM 650, an initial letter indicates a region; the two digit number which follows indicates a relative position in the region. After the programmer has written his routine in assembly language, he may find that the regions are defined as follows:

1. Program P00–P89
2. Constants C00–C22
3. Coefficients K00–K10
4. Working Storage W00–W29
   etc.

If he submits this list to the assembler at the start of assembly, the allocation is made automatically.

The limit in the size of the region is the number of digits provided for spots in the region. (For SOAP this is 100.) The programmer can define a larger region simply by making two regions contiguous, thus:

Program P00–P99,   Q00–Q59

Regional Addressing is a compromise between absolute addressing and symbolic addressing. When symbolic addressing is furnished, regional addressing serves no purpose. It is absent from FLAP.

SYMBOLIC

A set of letters or letter/digit combinations is used to distinguish each datum. The programmer assigns no absolute location to this symbol; this is left to the assembler. The assembly language contains a convention which dictates the permissible combinations of letters and symbols. This is necessary to distinguish a symbolic address from mnemonics, pseudos, subroutines, and literals.

As examples of symbolic data designators in a payroll computation, the tax deductions might be designated as TAX1, TAX2; the bond deduction as BOND; the gross pay as GROPAY; the paycheck quantity as NETPAY; and so forth.

RELATIVE ADDRESSING

When a step in the program is labeled, it is possible to refer to steps that follow by calling forth the label and adding the proper increment to it. Thus if the first step of a routine to calculate the net pay is called FINDPA, then the *fourth* step of this routine is designated as FINDPA + 3. That is, it is the third step *after* the step labeled FINDPA.

A similar convention is applied to symbolically define sets of data. Thus a set of data may be defined to consist of six cells in memory. Since these are different kinds of deductions, the first cell is labeled DEDUCT. The third cell is therefore DEDUCT + 2; the last cell is DEDUCT + 5.

The **self-relative address** permits the programmer to designate the program step displaced a fixed amount from the one he is using now. Thus, if he gives a command, JOE * + 3, the *jump on equal* takes us three steps from *this* step when the equal condition is met. Here the asterisk stands for the address of the command itself. This is the preferred assembler form, and it produces the scheme of Section 2.6, in which we proposed the FLAP form, JOE,*   3.

Some assemblers permit the use of an arithmetic expression as an address: 3 × ALPHA + 2 × BETA − GAMMA. The calculation of such an address involves an evaluation which we classify as the job of a compiler. In FLAP only addition and subtraction are permitted in a symbolic address.

The assembler allows the programmer to *address immediately* data to be used by the program. These references to data are called **literals**. To use a known constant, it is named in the command as *the* operand (not its address). Hence there is no need to address the quantity symbolically and then later declare the symbol.

The literal must be distinguished from operand address. It is usually prefixed by a special character such as "=" which prefixes the FLAP literal. Another assembler recognizes as literals all operands which are numbers; but it requires alphanumeric literals to be prefixed by "@".

ARRAYS

The linear array is a direct result of regional or relative symbolic addressing. In the assembler the programmer must impose his own format upon the array; in other words, he does the linearization.

In compilers, an array may be simply specified or designated and as long as the proper limits are supplied to the compiler, it allocates storage automatically. This may be a disadvantage in disguise.

Advantages of Symbolic Addressing

The usefulness of the SAL assembler is best exploited with *symbolic addressing*. It relieves the programmer of all data accounting chores. It easily takes the place of most other data types except literals:

- ABSOLUTE   Much too cumbersome
- RELATIVE   Of course, but relative to symbols
- REGIONAL   Yes, but initialize the region with a *symbol* as DATA, DATA + 1, etc.

5.2 WHAT IS TO BE DONE?

Summary

Each item in the AL must be translated before it appears in the machine language program. Each command code has a binary equivalent which is substituted for it at the proper location in the object program. Even in a decimal or alpha machine, the character is *actually* coded as a set of bits; there is no truly decimal machine extant. Index specification, addressing mode and supplementary information are similarly translated on a dictionary lookup basis, if not by direct substitution. An allocation procedure precedes data translation. Once a symbol has been assigned a location, it is simple to place this location in the machine language command. A good part of the assembly process is spent in allocation.

Label in the assembly language command of (5.1.1) is not translated and does not appear in the machine language command. It is incorporated in the reference table. Another command using this label as an operand can now be translated into its machine language equivalent and inserted into the object program.

Comments appear with the assembly command at *comment* for printout.

The Allocation Problem

The allocation routine of the assembly program contends with the five kinds of data and also manages the location labels which reference program steps. Its greatest obligation is to prevent conflicts—to assure that no two data are assigned the same address by mistake. An additional condition imposed by the nature of the computer is that, in most instances, the sequential program steps must occupy sequential memory cells. Further, there is a limit to the memory available for any program. The physical memory provides an upper boundary to this limit. Much software and the subroutines required by the problem fill up a sizable portion of memory. What is left over is assignable to the program. If it is exceeded, some of the program will be hanging in the air and not accessible to the computer; this situation is intolerable. Segmentation, the cure for large programs, is encountered in Chapter 7.

The main difficulty in analyzing the source program is that, customarily, source language steps are supplied sequentially to the assembler: the whole program is not available to the assembler at once. Reference may be made in one portion of the program to labels which have not been defined or allocated as yet. This, together with the sequential nature of command execution, makes almost mandatory the two-pass solution.

The Two-Pass Solution

These storage assignments must be made by the assembler:

1. Absolute and regional data

2. Symbolic data

3. Object language program origin

4. Subdivision orientation

5. Each program step whether labeled or not

6. Literals (preferably without duplicates)

In addition, other allocations are necessary when the assembler is broadened to include macros, quasis and such. These needs are discussed in detail in Chapters 6 and 7. They are mentioned here in passing to ensure that the reader will not forget them in this attempt to simplify the initial presentation of the assembly task:

7. Multiple steps for macro commands

8. Data allocation pertinent to macro commands

9. Library subroutine links

10. Subroutines

11. Conditional assembly

12. Processing during assembly

Because of the sequential nature of entry review, most assemblers perform the assembly operation by reviewing the source language program in two operations called passes. A **pass** is a separate review of the data.

The purpose of the first pass is to make data allocation and assignment. It also checks the source language program for consistency, regularity, and overdefinition and underdefinition of symbols. This provides the programmer with a number of checks and enables him to make corrections if a successful translation is not forthcoming.

The second pass does the translation of the mnemonics and of the data assignments made in the first pass. An output listing of source and object commands, data assignments, and possible sources of errors is also produced.

Data Availability Within the Object Program

There are two classes of data:

- built into the program
- brought in from outside as a program is run

Data incorporated into the program are called **built-in data**, for lack of a better term. One example is the literal; another is the declared constant. Building them into the program saves bringing them in with each new data set. More "intelligent" assemblers even eliminate duplicate literals.

What is variable for one program might be fixed for another. Let us see some examples of constants which *might* be fixed for some program. A quadratic equation of fixed parameters may recur, such as $AX^2 + BX + C$. We expect the constants A, B and C to remain fixed as the program is run, whereas X could be expected to vary. For the commercial application, such as a payroll, we might expect such things as tax percentages and witholding tax brackets to remain constant. The initialization of subroutines is also usually fixed.

Variable data is that which is supplied when the program is run. It can be subclassified:

- **run data**—parameters which apply for this data set
- **record data**—different each time the program is performed

For run data in the commercial installation, we output the date with each check of the payroll; we output the operator's name or number with each summary sheet; etc. For the scientific installation, a program may be used for processing matrices. Each record may be a matrix for inversion. The run parameter will give the size or dimension of the matrix and the maximum or minimum size of the element.

How the Assembler Handles Data

BUILT-IN DATA

Program-fixed information can be supplied in several ways in the source program. We are acquainted with both immediate addressing and literals from Chapter 3. In source language, the immediately addressed quantity is written in the address field in decimal and converted by the assembler to binary or BCD form. Occasionally it is written in octal and, rarely, directly in binary. In these special cases it must be prefixed by some identifying mark. As an example, the command;

$$\text{XPN, } 2 \qquad 3 \qquad\qquad (5.2.1)$$

inserts the decimal number 3 into index register 2.

A quantity may be named but defined someplace within the source language program. Thus we have the two not necessarily sequential entries:

$$\text{XMA} \qquad \text{PI} \qquad\qquad (5.2.2)$$

$$\text{PI} \quad \text{DEF} \qquad 3.14519 \qquad\qquad (5.2.3)$$

(5.2.2) is a transfer into the accumulator. The quantity to be transferred is assigned a location by the assembler. Since the number for that location is furnished to the assembler, this number is imbedded in the program.

A third alternative is to use direct addressing and indicate a literal with a special character ("=" in FLAP and FAP):

$$\text{XMA} \qquad =3.14159 \qquad\qquad (5.2.4)$$

The assembler provides a cell in the object program where it stores 3.14159 in binary (or BCD). The address of this cell is placed in operand portion of XMA in (5.2.4). This is essentially the object of (5.2.2) and (5.2.3); there, however, PI may be referenced again using its name.

The cell where the literal is stored may have no name or, alternatively, may have a name identical to its contents.

VARIABLE DATA

Run and record data are brought into the computer memory at run time by steps in the program. The programmer distinguishes the two kinds of data by the way he sets up his program. For instance, the program may bring in two records, A1 and B1. When the program is finished it writes out the results and seeks new data. The new data is only of the B-type block for a given run.

After writing results, the program returns to a section where record B2 is brought in. We continue thus, bringing in records B3, B4, etc., until the record brought in contains an end-of-file mark indicating that this program run is complete. Control then goes over to the monitor. The A blocks contain run data, and the B blocks, record data. The assembler need not distinguish between them.

Data Tables

As the assembler is producing the object program, it makes up many tables to keep track of its activities.

DATA SYMBOL TABLE

Each time a new symbol is used an entry is made in the data symbol table. If and when the symbol is defined, it is so tagged in the table. A symbol should be defined once and only once.

5.3   PSEUDOS

Need

Pseudos are used mainly to keep track of data. They also provide a means for making restrictions on the object program. They are called **pseudos** because they are not translated into the object program; rather, they are instructions to the assembler itself.

Pseudos may be inserted any place in the program for some assemblers although others have placement restrictions. When the assembler encounters a pseudo, it performs a bookkeeping operation instead of a translation.

The following subsections describe FLAP pseudos which are also common to many assemblers. The names for the pseudos differ from one source language to another, as does the precise description. With each of the following pseudo descriptions is included a statement of purpose, need, operation, result and an example.

Origin Set, ORG

$$\text{label} \quad \text{ORG} \quad \text{number} \qquad (5.3.1)$$

This pseudo tells the assembler the nominal beginning of the object program, i.e., it sets up the origin of the object program when no relocation is done by the loader. The need for setting the origin stems from variable placement of other software, programs and subroutines. When the assembler recognizes this command, it sets the object program step counter to the value designated by *number*. The first command generated by the assembler is assigned this step number and is also designated symbolically by *label*. This should be the first command furnished the assembler, to initialize the step counter. The object program begins at step 105 for the pseudo:

$$\text{ORG} \quad 0105 \qquad (5.3.2)$$

Reserve, RSRV

$$\text{label} \quad \text{RSRV} \quad \text{number} \qquad (5.3.3)$$

This pseudocommand reserves a block of cells in the object program where data will be stored. It functions in different ways according to the assembler design. In SOAP, for instance, specific allocations of object memory cells are made in this command. In FAP, a block of cells in the middle of the program just after the last translated command, is allocated. Another alternative, used here, is to reserve a number of cells by advancing the *cells used* counter and by making a symbolic entry in a table. After the first pass when all the program steps have been assigned absolute locations, the reserved blocks will be assigned from the remaining space. To reserve a region of fifty cells called ALPHA, we give the pseudo:

$$\text{ALPHA} \quad \text{RSRV} \quad 0050 \qquad (5.3.4)$$

A single symbol may be reserved in the same fashion:

$$\text{DATE} \quad \text{RSRV} \quad 1 \qquad (5.3.5)$$

Unreserve, NRSRV

$$\text{label} \quad \text{NRSRV} \quad \text{number, number} \qquad (5.3.6)$$

Some assemblers include this emergency measure should the program become large and the programmer find that he has reserved too many steps previously. This frees memory locations for program steps. Thus, if we find near the end of the source language program that only 38 steps were required in the ALPHA region, and if the program seems long enough to need all the spaces we can spare, then we give this command to reduce the allocation for ALPHA:

$$\text{ALPHA} \quad \text{NRSRV} \quad 50,\ 38 \qquad (5.3.7)$$

Define Symbol, DEF

$$\text{symbol} \quad \text{DEF} \quad \text{number } and/or \text{ letters}$$

This pseudo, which is an alternative to the literal, supplies a constant and names it. The pseudo enters *symbol* into the symbol table, tags it as defined, and incorporates it in the program at the allocated position. Thus space is reserved for symbol and *number* or *letters* is stored there. For some assemblers the pseudo consists simply of a label with a blank operation code followed by the literal value. An example of a FLAP definition is:

$$\text{PI} \quad \text{DEF} \quad 3.1459 \qquad (5.3.8)$$

Some assemblers, including ours, permit the definition of literals directly in the address portion of the command:

$$\text{XMA} \quad = 3.141590 \qquad (5.3.9)$$

The literal has the advantage that it is written down immediately with no fuss. The defined symbol, however, permits us to postpone a definition until after writing. Further, changing a single definition allows us to change every occurrence of the constant at once, an advantage if this modification is ever required.

A distinction might be made between a pseudo defining an octal constant and one defining a decimal constant. Further, alphabetic and alphanumeric defining pseudos may be set apart. Hereafter, it is assumed that decimal alphanumeric data is permissible for the DEF pseudo.

End of Program, END

$$\text{label} \quad \text{END} \quad blank \qquad (5.3.10)$$

This last command in the source language program indicates that this is the end of the program to be assembled. It is necessary when submitting several programs. After the assembler has run through the first source program, it encounters the END card. Hence the preceding command was the last one belonging to the first source program. What follows belongs to the *next* source program. When the first program assembly is complete, END is a signal to destroy all the old tables and construct new ones.

Equality, EQL

$$symbol \quad EQL \quad symbol \qquad (5.3.11)$$

The purpose of this pseudo is to permit two names to apply to the same datum. Occasionally the programmer wishes to designate a datum temporarily by one name until he finds a suitable name later. In the construction of a large program the work may be split into several parts or segments. When the parts are put together, the same variable may have different names. EQL permits the same variable to be identified by two or more names. The assembler sets up an equivalence table, preferably cross-referenced to prevent ambiguity. Only one cell assignment in the object program must be made and this assignment used for either variable name occurrence. To make X1 and POLY stand for the same variable (the same cell in the object program), this pseudo is given:

$$POLY \quad EQL \quad X1 \qquad (5.3.12)$$

Comment, CMNT

$$label \quad CMNT \quad text \qquad (5.3.13)$$

This pseudo is used to print information in the assembly printout for the programmer's convenience and for documentation. It is otherwise ignored by the assembler.

Others

Other pseudos associated with macros and conditional assembly are discussed in Chapters 6 and 7. They would not be included in the early or middle assembler. Specific assemblers may have additional unique and characteristic pseudos.

5.4   FIRST PASS, ANALYSIS PHASE

Introduction

The FLAP assembler comprises two passes. The first pass sets up many tables from the source program. On the second pass the program is reexamined; each step is completely translated in conjunction with the tables and a printout is produced. The conditions required to assemble a program in a single pass are discussed in Section 5.7.

Before the first pass the memory is cleared of old information by one of the following methods:

- *physically*, by entering 0's in all old tables
- *symbolically*, by eliminating all references to such tables
  (This has the effect of indicating that trash is stored there.)

A table, for instance, is effectively cleared when the *last entry* pointer is reset so that it indicates the *beginning* instead of the *end* of the table. When the beginning and end of the table correspond, the table is effectively empty.

Next, commands in the source language program are examined in sequence. For each command an entry is made in one or more of the assembler's reference tables. As each step of the program is examined, it is assigned a step number, starting with the assigned origin. This number is entered in the appropriate tables when a program step has a label associated with it.

At the end of the first pass, since some of the data assignments remain to be made the tables are reviewed.

Memory Layout

Figure 5.4.1 shows a diagrammatic layout of the computer memory when it is ready to do an assembly program. For the two-pass assembler it is assumed that the memory requirements are so stringent that there is little space left for any of the source language program. Of course, there is enough room to review the program a step at a time, but the assembler presents a crowded picture of memory. Whether this limitation is realistic is another question. Assemblers are usually designed for the minimum configuration of the manufacturer's machine. Thus, if the least amount of memory he supplies is $2K$, he designs the assembler for this amount of memory. If the user actually has $16K$ of memory, then for many short source programs, he could fit both the source language program and the binary output into the memory with the assembler.

In Fig. 5.4.1, the assembly program takes up a good portion of memory. Next there are a number of tables; the purpose of each is introduced later. The input area receives source language statements one at a time. These are interpreted by the assembly program and posted to one or more of the tables. When the assembler is done with *this* source language step it is sent to the intermediate output area. From this area it is entered onto an intermediate tape or other medium so that it is available when required for the second pass.

Two other output areas are provided for the second pass. One of these is used for the final binary output, referred to as OCTOUT for *octal output* (the same as binary). For the decimal computer this might be DECOUT. The second area called PRINTOUT prints out the assembled program for the programmer's record. Information may be printed out directly or it may be stored on an intermediate tape for later printout.

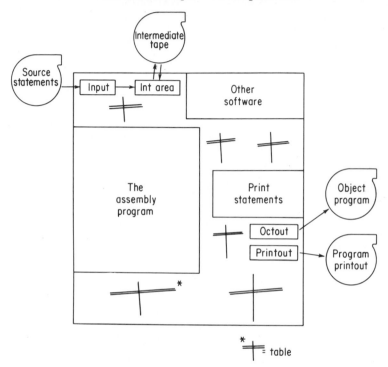

FIGURE 5.4.1. The contents of memory during an assembly run.

Error statements for errors discovered on either pass are prepackaged and stored in the area labeled *print statements*. Appropriate statements together with identification for correlation with the source program are furnished with the printout.

The rest of memory is occupied by the loader, the control monitor and other software.

Tables

A list of the tables (used during assembly of Middle FLAP or its equivalent,) and their contents are presented in Table 5.4. A particular assembly

TABLE 5.4   Tables of Pass I Assembly

Table name	Entries	Built by
Command†	Command mnemonic, order code.	System programmer.
Symbol†	Symbol name, address (space for second address). Undefined? Overdefined? Used? Equivalent symbol? Name, if so.	Assembler.
Error	Command used, location. Other error specification.	Assembler.
Region	Symbol, starting address, number of words.	Assembler. May be incorporated in symbol table.
Defined symbol	Symbol, location. Quantity (binary).	Assembler. May be incorporated in symbol table.
Equivalence	Symbol, symbol (equivalent; cross-referenced).	Assembler.
Assignment	Memory map.	Assembler.
Literal	Literal name, quantity, assignment.	Assembler.

† Absolute minimum

program may require more or fewer tables. Tables for macros or other advanced features are lacking at this stage of discussion. The first pass requires a number of additional assembly *subroutines* to take care of these situations, as well as additional *tables*.

Let us examine the purpose of the tables outlined in Table 5.4.

COMMAND TABLE

This table, built into the assembler, translates mnemonics into command codes on pass II.

THE SYMBOL TABLE

This table contains a list of all symbols encountered in the source language program either as labels for program steps, as operand addresses of commands or as literal names. We want to know whether the symbol has been assigned a space in memory, whether it has been used and whether it has been over-defined (defined more than once, and differently). Tags keep track of these facts.

ERROR TABLE

When an error is detected it is written into this table for printout at the end of the first pass. In some assemblers an error printout tape is substituted.

REGION TABLE

When a block of memory has been assigned it can be noted most compactly in a region table if the beginning address of the block and the number of cells provided for it are recorded.

DEFINED SYMBOL TABLE

This stores symbols, definitions and assignments.

EQUIVALENT SYMBOL TABLE

It cross-references equivalent symbols.

THE ASSIGNMENT TABLE

This table keeps track of all the memory cells which have been assigned so far. It is a map of memory for the compiled object program at run time. In order to make such a map without using up too much memory, we must shrink the cell size down to a single bit and record in that bit space whether the cell has been assigned. Thus the table contains one bit per actual memory word, and the subroutine for using the table contains a formula for finding the appropriate bit.

Really all we want to do is keep complete track of memory allocation. If nonsequential assignment is made, this table is required. Otherwise two or three counters will suffice. A **total counter** tallies all assignments, including program and data, up to now; a **data counter** and a **program counter** monitor those respective areas.

LITERAL

A list of literals and their addresses are provided in this table.

Command Analysis

The flow diagram of the first pass of the Middle FLAP assembler is shown in Fig. 5.4.2. After the tables and assembler are cleared (0), we get the first command. The first job is to determine the type of command (1).

For macro, quasi, and conditional assembly commands, separate subroutines are entered. The other alternatives are handled here. If there are no more commands left when END is encountered we go to the second phase of pass I, designated here as WINDUP. The remaining types of commands are discussed in the following paragraphs.

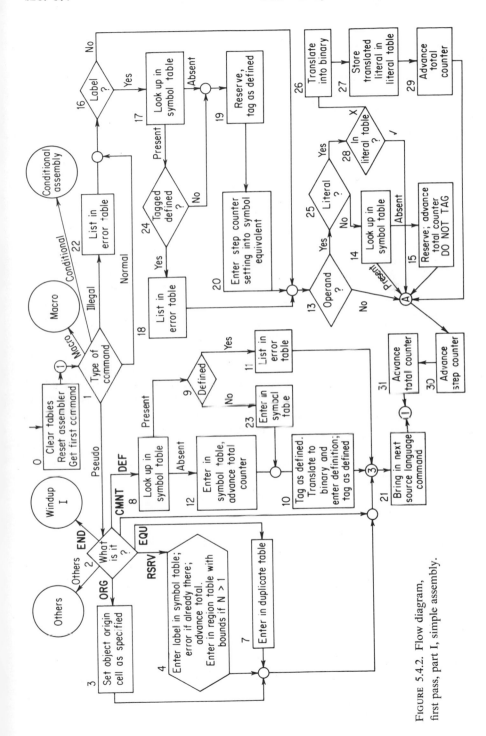

FIGURE 5.4.2. Flow diagram,
first pass, part I, simple assembly.

Pseudos (Simple ones)

If the command is a simple pseudo (1) in Fig. 5.4.2, its nature is determined (2).

ORG

The total counter is set to 0(0). The pseudo ORG is called at the beginning of the program to enter *number* into the step counter (3); otherwise, the origin remains set to 0.

RSRV

When a block of cells is reserved, the label and the number of cells reserved are placed in the region table. The total counter is increased by the number of cells reserved.

CMNT

Comments are ignored in this pass.

EQU

Both symbols indicated as equivalent are entered and cross-referenced in a duplicate table (7). If an assignment has been made to either, as indicated in the symbol table, then that assignment must be duplicated for the other. If both of them have been assigned and assigned differently, an error is recorded. If neither has been assigned, this may be done at the end of the pass. As long as the assignment is the same for both symbols, then during the second pass, no matter which symbol is used, the same address will be entered into the fabricated command.

END

This pseudo signals the end of the first part of pass I.

DEF

When DEF is found, *label* preceding it is looked up in the symbol table (8). If it is already present in the symbol table with a definition following it (9), then it is overdefined and is listed in the error table (11). To expedite assembly, a rule may be incorporated dictating that the first (or last) definition is binding. If *label* is found in the symbol table but a definition is absent (9), then *number* and/or *letters* become the definition entered there (23); the entry is tagged to indicate that it has been defined.

When *label* is absent from the symbol table (8), both *label* and *numbers* and/or *letters* (the latter *is* the definition) are entered there and the total counter is advanced (12). The entry is tagged as defined (10).

Number and *letters* are translated into binary (or BCD) before they are stored in the definition table.

Mnemonic

We look for a label (16) which implies that this command is referred to by another part of the program—as the object of a jump, for instance. The label is looked up in the symbol table (17). If it is already listed, we see if it is tagged as defined (24). If the label is absent or present and undefined, we enter the present step counter setting as the label address and tag it as defined (19, 20).

If *label* is tagged as defined in the symbol table, then it is overdefined and is listed in the error table (18).

The treatment of the mnemonic depends upon whether it has an operand (13). If it does, is the operand a literal (25)? If so, is it in the literal table (28)? For present literals, we may skip to (A); otherwise the literal must be translated into binary. In the figure this is done in pass I (26), although this may be left until the second pass. Then the literal symbol and the translated literal are placed in the literal table (27) and we advance the total counter (29).

The literal is an interesting case; we distinguish three separate descriptions associated with it. There is the original reference to it in the program; this also acts as a symbol label in order to record it in the literal table. There is the binary, octal or BCD quantity into which it is translated. Finally there is the address where the literal is stored as a *built-in datum*.

The same literal (value) may be used many times in a program. It would be wasteful to redefine it upon each appearance. Therefore, it is looked up in the literal table (28) before processing is attempted (26, 27).

An operand is looked for in the symbol table (14). If absent, *address* is entered and the total counter is advanced so that a space in the program is reserved (15). So that we know it is undefined the entry must not be tagged. If there is no operand (13) or if the operand is listed in the symbol table (13, 14), nothing is done.

An entry in the error table is made (22) when an illegal command is detected (1). All pseudos, literals, and mnemonics lead to ③ so that, eventually, the next command will be examined (21) and classified (1). Commands are examined until END is encountered.

Errors and labeled mnemonics exit through the path (A) (30) and (31). This advances both the step and total counter. The total counter advances for any memory cell reservation; the step counter advances for any tabulated source program step. When a new data allocation is associated with a program, the total counter is advanced immediately (15) or (29).

5.5   WINDUP OF FIRST PASS

The second phase of the first pass involves three main tasks:

- In some assemblers (including ours), the human is now informed by a printout of obvious errors that the assembler has detected; other assemblers wait until the end of pass II to furnish this printout.
- Unassigned entries in the symbol table are assigned addresses as yet unassigned.
- If no disabling errors have occurred, the second pass is entered; otherwise, the assembler goes on the next job noting this fact first.

The flow diagram for the windup portion of the first pass of the assembler program is found in Fig. 5.5.1.

Illegal Commands

If there are any entries in the illegal command table (1), then the entries from the illegal command table are printed (2). Blanks replace the illegal command code and assembly continues.

Symbol Analysis

Entries in the symbol table are divided into four categories (4), two of which produce difficulties:

- A symbol tagged as undefined is entered into the *underdefined symbol* table (5).
- A symbol defined more than once is entered in the *overdefined* table.
- Symbols tagged as never used are collected in the *unused* table. When the programmer labels a step but never refers to that label an entry appears in this table.
- Symbols defined only once and used at least once are looked on with the most favor.

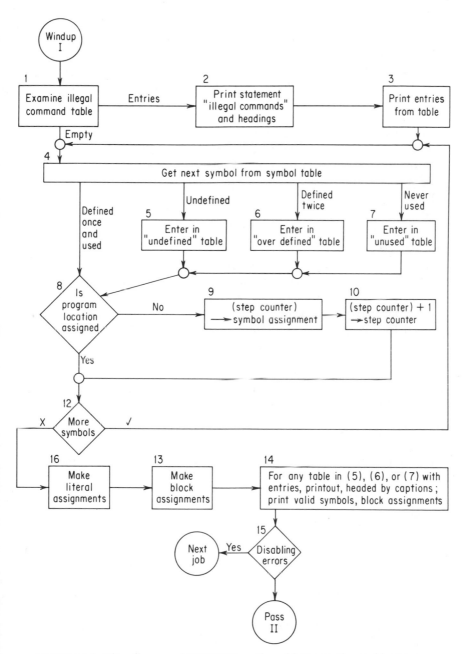

FIGURE 5.5.1. Flow diagram of WINDUP portion of first pass of assembly program.

Address Assignment

As each symbol table entry is reviewed for possible copying into a *use* table, its assignment status is noted. If unassigned, an assignment algorithm for the particular assembler is employed. For FLAP, successive locations in the remainder of the program are allocated to successive symbols. This space is known to be available because the total counter monitors *total* space usage regardless of whether the space had been assigned.

In (8) we check for symbol assignment. The present step counter reading is given to an unassigned symbol (9) the step counter is advanced (10). If there are more symbols in the symbol table (12), we return to (4) and get the next symbol. Otherwise, we go on and make literal and block assignments (13).

Literals

All literals required by the program have been listed in the *literal* table including the original meaning and the machine language equivalent. Each machine language equivalent is entered into a cell—enough cells were provided by advancing the total and step counters as each literal was encountered. Now (16) cells are allocated and the literals are entered. Then in pass II, references to literals can have their address fields replaced by the address in the literal table.

Block Assignments

It is usually desirable to constitute a block from contiguous locations.

Printout

The tables developed in (5), (6) and (7) may now be printed out. They are properly headed so the human can interpret them. In addition, a table of valid symbols may be printed from the symbol table, skipping those entries which are covered by the other error tables. A list of block assignments also may be produced.

Naturally, the format and detail produced depend upon the assemblers; for instance, one may subdivide illegal symbols into those associated with pseudos, mnemonics, macros, etc.

Cross Reference

On pass II the object program is produced. Data space is provided for input and output data. Built-in data and literals must be included in the object program string. The cross reference table indicates which data outputs must be filled in.

Continuation

When to continue to pass II is designed into the assembler. Some assemblers always assemble! When a decision is made by the assembler it is done in (15).

5.6   THE SECOND PASS

Procedure

The purpose of this pass is to review each command, replacing it by the final machine language command which contains a command code, tags and an address and equivalent to the source command. All addresses have been allocated so that a symbolic address may be replaced with its assignment.

How to review

The most effective way to review the source commands depends upon the assembler input medium. If magnetic tape is the source of assembly input, then the tape must be rewound. If punchcards are the input medium, which is most frequently the case, the problem is different. Card reading equipment is not capable of automatically restacking the input cards for another pass through the input. This must be done physically by the human and takes much too much time. The most popular solution is to copy information from the cards to an intermediate magnetic tape during pass I.

Double intermediate magnetic tape system

A problem occurs for both magnetic tape input and card input with a single intermediate magnetic tape. When the first pass is finished, the magnetic tape containing the command information is sitting at the end of the source language program. To review the information the tape must be rewound and restarted; this is time consuming.

A double intermediate tape is used in the IBM 7090 FAP assembler. This system has an initial punchcard source program input. The input is headed by a card indicating the number of program steps. During the first pass the program steps are copied from the cards into the first intermediate tape until the halfway mark. At this point, intermediate tape 1 is rewound and the remaining program steps are entered onto tape 2. At the end of pass I, tape 2 is rewound also; but now, while tape 2 is rewinding, pass II can begin with the already rewound intermediate tape 1 (it contains the first half of the source language program steps).

Output

The output of the assembly program is, most important, the binary object program, ready to be loaded by the loader. A documentation of both the source language and object language program is of importance in debugging the program. The two should be correlated so that each object program step matches an original source language step. Such a printout which may be printed off line.

A portion of a typical (FLAP) printout is found in Fig. 5.6.1. Binary

| | OCTAL | | | | SYMBOLIC | | |
Heading:	Step Number	Command Code	Supplementary Information	Operand Address	Location	Command	Supplementary Address	Comments
Example:	00004	0500	000	00011	TEMPCAL	XMA	TMP	START
	00005	0774	004	00014		XPI	012,4	TEMPERATURE
	00006	0400	004	00031		ADD	FUNC + 12,4	CALC.

FIGURE 5.6.1. Typical assembly printout format.

object language furnished the computer is most easily understood when printed in octal. Here three bits of object language are replaced by their octal equivalent in the style followed in the figure.

The first column in Fig. 5.6.1 is the step number assigned to the command. The remainder of the octal information in the first column is the actual word stored at the location. This word is broken up with blanks simply to improve comprehension. The remainder of each row contains the source language command to the assembler, be it mnemonic, pseudo or whatever.

Below we discuss how the information for transmission to the object language tape is gathered in the location designated OCTOUT. The information for printout, which always includes the information at OCTOUT, is designated PRINTOUT.

Command Review

The startup and command review portion of the second pass is illustrated in the flow diagram in Fig. 5.6.2.

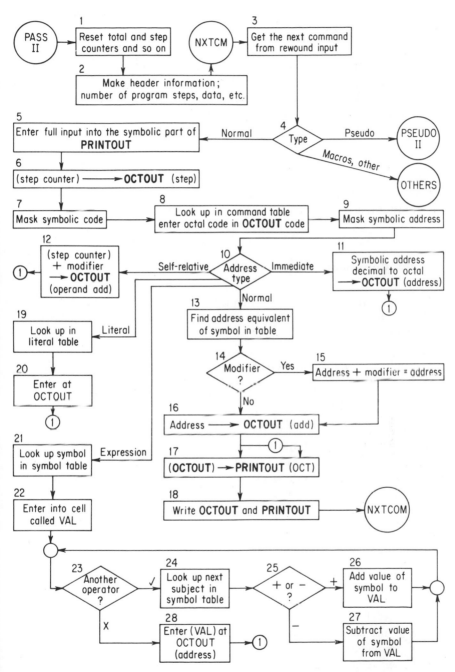

FIGURE 5.6.2. Repetitive portion of second pass of assembly program.

Startup

Reset functions are performed at the beginning of the second pass. Both the total counter and the step counter must be reset to 0 or the proper origin setting (ORG). A record is kept of the final settings of these counters. Other cells and registers must be cleared and housekeeping functions performed.

Header information, highly dependent on both the assembler and loader design, must be fabricated. All information initially required by the loader is furnished in the header of the object language program. It might contain, for instance, the number of steps in the program, the breakdown between program steps and data cells, the number and name of subroutines required. This information is accumulated in the first pass.

For Each Command

The next (first) command is brought from the input (3) and its type is determined (4). The treatment of pseudocommands is examined later in this section. Macros and other special commands are discussed in Chapters 6 and 7.

The full command in symbolic form is entered into the symbolic portion of PRINTOUT (5). The present setting of the step counter is the cell location for this command in the object program. This is entered in the step number portion of OCTOUT (6).

The mnemonic is extracted (7) and looked up in the command code table (8), then it is entered into the code portion of OCTOUT.

Next the symbolic address is extracted from the command. What follows depends on the type of address (10). This is determined by the command type which was obtained when the command was looked up (8).

Address Processors

There are five kinds of addresses:

- literal
- symbolic expressions
- immediate
- self-relative
- direct (and indirect)

The address translation is inserted immediately in the object command. Usually the source language address is decimal and must be translated into octal before being placed in the address portion of OCTOUT (11).

SELF-RELATIVE

Such commands refer addresses to the step number in execution. The final address is obtained when the modifier is added to the contents of the step counter and this is placed in the address portion of OCTOUT. Thus if the programmer has called for the address ∗ + 3 in this command, 3 is added to the step counter (in binary or BCD).

DIRECT

The symbol in the address field of the source language command is looked up in the symbol table (13). All symbols now have locations assigned to them. If there is a modifier associated with the address (indirect addressing or index tag, for instance) (14), this modifier must be included with the address field (15) of OCTOUT (15, 16).

LITERAL

A cell in the literal table stores the BCD literal and its binary translation (in binary machines). The *name* of the entry in the literal table *is* the literal in its original symbolic form; early in pass I its machine language equivalent was placed there. During WINDUP, this was replaced by a cell number That is what we need now.

We replace the literal name in the command by the address of the cell where the machine representation of the literal is stored.

SYMBOLIC EXPRESSIONS

These are arithmetic functions of symbolic addresses. The assembler looks up *each* symbol and replaces it with the *value* in the table. The arithmetic expression is evaluated concurrently with lookup or thereafter. Since such evaluation is a compiler function, FLAP is limited to expressions involving only addition and subtraction.

Table Reference Simplification

Address evaluation involves much time consuming table reference. It is expedited by:

- table lookup hardware
- list processing hardware or software facilitation
- interpass sorting

The latter is most frequently practiced. Ordered tables facilitate lookup; binary search reduces the number of entries referred to.

Printout

The symbolic portion of PRINTOUT has already been supplied. The octal portion is transferred *in toto* from OCTOUT (17). Now we write out both records (18) and go on to get the next command.

Pseudos, End-of-Pass

The treatment of pseudos and the end-of-pass is presented in Fig. 5.6.3.

Pseudos are no problem. COMMENT (1) requires that everything in the address field be printed out (2). END indicates that the examination of commands now terminates and the pass is almost over. All other pseudos except special ones are ignored (1)—we get the next command.

END

A check may be made at this point to see if the present contents of the step counter correspond with the termination step during the first pass; otherwise we might suspect something is wrong. The cross-reference table is now reviewed (3). Literals and built-in data appear in the table with both a cell number and a cell content (4). Both of these are passed over to OCTOUT (5). The entry is duplicated in PRINTOUT (6). Also, when present from a data definition, the data symbol or literal obtained from the table is entered in the symbolic label portion of PRINTOUT. The alphanumeric equivalents of binary literals are printed by some assemblers. Both OCTOUT and PRINTOUT are written (7), and we continue to examine the cross-reference table.

If the item is not a literal or built-in datum, it should be an inputted datum or block (8). The location number associated with the symbol and/or the blocks is entered into the cell number portion of OCTOUT which is tagged to indicate that these locations will hold data. The rest of the entry is left blank since the data is not presently available (9). The contents of OCTOUT are entered into PRINTOUT. The label is also placed there (10). Both units are then printed out (11).

When there are no more cross-reference table entries (8), the printouts for macros, subroutines and other special tables are produced in (12).

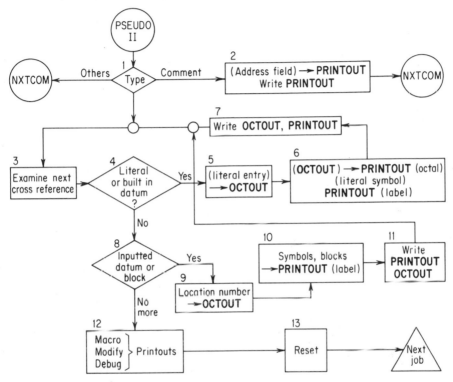

FIGURE 5.6.3. Processing the pseudos and completion for the second pass of the assembly program.

These are discussed in subsequent chapters. The assembly program is then reset (13), and we continue to the next job.

Printout

Figure 5.6.4 presents a printout of the data portion of an assembly. Data entries are given step numbers, but the octal portion is blank. Data blocks have step numbers and only one entry. In the figure, 64 locations are reserved for DELTA. Incidentally, decimal 64 becomes octal 100, accounting for the hiatus of one hundred spaces.

Entry Type	Step	Octal	Symbolic
Command	01347	050000061811	XMA RESULT
Datum	01350		ALPHA
Datum	01351		BETA
Datum	01352		GAMMA
Data Block	01353		DELTA RSRV 064
Data Block	01453		EPSLN RSRV 008
Literal	01463	000000000001	ONE
Literal	01464	016314000000	TAXLIM 0048000000

FIGURE 5.6.4. Data printout for typical assembly program illustrating three types.

Literal entries have an octal translation next to the step number.

Printout can be done on-line or written on magtape for later printout of line.

5.7   THE ONE-PASS ASSEMBLER

Feasibility

TWO PASS METHOD

The first pass of the two pass system accounts for all the labels and symbols addressed by the source language program. It makes all the allocations so that when the second pass begins, every symbol encountered has been assigned a location. Two passes are required because if a symbol is referred to before it is defined and a cell allocated to it, the command containing the symbol cannot be fully translated.

When a symbol is described after it has occurred in the program, it may be necessary to defer assignment. Similarly, when a command refers to another command further ahead in the program and for which space has not been allocated, the same problem arises. How then is it feasible to do assembly in one pass?

SOLUTIONS

There are at least three one-pass solutions:

- An assembler for a two-address machine (really one-plus-one address machine) does not require sequential allocation of storage and can use a one-pass assembler.
- If the entire source program can be stored in memory during assembly, only a single input operation is needed.
- If more stringent rules are imposed upon the source language, it is possible with a different assembler philosophy to do the job in one pass.

One-Plus-One Address Machine

Drum computers, such as the IBM 650 and the Univac Solid-State 90, commonly use a 1 + 1 addressing format. They do not comply with our original assumption: they are not random-access memory machines. Memory cells are laid out on the drum as shown in Fig. 5.7. A number of sets of reading heads are provided. As the drum revolves, the area that passes beneath a given set of reading heads is called the channel. Each channel contains a number of cells. To find a given cell, we must do two things: we must select a channel; we must wait until the cell selected passes beneath the reading head.

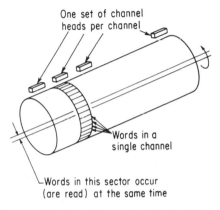

Cells in a given channel may be classified according to their positions around the drum. Each is set to lie in a different sector. All cells that lie in the same sector pass under the reading heads at the same time. To provide optimum programming, the 1 + 1 address system is selected. The first address is the operand address; the

FIGURE 5.7. Pictorial representation of the drum memory.

second is the address of the next instruction. Permitting this second address to be variable allows us to fix the position of the next instruction on the drum according to the length of the command now in process. If we know the time required to execute *this* command, we can place the next command in a section which comes beneath the reading heads right after this command is performed.

Since the next instruction address is included in the command word, commands need not occupy sequential locations. In fact, it is to avoid the sequential arrangement that this addressing format is chosen.

HOW DOES THIS HELP THE ASSEMBLER?

Data can be assigned to any cell on the drum not previously used. Further, when a later program step is referred to, this step can be assigned immediately and reserved. Thus all assignments can be made as soon as needed. This is the reason that SOAP, the assembler for the IBM 650, one of the first small scientific computers, does its assembly in a single pass, whereas many of today's faster computers require two or more passes.

Source Program in Memory

If the entire source program is placed in core memory, it is completely and immediately available to the assembler. The question now arises, what do we mean a pass to be? If this is the number of times commands are reviewed, then placing the source program in memory will not eliminate a second pass. However, if we refer to the number of times information is entered from outside (from an intermediate medium) to the assembler, then this need be done only once.

Since the input and output operations consume most of the time, a large improvement will accrue from storing the source program entirely in memory.

Is this possible? Manufacturers usually design their assemblers to go on the minimum machine configuration. Thus if an assembler is designed for 4K of memory, the customer with 32K of memory might easily fit the assembler and his entire source language program into memory and hence reduce his total assembly time. But the 4K assembler cannot be used this way; either the manufacturer must supply two assemblers or else the user with the large installation must design his own assembler.

Rule Change

Two things cause difficulty with the assembler: data definitions are at arbitrary points within the source program; labeled program steps are referred to before being counted.

The first difficulty is eliminated if all data definitions precede the main program. If this rule is not imposed upon the programmer, we might tag data cards and presort the deck before it is entered into the computer.

The second obstacle can be overcome by preassigning program regions so that, when an unassigned step in the program is referred to, an assignment is made to the beginning of a new region. Later, when commands whose labels were previously assigned are encountered, they follow the assignment made previously to this region. Should the program segment be larger than the region provided, another region assignment is made and the program is continued. This requires a slight alteration in the assembler design, but the advantage is probably worth the change.

PROBLEMS

5.1   Name and characterize the five kinds of assembly commands.

5.2   Repeat problem 5.1 for five kinds of data.

5.3   What are the main tasks of the simple assembler?

5.4   Explain *built-in data*, *nonvariable data*, *record-variable data*, and *literal*.

5.5   Write one FLAP program which finds the volume
       (a) of a sphere if (FIGURE) = SPHERE.
       (b) of a cone if (FIGURE) = CONE.
       (c) of a cylinder if (FIGURE) = CYLIND.
       Use RADIUS in (a), RAD in (b), and R in (c) for the radius. Use EQL to
       equate them. Employ all the other pseudos if possible.

5.6   Write another FLAP program as before, but this time to find the surface
       area of the figure. Use the three forms of *radius* as in problem 5.5.

5.7   Combine problems 5.5 and 5.6 into a single program to find area for
       (MENS) = AREA and volume for (MENS) = VOL.

5.8   Review the assembler tables in Table 5.4, indicating why each is needed,
       what kind of assembler needs it and when, if ever, it may be dispensed with.

5.9   How does the assembler react to each of the pseudos of Section 5.3?

5.10   Why is it necessary to have a separate phase of the pass I directed to
       WINDUP?

5.11   Why is a second pass required in most assemblers?

5.12   What can be done to make a one-pass assembler
       (a) for a 1 + 1 address machine?
       (b) for a single address machine?

6

MACROS

6.1 WHAT ARE MACROS?

Macros As Subroutines

The **macrocommand,** or simply **macro**, is a subroutine (generally an open one) with which a name, the **macro name**, is associated. The programmer can use subroutines more profitably by simplifying reference to them. The macro name for the subroutine saves time since this single referent ellicits the entire set of commands from the associated software—the assembler, loader, etc.

Where Are The Macros Defined?

Macros and subroutines may be defined in

- the library
- the assembler
- the program

A **library** is a large collection of subroutines. Access to the library may be made when the program is ready to run. Subroutines for the library may be prepared by programmers all over the country who use this particular machine and have need to solve a particular problem or subproblem. Any program may be looked upon as a subroutine and incorporated into the library so long as the control and naming conventions of the library are maintained in the subroutines. After all, any problem may be thought of as a subproblem of a larger problem which has recourse to the method of solution provided by the subproblem.

LIBRARY

Library macros are externally defined subroutines available for the programmer to request for incorporation when the program is loaded. To facilitate use of a library subroutine, it should be properly documented. Then the programmer will know what, if any, parameters are required and their order and format. The documentation should specify the form and quantity of results and how the subroutine should be employed, as well as the intimate details of incorporation.

ASSEMBLY DEFINED MACROS

Some assemblers furnish subroutine skeletons which they can incorporate into the object program in either open or closed form when the programmer requests this by using the macro name. Documentation requirements for **assembly defined macros** parallel those of library defined macros; the difference is only *where* the subroutine is made available. Here they are produced as part of the assembly language output. Many assemblers provide assembly defined macros to facilitate library calls; these are discussed in Chapter 7.

PROGRAMMER DEFINED MACROS

The programmer may define a macro within his source language program in some assemblers. This permits him to have the assistance of the assembler in incorporating the subroutine into his program and it eliminates repetition of the command sequence and the link management required for closed subroutines. The programmer defined macro dominates the remainder of this chapter.

The Programmer Defined Macro

The name of the **programmer defined macro** appears in the source language programs in two ways. In the **macro definition prototype,** or simply **macro prototype**, the subroutine is named by the programmer and he enumerates all the steps which comprise it. The macro name and the sequence of instructions to which the name applies are supplied by the programmer in source language.

After defining his macro the programmer may *use* it at any time with a **macro call**. He enters the macro name in his assembly program as though it were a normal command mnemonic. He provides in the address field an argument list, discussed later.

Classification of Macros

One classification is the *time* at which the macro sequence is defined:

- at any time *before* the subroutine is entered into the external (library defined)
- when the assembler was constructed (assembler defined)
- when the source program is written (programmer defined)

Second, we distinguish:

- closed
- open

Third, we note the time at which they are incorporated:

- assembly time
- between assembly and load time
- load time
- run time

Finally, we classify subroutines according to their variability:

- fixed length whenever called
- variable length dependent upon the parameters supplied

CLOSED OR OPEN

At run time, a duplicate of the open subroutine appears whenever required in the program; the closed subroutine appears only once in memory.

TIME OF INCORPORATION

The assembler may furnish the coding to the object program during assembly. The object program is stored on an intermediate medium until we are ready to run it. The program including the subroutine is then entered into memory by the loader.

The assembler may indicate to the combined loader-allocator what subroutines are required at run time but may omit the object language subroutine per se. When we are ready to run, the loader not only places the object program into memory, but also finds in the library the subroutines requested, enters them in memory and collates them with the requests.

When a separate allocator and loader are provided as with UTMOST for UNIVAC III, the subroutine may be incorporated after assembly time but before run time. For UTMOST this allocation and incorporation time is called *designation time.*

FIXED OR VARIABLE OBJECT SUBROUTINES

When a fixed sequence of steps is requested by the macro call, the assembler merely has to fill in a series of blanks provided for by a table which it incorporated during macro definition.

In contrast the number of steps produced by the variable macro depends upon one or more of the input parameters.

Combinations of Characteristics

Table 6.1 classifies subroutines according to the above characteristics.

TABLE 6.1   Macro Classification Table

Subroutine source	Fixed sequence		Sequence variable generated		Time
	Open	Closed	Open	Closed	Incorporated
Source language defined	Yes	Possible	No	No	Assembly
Part of assembler	Yes	Possible	Yes	Possible	Assembly
Part of subroutine library	Possible	Yes	Possible	Possible	Run

Note: "Possible" means not generally used but theoretically possible.

SOURCE LANGUAGE DEFINED

When the subroutine is incorporated at assembly time, we transmit to the assembler a macro definition in source language. This is the basis of the output command sequence produced by the assembler in response to a later macro call.

It is possible to produce the macro in object language as a closed subroutine. This introduces complications into the assembler. The loss of efficiency in the assembler and the subroutine operation may be compensated for by the release of memory for the segments which need not be duplicated. In any case, the complication would overtax the explanation; hence we confine the discussion of macros to the programmer defined macro—to open fixed length sequences incorporated at assembly time.

ASSEMBLY DEFINED MACROS

Macros such as GET and SAVE for FLAP (Sections 7.2 and 7.3) are incorporated at assembly time. Fixed or variable sequences of commands may be supplied by assembly defined macros.

LIBRARY MACROS

Although libraries of subroutines might be available to the assembler for incorporation during assembly, this is not customary. Hence, library subroutines by definition are incorporated at post assembly time or load time. The means to get hold of subroutines must be provided in the assembler—but the routine itself is provided by the library under the egis of the allocator or loader.

It is simple for the allocator to provide closed library subroutines. Fabrication of links is done through cooperation of the assembler and the loader.

The *subroutine* from the library is a fixed sequence of commands. To produce a variable sequence, we might withdraw a **macro generator**—a sequence to construct the SR—from the library. This eventuality is beyond our present scope.

Sections 6.2 through 6.5 are devoted to programmer defined macro generation. Section 6.6 discusses the nesting of programmer defined macros.

6.2   FLAP MACRO DEFINITION

Defining The Macro

The programmer conveys to the assembler:

- The macro name.
- The names by which the programmer refers to the variables within the prototype structure. These variables' names are called the **prototype arguments** or **prototype parameters**.
- One command and operand for each step of the subroutine.

To convey the macro definition to the assembler, the source language often provides two pseudos. In FLAP these are MCDEF and MCEND. They bracket the prototype subroutine as shown in Fig. 6.2.1. Their format is:

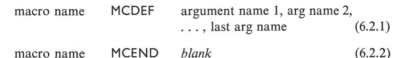

$$\text{macro name} \quad \text{MCDEF} \quad \text{argument name 1, arg name 2,} \quad \ldots, \text{last arg name} \qquad (6.2.1)$$

$$\text{macro name} \quad \text{MCEND} \quad \textit{blank} \qquad (6.2.2)$$

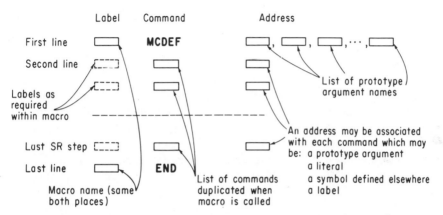

FIGURE 6.2.1. The macro definition or prototype using the pseudos *MCDEF* and *END*.

The Prototype Macro

FIRST LINE

The assembler detects the presence of a macro definition when it encounters (6.2.1) as at the top of Fig. 6.2.1. The command field contains MCDEF. The name of the macro being defined is macro name (6.2.1). The address field contains a list of prototype arguments. The number of argument names is the same as the number of variables provided in the corresponding fields of the *macro call*. This is limited only by the assembler structure. An argument is a constant or a symbol address according to its use in the macro definition.

SUBROUTINE STEPS

Lines of the source program that follow may be labeled. The command field preferably contains mnemonics. It may also contain a pseudo or previously defined macros if the assembler provides for nesting macros. This is discussed in Section 6.6.

The address field of each definition step contains a valid address. It may,

- refer to a prototype argument, one of those listed in the initial line containing MCDEF,
- contain a literal, if this is permissible,
- contain a symbol defined elsewhere in the program,
- contain a label previously defined or refer to a step within the macro itself,
- use a self-relative address,
- be blank for some mnemonics.

MCEND

As long as commands continue, the assembler assumes that they are part of the macro definition prototype and will incorporate them. Improper mnemonics are accepted but printed out for later correction by the programmer, just as anywhere else in the program. The macro definition is terminated when MCEND is encountered. The name of the macro whose definition is terminated appears in the label portion of MCEND.

Some assemblers use END to end a macro definition or permit MCEND to be unlabeled. MCEND makes the definition unambiguous and helps with nested definitions (see Section 6.6).

Evaluating a Quadratic

To illustrate this principle we define a macro to evaluate a quadratic equation. The six mnemonics to do this appear in Fig. 6.2.2. They were

Equation:	$Y = AX^2 + BX + C$	
Subroutine:	1	XMD X
	2	MUL A
	3	ADD B
	4	MUL X
	5	ADD C
	6	XAM Y

FIGURE 6.2.2. A quadratic and a symbolic subroutine to solve it.

obtained from the equivalence:

$$AX^2 + BX + C = X(AX + B) + C$$

QUAD DEFINITION

We name the macro QUAD. Its definition in FLAP is in Fig. 6.2.3. The first line of the definition consists of the title QUAD, the pseudo for macro definition, MCDEF, and a list of the five arguments used in the subroutine.

```
QUAD      MCDEF  A, B, C, X, Y
          XMD    X
          MUL    A
          ADD    B
          MUL    X
          ADD    C
          XAM    Y
QUAD      MCEND
```

FIGURE 6.2.3. A macro definition for the quadratic equation of Fig. 6.2.2.

All arguments represent symbolic addresses. We could have designed the macro so that some parameters, perhaps *A*, *B*, and *C*, are literals supplied in the definition.

The next six entries are duplicates of those in Fig. 6.2.2. They are mnemonics with prototype arguments associated with them. The last step in the definition uses MCEND to indicate that the definition is now complete.

Using The Macro

Later in the program we call the SR as shown in Fig. 6.2.4.

```
          XAM   ZETA
SOLVE     QUAD  ALPHA, BETA, PHI, VOL, TEMP
NEXT      XMD   TEMP
          MUL   TIME
```

FIGURE 6.2.4. Call for the macro QUAD in a program for assembly.

The assembler is notified to employ this SR when it recognizes the macro name QUAD in a command field. This macro call can be labeled; in our illustration it is called SOLVE. The number of arguments in the macro call QUAD should be five as in the prototype. The arguments can be given any symbolic name previously defined or, in some cases, to be defined, as shown in the figure. Only the macro name QUAD and an argument list are required to call forth the subroutine.

Figure 6.2.5 shows the printout of the assembled program (when a macro call is totally printed). The object program contains a series of steps identical

```
          XAM   ZETA
SOLVE     XMD   VOL     ⎫  In some assemblies the
          MUL   ALPHA   ⎪  symbolic command and address
          ADD   BETA    ⎪  within the macro are omitted
          MUL   VOL     ⎬  from the printout.
          ADD   PHI     ⎪  Only the binary equivalent
          XAM   TEMP    ⎪  is transferred to the binary
NEXT      XMD   TEMP    ⎪  output. This also appears
          MUL   TIME    ⎭  in the printout.
```

FIGURE 6.2.5. Printout of the program assembled from Fig. 6.2.4.

with those which would be produced if the source program sequence of Fig. 6.2.5 were presented to it. For some assemblers, the symbolic names in the macro call appear in the printout.

6.3 THE FIXED MACRO GENERATOR, QUAD

Calling The Macro

QUAD is called using the source language word dissected in Table 6.3.1, which shows and labels the command fields of the QUAD call.

TABLE 6.3.1   Fields of Incoming QUAD Macro Command
Command Fields

	INCOM	+1	+2	+3	+4	+5	+6
Content	label	QUAD	l(A)	l(B)	l(C)	l(X)	l(Y)

Note: l(A) means one label in this macro call for QUAD, corresponding to the argument A in the macro definition for QUAD.

The assembler routine which produces the object language code (or supplies sufficient information for its production) once the assembler has recognized the macro call, is a **generator**.

The first field, INCOM, in the macro call contains a label which is ignored now by the assembler. The second field INCOM + 1 contains the name of the macro. It is identified as a macro since:

1. It is looked up in the command table from which it is absent.

2. It is, therefore, not a suitable mnemonic or pseudocommand.

3. It is looked up and found in the macro name table.

The next job is turned over to the *generator*.

In the following five fields, INCOM + 2 through INCOM + 6, are labels of the arguments used in producing this macro.

WHAT THE GENERATOR DOES

The QUAD generator performs a number of tasks. The argument labels provided are not satisfactory for the object program. They must be translated

from symbolic addresses into previously assigned numerical addresses before object commands can be produced. The generator

- looks up the labels and finds their
  correspondents.
- lists the addresses in the order of
  appearance of the argument labels.
- creates a list of output commands.
- supplies a suitable address for each
  command.
- outputs the commands as part of the
  object program.

Argument Management

The generator might set up a table of
arguments for the QUAD macro as in the flow
chart of Fig. 6.3.1. The task to be performed
is to set up computer equivalent of Table 6.3.2.
Since the table is the argument table for the
QUAD macro, we call it QUADRG. The
first location in the table is referred to as
QUADRG. One cell is allocated to each argument symbol that appears in the macro definition argument list; space is also provided to
store the address corresponding to each symbol.

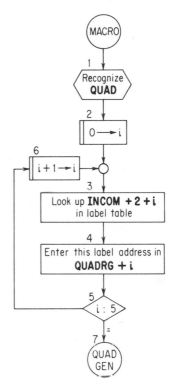

FIGURE 6.3.1. Flow chart
for the construction of the
QUADRG table.

In the flow chart we first recognize the QUAD macro (1) after setting an
index, i, to 0 (2), we obtain an argument field (3) and look it up in the
assembler symbol table. The symbol and its address are entered in the
corresponding positions in the argument QUADRG. Are there any more
of the five argument fields left to be analyzed (5)? If so, the index is advanced
(6) and the next argument label looked up. Otherwise we go on to the
generation routine.

TABLE 6.3.2   QUAD Argument Table

Location	Space for
QUADRG	First argument symbol and address
+1	Second argument symbol and address
+2	Third argument symbol and address
+3	Fourth argument symbol and address
+4	Fifth argument symbol and address

Command Generation

Command generation is performed by referring to the command table or this macro. The command table is the computer equivalent of Table 6.3.3. The table contains, in order, the commands which produce the macro. They are tagged to indicate the kind of addressing required with the command. In the address field is an address or argument number. For instance, the first entry in the QUAD command table is XMD which requires the fourth

TABLE 6.3.3   QUAD Command Table

Location	Command field	Tag field	Address referent field
QUADCM	XMD	A	3
+1	MUL	A	0
+2	ADD	A	1
+3	MUL	A	3
+4	ADD	A	2
+5	XAM	A	4

Note: All symbolic entries in this table should actually be binary codes, binary address, or binary tags.

argument supplied in the macroc all at INCOM + 5. The QUAD command table entry is tagged as an argument with address A. Operand address for the command appears as the fourth entry in QUADRG, QUADRG + 3. It is the address corresponding to the label which must be finally produced for the object language command.

For further clarification, let us look at the macro call, QUAD, at SOLVE in Fig. 6.2.4. The fourth item in the argument list is the label VOL. In the address of the object command XMD, the first command in the macro sequence, is the address allocated to the symbol VOL.

Let us now see how the QUAD generator operates to produce the command sequence.

QUAD Generator Flow Diagram

The flow chart for the command generation of the sequence QUAD is shown in Fig. 6.3.2. It begins by setting an index to 6 (1) because there are exactly six commands in the sequence. The next entry is obtained from the command table called QUADCM (2). We extract the command code from the command by masking it into a register. From the register it is sent to the binary output called OCTOUT (3). Next the argument number is extracted from the entry of QUADCM that we have been using: this quantity is used as an index called j (4). The index quantity just procured is used to augment the starting position QUADRG of the argument table, QUADRG. This table is entered and the argument address is obtained (5). This address is now entered into the binary output (6).

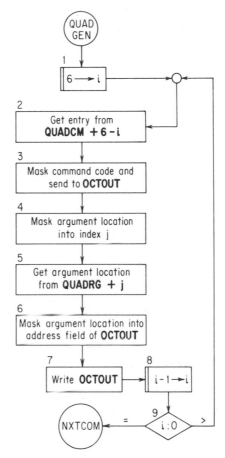

The command is now completely assembled and can be written out (7). A symbolic output may also be produced at this time, although this is not shown. The command number just generated is incremented (8), and we check to see if there are any more commands left (9). If there are, we return to the sequence beginning at (1). Otherwise, we reset the macro generation mechanism and continue by examining the next source language command.

An Assembly Program.
QUADGEN

Figure 6.3.3 shows a program to generate the QUAD routine with FLAP mnemonics for the assembler.

The first command sets up index 1 for five arguments. The second command at GETFIELD brings the next (first) field of the macro call into the A register. Table 6.3.1 shows that the first argument field is at INCOM + 2. The first time used $((N1) = -5)$, INCOM + 7 in GETFIELD

FIGURE 6.3.2. Flow chart for the construction and output of the commands required for the macro call QUAD.

will get the first argument.

GETFIELD + 1 is a jump to the table search SR which looks up the argument in the symbol table. When finished the SR leaves the address corresponding to the furnished symbol in the A register. GETFIELD + 2 is not a command but an indication that the table to be used is called *LABEL*— it is part of the calling sequence for TBLSRCH.

At GETFIELD + 3 the argument address in the A register is inserted in QUADRG. Indexing points to the table entry. The negative index is incremented in command GETFIELD + 4; we continue to fill the argument table until the index register reads 0.

The generator proper is initialized at QUADGEN. The QUAD command table starts at QUADCM. The next command is withdrawn from QUADCM

Step	*Command*		*Use*
−1	XPN,1	−5	There are 5 arguments
GETFIELD	XMA,1	INCOM + 7	Get next field
+1	JSN,4	TBLSRCH,4	Go to subroutine which looks up (A) in table whose name appears in the next command.
+2	NOOP	LABEL	Use *label table*
+3	XAM,1	QUADRG + 5	Store argument location
+4	TUN,1	GETFIELD	Fill entire argument table
QUADGEN	XPN,1	−6	There are 6 commands
+1	XMA,1	QUADCM + 6 ⎫	Get command portion of
+2	ANDTA	MASKCM ⎬	this command from table
+3	XAM	OCTOUT ⎭	and put it in output.
+4	XMA,1	QUADCM + 6 ⎫	Put argument location in
+5	ANDTA	MASKAD ⎬	index 2.
+6	XAN,2	⎭	
+7	XMA,2	QUADRG ⎫	Put argument address into
+8	ORTM	OCTOUT ⎬	command.
+9	WRITE	OCTOUT	
+10	TUN,1	QUADGEN + 1	Output all 6 commands
+11	UCJ	NXTCM	Exit

FIGURE 6.3.3. Assembly program to generate QUAD.

by QUADGEN + 1. We mask out the command portion of the QUADCM entry using ANDTA. The mask *command* is at MASKCM. Where it contains 1's, the quantity in the A register will be preserved; where there are 0's in the mask, the quantity in the A register will be set to 0. The extracted command code is placed in OCTOUT by QUADGEN + 3.

A sequence of three commands at QUADGEN + 3 masks the address portion of the entry in QUADCM into the A register and from there into *index 2*. Now we have the ordinal number of the argument in *index 2*.

At QUADGEN + 7 we enter QUADRG and withdraw the entry which has the ordinal number of the address found for this command in QUADCM. Presently OCTOUT contains all 0's except for its command code. By *OR*ing the address is masked from the accumulator into OCTOUT in QUADGEN + 8. This completes the assembly of a single command.

In QUADGEN + 9 the assembled command is written out. In QUADGEN + 10 we check to see if more commands are to be assembled.

If there are, we return to QUADGEN + 1 and get the next command from the command table. If not, QUADGEN + 11 jumps to the sequence which inputs the next command for assembly.

SYMBOLIC OUTPUT

It is simple to include a few more orders to assemble the symbolic output to be entered into PRINTOUT in order to produce a record for the programmer. The argument symbol as well as its address must be stored in the argument table and the mnemonic must be stored in the command table along with the command code.

6.4   THE UNIVERSAL MACRO GENERATOR

What Is It?

In the previous section we examined a generator for a specific macro, QUAD. The generality of this process can be discovered if we scrutinize the generator flow chart. What must be changed to accommodate a different macro?

- A different command table and a different argument table are needed.
- The number of commands for the new macro is probably different from that for QUAD.
- The number of arguments is also probably different.

We specify the number of items in each table for *each* macro required in a new table where it is available to the generator:

- the location of each table
- the number of entries in each table

We now examine a generator which will produce any macro after it has been defined by the programmer using the prototype macro definition.

TABLES

The macro definition routine produces a number of tables:

- For each macro, a macro command table unique to that definition.
- A directory, called here MCNAME, which lists
  * each macro by name.
  * where that macro command table is stored.

We find later that one argument table serves for all macros.

TABLE 6.4   Tables Required for Generation of the Macro and Their Entries

Table	Entries
MCNAME	1. Macro Name 2. Starting address of macro command table 3. Length of macro command table 4. Number of arguments required
Macro command table	1. Command type tag 2. Command mnemonic 3. Command code 4. Address type tag 5. Address part 6. Index designation and supplementary information
ARGTAB	1. Argument symbol 2. Argument address

A list of tables required in the production of a macro and their contents appears as Table 6.4.

MCNAME

Figure 6.4.1 provides a first look at MCNAME. The left-hand column contains a current list of defined macros. There are pointers to macro command tables for each macro. The figure shows macro command tables for four macros which provide, respectively, polynomial solution, quadratic equation evaluation, matrix inversion and square root.

Other entries in the directory supply a quantitative description of each macro:

- the number of arguments required for the macro
- the number of commands to be produced by this macro

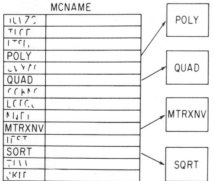

FIGURE 6.4.1. How MCNAME points to all the macro command tables listed therein.

Relation of the Generator to the Other Tables

Figure 6.4.2 shows the relation of the generalized generator, called

MCGEN, to the other tables. We examine it with respect to a specific macro called QUAD. The listing in MCNAME for QUAD at quad specifies four quantities:

- the macro name, QUAD
- the starting point of the command table, QUADCM
- the length of the command table, QUADLN
- the number of arguments required, QUADAR

The setup portion of the generator will set these quantities into the generator proper so that it becomes a specific generator tailored to the

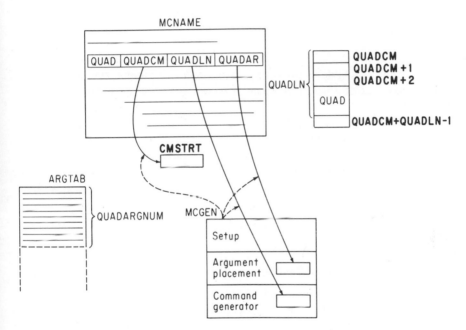

FIGURE 6.4.2. MCNAME is used to set up the generator MCGEN.

macro QUAD. Knowing the number of arguments, we can create an argument table as in the previous section, by examining each argument field of the incoming macro call. Each symbolic address is then looked up in the symbol table and an entry made in the argument table providing the address assignment to the generator.

When this table is complete the generator can produce commands by referring to the command table. Indexed indirect addressing provides simple entry to the command table when its starting address is stored in some known position, such as CMSTRT.

Table Makeup

This directory table is made up in the first pass. An entry is made there for each new macro definition as described in Section 6.5. For each, these particulars are entered there

- name
- start
- the command table
- length of command table
- number of arguments

Thereafter, when a macro call is encountered in the first pass, MCNAME is referenced to reserve cells for the commands produced by the generator. For this reason, the macro should be defined before use. We advance the step and total counters by *number of commands* in MCNAME.

The argument table provides room for each argument symbol and its address. It is constructed during pass II by the generator. Its length depends upon the number of arguments specified for the macro. The same table is used for all macros. It is constructed anew as each macro call is encountered. We provide a maximum length for the table so that it can store the largest permissible number of arguments and, in the case of nested macros (Section 6.6), for maximum nesting depth.

This table contains:

- the command code
- the argument reference

Additionally a number of other things may be contained there:

* The command mnemonic for printout.
* A type tag pinpoints the lookup procedure and allows the generator to handle different types of commands in different ways.
* An address type tag is a necessity for, although all we encountered in the QUAD macro was direct argument addresses, several other kinds are discussed later.
* Index register and supplementary address designation.

Command Operands

The normal referent for a command in a macro is an argument. The macro call contains a list of arguments, symbols for which memory cells have probably been previously assigned. During generation, the assignment is incorporated into the command, requiring that the symbol table is referenced to match the symbol with its assignment.

LITERALS

The literal is identified by $=$ in the macro definition. The literal quantity is replaced by its binary or BCD equivalent when the prototype command is stored in the command table and the command is tagged to show its address is a literal.

Any symbol may be used in the macro definition in the operand address of a command. There are at least three places where such a symbol may be defined:

- within the macro by DEF (then why not use a literal?)
- within the program by the pseudo DEF
- external to the program by a subroutine or such (In this case *our* program should use the pseudo EXT to indicate an external definition.)

In the first two cases the command referring to the symbol is placed in the command table with an operand address obtained from a lookup in the symbol table. For the last case the assembler must rely on the loader or the subroutine to supply the missing information. This is messy and is prohibited in most assemblers.

LABELS

Another command referent is a command in the generated macro sequence. In looping we jump to a preceding or following command in the macro sequence. This can be done in two ways:

- Relative addressing is the simplest
- Label the commands within the macro, and then use the label as a symbolic address for the jump command. The result is the same. In fact, even when the programmer uses the label method, the final entry in the command table should be a relative one.

Setup

The generator is set up and produces the argument table shown in Fig. 6.4.3. During pass II, as a command is examined, its type is determined. First the mnemonic translation table is searched and then the pseudo table.

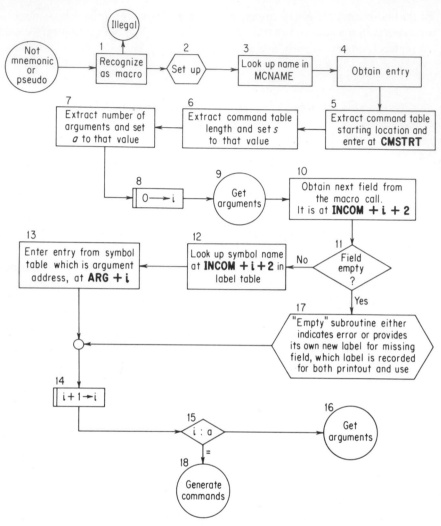

FIGURE 6.4.3. Setting up and filling the argument table for the general macro generator.

If the command is absent from both, it is probably a macro; so we enter the setup routine (1). If it is absent from MCNAME, it is an illegal command (2). If it is present, we obtain the full entry (3, 4).

The three quantities in MCNAME are extracted:

- the start of the command table
- the number of commands
- the number of arguments

The starting location of the command table goes to a cell called CMSTRT (5) to indirectly address the table. The number of commands to be performed, s, is entered into an index to fix the number of times the command generation loop is done (6). The number of arguments, a, is also entered into the argument table production portion of the generator (7) and the index is set to 0 (8) so that we can begin to get the arguments (9).

The next field of the macro call is obtained for analysis (10). A non-empty field symbol is looked up in the main symbol table (12). The address is placed in the next argument table entry (13). The index is advanced (14) and checked (15) and, as long as there is another argument field, it is examined (16).

EMPTY ARGUMENTS

A subroutine is provided (17) to take care of empty arguments. One way is to assign locations for the arguments which the programmer can fill in at a later date. The assembler creates symbols for these empty fields so that the programmer can identify the missing arguments symbolically. Some assemblers even provide special argument symbol allocation pseudos (Section 7.8).

This setup phase produces the argument table and specifies variable parameters within the generator.

Generation

After clearing an index (1) in Fig. 6.4.4, we prepare to generate a new command (2). The next entry in the command table by indexing and indirect addressing (3) is made available in both its symbolic and binary form and is typed (5). A pseudo is executed. For instance, a block of storage may be reserved.

A macro in the table indicates nesting, which is discussed in Section 6.6.

For mnemonics, the symbolic definition and its binary equivalent are transferred to the respective output words (4).

The tag in the address portion of the command indicates one of four types of addresses (8): argument; literal; self-relative; external.

ARGUMENT

Arguments are handled just as they were for QUAD. The address portion is masked into an index register (10). The argument is then procured by entering the argument table indexed by this quantity. The argument address is entered into OCTOUT and the symbol into PRINTOUT (11).

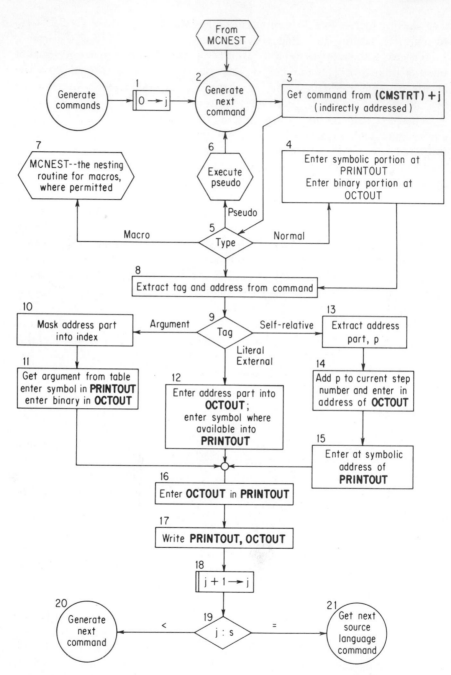

FIGURE 6.4.4. Producing the actual commands of the macro called for the object program via OCTOUT and the record PRINTOUT.

LITERAL

The address where the literal is stored (in binary form) is in the command table. It is entered into OCTOUT. Its decimal equivalent from the table is at PRINTOUT (12).

SELF-RELATIVE

The address indicates the position of the operand relative to the command in production. This number is extracted (13) and is added to the present contents of the address counter to obtain the proper address (14). This number is entered into OCTOUT. The symbolic printout is formed by printing * followed by the adjustment quantity (15).

EXTERNAL

Symbols defined outside of the macro but within the program have had space allotted to them by the definition routine (see Section 6.5). The address corresponding to the symbol was entered into the command word when it was prepared. The command word is used *in toto* in the same way a literal is handled.

When the definition of a symbol is supplied from a subroutine or foreign program segment, the pseudo EXT in the main program requires the creation of communication between the macro and the defining segment. One way to do this is through a cell in the main program and with indirect addressing. Thus if GRACE is defined in PIGEON, our macro might incorporate:

$$ADD \quad GRACE \tag{6.4.1}$$

our program would contain:

$$EXT \quad GRACE \tag{6.4.2}$$

and PIGEON would contain:

$$GRACE \quad DEF \quad definition \tag{6.4.3}$$

When the command table for the macro is fabricated, the reference to (6.4.1) is made indirect because lookup of GRACE in the program symbol table shows it to be *external*. The cell designated for this purpose is assigned by the pseudo EXT let us call XGRACE. During loading, the address of the definition of GRACE is obtained from the foreign segment. This is entered into XGRACE.

As the command table is prepared, for (6.4.1) we have substituted:

$$ADD, 1 \quad XGRACE \tag{6.4.4}$$

At run time, since:

$$(XGRACE) = GRACE \tag{6.4.5}$$

the command of (6.4.4) correctly references GRACE.

This technique permits several references to GRACE within the macro with only one housekeeping function at load time.

Printout

For the programmer the octal output is also entered in PRINTOUT (15). The words for both the binary output and for the printout have now been completely prepared and we write them out (17). We now check to see if there are any more commands left in the table (18) (19). If there are, the next command is generated (20). Otherwise we go on and get the next source language command in sequence for assembly (21).

6.5   MACRO DEFINITION TABLES

Introduction

During the first pass of assembly, space accounting takes place. It is preferable to prepare the tables associated with macros on pass I so that the number of steps for each is known.

When a new definition is encountered several entries are made for the new macro in the macro name table, MCNAME directly:

1. The starting place of the command table for the new macro.

2. The number of commands in the table.

3. The number of arguments in the call.

One philosophy for both MCNAME and the command tables is presented in Fig. 6.5.1. Pointers indicate the next entry in MCNAME and the next starting word allocated for command tables. These pointer words are referred to respectively as MCNXTNAM and MCNXTCOM.

The diagram contains two more boxes. The one called ARGTAB is the general argument table which is used when a macro is called to store the arguments during generation. It may be alternatively used to store arguments for the definition period and, in that case, is renamed MCARG. A label table, MCLBL, is required to contain labels which arise as commands are examined. Substitutions are made for labels where appropriate, as discussed later.

Sequence of Steps

To create the appropriate tables, the macro definition generator makes intermediate tables. First it prepares the table of arguments, MCARG. A command in the definition string which refers to the arguments will have its address field changed to the ordinal number of the argument relative to the argument table. During the macro call the commands refer to the call argument table. But the operand addresses stored in the call argument table are in the same order as the labels stored in the definition argument table, MCARG.

Next, commands are fabricated. They correspond exactly with the definition prototype. However, the operand address portion may require

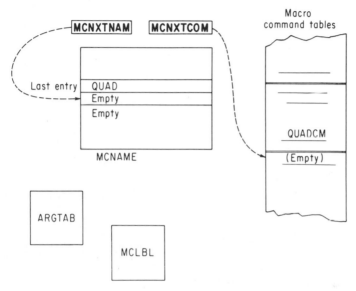

FIGURE 6.5.1. To record a macro definition the pointer MCNXTNAM indicates the next empty spot in MCNAME; MCNXTCOM points to where the next command table should begin.

change according to its referent type. An intermediate label table is required to keep track of labeled jumps within the macro, as well as literals and references to defined symbols.

The command table is produced in the same order as the commands are introduced within the definition beginning at MCDEF. When MCEND is reached, the address entry in MCNAME can be filled in, for then we know the number of commands as well as the number of arguments in the macro. Finally, the pointers are reset for use for the next macro definition.

Argument Table

Figure 6.5.2 shows the first steps in the macro definition process. The first field of the definition pseudo is the name of the macro. The first field is called INCOM. This must be inserted in the label portion of the next entry in MCNAME. This is done in (1) by indirectly addressing the entry using MCNXTNAM.

The argument entry loop is then initialized (2) and arguments are placed in ARGTAB, the temporary argument table. The first field at INCOM + 2

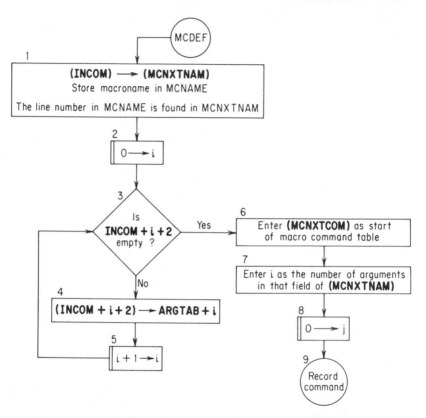

FIGURE 6.5.2. The first phase of recording a macro definition: setting up the argument table.

is the first entry for ARGTAB (INCOM + 1 is the pseudo, MCDEF). We continue to enter fields into the argument table until no comma is detected following the field.

We set up to create the command table by indexed indirect addressing. The address of first entry of this table is at MCNXTCOM (6).

Having finished the table MCARG (3), we know how many arguments the macro uses and can place this number, i, in the proper field of this entry in MCNAME. Again, this is done by indirectly addressing the entry using MCNXTNAM (7).

Recording the Commands

The next phase of recording the definition in Fig. 6.5.3 begins with initialization (1). We examine the next command to see if it is labeled (23). If so, the label table, MCLBL, is referred to (4). If this label already has a step number associated with it (5), an entry is made in the error table (6). If a step number is not associated with the label or the label is absent (5), the step number is now entered into MCLBL (8). A review is required either now or in the final phase of the definition process so that references to this label can be replaced by a number indicating the relative position of this command within the command set (9).

If the label is not present at all (4), then it is entered into the next free space in MCLBL (7), and the label entry counter advances (10). Finally, *this* step number (relative) is inserted in the entry (11).

Now we type the command (12). Nested macro commands are described in detail in the next section (13). If MCEND is encountered, the next phase is entered (14). Both mnemonics and pseudos are permissible. The command is classified using the mnemonic table (15). The command code class, index, supplementary information and machine code are entered in the command table (16) using MCNXTCOM indirectly.

The operand address processing depends upon the command classification (17). Immediate and self-relative commands are simply tagged (18, 19). Then the address part is entered into the operand portion in the command table (20). For the relative address the address quantity is added to the setting of the step counter. Immediately addressed commands, such as index-setting orders, simply enter the command operand address in the command table.

Directly addressed commands (17) may or may not refer to arguments. This is determined by looking up the operand label in MCARG (23). If the symbolic address is there, the command address is tagged as an argument and filled with the ordinal position of the argument in the argument table (25).

Reference might be to a label in MCLBL which is scanned (26). If the entry is present, we check the step number (27). When a step number is present, this is a self-relative command. It is so tagged (28) and the relativity number is calculated and entered into the address portion in the command table (29).

If the referent is listed in MCLBL (26) without a step number (27), the command is listed for later review (30) and the address portion is not filled in for the command table (31).

If the operand is not an argument (23) and is not listed in the label table (26), the main symbol table is searched. If an entry is found (32), the address

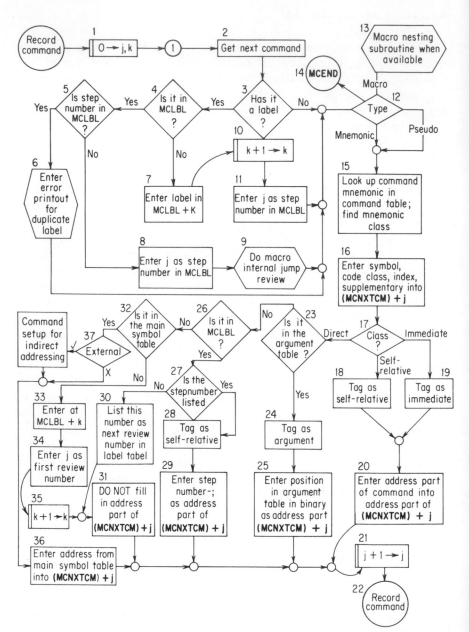

FIGURE 6.5.3. The second phase of recording a macro definition: making the command and label tables.

in that table is entered in the operand portion in the command table (36). Reference is to an external datum, a literal or a defined symbol, probably.

When the main symbol table indicates an externally defined symbol (37), the command is tagged for indirect addressing using the symbol cell address (38).

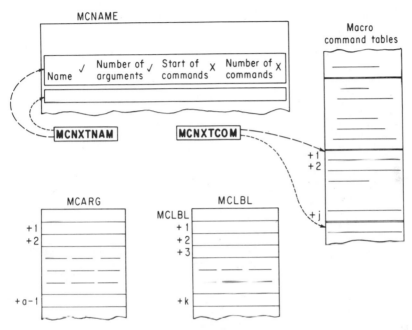

FIGURE 6.5.4. The situation just after reading MCEND. The entry in MCNAME must be completed; some labels in MCLBL still must be posted in the command table; the pointers must be adjusted.

When the symbol is not located anywhere (23) (26) (32), it is stored in MCLBL (33) and the command is posted for review (34). When entries are made in MCLBL, the pointer to it is advanced (35).

Conclusion

After finishing the last phase, the portion of memory devoted to macro definitions appears schematically as shown in Fig. 6.5.4. To conclude the process, we must make sure all commands in the command table have operand addresses filled in. Hand in hand with this goes the listing of labels not otherwise accounted for in MCLBL. These are posted into the external symbol table. Then the entry in MCNAME must be completed (note the

X's for that entry in Fig. 6.5.4). Finally, the pointers, MCNXTNAM and MCNXTCOM, must be adjusted, as shown in dashed lines in the figure.

FLOW CHART

Figure 6.5.5 shows the completion of the macro definition process. After initialization (1) the next label in MCLBL is examined (2) to determine if an address is listed for the label (3). If so, and a command review is necessary

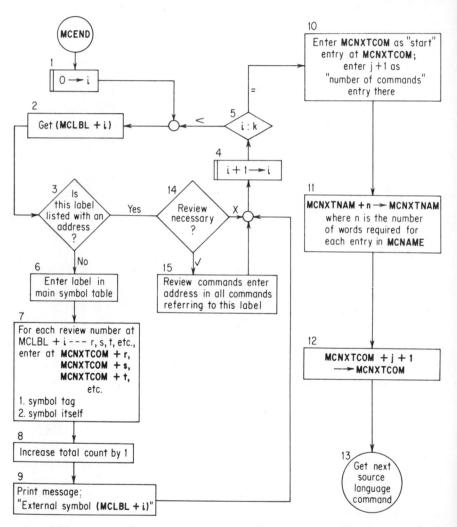

FIGURE 6.5.5. The completion of macro definition by the assembler when the pseudo MCEND is encountered.

(14), this is done (15). If the label has had an address associated with it and subsequently has been reviewed (14) then we continue to the next label (4) (5).

Labels not allocated (3) are entered into the symbol table (6). An address assignment is made for the symbol as it is entered. In MCLBL there is a list of commands which refers to this symbol. These commands must now be reviewed and the address assigned to the symbol inserted in the operand address portion of the command (7). A symbol tag is also inserted to indicate that this is a symbol, not an argument.

An entry in the symbol table increases the total counter by one (8). Further, the programmer should know if his macro definition contains undefined symbols and a message is printed out (9).

After label review, we complete the entry in MCNAME. The start of the command table, the present contents of MCNXTCOM and the number of commands are placed there (10).

The pointers are advanced. We obtain the address of the next entry in the name table by adding the number of words entered to the contents of MCNXTNAM; this is returned to MCNXTNAM (11). To form the beginning of the new command table, we take the present starting address and add the number of commands in the table (12).

We have now completed the processing associated with MCEND. The next command in the source language sequence is now obtained (13).

6.6   NESTED MACROS

Principle

The programmer may define a number of macros as required instead of writing a sequence of commands. Along the way he may find that he requires another new macro. Within the sequence of commands which defines this new macro he may come across a subsequence which could be replaced by an old macro. For instance, he may be writing a macro to take the standard deviation of a number of quantities in a statistical analysis. This process requires the square root. If he has a macro for the square root, this can be incorporated into his definition of standard deviation. When the programmer uses his new macro call, the assembler builds a set of commands within which is another macro which is, in turn, replaced by its subsequence of commands.

Once we permit macros within macros, there is no reason why we should not permit macros within macros within macros, and so forth. In other words, we permit indefinite **nesting** of macros limited only by assembler table storage provisions.

Pictorial Example

Figure 6.6.1 shows an example of a program which contains a nested macro. The source program contains a sequence of mnemonics labeled *A*. It is followed by a macro, MACROB. Another sequence of mnemonics follows which is labeled *A′*.

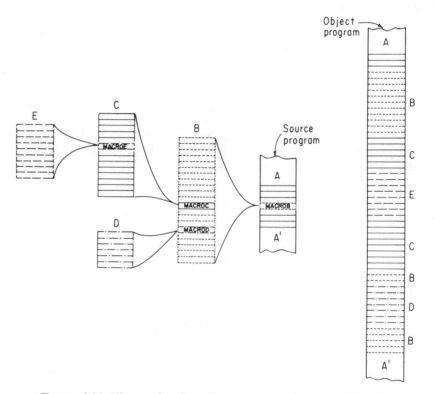

FIGURE 6.6.1. The result of nesting macros in the source-language program.

To the left is an expansion of MACROB. It consists of a number of mnemonics but also contains nested within it two other macros, MACROC and MACROD.

Further to the left we see the expansion of these two macros. MACROD consists entirely of mnemonics—MACROC includes another macro, MACROE, which consists entirely of mnemonics. Shading distinguishes the macro sequences from one another.

In this example the assembler:

- inserts the sequence E into the sequence C.
- pushes the sequences C and D into their slots in the sequence B.
- places this whole composition in the object program between A and A'.

The result is the object program shown on the extreme right of Fig. 6.6.1.

Nesting Hierarchy

In writing a new macro, one can draw upon old macros he has already defined. It is hardly feasible to consider inserting a *new* macro into an *older* definition. Thus all lower-level macros or inner macros are assumed to be defined before they are used in a new or outer macro.

Some assemblers permit the **nesting of macro definitions**: an inner macro is *defined* within an outer macro definition. The resulting complication in assembler design does provide a benefit to the programmer through the unambiguous and explicit statement of the nesting sequence.

The Mechanics of Interpretation

We examine how the assembler interprets nested macros—how it builds the object program when it is presented with macro calls which include nested macros.

We use a macro definition for an outer macro which includes within it a middle macro which, in turn, includes within it an inner macro.

In the upper left part of Fig. 6.6.2 we see the command table for the outer macro MCOUTR. The macro generator reviews the commands in the command table and forms the object program as described in Section 6.4.

When the generator finds a reference in the table to another macro, the middle one named MCMID, it switches to the macro command table for the middle macro. To find this command table, the generator looks up *MCMID* in the macro directory, MCNAME. It enters commands in the object string from the *MCMID* command table as described in Section 6.4.

Down the line within the MCMID macro command table it encounters another macro call, MCINR. The start of the command table for MCINR is looked up in the macro directory, MCNAME. The generator produces commands in the object string from the MCINR command table. Since MCINR contains no nested macros, all the entries from the MCINR command table are entered to the object language string.

Climbing Up the Hill

After assembling the innermost macro, there are still commands in the middle macro command table to be entered. Where does the assembly

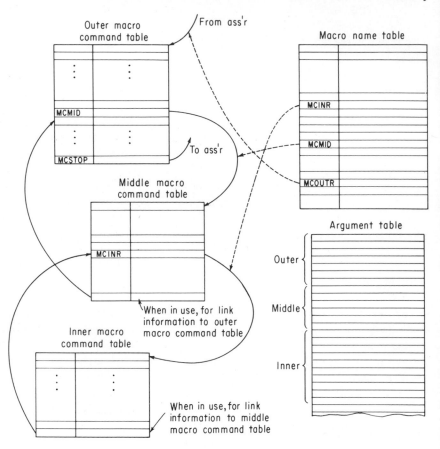

FIGURE 6.6.2. How information for linking a lower level nestal macro to a higher level macro is stored at the end of the command table. A nest of three macros is shown.

process continue? A link must be left to finish the operation. One of the many ways to do this, indicated in Fig. 6.6.2, is to place the linking information to the next higher level macro in a vacant space provided at the end of every macro command table.

With this feature, after generating all the MCINR commands, we return to the next command after the macro call, MCINR, in the *MCMID* command table. We continue to generate commands until, at the end of MCMID, we find a link to the next command past the macro call, MCMID, in the *MCOUTR* command table. We use up all the commands in the outer command table. The link space in the *MCOUTR* command table now contains termination information telling the generator that the nested macro is constructed. It returns to the source program to examine the next source language command.

ARGUMENTS

Arguments for the outer macro are entered into the argument table. When an inner macro is encountered, its arguments are entered into the same table in sequence following those for the outer ones. We re-reference the argument table for the inner macros. When the inner command table is exhausted and we switch to an outer one, we find the arguments for the outer macro are present in the upper entries of our argument table. It is only necessary to reset the pointer to this table so that the old arguments are now referenced.

Inward Processing of Nested Macros

LOOKUP

Assuming proper definitions, we examine how the generator *processes* nested macros flow-charted in Fig. 6.6.3. Nested processing is initiated when a new command from the macro command table is classified (1) as one of three special commands:

- the pseudo MCSTOP
- the pseudo LEVEL
- the name of the inner macro

The pseudos are special, for they are *not* programmer's commands! They are used only by the assembler and serve more like flags.

LEVEL

A macro appearing in the macro command table is looked up in the macro directory, MCNAME (2). The entry in MCNAME indicates how many commands there are in the macro and, hence, the last cell in the command table. For FLAP conventionally, the last step in all macro command tables contains MCSTOP. When a macro is not part of a nest, this remains unchanged. When a macro is nested within other macros, the assembler augments temporarily this last command table entry (3) by replacing MCSTOP with LEVEL. We provide information for return to the outer level by placing the name or location of the outer macro in the first field of LEVEL (4). We keep track of the command number within the outer macro where we have left off in the next field of LEVEL (5).

ARGUMENTS

The argument table is set up for the inner macro. We preserve the old portion of the argument table (6) by entering as the next field of LEVEL the

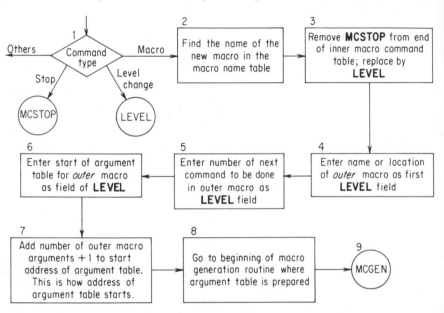

FIGURE 6.6.3. When a macro is encountered within a macro, the above steps are taken to move *inward*.

starting position of the first outer macro argument. This would not be necessary if we could be assured that the outer macro were outermost; it, too, might be nested. The new argument list starts right after the old list (7).

To prepare the argument list for the inner macro (8), we return to the beginning of the generation routine where the list preparation SR is located (9).

COMMANDS

The generation of object language commands proceeds as for an unnested macro. The difference occurs only when another nested macro is found or LEVEL or MCSTOP is encountered at the end of the command table.

Outward Processing of Nested Macros

When an inner macro is fully processed, LEVEL is encountered (1). We groeed outward to finish off the next outward-going macro as shown in Fig. 6.6.4. We reset the argument table for the outer macro (2) by procuring

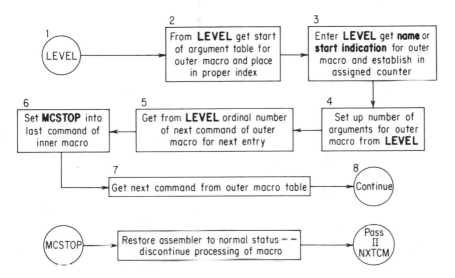

FIGURE 6.6.4. Moving outward when LEVEL is encountered for assembling a nestal macro (above). Resuming normal assembly when the end of the outer macro is encountered (below).

the new starting address from a field of LEVEL. The remainder of the argument table used for the inner macro is no longer required. In fact, if another inner macro should arise, it would be handled as in Fig. 6.6.3, and the space occupied in the argument table by the last inner macro would be used for the new one.

The starting point of the command table is reset from the next field of LEVEL (3) as well as the relative position in the command table (5).

The number of arguments is reset, for other inner macros may be found (4).

Resetting inner macros

In entering the inner macro table we changed MCSTOP to LEVEL. If we left the table thus, it would mess up all non-nested macros that refer to that table. Hence the final command in the inner macro table must be restored to MCSTOP and previous entries obliterated (6).

We are now finished with the inner macro and continue to generate the outer macro. We procure commands from the command table (7) until another LEVEL or MCSTOP is encountered.

Nested Macro Generation Termination

The outermost macro does not have its terminal command altered. It therefore remains as MCSTOP which, when encountered in Fig. 6.6.3, terminates the operation of the generator. In fact, this is the way all unnested macros are terminated. Recognition of MCSTOP returns the assembler to normal status and discharges the macro generator as illustrated at the bottom of Fig. 6.6.4.

Definition of Macros Containing Macros

The procedure for constructing the tables associated with the nest-containing macro is similar to the description in Section 6.5. One difference is that inner macro commands must be recognized and tagged. Another difference is in the space allotted to the nested macro. The number of commands in the object string is not the same as the number of commands in the definition string. Each inner macro is replaced by a subsequence of commands. Enough space must be allotted for each subsequence. This is easily done since all inner macros have been previously defined. By reference to MCNAME we can determine the number of commands generated by an inner macro and add this as it occurs to the total provided for the outer macro in MCNAME.

Of course, inner macros may in turn contain inner macros. How do we account for the extra commands introduced by the innermost macros? Well, these have already been accounted for. Any macro called by the outer macro has a listing in MCNAME which includes not only the steps of the prescribed macro, but all macros nested.

Transmitting Values

The purpose of a subroutine is to calculate a value or set of values for use by another program segment. How are these values transmitted from one SR to another in the case of nested macros? This is usually done using cells which were defined outside of the macros. Another alternative is the SET pseudo described in Section 7.5.

Macro-external definitions provide space for answers produced by one macro so that it may be accessed by another macro. For instance, suppose we have a product routine, PRODSR. It is nested in a sum routine, SUMSR, used by a program. The program furnishes sets of sets of values to SUMSR. Sets are furnished one at a time to PRODSR which finds the product and places it at some symbolic location, say PROD. Then SUMSR adds PROD to its sum. It gets a new set of values for PRODSR and calls it in again. Finally, the sum of products is furnished to the program by the use of some program defined location such as SUM.

6.7 COMMANDS AS ARGUMENTS

Need

The versatility of the macro assembler can be expanded further if we incorporate the ability to specify *commands* as arguments in the macro call. This permits the programmer to call forth more machine language statements with fewer assembly language statements; any such device which reduces the programmer's toil is attractive so long as it is bought at not too high a cost. In this case the cost is in the greater complexity of the macro generator.

Principle

The prototype macro now may have in its structure a place where a command specified in the call will replace a prototype argument. The procedure is best explained with an example.

Example:
We wish a subprogram to evaluate the function, G, given as:

$$G = \sum_{i=1}^{N} F(X_i) \qquad (6.7.1)$$

where it is desired to specify F at the time of call. We design a macro, FADD, to do this task (Fig. 6.7.1). The N values of the independent variables are in cells starting at ITEM; the function F is specified by commands which replace F1, F2 and F3 when FADD is called.

On lines 2–4 in Fig. 6.7.1, we fill index 3, clear RESULT and adjust the index. Lines 5–7 find $F(X_i)$; lines 8–10 add it to the result so far. Line 11 completes the loop; line 12 completes the macro definition.

```
line
   1    FADD    MCNAME    ITEM, N, F1, F2, F3, RESULT
   2            XPN, 3    N
   3            XOM       RESULT
   4            TUN, 3    * + 1
   5            F1, 3     ITEM
   6            F2, 3     ITEM
   7            F3, 3     ITEM
   8            XMA, 3    RESULT
   9            ADD, 3    ITEM
  10            XMA, 3    RESULT
  11            TDN, 3    * − 6
  12    FADD    MCEND
```

FIGURE 6.7.1. The macro FADD containing three commands as arguments.

Using FADD

We employ FADD to find the sum of numbers, the sum of squares, and the sum of roots.

If F1, F2 and F3 are replaced by NOOPS we have:

$$F(X_i) = X_i; \qquad G = \sum_{i=1}^{N} X_i \qquad (6.7.2)$$

The call for this is then:

FADD   X, 17, NOOP, NOOP, NOOP, SUM   (6.7.3)

where seventeen items are stored starting at X, with the result to be placed in SUM.

Now the macro is performed as though lines 5–7 (Fig. 6.2.1) were omitted.

SQUARE SUM

To square an item before adding to the result so far, we need a series of three items to (1) get the item, (2) multiply by the item and (3) return it to its cell:

```
XMD, 3    ITEM
MUL, 3    ITEM
XAM, 3    ITEM          (6.7.4)
```

Since the index and address are already specified in FADD, only the commands need be specified in the call:

FADD   X, 17, XMD, MUL, XAM, SUM   (6.7.5)

for seventeen items starting at X, with the result placed in SUM. It solves:

$$F(X_i) = X^2; \qquad G = \sum_{i=1}^{N} X_i^2 \qquad (6.7.6)$$

ROOT SUM

Finally let us specify a macro within the macro FADD: this is not a simple nested macro for the command arguments of FADD are not fixed. Suppose that SQRT is a macro which finds the square root of the number in the accumulator and returns the answer to the accumulator. We assume that an index tag appended to the macro call, SQRT, will not affect its performance. We are going to solve:

$$F(X_i) = \sqrt{X_i}; \qquad G = \sum_{i=1}^{N} \sqrt{X_i} \qquad (6.7.7)$$

Our call is thus:

$$\text{FADD} \qquad \text{X, 17, XMA, SQRT, XAM, SUM} \qquad (6.7.8)$$

to sum seventeen square roots of numbers starting at the cell labeled X and to place the sum at SUM. It inserts the machine language equivalent of the sequence:

XAM, 3	ITEM
SQRT, 3	ITEM
XMA, 3	ITEM (6.7.9)

in the program.

However, SQRT is a macro call and must be replaced by its equivalent coding. This is done by the nesting portion of the macro generator.

The Generator Table Preparation

The command table is the key to the generation of call-specified commands.

Before a command is placed in the command table, it is classified using the mnemonic table (see Section 6.5 and Fig. 6.5.3). Now, however, if absent it is not necessarily an error; an argument may be found in the process portion of the command. The table preparation portion of the generator makes a check of the unfound command in the argument table.

A command which is an argument is uniquely tagged as such and supplied a number to show which argument is used there.

Generator Uses Table

Code generation proceeds as described in Section 6.4 until a command is encountered in the command table which is tagged as an argument. It is looked up there. Before use, its type must be ascertained MNEMONIC. When the command name is listed in the mnemonic table it is translated directly: the command code is substituted for the argument.

PSEUDO

The task required by the pseudo is performed by the generator, e.g., data definition.

MACRO

When the command name is missing from the mnemonic table, it is looked up in MCNAME. A defined macro is found there. It calls the nesting sequence described in Section 6.6. LEVEL is set and the inner macro is furnished as an argument is performed. It, in turn, may contain fixed or argument-specified macros. The nesting sequence remains in control until MCSTOP is found. The generator is then reset and generation continues.

ERROR

When the argument-specified command is missing from all tables, this is an error. The command in the printout may be replaced by a *created symbol* or some other error indication maybe employed.

PROBLEMS

6.1 Distinguish library, assembler and program macros.

6.2 Discuss when the macro sequence is placed in the program and the reasons why one might choose a given time for inclusion.

6.3 How are variable length SR's generated?

6.4 Define a macro, SQRT, to take the square root of a number as in problem 3.9.

6.5 Define a macro, QUADRT, to find the roots of a quadratic as in problem 3.10. Use the macro, SQRT, defined in problem 6.4.

6.6 Define a macro, RECT, to solve problem 3.11. Use the calling sequence: P, Q, T, ANS1, ANS2. The macro, QUADRT, should be used here.

6.7 Write a fixed generator for problem 6.4.

6.8 Write a fixed generator for problem 6.5.

6.9 For a generalized generator show the argument and command tables for problem 6.4.

6.10   As before, show the argument and command tables for problem 6.5.

6.11   As before, show the argument and command tables for problem 6.6.

6.12   Show the interaction of SQRT and QUADRT when RECT is called by using the command tables in problems 6.9–6.11 and by indicating how they are used by the generator. Show the triple argument table built for RECT.

6.13   Write an SR TBLSRCH to do the job required in Fig. 6.3.3.

6.14   Write a FLAP subprogram to fill the argument table for a generator as shown in Fig. 6.4.3.

6.15   Write a FLAP subprogram to produce machine language commands from the command table as shown in Fig. 6.4.4.

6.16   Flow chart and program in FLAP the lookup in MCNAME and the setup of the other macro generator phases.

6.17   Interconnect the subprograms of problems 6.14 through 6.16 to make a macro generator.

6.18   Program in FLAP phase 1 of macro definition (Fig. 6.5.2).

6.19   Program in FLAP phase 2 of macro definition (Fig. 6.5.3).

6.20   Program in FLAP phase 3 of macro definition (Fig. 6.5.5).

6.21   Interconnect the macro definer using problems 6.18 through 6.20.

6.22   Discuss and flow chart the changes required to accommodate a nested macro definition.

6.23   Change the program of problem 6.21 to handle nested definition. Do this piecewise.

6.24   Write a FLAP subprogram for *inward* nested macro generation as in Fig. 6.6.3.

6.25   Write a subprogram for *outward* nested generation as in Fig. 6.6.4.

6.26   Make a complete nested macro generator using the results of problems 6.14, 6.15, 6.16, 6.17, 6.24, and 6.25.

7

ASSEMBLER
SUBROUTINES

7.1 MORE ON SUBROUTINES

Table 6.1 summarizes the classification of subroutines by reference in assembly language. This section discusses the other kinds of subroutines available to the assembly programmer.

Source Language Subroutines

An open subroutine in source language is duplicated at frequent intervals in the input source language stream. Only a few parameters are subject to change from one occurrence to another.

A closed subroutine is used as demonstrated in Fig. 7.1.1. In the source program, the square root sequence is labeled as SQROOT but defined by a sequence of assembly language statements at another point. The label of the first of these statements permits the sequence to be entered from any point in the program. The final statement of the subroutine is a return to the source sequence in the main program by an indexed unconditional jump.

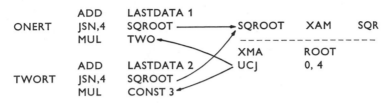

FIGURE 7.1.1. The programmer can include closed subroutines in his source program without the aid of macros.

Programmer Defined Subroutines

A generator produces object commands when macros (open SR's) are defined by the programmer. Figure 7.1.2 shows the sequence the programmer might use to obtain results produced by Fig. 7.1.1.

Whenever the programmer needs a subroutine he defines it by writing a prototype directly into the program using MCDEF and MCEND as parentheses to the defining sequence. When he needs a copy of this macro, he calls it by name, and the assembler automatically packs the proper set of commands into the object program. He calls for SQRT in Fig. 7.1.3, at ONERT and TWORT.

The prototype macro definition does not produce any object command; only later calls using the macro name cause generation of the command set. Figure 7.1.3 shows the assembly language equivalent of the object program for a macro call of SQRT shown in Fig. 7.1.2.

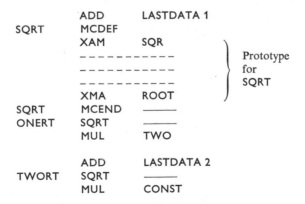

FIGURE 7.1.2. The MCDEF pseudo is used to define a subroutine incorporated at ONERT and TWORT as an open subroutine, thus accomplishing the same task as Fig. 7.1.1.

```
            ADD      LASTDATA
ONERT       XAM      SQR
            ─────
            XMA      ROOT
            MLR      TWO
TWORT       XAM      SQR
            ─────    ─────
            XMA      ROOT
            MLR      CONST 3
```

FIGURE 7.1.3. The coding of Fig. 7.1.2 produces object language codes, as though *this* program had been submitted to the assembler.

Assembler Contained Macros

The entries in the second line of Table 6.1 indicate the cases where the assembler already includes subroutine skeletons which the programmer can refer to simply by making the proper call. For instance, if the square root skeleton were available within the assembler, the programmer would not have to define it in his source program; he would simply write it as in Fig. 7.1.4.

The assembler searches its internal tables for this command combination as for any other. SQRT is not found in the (FLAP) mnemonic table, the pseudo table nor the macro table, but it *is* in the library table. This is a directory for the library of subroutines. This library is on a separate tape which can be scanned, and a prototype can be recovered from it for use by the universal library generator incorporated in the assembler.

An alternative to the prototype is to have a number of generators in the library. A generator, when called, produces the required object program. The contrast is between a skeleton which is filled in by a generalized subroutine generator and a unique generator for each subroutine. Such a unique generator can produce a variable sequence of steps communicated by the parameters in the subroutine call.

Loadtime Subroutine Libraries

The last line in Table 6.1 applies to a program which contains a reference to a subroutine unavailable to the assembler. It is specified by a call to be

```
            ADD      LASTDATA 1
ONERT       SQRT     ─────
            MLR      TWO
            ─────    ─────
            ADD      LASTDATA 2
TWORT       SQRT     ─────
            MUL      CONST 3
```

FIGURE 7.1.4. If the assembler includes a built-in macro for the square root, this source coding suffices to produce an output equivalent to Fig. 7.1.3.

loaded with the assembled program. The loader is responsible for obtaining the SR from the library and incorporating it into the memory with the proper links.

This problem is examined in Fig. 7.1.5. The source program contains two references to a single subroutine in the runtime library. The commands

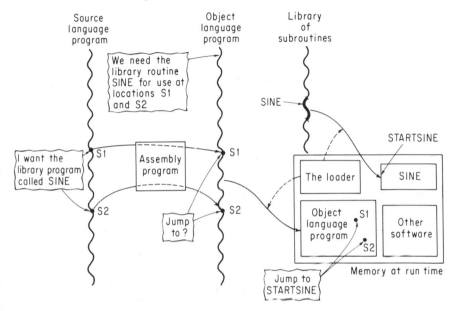

FIGURE 7.1.5. How the library subroutine call appears in the source program, in the object program and in the memory at run time. The captions convey the spirit of the information rather than its form.

which indicate these needs are figuratively indicated by, "I want the library program called SINE."

The assembly program does two things with this statement:

- At the position in the program where the need was made known, it places an object language command *jump-and-set-index*, JSN.
- It enters the name of the SR in a list at the head of the object program.

The place to jump to is the beginning of the SINE subroutine; but this sequence is not available and so the jump address is left blank.

The SINE routine is loaded with the object program by the loader which:

- determines what subroutines are required (this includes SINE)
- obtains them from the library
- assigns them a position and places them there

The loader does these *before* the program is loaded to be sure that enough space is available for both the program subroutines. The names of the subprograms and subroutines in the header information of the object program which is to be loaded tell the allocator how much space the program needs, figuratively shown in Fig. 7.1.5.

At the top of the object language string the statement appears: "We need the library routine, SINE, for use at locations S1 and S2." This statement is a new entity for us. It exists in the object program before loading but is not in the object program during running. It is different in nature from the object language statements or constants which are incorporated into the object language string. It is also different from spaces allocated for incoming or outgoing data. The sole purpose of this statement is communication with the loader.

A special name is applied to assembly language commands which create this kind of information in the object language string. So far, we have encountered:

- *mnemonics* which are translated directly
- *pseudos* which instruct the assembler
- *macros* which cause several object language commands to be produced

A **quasicommand** (or simply **quasi**) produces an entry in the object language string for use by the loader, monitor or other software during loading into memory the **quasi entry** to transmit information to the loader about its task. This entry, corresponding to the quasi, does not appear in the object language program in memory at run time.

Quasis, while producing an entry may also produce object code. In Fig. 7.1.5 the quasis at S1 and S2 are replaced by jump commands to be executed in the object program during run time. In some assemblers the same quasi produces the jump command and the header information; other assemblers require a quasi for the header and a mnemonic for the jump command at S1 and S2.

7.2   CALLING LIBRARY SUBROUTINES

The Simple Task

We communicate to the loader the need to bring in a subroutine from the library by incorporating in the source program a macro, GET. This command is both a quasi and an assembly defined macro. For specific assemblers other names are used for our GET: FAP for the IBM 7090 uses the word CALL and BOSS III for the Remington Rand Univac III uses EXT described in Section 8.6. The achievements are similar.

On encountering GET, our assembler does two things: it makes an entry in the **subroutine jump table, SRJ table** (sometimes referred to elsewhere as the transfer vector list), a list containing the name of each subroutine requested and, sometimes, the step in the object program requesting it. The latter is the setting of the step counter when GET is encountered; it determines the ordinal number of the entry in that table.

Next an object command is prepared with the code for *jump and set index*, JSN. The jump location is the ordinal number of the entry in the SRJ table offset by the origin setting if one was defined. It is tagged for the index allocated to the linkage function—in our case index 4.

As other GET commands appear, the process is repeated. Before an entry is made in the subroutine jump table, however, the table is checked to see if an identical entry is already present. Thus, although the same subroutine may be called several times in a given program, it need be procured only once from the subroutine library. If the name is present in the table, the present step counter setting for the GET quasi is stored with this name in the table. As before, the JSN is prepared; the jump location is the ordinal number in the table; the index tag is 4.

The Object Program

The object program is prefixed by the subroutine jump table, a single step devoted to each subroutine required. The step numbers of all commands are advanced by the number of entries in the SRJ table at the *start* of pass II so that everything will come out right.

LOADING

The first thing the loader finds in the object program is a message indicating the number of steps in the program and the number of subroutines required by it. Next is the SRJ table with names of subroutines which the loader is to get from the subroutine library. It places the first SR in a previously unassigned spot: the top of memory or the area just following where the program will end. The loader continues thus:

- It gets the next subroutine.
- It locates a free area and puts the subroutine there.
- It replaces the table entry by an unconditional jump to the subroutine.

The problems of search and memory space are discussed in Chapter 14 on loaders.

RUN TIME

The program is initiated when control is turned over to the first command in the program proper. Successive commands are executed. When a subroutine is needed JSN causes a jump to the entry in the SRJ table and sets index 4 to the number of the step just left.

In the SRJ table is found another jump, this one to the beginning of the subroutine. At the end of the SR is a jump, indexed by index 4, returning to the main program. The procedure could be simplified further for some computers if we use:

$$\text{JSN,I,4} \qquad \text{name} \qquad\qquad (7.2.1)$$

Then only the SR starting address replaces the SR name in the SRJ table; the SR is reached by indexed indirection of the SRJ entry.

Example:

Figure 7.2.1 shows an example of how GET is used. On the left is the source program. To make the explanation simpler, no macros appear there. The program includes exactly three SR calls: HARRY, TOM and DICK.

Source				Object			Run	
				Steps 537;	SRs 3			
1	START	XPN	ZERO, 3	1 HARRY	26		1 UCJ	538
	———————————			2 TOM	52		2 UCJ	603
23	CALL 1	GET	HARRY	3 DICK	61		3 UCJ	667
	———————————			4 XPN,3	ZERO,		4 XPN,3	ZERO,
49	CALL 2	GET	TOM	—————————			—————————	
	———————————			26 JSN,4	1		26 JSN,4	1
58	CALL 3	GET	DICK	—————————			—————————	
	———————————			52 JSN,4	2		52 JSN,4	2
533	FINIS	XMA	RESULT	—————————			—————————	
534	NEW	END	——	61 JSN,4	3		61 JSN,4	3
				—————————			—————————	
				536 XMA	RESULT		536 XMA	RESULT
				537 UCJ	SYSTEM		537 UCJ	SYSTEM
							538 (HARRY)	
		ASSEMBLY			LOAD		602 UCJ,4	1
							603 (TOM)	
							666 UCJ,4	1
							667 (DICK)	
							681 UCJ,4	1

FIGURE 7.2.1. A source language program with links using GET to a subroutine library. The program contains only *three* calls and *no* macros so that its expansion is evident. In the center are the steps which would have also generated the object code. In other words, the equivalent of the center column is assembled from the left column. Similarly, the equivalent of the right column is loaded from the object code.

During the first pass the subroutine jump table is filled with three entries, one each for HARRY, TOM and DICK, for steps respectively numbered 23, 49 and 58.

At step 534, END is encountered, indicating the end of the source program. This initiates the second pass.

On the second pass, the number of entries in the subroutine jump table recorded as 3. It is added to the step counter and to all relocatable operand addresses.

The object program is headed by an entry indicating that the number of steps in the program is 537 and that it includes the number of entries in the SRJ table. The program in the center of Fig. 7.2.1 is not the object program but its equivalent written in assembly language.

After the heading information we have the three entries of the table. All the remaining program steps have been offset by 3, the number of entries in the table. Thus 23 now appears as 26, and so forth. The GET commands have been advanced three places and now appear as JSN's. Each has an address, the corresponding entry in the subroutine table. Standard index 4 is used. The final command inserted by the assembler is not a halt, but rather, an unconditional jump to a standard location reserved in the system software for the monitor called $\mathscr{SYSTEM}$.

LOADER

In the memory at run time, shown in the right column in assembly language equivalent, the three subroutines, HARRY, TOM and DICK, are at locations 538, 603 and 667. The three entries in the subroutine jump table are replaced by unconditional jumps to these locations. Further, the last command in each subroutine is an unconditional jump indexed by the standard jump index location, 4. This returns control to the main program one step beyond where the subroutine was called.

The Calling Sequence

Usually information is passed from the main program to the subroutine, and vice versa. To simplify the situation, let us examine a source program identical with that of Fig. 7.2.1, with the single exception that the subroutine DICK now requires the additional information: LIZ, DOT and JANE.

A portion of the source program for this new setup is found in Fig. 7.2.2. At step 58, CALL3, GET is found calling for the SR DICK with the data specification, LIZ, DOT, JANE:

$$\text{CALL3} \quad \text{GET} \quad \text{DICK, LIZ, DOT, JANE} \qquad (7.2.1)$$

Source				Object			Run	
				Step 540	SR's 3			
1 START	XPN	ZERO,	3	1 HARRY	26		1 UCJ	541
----------------							2 UCJ	606
58 CALL 3	GET	DICK,		2 TOM	52		3 UCJ	670
LIZ,	DOT,	JANE		3 DICK	61		4 XPN,3	=0
				4 XPN,3	=0			
----------------				----------			----------	
533 FINIS	XMA	RESULT		61 JSN,4	3		61 JSN,4	3
534 NEW	END	-----		62 NOOP	LIZ		62 NOOP	LIZ
				63 NOOP	DOT		63 NOOP	DOT
				64 NOOP	JANE		64 NOOP	JANE
				----------			----------	
				539 XMA	RESULT		539 XMA	RESULT
				540 UCJ	SYSTEM		540 UCJ	SYSTEM
							541 (HARRY)	
		ASSEMBLY			LOAD		605 UCJ,4	1
		$\Longrightarrow$			$\Longrightarrow$		606 (TOM)	
							669 UCJ,4	1
							670 (DICK)	
							684 UCJ,4	4

FIGURE 7.2.2. The source program of Fig. 7.2.1, this time where CALL3 (DICK) contains a calling sequence. The assembler must provide addresses and space for the calling sequence in the object program—steps 62, 63 and 64. Return to main program is provided by step 684 of the loaded object program.

ASSEMBLY

Assembly proceeds just as before. When we reach CALL3, DICK is entered into the subroutine jump table with his location, 58:

Jump Table

Entry	SR name	user	
1	-------	---	(7.2.2)
2	-------	---	
3	DICK	58	

We replace the GET sequence by the JSN command with address 3 (for entry number 3 in the SRJ table) and index 4.

Something new happens when the calling sequence is noted: a space is provided in successive cells of the program for each girl, found in the calling sequence, thus:

step	label	command	
058	CALL3	JSN,4	003
059		NOOP	LIZ
060		NOOP	DOT	(7.2.3)
061		NOOP	JANE

Further, on the second pass the assembler replaces LIZ, DOT and JANE by the cell numbers assigned to them. This procedure is followed whenever GET includes a calling sequence.

When GET DICK is encountered again at step 217, an additional entry is made to the SR jump table:

$$217 \quad CALL8 \quad GET \quad DICK, MARY, DOT, JANE \qquad (7.2.4)$$

We revise the jump table entry to:

$$3 \quad DICK \quad 58, 217 \qquad (7.2.5)$$

and replace GET by:

$$
\begin{array}{lll}
217 & CALL8 & JSN,4 \quad 003 \\
     &   & NOOP \quad MARY \qquad (7.2.6) \\
     &   & NOOP \quad DOT \\
     &   & NOOP \quad JANE
\end{array}
$$

A similar procedure is required for any other calling sequence.

User references—the places where the subroutine was requested—can be omitted from the SR table for most assemblers, where cross-referencing is automatic.

LOADING

Loading is performed as before. The main program is a little longer now, for each entry in a calling sequence has lengthened the program by a step. Subroutines are brought in and each call is replaced by an unconditional jump to the SR start. Running follows.

Using GET in Macros

It is possible to request a subroutine within a macro as in Fig. 7.2.3, which contains a definition of COMPLEX, a macro to evaluate a complex

$$W = \exp(x + iy) = \exp x(\cos y + i \sin y)$$

```
COMPLEX    MCDEF    X,  Y,  REALW,  IMAGW
           GET      EXP,  X
           XAM      EXPX
           GET      COS,  Y
           XAD      ——
           MUL      EXPX
           XAM      REALW
           GET      SIN,  Y
           XAD      ——
           MUL      EXPX
           XAM      IMAGW
COMPLEX    MCEND
```

FIGURE 7.2.3. A macro to find a complex exponential. It includes library subroutines calls (GET).

exponential. COMPLEX uses four arguments: X and Y, the real and imaginary portions of the exponent; REALW and IMAGW, the real and imaginary portions of the result.

Three subroutines are called in this macro definition: the exponential, EXP, the sine, SIN and the cosine, COS. The expansion of Fig. 7.2.3 into its assembly language equivalent, including the SRJ table entries and the calling sequence, is left to the reader as an exercise.

Flow Chart for GET

Figure 7.2.4 shows a flow chart of the typical assembly activity in one pass or the other to translate GET. The name of the subroutine is found in

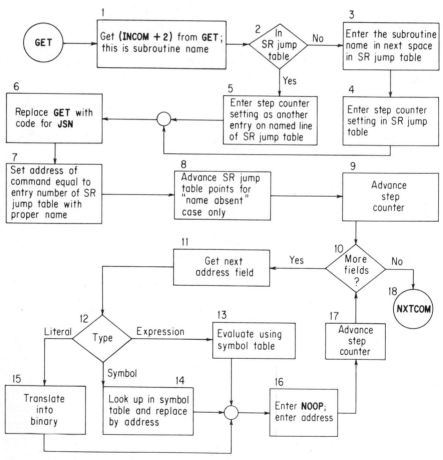

FIGURE 7.2.4. Flow chart of assembler activity to translate GET.

the first address field of the GET command (1). We look at the SRJ table to see if the SR name is there (2). *During* assembly the SRJ table is stored within the assembler rather than at the head of the program. If the SR name is absent, we enter it in the next space in the subroutine table (3). The step counter setting is entered there too (4). If the SR name is in the table (2), then we may enter the current setting of the step counter as another entry in this line of the SRJ table (5).

Now we make up the command code JSN (6). Its address is the entry number either where the SR name was found or where the name was placed in the SRJ table (7). The SRJ table pointer is advanced if a new entry has been made in that table (8). The object language command is prepared for output and we advance the step counter (9).

Next we check GET to see if it contains more fields (10). If so, a calling sequence is involved; we get the next field (11) and check its type (12). An expression must be evaluated by the use of the symbol table (13). A defined symbol should be in the symbol table which is complete after the second pass; the symbol is looked up and replaced by an address equivalent (14). A literal is translated into binary (15). The symbol equivalent just determined becomes the address field of the next command, a NOOP. For the literal, the entire word may be the binary equivalent of the literal. The step counter is advanced.

When there are no more fields in GET we continue with the source-language analysis (18).

Assembler Defined Macros

We have discussed assembler defined macros as being similar to the programmer defined macros. The difference is that, for the former, the programmer need not supply a definition: it is incorporated into the assembler.

There is no reason why assembler defined macros cannot include subroutine calls since this facility is provided in the assembler anyway. It is possible to carry this reasoning another step further. The programmer can define macros which include assembler defined macros which, in turn, include subroutine calls. In fact, most combinations of these three tools can be employed. The exception is that the subroutines and assembler defined macros perforce cannot contain programmer defined macros; the former are defined before the programmer comes on the scene.

A most powerful tool is the assembler defined macro which includes library subroutines. This is one way to implement an input-output control system (Chapters 8 and 9). A single call is replaced by a calling sequence to the library. The latter is then brought to bear at run time, providing as long a routine as necessary to perform the IO operation.

7.3   ASSEMBLING SUBROUTINES

Assembler defined macros are usually short. If one wishes to make frequent references in many programs to important subroutines, it is a good idea to incorporate them into the SR library. Subroutines are assembled almost the same as any other program. They are incorporated into the subroutine library using service routines, as discussed later. Two important macros which facilitate the assembly of SR's are now introduced.

Saving Index Registers

The obligation for leaving index registers intact is usually placed upon the SR rather than the main program. By having the SR save the indexes, we remove these program steps from the main program and store them in the subroutine.

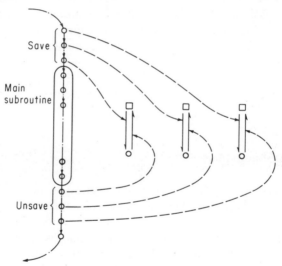

FIGURE 7.3.1. The job of SAVE: temporarily store the contacts of indexes and supplementary bits in special cells (above); reinstate these indexes and bits after use (below).

Another good convention is to have the SR save the contents of any register before the SR uses it, whether used by the main program or not. Computers which provide few index registers allow any index to be used by a SR. We suppose here that index 4 is sacrosanct, is never used by any SR and hence, need not be saved. On the other hand, the FAP assembler is built for a machine with only three index registers, and its convention is to store index 4 regardless of whether the SR uses it.

When to Save

The first approach to saving the index registers is shown in Fig. 7.3.1. The indexes (squares) have their contents passed over to some specified cell by steps which precede the SR. Before returning to the main program, the steps follow the subroutine to return the quantities from the cells to the index register from which they came. After index restoration, the final SR command returns control to the main program.

The trouble with this procedure is that we place a number of steps both *before* and *after* the subroutine proper. We probably don't know the number of steps as we start to write the subroutine; we may forget this extra macro if it must go at the end. To circumvent these difficulties, we use a scheme for placing the *save* and *unsave* steps before the subroutine proper, as in Fig. 7.3.2: the *save* phase directly precedes the subroutine; the *unsave* phase precedes the save phase.

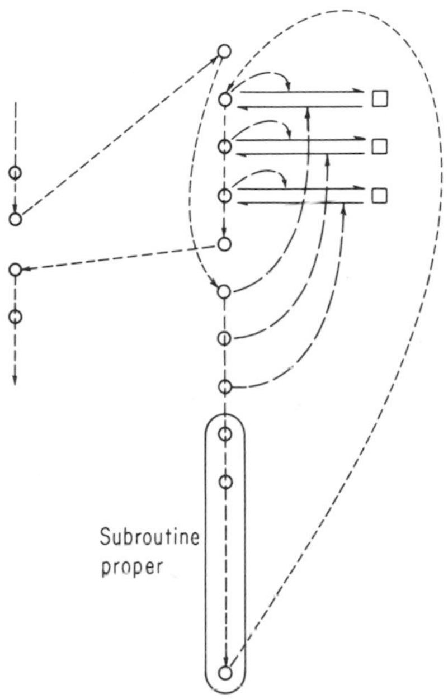

In Fig. 7.3.2 the main program jumps us to the beginning of the *save-unsave* sequence which, in turn, jumps to the *save* phase. This is a sequence of transfers which places the contents of each index into the address portion of one of the *unsave* commands. To save index 3, we place its contents in a cell which contains the command:

FIGURE 7.3.2. The SAVE job is done by the insertion of the contents of chosen indexes in XPN commands; these same commands are later used to reinstate the indexes.

$$\text{XPN,3} \qquad blank \qquad\qquad (7.3.1)$$

The contents of N3 replaces the blank. When XPN is performed, it places the quantity where the blank was back into index 3, thus *unsaving* it.

After the *save* sequence the subroutine is performed; at its end, a jump takes us to the *unsave* phase. This set of commands, each like (7.3.1), restores the indexes. A return to the main program is at the end of the *unsave* phase; its address field is one more than the number of arguments in the subroutine.

Expansion of the Save Macro

Figure 7.3.3 shows how SAVE is used to place the steps of both the *save* and *unsave* phase before a subroutine; this one for taking the sum of squares is called SUMSQ. SAVE is formatted thus:

label SAVE number of parameters, index list, indicator list   (7.3.2)

Number of parameters is the length of the argument list provided by the main program. The return jump must skip past these parameters to land properly in the main program.

```
                                      length of parameter list
                                      index list
                                      list of other indicators
SUMSQ      SAVE     3,  2,  5,  6
SUMSQ1     XMN,4              2


SUMSQ      UJIT     * + 5
           XPN,2           blank
           XPN,5           blank
           XPN,6           blank
           UCJ,4        4
           XNM,2    * — 4
           XNM,5    * — 4
           XMN,6    * — 4
SUMSQ1     XMN,4        2
```

FIGURE 7.3.3. Expansion of the SAVE macro for a subroutine with three parameters where indexes 2, 5 and 6 are to be saved. *Note:* The UJIT (*unconditional jump ignore tag*) command is used here instead of UCJ in order to coordinate with the macro ERROR described later.

Index list for FLAP contains a digit for each index for which storage is required: indexes 2, 5 and 6 in the figure. FAP employs a single number here, for the IBM 709/90/94 series has just three index registers; this provides full knowledge of which and how many of the three are to be saved.

Indicator list, empty in the figure, refers to sense switches, IO indicators, overflow indicators, and so forth. If such indicators are to be used by the subroutine, the setting they have up to this point in the main program must be *saved*. SAVE does this and also restores them when the SR is done. Type number, function and presence of indicator is subject to extreme variation from one machine to another. Indicators in one machine may be absent in another. Commands to save and reset indicators also may differ widely. Indicators are usually listed symbolically in SAVE to distinguish them from the indexes.

The first working step of the subroutine is indicated in Fig. 7.3.3 as SUMSQ1. Everything before this step is provided for by SAVE in the assembler.

Assembled Subroutine

START

Into what commands is the original SAVE instruction translated? In Fig. 7.3.2, note that the first command jumps over the restoring string of commands to be performed after the subroutine. Then follows a number of *save* operations, followed finally by the main program.

The string produced in Fig. 7.3.3 begins at SUMSQ with a jump to the *save* group. The number of intervening commands is 5, so the address portion is $* + 5$. The command mnemonic could be an *unconditional jump*, UCJ, but UJIT, *unconditional jump ignore tag* coordinates with the error routine discussed later.

STORING

Starting at SUMSQ $+ 5$ we find three XNM commands to store the contents of N2, N5 and N6 in consecutive spots right after SUMSQ. The index contents are inserted into the address portion of XPN commands which ultimately restore the indexes that have just been saved. Since each of the *unsave* commands is just four steps behind the corresponding *save* command, the address for *each* XNM *save* command is $* - 4$.

Because no indicators need be saved, the first command of the main subroutine at SUMSQ1 is entered.

RESTORATION

To make use of SAVE, all subroutines are set up so that normal return is made to the *second* step of the total subroutine. In other words, for the subroutine at SUMSQ, return is made to SUMSQ $+ 1$ (not to be confused with SUMSQ1). Notice in Fig. 7.3.2 that at the end of the subroutine there is a jump to the second step in the total subroutine. The *unsave* sequence follows, concluding with a return to the main program, jumping over the calling sequence provided by the main program.

Beginning at SUMSQ $+ 1$, XPN commands restore the contents of the address portion of the command word into the index indicated. After restoring the indexes, the indicators that were saved are reset and, finally, return is made to the main program.

In Fig. 7.3.3 the main program return is from SUMSQ $+ 4$. By convention here, index 4 stores the contents of the instruction counter when the jump to the subroutine was made. If no calling sequence or parameters were present, the proper command would be UCJ,4 1. The SAVE command indicates a parameter list of three items. To avoid the parameter list, we must jump four places instead of one with UCJ,4 4.

Operation of the Assembler for SAVE

The macro SAVE is flow-charted in Fig. 7.3.4. The number of items to be saved is the same as the number of commas in the address field of the macro (ignoring indicators). The assembler resets i and j, to 0(1). The indicator i stores the number of commas. From this we construct the first command (5).

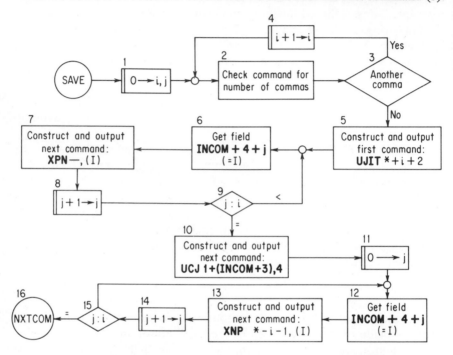

FIGURE 7.3.4. Flow chart for the SAVE generator, a variable, assembler-defined generator.

Next we construct the restore commands; XPN's with blank addresses tagged by the index or indicator contained in SAVE. One command is created for each index and indicator in SAVE. Successive fields of the SAVE command are obtained (6) to construct the commands (7), until all the fields of SAVE have been used (8) (9). *Unsave* commands for the indicators are then provided (not shown).

The next command is UCJ indexed by 4 and with an address one more than *number of parameter* in Fig. 7.3.2 (10). After resetting j (11), we prepare commands. We procure index fields in order (12) and construct XPN's with address $* - i - 1$ (13) for each (14) (15). The construction of the subroutine continues with the next command (16).

7.4   SUBROUTINE ERRORS

SR Limitations

A subroutine has limitations in the things it can do and the data it deals with. It is not always possible nor even desirable to check all information supplied to the SR. For instance, we could make sure that no number supplied a square root subroutine was negative; but it would be much more difficult to determine that the numbers supplied to SUMSQ did not form a sum which exceeds the capacity of the computer word. Therefore, the subroutine should have precautions built into it to inform the main program that it did not reach successful completion.

Different conventions prevail. We investigate an error scheme which is easy to implement and has been incorporated into FAP, IBMAP and FLAP.

A convention requires that one cell of the main program calling sequence be reserved for an error jump; normal return is one position after the error return or two steps after the parameter list as illustrated in Fig. 7.4.1. The main program contains:

- a jump to the subroutine
- a list of three parameter values
- a position for the error jump
- the remainder of the main program

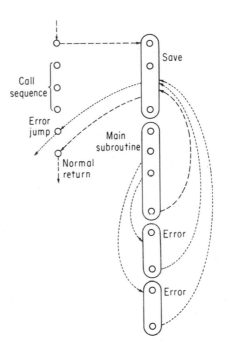

FIGURE 7.4.1. When ERROR is called, besides setting an indicator at the initial address, the assembly must verify that return is made to the main program one step earlier than normal—to where the error jump is placed.

Normal sequence follows the dashed arrows from the main program, through the subroutine to the normal return, ignoring the error return; a *detected error* sequence is shown in dotted lines.

Error Indication

If there is but one kind of error the subroutine can encounter, then the foregoing solution is adequate. When the error jump is taken, since only one kind of error is possible, this is it!

When an SR might encounter several difficulties, something should convey to the program which error has occurred. Then an error-correcting subroutine entered from the error jump could determine where the fault lies before attempting to correct it. In Fig. 7.4.1, the subroutine consists of four segments:

- *save* and *unsave*
- main subroutine
- two error segments

The subroutine contains points where exceptions are checked for. Should faults arise, the subroutine is discontinued and an *error* segment is entered. The object of each *error* segment is to set an indicator and return to the main program at the error jump.

Now we see why the first command produced by SAVE is UJIT instead of UCJ. UJIT is a nonindexable unconditional jump (*Unconditional Jump, Ignore Tag*), shown on line 40, Table 2.3.1; it does not have its address augmented by the index associated with the tag, whereas UCJ would. Hence the index tag of UJIT can store an error indicator without affecting its execution.

The error segment (Fig. 7.4.1) enters an indicator in the tag of the first command, UJIT, of the subroutine. The error sequence also augments the final jump command to make return one step earlier in the main program, the error return point. This is done when 1 is subtracted from the return index.

ERROR JUMP FUNCTION

It is up to the programmer to make use of the error jump function. When an error is found in using the subroutine, the error jump is entered. The programmer inserts a jump at the error return to a repair subroutine generally unique to the subroutine just attempted. The programmer also furnishes the proper repair function.

In a case such as overflow the repair may consist of rescaling. When the square root SR detects a negative operand, several alternatives exist, including the recording of imaginary numbers. To investigate this topic more fully would be a digression.

Error type is distinguished by the repair SR from the tag of UJIT in the original SR.

The Macro ERROR

The segment of the subroutine devoted to indicating the error and causing return to the error jump can be completely fabricated with a single FLAP macro, ERROR, with format:

$$\text{label} \quad \text{ERROR} \quad \text{subroutine name, number} \qquad (7.4.1)$$

Subroutine name is the name of the subroutine; *number* is a digit to replace the index tag of UJIT in the subroutine when an error is detected. On assembly this macro applied to SUMSQ results in the steps shown in the lower portion of Fig. 7.4.2.

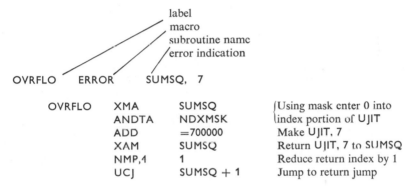

OVRFLO	XMA	SUMSQ	⎰Using mask enter 0 into
	ANDTA	NDXMSK	⎱index portion of UJIT
	ADD	=700000	Make UJIT, 7
	XAM	SUMSQ	Return UJIT, 7 to SUMSQ
	NMP,4	1	Reduce return index by 1
	UCJ	SUMSQ + 1	Jump to return jump

FIGURE 7.4.2. Assembly of the macro ERROR.

At OVRFLO we put in the accumulator UJIT, n from SUMSQ. The tag, n, may have been set by a previous error exit. This position is reset to 0 by the logical ANDTA which refers to NDXMSK. This is a mask which contains 1's everywhere except in the index tag position, which contains 0's. UJIT with 0 tag is now in the accumulator.

At OVRFLO + 2 the error tag from ERROR is added to the UJIT command. Since the tag position is 0, this acts like a transfer of the constant to the tag position. The constant corresponds to *number* in ERROR. The augmented UJIT is returned to SUMSQ by XAM at OVRFLO + 3.

Return to the main program still uses the UCJ,4 at SUMSQ + 1. But to make this return one step earlier, the contents of index 4 are reduced by 1 by NMP,4 at OVRFLO + 4.

To leave the error, request UCJ at OVRFLO + 5 goes directly to SUMSQ + 1 where UCJ,4 takes us to the error return in the main program.

The next time the subroutine is used, the index tag of UJIT retains the 7 entered by *this* error sequence. If no error occurs, the tag of UJIT is not referred to, so it doesn't matter. If an error should appear, the tag is positively set to record this, so again, the present setting is disregarded.

Example and Summary

A portion of a source program which uses a subroutine is found in Fig. 7.4.3. To call the first subroutine, SUMSQ, we simply use GET at

Main				Subroutine	
			SUMSQ	SAVE	4,1,2
CALL1	GET	SUMSQ, LISTART,	SMSQ1	XMA,4	2
		LENGTH, SUM		XAN,2	*blank*
	UCJ	SUMSQERR		XMA,4	1
	XMA	SUM		XAN,1	*blank*
CALL2	GET	ROOT		XOM	TOTAL
	UCJ	ROOTERR	SUMSQ2	XMD,1	0
	XMA	DATUM		MLR,1	0
				ADD	TOTAL
				JOO	OVRFLO
				XAM	TOTAL
				TUN,1	* + 1
				TDN,2	* − 6
				XAM,1,4	3
				UCJ	SUMSQ + 1
			OVRFLO	ERROR	SUMSQ, 7

FIGURE 7.4.3. Source language portion of main program and subroutines.

CALL1 which contains the name of the subroutine, SUMSQ, and the names of the three parameters used by the subroutine.

The programmer knows that this subroutine can encounter an error and provides a jump to a corrective SR, SUMSQERR at CALL1 + 1. If no error is made, normal return is made CALL1 + 2 which contains the XMA command.

Another SR ROOT contains no parameters because the number to be recorded is left in the accumulator. Hence, GET at CALL2 contains only ROOT in its address field. An error can occur in this subroutine, so the programmer places a jump to the repair SR, ROOTERR, at CALL2 + 1. The program continues at CALL2 + 2.

The subroutine at SUMSQ begins with SAVE. There are four items in the parameter list: three are parameters; one is a space for the error jump. At SMSQ1 and SMSQ1 + 1, we enter the list length (the second item in the parameter list) into index 2 by indexing 2 by the contents of index 4. The starting point of the list, the first parameter, is transferred via accumulator to index 1 at SMSQ1 + 2 and SMSQ1 + 3. The cell called TOTAL is cleared at SMSQ1 + 4.

The actual work of the subroutine begins at SMSQ2. We find the square of the next item by referring to the list through index 1. We add square to TOTAL but, should the total overflow, the command at SMSQ2 + 3 causes a jump to OVRFLO. For no overflow the total is returned to memory. We note the next list item to be squared by tallying up index 1; the number of items is kept track of in index 2. When it is reduced to 0, the whole list has been processed.

When the list of items is exhausted, we have found the sum of the squares and, although it has been replaced in memory at TOTAL, it is still in the accumulator. It is to be placed at the location SUM, addressed indirectly at SMSQ2 + 7.

Return to the main program is made, using a convention, by a jump to SUMSQ + 1. Remember that the SAVE macro, when expanded, will start the *unsave* sequence at SUMSQ + 1.

In ERROR we list the name of the subroutine and the index tag setting for an error.

Assembly of Example

Figure 7.4.4 is the assembly language equivalent of the expansion by the assembler of Fig. 7.4.3.

MAIN PROGRAM

JSN,4 is substituted for GET. The SRJ table entry for SUMSQ is the address for JSN. NOOP entries are provided for LISTART, LENGTH and SUM.

The unconditional jump command remains intact. GET ROOT is replaced by JSN,4 with the address of the SRJ table entry.

SUBROUTINE EXPANSION

The expansion of SAVE is found on the right of the figure. Notice the expansion of ERROR. XAM at OVRFLO + 3 returns UJIT augmented to

Main			Subroutine		
CALL1	JSN,4	SR jump entry	SUMSQ	UJIT	* + 4
	NOOP	LISTART		XPN,1	blank
	NOOP	LENGTH		XPN,2	blank
	NOOP	SUM		UCJ,4	5
	UCJ	SUMSQERR		XNM,1	* − 3
CALL2	JSN,4	SR jump entry		XNM,2	* − 3
	UCJ	ROOTERR	SMSQ1	XMA,4	2
	XMA	DATUM		XAN,2	blank
				XMA,4	1
				XAN,1	blank
				XOM	TOTAL
			SMSQ2	XMD,1	0
				MLR,1	0
				ADD	TOTAL
				JOO	OVRFLO
				XAM	TOTAL
				TUN,1	* + 1
				TDN,2	* − 6
				XAM,1,4	3
				UCJ	SMSQ + 1
			OVRFLO	XMA	SUMSQ
				ANDTA	NDXMSK
				ADD	700000
				XAM	SUMSQ
				NMP,4	1
				UC1	SUMSQ + 1

FIGURE 7.4.4. Source language equivalent of object program translated from Fig. 7.4.3.

have a tag 7, to SUMSQ. The decrement command, NMP at OVRFLO + 4 reduces the contents of index 4 by 1. UCJ, at OVRFLO + 5 returns to SUMSQ + 1. Indexes 1 and 2 are restored and return is made to the main program to 5 plus the contents of index 4. Normally this would bring us to the location CALL2. Since index 4 has been decremented, we return to CALL1 + 4, the jump to the error routine.

Expansion of GET causes an entry in the SRJ table because the SR called is in a library to be entered at run time.

PROBLEMS

7.1   Why are assembler defined macros required?

7.2   Show how the GET flow chart of Fig. 7.2.4 fits into the general flow chart of the assembler, Figs. 5.4.2, 5.5.1, 5.6.2, and 5.6.3.

7.3   Write a FLAP subprogram for GET using Fig. 7.2.4.

7.4   Show and flow chart how GET can be called for in a macro definition. Indicate all changes required either in the GET generator, in the macro definer or in the generalized macro generator.

7.5   Make changes in GET, the macro definer and the macro generator sub-programs as required by problem 7.4.

7.6   Subprogram SAVE in FLAP using Fig. 7.3.4.

7.7   Flow chart ERROR.

7.8   Subprogram ERROR in FLAP using problem 7.7.

7.9   Rewrite SQRT (problem 6.4) incorporating SAVE for indexes 3, 5, 8 and ERROR for negative arguments (enter a test in the SR) using tag 1 for this case.

7.10   Rewrite QUADRT (problem 6.5) using SAVE and ERROR with an error exit tagged 2 when there are no real roots.

7.11   Rewrite RECT (problem 6.6) using SAVE and ERROR tagged 9 when there are no solutions.

7.12   Flow chart an SR to find the roots of a cubic equation, CBCRT, using CBRT [no error exit (why?)] and SQRT (problem 7.9) and providing any error exits required.

7.13   Program problem 7.12.

7.14   Expand Fig. 7.2.3 into the assembly language equivalent of the translation produced by the assembler. Include the SR entries and the calling sequences.

8

ASSEMBLER
REFINEMENTS

8.1   REPETITION COMMANDS

A command which duplicates a string of commands, while changing one of the parameters in the string, can be obtained by the use of macros. As a built-in assembly facility it is very useful, especially in defining repetitive data sets.

The Duplicate Pseudo

A pseudo which duplicates a string of commands is:

$$\text{label} \quad \textbf{DUP} \quad \text{length, times} \tag{8.1.1}$$

Length is the number of commands in the string to be repeated; *times* is the number of repetitions of the string. Parameters variable in the command list that follows are distinguished with the special symbol #. The first time the sequence appears, we substitute 1 for #; the second time the sequence is repeated, we substitute 2 for #. We continue thus, substituting *times* for # the last time the sequence is reproduced.

Example:

The use of DUP is shown in Fig. 8.1.1. At NOW we find DUP 4, 3. The next four commands are to be repeated three times. At the right of the figure is the equivalent of the object language program produced. The first time # appears we replace it by 1. For each duplication of the sequence

	XAM	A		XAM	A
NOW	DUP	4, 3	NOW	ADD	1
	ADD	#		SUB	R
	SUB	R		MUL	5
	MUL	4 + #		DIV	9
	DIV	8 + #			...
	ADD	B		ADD	2
				SUB	R
				MUL	6
				DIV	10
					...
				ADD	3
				SUB	R
				MUL	7
				DIV	11
					...
				ADD	B

FIGURE 8.1.1. The DUP pseudo duplicates sets of commands and substitutes 1 through N (here 3) successively for appearances of #.

its value is increased by 1. The power of this pseudo is increased further when the permissible expressions in the assembler include multiplication and division.

A Duplicating Command for Macros

For the macro, it is useful to duplicate a sequence of commands with a change in a single parameter. This procedure is magnified if, instead of incrementing the parameter, we reference a list.

MCDUP reproduces a string of commands, making substitutions for a given parameter from a list supplied MCDUP thus:

$$\text{label} \qquad \text{MCDUP} \qquad \text{list name } or \text{ list} \qquad (8.1.2)$$

In Fig. 8.1.2 we see a macro definition within which is a sequence of commands surrounded by the rectangle. The rectangle is bounded by a pair of MCDUP's. The first MCDUP contains a list referred to in duplicating the string which follows MCDUP.

MCDUP LIST INCLUDED

A set of symbols follows MCDUP which is the list; thus:

$$\text{MCDUP} \qquad \text{JOE, JIM, JACK} \qquad\qquad (8.1.3)$$

The commands which follow to the next MCDUP are repeated three times:

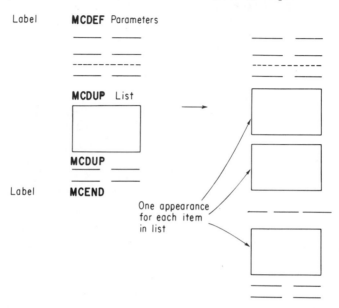

FIGURE 8.1.2. The macro definition duplicating pseudo. MCDUP is used to repeat a set of commands parenthesized by it for a list indicated with its first appearance.

the symbol # is replaced successively by JOE, JIM, JACK in sequence. An example appears in Fig. 8.1.3.

NAMED LIST

Another alternative is to *name* a list. The pseudo does not look any different:

$$\text{MCDUP} \qquad \text{LARRY} \qquad\qquad (8.1.4)$$

However, LARRY is now a *list name*! How does the assembler tell that LARRY is a list name? Not from the prototype statement which might appear as:

$$\text{SUMSQ} \qquad \text{MCDEF} \qquad \text{LARRY, SID} \qquad (8.1.5)$$

But when SUMSQ is called, LARRY may be replaced by another symbol as:

$$\text{SQ} \qquad \text{SUMSQ} \qquad \text{ONCE, TOT} \qquad\qquad (8.1.6)$$

in which case, for all commands after (8.1.4) in which LARRY appears, he is replaced by ONCE until the next MCDUP, and the sequence is *not* repeated.

LARRY may be replaced by a list of symbols only if these are placed in parentheses. Thus for the call:

SQ   SUMSQ   (TED, TOM, TONY, TOD), TOT   (8.1.7)

the sequence after MCDUP in (8.1.4) appears four times: once for each of the fellas.

```
SQUAR3    MCDEF    X, Y, Z, T
          XOM      T
          MCDUP    X, Y, Z
          XMD      #
          MUL      #
          ADD      T
          XAM      T
          MCDUP
SQUAR3    MCEND
          a. prototype
CALLS     SQUAR3   ONE, TWO, THREE, TOTAL
NEXTS     XMA      TOTAL
          b. call
CALLS     XOM      TOTAL
          XMD      ONE
          MUL      ONE
          ADD      TOTAL
          XAM      TOTAL
          XMD      TWO
          MUL      TWO
          ADD      TOTAL
          XAM      TOTAL
          XMD      THREE
          MUL      THREE
          ADD      TOTAL
          XAM      TOTAL
NEXTS     XMA      TOTAL
```
          c. AL equivalent of code generated by call in b.

FIGURE 8.1.3. Use of MCDUP in defining a macro where the list is included with MCDUP. The call and its assembly are shown.

Example of the Use of MCDUP

We examine three aspects of the occurrence of MCDUP:

- definition
- source language appearance
- object language appearance

The purpose of the macro SQUARE, defined in Fig. 8.1.4, is to find the sum of squares of items provided in the list of addresses supplied when the macro is called.

At SQUARE + 1 we clear SUM to hold the result. SQUARE + 2 is the MCDUP command and refers to a list named LIST. The commands that follow are to be performed for each item whose name appears in LIST.

	Definition				*Use*	
SQUARE	MCDEF	LIST,	SUM		XAM	DATA 1
	XOM	SUM		SQ	SQUARE	(FIRST,SECOND,THIRD),
	MCDUP	LIST				TOTAL
	XMD	LIST			XMA	TOTAL
	MUL	LIST				⇓
	ADD	SUM			XAM	DATA 1
	XAM	SUM		SQ	XOM	TOTAL
	MCDUP				XMD	FIRST
SQUARE	MCEND				MUL	FIRST
					ADD	TOTAL
					XAM	TOTAL
					XMD	SECOND
					MUL	SECOND
					ADD	TOTAL
					XAM	TOTAL
					XMD	THIRD
					MUL	THIRD
					ADD	TOTAL
					XAM	TOTAL
					XMA	TOTAL

FIGURE 8.1.4. Using the pseudo MCDUP in a macro definition. The main program calls the macro SUMSQ at right. The object to language equivalent appears below the double arrow.

An item is squared at SQUARE + 3 and SUMSQ + 4. It is added to the result so far at SQUARE + 5 and SQUARE + 6. We end the duplication sequence with MCDUP, and end the prototype structure with MCEND.

To use SQUARE, we enter it into a source language string, as at the top right of Fig. 8.1.4. SQUARE is requested at SQ. The commands above and below are simple FLAP mnemonics.

In the call, the list to be duplicated within the macro is furnished in the *parameter list* as a parenthesized set of symbols set off within the parentheses by commas. Next in the call we encounter TOTAL; it corresponds to the parameter called SUM in the prototype.

The assembly language equivalent of the object string produced by the macro call is shown in the bottom right of Fig. 8.1.4. The command at SQ clears the cell TOTAL.

The string to be duplicated contains four commands. The referents from the first two commands are taken from the list; the referent of the other two commands is the argument TOTAL. The commands at SQ + 1 through SQ + 4 are the same as those under MCDUP in the prototype, except that for LIST we substitute FIRST, and for SUM we substitute TOTAL.

The string appears again at SQ + 5 through SQ + 8, this time with SECOND substituted for LIST, but TOTAL still replaces SUM. Finally, since there are only three item names in the list, we find the commands at SQ + 9 through SQ + 12 have had THIRD substituted for LIST. The command at SQ + 13 is not part of the macro but is the next step after SQ in the main program.

Another example of the use of MCDUP is shown in Section 8.2 in connection with the SET command.

8.2 PROCESSING WITHIN ASSEMBLY

Conditional Assembly

Conditional assembly permits us to instruct the assembler whether a given source language command should be assembled. If the source language programmer is supplying the assembler with a set of source language commands for which he desires translation, why would he wish to furnish a command that would inhibit assembly? For short simple programs this facility finds little use.

Suppose that, instead of a simple program, we wish a generalized program to be assembled into one of several output programs according to conditions or parameters that are supplied with the source language program. For instance, we could write a generalized payroll program. We leave room in it for parameters peculiar to different departments. We make allowances for different kinds of employees. For one employee type certain processing steps are included; for another type they are omitted. If the payroll program is for a division without one type of employee, that sequence is omitted.

Conditional assembly is useful when a generalized source program is provided which can produce two or more object programs according to conditions supplied with the source program.

Use

A conditional assembly command is a pseudo since it talks to the assembler. It is an instruction to the assembler to either do or skip the succeeding command. We postulate two pseudos, IFTRU and IFALS, explained below.

IFTRU

This pseudo takes the form;

          label   IFTRU   relation, symbol 1, symbol 2   (8.2.1)

If *symbol 1* is related to *symbol 2* by *relation*, we assemble the commands which follow normally; otherwise we skip exactly one command.

IFTRU can be used anywhere in the source language program. If it is followed by a macro, then of course it dictates the inclusion or exclusion of that macro.

IFALS

This pseudo takes the same form:

          label   IFALS   relation, symbol 1, symbol 2   (8.2.2)

This time, if *symbol 1* is not related to *symbol 2* by *relation*, we assemble the next command; we omit the next command from assembly if *relation* is true.

Conditional assembly pseudos can be included in macro definitions. When that macro is called, one or another sequence will be included in the object program. An example of this procedure follows.

IFTRU Example

To explain the use of IFTRU, we examine the construction of several macro definitions.

INCLUD

The definition for INCLUD is found in Fig. 8.2.1. The purpose of this macro is simply to include or exclude *another* macro. The identity of the other macro is furnished when INCLUD is called. Here is an example of an argument defined command discussed in Section 6.7.

```
        INCLUD    MCDEF     MACRO, COND1, COND2
                  IFTRU     =,  COND1, COND2
                  MACRO
        INCLUD    MCEND
```

FIGURE 8.2.1. Defining a macro INCLUD which uses the conditional assembly pseudo IFTRU.

Three parameters are furnished on the first line of the definition. They name the macro and the two symbolic expressions to be compared. At INCLUD + 1 we find the IFTRU pseudo. It indicates *relation* is equality given by "=". The expressions to be compared are those furnished in the definition of INCLUD. At INCLUD + 2 the macro call which may be included is now presented for possible assembly. That is all there is to this definition.

CALCGROSS

This macro multiplies *rate* times *hours* to get *gross pay*, as presented in Fig. 8.2 2.

```
CALCGROSS      MCDEF      R,  H,  P
               XMD        R
               MUL        H
               XAM        P
CALCGROSS      MCEND
```

FIGURE 8.2.2. A simple marco to calculate gross pay from hours and rate.

USING INCLUD

Suppose we are writing the generalized payroll problem discussed earlier. We have just calculated one of the quantities for output in HOURLY − 1 in Fig. 8.2.3. To find the gross pay of the hourly worker we calculate using CALCGROSS. For the monthly employee all we do is get his gross pay amount from the proper field of the incoming record. At this point in the program we wish to assemble the proper steps to get the gross pay according to which type of payroll problem we are doing.

At the step labeled HOURLY, we have an INCLUD macro which includes another macro, CALCGROSS, for the hourly program; it is omitted otherwise.

```
              XAM        OUTPUT
HOURLY        INCLUD     (CALCGROSS,  RATE,  HOURS,  GROSPAY),
                         TYPE,  HOUR
MONTHLY       INCLUD     (BRINGROSS),  TYPE, MNTH
              XMA        GROSPAY

                         ↓        for  TYPE = HOUR
              XAM        OUTPUT
HOURLY        XMD        RATE
              MUL        HOURS
              XAM        GROSPAY
              XMA        GROSPAY
```

FIGURE 8.2.3. A portion of a source program (above) for conditional assembly. It produces an object program for hourly or monthly workers, depending upon parameters. This portion is expanded (below) for hourly workers.

On the next line labeled MONTHLY, we include another macro BRINGROSS, if the type of employee is monthly.

With two INCLUDs we include one macro or another, according to the type of employee specified with the source language program.

In the lower half of Fig. 8.2.3 we see the result of assembly when the task is done for an hourly payroll. When the assembler hits the first INCLUD, it looks up this macro name in the name table. The prototype command table for INCLUD is entered. The first command there is the IFTRU pseudo. This is performed by comparing the symbol in the field called TYPE with the symbol HOUR. Since the relation "=" prevails, the command which follows is assembled.

The command which follows IFTRU in the INCLUD command table is a macro whose name is obtained from the first field of the INCLUD call. Because HOUR = HOUR, the three commands which make up CALCGROSS are entered into the program string. The name of the macro and its three parameters, RATE, HOURS and GROSPAY are a list which is parenthesized to appear as a single field for the macro, INCLUD.

The assembler looks up the macro, CALCGROSS, and writes up the commands pertaining to it, replacing the prototype parameters by the labels in the parameter list of CALCGROSS. The latter is a sublist of the list for INCLUD. This accounts for the commands at HOURLY, HOURLY + 1 and HOURLY + 2 in Fig. 8.2.3.

Next the assembler encounters the macro INCLUD at MONTHLY. Again the command table for INCLUD is found. The first command, the pseudo IFTRU, is examined. Since TYPE represents the letters HOUR, which is not equal to MNTH, the relation "=" is false and the macro BRINGROSS is not assembled. The next command XMA GROSPAY (a mnemonic) from the source language string is translated and entered below.

Assembler Operation

Figure 8.2.4 shows the operation of the assembler when it encounters a conditional assembly command. First it obtains the relation and the two symbolic expressions, which we call respectively R, B and C, from the incoming command (1). The symbolic expressions B and C are compared (2) to determine their relation.

Next the relation prevailing is compared with the relation supplied in the field of the macro called R (3), (4), (5).

If the two relations are the same, we assemble the next command if the macro is IFTRU (6); on the other hand, if the command under consideration is IFALS, the two relations must be different for the next command to be assembled (7).

For IFTRU and different relations (6) or IFALS and the same relations (7), the assembler obtains the next source language command and ignores it (8). It gets the one after that one and analyzes it in a normal fashion (9). The flow chart has not considered the relations $\leqslant$ or $\geqslant$ which should also be permissible.

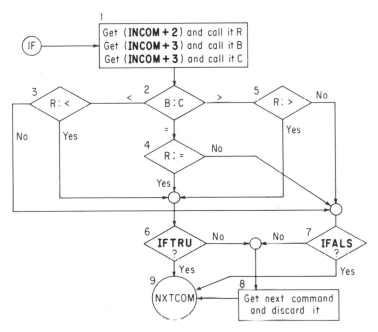

FIGURE 8.2.4. Operation of the assembler for the conditional assembly pseudos, IFTRU and IFALS.

SET

SET is useful in both source language strings and in macros. It is an assignment statement which may be used for counting events. The format is:

$$\text{symbol} \quad \textbf{SET} \quad \text{expression} \qquad (8.2.3)$$

Symbol is set to the value of *expression*. The beauty of this type of command is that it provides processing capability during assembly.

Example:

As a synthetic example, we define a macro prototype RTMNSQ in Fig. 8.2.5 to find the standard deviation of a list of items.

The parameters are supplied to RTMNSQ by LIST and a result is produced called SIGMA. The length of the list is stored in LENGTH. Probably it would be just as easy to supply this as a parameter in the definition; that is why the example is synthetic. We count the number of items as they are processed using SET, at RTMNSQ + 7. We clear LENGTH with SET at RTMNSQ + 1, and SIGMA at RTMNSQ + 2. .

Now we wish to perform a duplicate string of commands for each item in the list. Thus at RTMNSQ + 3 we find MCDUP with the referent, LIST. The next four commands are used to square the next item on the list, add this to the sum so far, and return this sum to the cell, SIGMA. Then another

RTMNSQ	MCDEF	LIST, SIGMA
LENGTH	SET	0
	MCDUP	LIST
	XMD	LIST
	MUL	LIST
	ADD	SIGMA
	XAM	SIGMA
LENGTH	SET	LENGTH + 1
	MCDUP	
LASTPART	XMA	SIGMA
	DIV	LENGTH
	XQA	*blank*
	SQROOT	*blank*
	XAM	SIGMA
RTMNSQ	MCEND	

FIGURE 8.2.5. Using SET to record the length of a list variable within a macro is a rather unplausible example for finding the root-mean-square (RTMNSQ).

command, SET, is used to add one to the count of items on the list. The second MCDUP completes the string of commands to be duplicated.

To find the root-mean-square, we take the sum of the squares, divide it by the number of items and find the square root thereof.

At LASTPART we bring in the sum of the squares. The cell labeled LENGTH contains the number of items on the list. Hence, at LASTPART + 1 we divide by LENGTH. The result is passed to the accumulator by XQA. We now perform a macro called SQROOT, which finds the square root of the item in the accumulator and returns it to the accumulator. That is the desired result which is now stored in SIGMA.

More Powerful Conditional Assembly Commands

It seems desirable to provide commands for the assembler equivalent to source commands which allow us to jump when a given relation prevails. Thus, referring to Fig. 8.2.6, we find that the assembler operates very similar to an actual program. When it reaches the first hexagon it looks for one of two conditions. If the first prevails, it jumps in the program being assembled to the desired string and assembles it. At the end of the string being assembled is an unconditional *assembly* jump returning us to where we left off in the source program. Thus, according to which conditions have been furnished as parameters to the assembler, one or the other object string will be produced, as shown in Fig. 8.2.6.

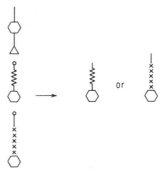

FIGURE 8.2.6. A more extensive macro definition might include closed subroutines.

It would be possible to incorporate such pseudos into the assembler, but it would avail us little, for his exact function can be performed with what we have. With conditional assembly the command we skip or assemble may be a macro. Therefore, we skip or assemble a full string of commands. This power is fully furnished by the two conditional skip commands, IFALS and IFTRU, without the need of conditional assembly jumps.

> In general, more powerful conditional assembly commands cost more than they are worth.

8.3   OUTPUT LISTING; MODIFICATION

Control of Listing

A most time-consuming task is printing source and object commands. It is important to give the programmer control over this activity. Suppose he has assembled his program and found it faulty due to his own error. He localizes the difficulty, changes a few source language statements and reassembles. There is no need to produce a *complete* copy of his output; he has interest only in those commands he has changed.

Listing Pseudos

These pseudos converse with the assembler about listing.

UNLIST

This pseudo has no referents. Its purpose is to suspend listing until otherwise notified by the LIST pseudo described next.

LIST

This pseudo reinitiates listing of commands. It has meaning only when it follows an UNLIST command. If there is no UNLIST pseudo preceding it, it is ignored.

LINE

This requests a line advance between assembly output listings. It helps the programmer find sections of the program for which he is searching.

PAGE

This pseudo advances the paper to a new page to further facilitate finding particular portions of the program.

CNTRLST

Normally control commands are not printed. We use the CNTRLST to produce a listing of itself and other control commands.

CNTRLOFF

This pseudo turns off the control listing turned on by CNTRLST.

MCXPND

When a macro command is encountered in the source program, the resulting commands in the object program are omitted from printout. To expand the macro, we use the pseudo MCXPND so that all commands produced by the macro are listed.

MCNTRCT

The purpose of this command is to turn off the foregoing feature so that no listing is made of the commands produced by the macro.

TABLE

This is the only control command which has referents. It is used to produce a table that lists relocatable numbers corresponding to the symbols which are referents in the pseudo.

Assembly Output

There are several options which the programmer can indicate about the object language output.

RELOCATABLE

To make the object language output relocatable, a tag is added to each command indicating the kind of operand contained in the command. The danger of relocation lies with the referent of a command. We must be sure that after moving, the command still refers to the same quantity that it did in source language.

ABSOLUTE

Some programs are loaded into a preassigned memory position. Economy in storage and loading time can be achieved if we produce output for these programs in absolute coding. Since tags are omitted, it is impossible to relocate such programs.

FORMAT

The format of the object program can be varied. As an example, if a pure binary output is produced, the bits can be arranged in sequence down each successive column of a punchcard, or they can be placed in sequence across each successive row. Naturally we must establish before output of the program and also before loading whether information is to be in **row binary** or **column binary**. Similar alternatives are possible for the format of output information for magnetic tape.

SPECIFICATION

Relocatable assembly is assumed unless an ABS card indicates absolute assembly:

$$\textit{blank} \quad \textbf{ABS} \quad \textit{blank} \qquad (8.3.1)$$

Symbolic Cross Reference

The assembler output need contain only command and address information in machine language form which may be relocatable. This is sufficient to run the program. It is a completely satisfactory arrangement for tried and tested programs for which no alteration is expected.

But this offers difficulty for two reasons:

- Programs do not usually work correctly after they are assembled.
- Written and running programs are not static—they are subject to change.

To change the object program, a way should exist to relate the source program to this object program. It is not too difficult to alter the source language statement to provide the new function, and then reassemble the program. However, debugging is a different story: if every time the program goes wrong, information must be extracted from it in the machine language and then translated and referenced to the original source language, we'll waste a lot of time.

SYMBOLIC DICTIONARY

One way to facilitate both modifying and debugging is to include with the object program a dictionary which cross-references operand addresses and program steps to their symbolic labels in the source program. This increases the cost and time of assembly and loading and uses up some of the memory space; the compensation is a symbolic output which so aids debugging and modifying and is well worth this extra cost.

Changes

Another instruction is introduced to tell the assembler to produce a symbolic dictionary.

blank   DICT   *blank*   (8.3.2)

Earlier we provided the assembler with a source program which it has dutifully assembled for us into object code. We discover, either in debugging or because of a modification in problem specification, that a change is to be made in the program. The question is how to initiate and cause the required alterations.

Alteration can be done to the object code by an experienced programmer by direct insertion or deletion in the object program. There are several objections to this procedure:

1. It requires an experienced programmer to interpret machine code instructions and to find the proper place for the alteration.

2. An alteration in the object code is not reflected in the source program since nothing has been done to it. Complete documentation must be kept of this kind of change to prevent it from wreaking havoc.

3. A patch often affects other commands in the sequence. If the programmer is not aware of *all* commands affected by the change, he may, in eliminating one error, produce several additional errors.

Despite these difficulties the patch is the fastest and easiest way to fix a miscreant program. It is difficult to discourage people from their habits, and many programmers find it a challenge to make this kind of correction. If they win, they save much time; if they lose, it provides a new challenge. But the disadvantages of patching far outweigh its occasional advantage: a successful patch *today* may be the roadblock of tomorrow when another change is required.

Source Language Changes

Patching seems to be an art not a science. A more methodical way to make changes is to enter them into the source program. The extra time for reassembly produces intransigent documentation. The rest of this section discusses means for entering these changes, classified according to the time when they become effective:

- before assembly
- during assembly
- after assembly

BEFORE ASSEMBLY

To fabricate a new source language program, assemble it, and run the new object program could be done in three ways:

- make a new deck
- manually make a few changes in the old desk
- make a change deck and have a service routine; together with the computer make a new deck or tape

We could alter the copy given to the cardpunch operator and produce a new set of cards. This is, comparatively, an expensive solution unless the changes are extensive.

When only a few source language statements are altered we can fix the source program card deck by deleting and inserting cards. The problem is to find the cards to be deleted or to find the place in the stack where new cards should be inserted. If each card has its content printed at the top and the cards are numbered consecutively, then it is not a difficult job to insert and delete cards manually. One may also enlist the aid of punchcard processing machines for collation and sorting.

An alternative is to make changes with service routines operating directly with the source language tapes produced after conversion by a card-to-tape routine. Each change is entered into a punchcard. The cards are converted to magnetic tape by a service routine. Another service routine, a library update routine, is used to produce a new tape by merging the original source language tape with the change tape. The resulting tape, when assembled, produces an output listing for that adequate documentation.

Change or alteration commands most frequently are not included for normal assembly but are associated only with the service routines for updating source language programs.

Another procedure takes the source deck which contains the original source program and appends to it a set of cards indicating the desired changes. After conversion this deck is presented to the assembler. The assembler notes what changes are required in the program, since these change cards are placed at the head of the deck. It examines each card of the old source deck and, if an alteration is required in it, it is made at this stage. On the second pass the corrected source program is presented to the assembler for translation.

This procedure is used by programs written in SLEUTH II for the Univac 1107B when associated with the EXEC II Supervisor.

Is it possible to alter object language code using source language statements? Only if symbolic cross reference is present. In that case we have the equivalent of both object and source language present at the same time. SHARE uses this system for making changes. This expands the loader to give it functions of the assembler besides a relocating and entry function. This permits us to take the object deck and follow it by *alter* statements in source language. The loader will assemble statements for insertion and place them in the proper positions in the object program. It will delete unnecessary statements from the object code. It will produce a new object deck if desired.

The *alter* statements supplied the loader are simple in form and indicate steps to be deleted and/or the entry for new steps.

8.4   SEGMENTATION AND OVERLAY

Program Subdivision

Some programs grow to such a tremendous size that it is impossible to fit the program into the memory of even the largest computer. In this case the whole program cannot be in memory at once. We divide the program into segments, placing in memory only those segments required for the particular portion of the program in progress.

Segmentation is dividing a program of subprograms, each of which is more or less a separate entity. **Overlay** is bringing into memory those segments of a program, those subroutines from the subroutine library and all the data applicable to them, so that a given phase of a program can proceed effectively and where several subsegments occupy the same memory area at different times.

We discuss segmentation, only touching upon the problem of overlay. The loader must deal with storage allocation, input and output during overlay.

NEED FOR SEGMENTATION

The most important reason for segmentation is that the program exceeds the amount of available memory. Segmentation is practical with less corpulent programs: to expedite writing, the program may be divided into sections so that several people can work on it. Otherwise it would be very difficult to have a group work on the program together; someone working alone might take years! These segments may now be debugged separately, a feature which simplifies the over-all program debugging.

Even when only one person is working on a program he can see the interrelation of its difficult aspects if it is broken into chunks. The best way to segment a program derives from the functional independence of the subsections. This is better than trying to divide the program into equal chunks for the participants according to some quantitative measure.

PROBLEMS

Each segment refers to symbolic addresses. Some of these addresses are unique to the segment; others conflict with those used in a different segment. Some means is necessary to distinguish between the same name appearing in two segments but with different meanings in each.

On the other side of the coin, we have one datum referred to in two segments by different names; here a single name would be preferable.

There is give and take between segments which make up a single program. If the program is regarded as a single entity, a symbol that stands for two data is over defined; a datum for which two symbols are used is ambiguous. Neither situation is tolerable. The latter has a remedy, the pseudo EQU. It permits us to equate NAME1 and NAME2 which both stand for one datum, thus:

$$\text{NAME1} \quad \text{EQU} \quad \text{NAME2} \tag{8.4.1}$$

The first problem is remedied by HEAD described next.

Symbols

To ensure that both program labels and address symbols are unique to a given segment, the segment is distinguished with HEAD formatted as:

$$\text{label} \quad \textsf{HEAD} \quad \text{letter} \tag{8.4.2}$$

This pseudo prefixes all referents and labels that follow by *letter*. In Fig. 8.4.1, A − 1 causes the segment to be headed by P. The pseudo at A reserves a block of two cells which are nominally labeled A. Since they appear in the segment P, the actual label is PA.

```
          HEAD    P
  A       RSRV    2
          XMA     A
          ADD     A + 1
          XAM     Q$A + 1
          HEAD    Q
  A       RSRV    1
          HEAD    0
```

FIGURE 8.4.1. Use of HEAD to define segments—external reference from one segment (P) to another (Q).

A + 1 in the figure refers to an item whose label seems to be A. Since the referent A lies in a segment headed by P, the actual command, XMA, refers to PA.

To summarize, the heading pseudo normally qualifies references within the segment which follows by prefixing references with the heading quantity, *letter*; this includes both labels and addresses.

INTERSEGMENTAL REFERENCES

Since all references within the segment are automatically prefixed by the heading quantity, how can we *ever* reference a quantity outside the segment? FLAP, FAP, IBMAP and several other assemblers use $, and UTMOST uses ∗ to reference another segment. One indicates the heading symbol for the foreign segment, followed by $, followed in turn by the symbol name within that segment. Although we refer to the cell A within the segment Q in which it was defined simply as A, we cannot do so in the segment headed by P. For the segment headed by P we refer to the label A in the segment headed Q by Q$A. The assembler looks this up in the symbol table under the definition for QA and then replaces it with the allocation for QA. If this device were not available, a reference to QA would turn out as a reference to PQA, and we could never make an external reference.

In Fig. 8.4.1, the fourth step of the segment headed P uses the symbol A + 1. This step actually refers to PA + 1 (not, of course PA + P1).

The fifth step in the program refers outside of this segment to the address A + 1 but this time headed by the character Q. This reference is therefore Q$A + 1 for the P segment.

SEGMENT TERMINATION

When the programmer is finished writing the segment, either permanently or for the nonce, the device he uses depends upon the assembler. One way is the UNHEAD pseudo. All steps belonging to a segment are bracketed by the commands HEAD and UNHEAD, each containing the heading *letter*. Two pseudos are necessary only when multiple heading is permissible, that is, when a headed segment may, in turn, contain a headed segment. The need for multiple heading is dubious and, hence, this topic is not discussed here.

If segments can be headed only by a single letter, the introduction of a new heading letter will terminate the production of the old segment. Thus in Fig. 8.4.1, HEAD Q terminates the production of the P segment and starts or reinstates the production of the Q segment. This is the expedient used in FLAP.

MAIN SEGMENT

We usually start writing a program without any heading and produce an unheaded segment. How do we refer to or return to such a segment? One solution to this is for the assembler to use a fixed number of characters in making up tables and dictionaries using a given symbol. The symbol is filled in with 0's to make up the proper number of characters for the label.

For instance, suppose we limit the format of all symbols to six characters. A reference in the main program or unheaded segment to the location DATA must be filled in with 0's (alphabetic zeros), so that it becomes 00DATA when the assembler makes up a symbol table.

In a segment headed by P, for instance, a reference to DATA would be used by the assemblers as though P0DATA had appeared. The fixed six-letter symbol imposes a limit of five letters to symbols within a headed segment.

To compensate for the limitation, we have the advantage that reference to the unheaded segment from within a headed segment is simplified. To refer to X in the main program from any other segment, we simply refer to 0$X, which the assembler interprets as 00000X.

Figure 8.4.2 shows a segment headed by R. The address referred to by the assembler is shown in the extreme right-hand column. Notice that referents which do not contain $ are prefixed by R before reference.

Reference to main program data requires in the source language a prefix of 0$ within the segment headed R. The step referencing T$DATA is formed into the six-character word, T0DATA, before use.

Notice that six letter characters cannot be headed nor deheaded (decapitated?). The following symbols are identical to this assembler, regardless where they appear: RSDATA; X$RSDATA; 0$RSDATA; R$SDATA. In the segment headed R they may be called SDATA.

			Actual Referent
T0P	HEAD	R	
	XMA	DATA 1	RDATA1
	MUL	DATA 2	RDATA2
	ADD	0$DATA 1	0DATA1
	XAM	T$DATA	T0DATA

FIGURE 8.4.2. Use of a fixed format (here six characters) to enable unheaded external reference using 0$.

Now FLAP does not limit the number of characters in a symbol. Hence RSDATA may be headed; X$RSDATA is recognized as XRSDATA and 0$RSDATA as RSDATA regardless of the heading of the segment containing it. SDATA in segment R is recognized as RSDATA.

COMMON

When a segment is present in memory, the data reserved by it is also present; when a segment is absent, the correspondingly headed data is also absent from memory. This is a deterrent to intercommunication. If the segment G wishes to transmit information to the segment R, it can do so by placing information in a spot prefixed by R$. However, suppose it wishes to make information available to all segments. This cannot be done by the prefix 0$, since that will transmit information only to the main program, the unheaded segment. If the unheaded segment is absent from memory, this information will not be available to any other segment.

A section of memory called COMMON is established which can store data regardless of any overlay in use. It is preserved as long as the program or any part thereof is in operation. Information may be entered into the COMMON section by the command:

$$\text{label} \quad \textbf{COMMON} \quad \text{number} \qquad (8.4.3)$$

This distinguishes a block, referred to by *label*, and of length, *number*, in the *common* section of storage. Entries in the *common* area are usually unprefixed. The main program, too, references this area as though it were using any other piece of normal information. A headed segment uses this area by prefixing the address with 0$. So long as the referent was declared to be COMMON by a previous pseudo command, it occupies memory even when the main program segment is removed. (Some assemblers require that *the main segment be always present*.)

Use of COMMON

A picture of memory after loading a given program might appear as in Fig. 8.4.3. There are four segments in memory at this time: the main program; two segments headed A and R; and COMMON. Part of the memory is also reserved for software.

With this particular memory configuration, those segments which are presently in memory can intercommunicate with each other. Thus the

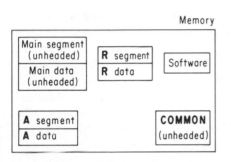

Memory

FIGURE 8.4.3. Initial overlay—memory contents—indicating intercommunication.

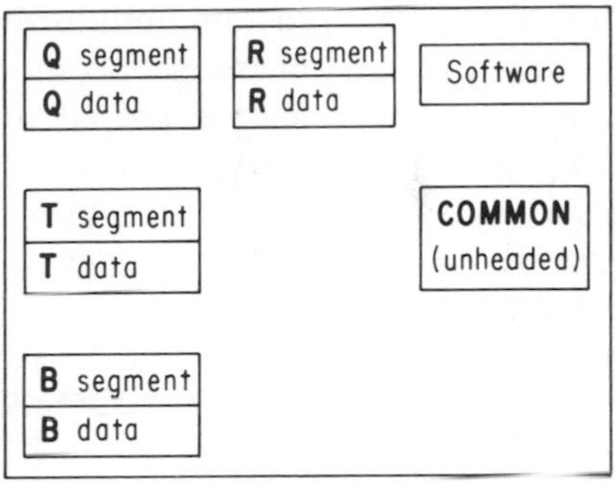

FIGURE 8.4.4. A subsequent overlay—memory contents—indicating intercommunications.

program segment A can refer to the main program, to segment R, but not to segment T, since it is somewhere on the input tape but not in memory. All segments also can communicate with COMMON. Information to be used by T can be entered into COMMON.

Later, an overlay is performed, and the resulting state of affairs is shown in Fig. 8.4.4. The main program and segment A no longer exist in memory. Instead, segments Q, T and B have been brought in. Segment R remains from the last figure. Of course, COMMON is also maintained. Now information for the segment T, provided by segment A, can be withdrawn from COMMON, since it has not been disturbed by the overlay.

To repeat, some assemblers require that the main segment of the program be retained in memory during all overlays.

DEFINITION OF COMMON

References prefixed by 0$ or those which are in the main program do not necessarily appear in COMMON. The pseudo COMMON is used to establish items in COMMON, the main program segment. It is encumbent upon the programmer to collect all references for COMMON between segments which are not referred to by the main segment so that these can be established during assembly of the main segment. More sophisticated methods which relieve a programmer of this responsibility are available but are not discussed here.

The Task of the Loader

Initially the loader brings in a segmented program just as it would any other. Of course, it must be informed of what other segments besides the main program must be brought in for this first phase. It then turns control over to the main program until further notice.

When the first phase of operation is completed, the loader must receive notification. Entering the second overlay is then delegated to the loader. It knows which segment has *expired*—that which is subject to replacement. It also knows those segments which are *required* for the next phase of operation. It supervises the procurement of these segments and assigns space in memory for them. The assembler or other system usually checks the allocation of overlay programs for consistency and memory size. The new segments, remaining segments, COMMON area and software should fit into the memory.

As the loader brings in new program segments it relocates them. The loader provides the proper sites and must make sure that any reference within the segment has had its referent resituated if necessary. The loader must provide complete cross referencing. When a segment communicates with another segment, the label it uses does not depend upon where the loader has placed the new segment. Therefore, all such cross references must be provided by the loader. Where all COMMON references are not provided in the main program segment, the loader has an expanded job. It must cross reference all COMMON references and be sure that space is allocated to the expanding COMMON area.

8.5   DATA DEFINITION

Intent

This section introduces assembly language refinements included or omitted from particular assemblers. Although these points could have been brought up more appropriately in connection with particular aspects of the language discussed previously, they were omitted for the sake of clarity of explanation.

Step Number

With each command included for assembly we have three fields: the step may be labeled with a symbol, following the format of other labels; the command can be any one of many mnemonics, pseudos, macros and so forth; the last field may consist of many subfields indicating the referent for the command. One command refers to another through labels, relative addressing or label arithmetic. Thus, if this command contains no label but the command preceding it three steps back is called START, then we refer to this one as START + 3.

There are several reasons why we might wish to number the steps of a program. First, it is a quite natural procedure and one that was once the standard. Second, the program is often supplied in the form of punchcards. If the deck should drop on the floor, it would be almost impossible to reorder the cards without having them specifically numbered. Finally, it is easy to describe changes to the program editor in terms of the step numbers. Of course, then the editor must renumber the cards if the changes would otherwise cause duplication of numbering.

ETC

The referents to a given command may be several subfields. In fact, so many subfields may be required that there is not enough room on the card for them all. We continue the list on another card containing the pseudo ETC in FAP and FLAP. For some assemblers this command field is empty for the extender function.

When do we require such a large number of subfields?

MACRO DEFINITIONS

The argument list for a macro definition must have room for all the parameters. Theoretically there is no limit to the number of parameters.

PROGRAMMER MACRO CALL

Naturally, if we define a macro having ten parameters, we have to leave room in the call for this macro for ten parameters.

EXTERNALLY DEFINED MACRO CALL

A library routine can also specify a large number of parameters whose values are furnished in GET and extended with ETC.

DATA DEFINITIONS

Data definitions may be chained so that a single DEF command can specify the contents of a number of cells by indicating these in the subfields of the command.

An example of the use of the ETC command with a programmer defined macro call is shown in Fig. 8.5.1. There is not enough room for the parameters of the macro call, SUMSQ; ETC supplies the remainder of the parameters for the call.

```
PART1    SUMSQ  FIRST,  THIRD,  THIRD + 1,  FOURTH,  FOURTH + 2
         ETC  FOURTH + 4,  NINTH,  NINTH + 3
```

FIGURE 8.5.1. The use of ETC as an extension of a macro call.

Data Definition

DEF is used to define data, providing a label for a cell or a set of cells and dictating the contents of the cell(s). There is only one thing a cell can hold—bits. But the human can define the bit configuration in different ways.

Let us examine just a few of the ways the human can convey this bit configuration within the framework of the assembly language. Since we are not really designing an assembler here but are simply investigating the principles of design, this topic receives a casual treatment.

BINARY DATA

For machines that use straight binary data, it is sometimes convenient for the programmer to define information directly in this form. He is interested in conveying the state of all the bits in the word, but it is easier to do so by grouping the bits in sets of three. An octal data definition command might take the following format:

$$\text{label} \quad \text{DEFOCT} \quad \text{number, number, . . . , number} \qquad (8.5.1)$$

Each *number* in this command format consists of up to twelve octal digits. A DEFOCT pseudo and the data it produces is shown in Fig. 8.5.2.

```
DATA     DEFOCT    23, 472, . . . , 77
DATA     0000. . . . . . .  0010011
         0000. . . . .00010111010
         0000. . . . . . .     000
         0000. . . . . .  00111111
```

FIGURE 8.5.2. Using DEFOCT to define four binary data words.

DECIMAL DATA

Decimal data definition is a requisite of most assemblers. The translation depends upon the machine used. Object code for the RCA 301 or the IBM 1401 produces binary-coded decimal or six-bit alphanumeric for each decimal character.

Decimal information is converted into straight binary for a machine such as the Univac 1107 or Philco 2000. Conversion to binary may be done in the assembler, increasing its load; it may be left for the loader or for a library subroutine called by the assembler.

Figure 8.5.3 shows the four bit NBCD output of the assembler when supplied with the decimal data definition command, DEFDEC.

```
NUDATA    DEFDEC    23, 472, . . . , 77
NUDATA    00. . . . . 027     0. . . . .0000  0010  0111
          00. . . . .0730     0. . . . .0111  0011  0000
          00. . . . .0000     0. . . . . . .             0
          00. . . . .0115     0. . . . .0001  0001  0101
```

FIGURE 8.5.3. Using DEFDEC to define four data words.

OTHERS

An assembler may use many other kinds of data definition, including:

1. Fixed-field alphabetic.
2. Variable-field alphabetic.
3. Variable-field alphanumeric.
4. Fractional floating-point.
5. Integral floating-point.
6. Mixed floating-point.
7. Multiple precision of various kinds.

Separate data-definition commands are required according to the way the data is presented.

8.6 MISCELLANEOUS CONSIDERATIONS

Macros

What does the assembler do when arguments are omitted in the call? Although such an omission is usually undesirable, we cannot prevent the programmer from doing it; we allow the assembler to continue, prescribing its conduct.

For one solution, the assembler creates symbols for those which are missing. It must use a symbol set which will not conflict with other uses. Prefixing created symbols with one or more special characters satisfies this requirement. *F L A P* prefixes created symbols with an apostrophe. It is forbidden for the programmer to create symbols that begin with anything other than a letter; hence, it will not conflict with him. When we detect '137, it can only be created by the assembler to provide an argument symbol neglected by the programmer.

FLAP creates new symbols beginning with '001.

EXAMPLE OF CREATED SYMBOLS

Suppose the programmer has defined a subroutine, DIFSQ, the prototype of which appears in Fig. 8.6.1. Further, suppose that somewhere in the

DIFSQ	MCDEF	A, B, C, D, E
	XMA	A
	SUB	B
	XAM	D
	XAD	—
	MUL	D
	XAM	A
	XMA	B
	SUB	C
	XAM	D
	XAD	—
	MUL	D
	ADD	A
	XAM	E
DIFSQ	MCEND	

FIGURE 8.6.1. A macro definition of the sum of the square of two differences.

program he calls upon this routine but omits, purposely or otherwise, the fourth parameter. The call appears as ASK3 in Fig. 8.6.2. The assembler notices that the fourth parameter is missing from the call and creates a symbol to substitute for it. Since this is the first time it has created a symbol in this assembly, it chooses for that symbol '001. The assembled output is the equivalent of the bottom half of Fig. 8.6.2.

ASK3	DIFSQ	X1, X2, X3, , X5
ASK3	XMA	X1
	SUB	X2
	XMA	'001
	XAD	—
	MUL	'001
	etc.	

FIGURE 8.6.2. The assembler creates symbols, namely '001 for argument *D* omitted in the macro call for DIFSQ of Figure 8.6.1.

NEW ORIGIN FOR CREATED SYMBOLS

The programmer may wish to distinguish and localize the macros for which arguments have been omitted. He may do so by adding a prefix of his choosing for the assembler to insert as it creates symbols. This is done by the FLAP pseudo, formatted:

blank   MCSYMB   character   (8.6.1)

All created symbols will be prefixed now by '*character* until another MCSYMB comes along. As an example, the upper two commands of Fig. 8.6.3 are translated as below in that figure.

		MCSYMB	M				
ASK4	DIFSQ	X1,	X2,	X3,		,	X5

ASK4	DIFSQ	X1
	SUB	X2
	XMA	'M001
	XAD	—
	MUL	'M001
		etc.

FIGURE 8.6.3. The programmer can cause the prefixing of created symbols. Here MCSYMBcauses the creation of the symbol 'M001 instead of '001 as in Fig. 8.6.2.

To suspend the creation of symbols, we give the command;

blank   MCSYMB   blank   (8.6.2)

The assembler will not create any missing symbols. It will indicate on the output listing that symbols are missing in certain places. The object program produced cannot be run until these blanks are filled in.

To reset the creation of symbols so that they are not prefixed by the programmer-designated character, one gives the command:

blank   MCSYMB   '   (8.6.3)

The assembler returns to its last count: if it previously created '137, it next creates '138.

Subroutines

Library subroutines are called in by the GET quasi. This causes the name of the subroutine to be incorporated in the subroutine jump table which the assembler produces. The subroutine name need not appear in the symbol table. Other symbols may be used which refer to externally defined information. For instance, other segments of the same program or segments of a different program may have names by which the program calls them. Symbolic addresses not appearing in the symbol table are repulsive to the assembler. To console it, the pseudo EXT explains that an externally defined symbol is being employed.

$$\text{blank}\quad\textbf{EXT}\quad\text{symbol list}\qquad\qquad(8.6.4)$$

Besides inhibiting an *undefined symbol* error, this causes an entry for this symbol to appear in the subroutine jump table if one is not already there. The loader replaces the symbol name by an address. The datum can then be reached by indirection.

Suppose, for instance, we wish to request a jump to another program segment, SEGQ at this point. We might use:

$$\begin{array}{ll}\textbf{EXT} & \textbf{SEGQ}\\ \textbf{UCJ} & \textbf{SEGQ}\end{array}\qquad\qquad(8.6.5)$$

FLAP puts SEGQ in the SR jump table and makes the UCJ address it indirectly; thus:

```
005    SEGQ
. . . . . . .
487    UCJ,1    005
```
$$\qquad\qquad(8.6.6)$$

Later the loader places SEGQ in memory beginning at 1256. It replaces the SR jump reference to SEGQ by this address:

```
005    NOOP    1256
. . . . . . .
487    UCJ,1    005
```
$$\qquad\qquad(8.6.7)$$

Hence during execution, when step 487 is reached, an UCJ takes the program through step 5 to step 1256, the start of SEGQ.

Subroutine Definitions

In defining subroutines or program segments to which the assembler will refer occasionally, the same subroutine or segment may find multiple uses. For instance, the subroutine to find the sine of an angle may also find the cosine of an angle if a simple adjustment in angle size precedes the routine. This can be effected if the same routine is supplied with two different entry points. To distinguish the entry points to the same subroutine:

- Label each entry point when it appears in the SR.
- Use the pseudo ENTRY to define these labels as entry points.

The pseudo for establishing entry points has the format:

blank   ENTRY   label   (8.6.8)

where *label* is the entry point.

The use of this pseudo for the sine/cosine subroutine is shown in Fig. 8.6.4.

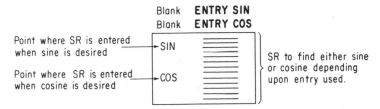

FIGURE 8.6.4. How the pseudo ENTRY is used to distinguish multiple entry points to a program.

Startup Information

Besides knowing the kind of assembly, absolute or relative, the assembler likes to know the number of source commands forthcoming. It would also like to know about overlay and segmentation, but this depth is not attempted here. From the command count, the assembler can distinguish the half-way point and start rewind of the intermediate tape.

The FLAP count pseudo, indicating the number of source language steps to the assembler, is formatted:

blank   COUNT   number   (8.6.9)

where *number* is the number of FLAP source steps presented for assembly, regardless of whether these are mnemonics, pseudos, macros, quasis or otherwise.

8.7 SUMMARY

Nature of the Assembler

The assembler translates a machine oriented source language input into object code for a given computer. The order of steps in the source language corresponds essentially with the order of translated steps in the object language. For the simplest assembler (AAL) using only mnemonics, a one-to-one correspondence exists between source and object commands.

Data definitions do not produce object commands. A *single* macro produces a *set* of object commands.

Language

The completeness of the assembly language determines the extensiveness of the assembler. FLAP contains these features:

1. Mnemonics. The mnemonics used by the assembler correspond exactly with the commands in the repertoire of the object computer. FLAP mnemonics are listed alphabetically in Table A and functionally in Table B in the inside front cover of the book. FLAP directives are found in Tables C and D in the inside rear cover.

2. Data pseudos. Pseudo operations define data to be used by the assembler and the object program. *External data* is supplied to the object program at run time. *Internal data* is entered by the assembler into the object program and resides there at run time. It consists of two subtypes, defined data and literals.

3. Programmer defined macros. These subroutines are provided by the programmer within the source language program. The macro definition is incorporated into tables and is used later at the macro call to prepare a duplicate tailored to the parameters in the call.

4. Nested macros. Macro definitions can include previously defined macros. This is a powerful way to abbreviate programs.

5. Assembler defined macros. Three examples from FLAP are GET, SAVE and ERROR, which are expanded by an assembler-incorporated variable generator.

6. Duplication. Here is a simple tool for duplicating strings of commands within the source language proper or within macros.

7. Assembler processing. We have seen how the assembler can use the computer to do calculations *while it assembles*. These calculations can be incorporated into the program with the SET command; it can be used to enter or delete commands conditionally from the object program according to the results of processing within the assembler.

8. Listing. List commands affect the details of the listing which the programmer receives. By abbreviating the listing, we reduce assembly time.

9. Segmentation. The program can be broken down into smaller, manageable pieces and later run as a whole. When the program is very large, it can be run by performing one or more overlays.

The Assembler System

The assembler *system* might appear as in Fig. 8.7.1. In some cases the source language program (1) can be entered directly into the computer where the assembler resides (2). Most large systems today provide a monitor (3) which allows assembly jobs to be intermixed with object programs and compiling jobs. When an assembly job appears, the monitor is responsible for getting the assembler into memory and submitting the source program to the assembler.

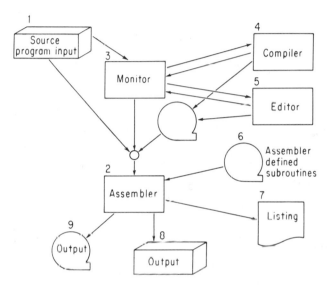

FIGURE 8.7.1. General block showing system interaction of the assembler.

A job that is compiled first is detected by the monitor which oversees the compilation (4). The full compilation may require that an assembly is performed thereafter. In that case the compiled program is turned over to the monitor which brings in the assembler and initiates assembly.

A job with corrections must have the source language edited by the editor (5). Upon completion, the edited source program is passed over to the monitor which delegates the assembly process. The main input to the assembler (2) is the source program furnished by the monitor (3). In some cases assembler defined subroutines are furnished to the assembler from a separate library (6). The assembler produces an output listing (7), an output card deck (8) and an output tape (9). Any of these items are optional. The object program may be returned to the monitor if a machine language run after assembly has been requested.

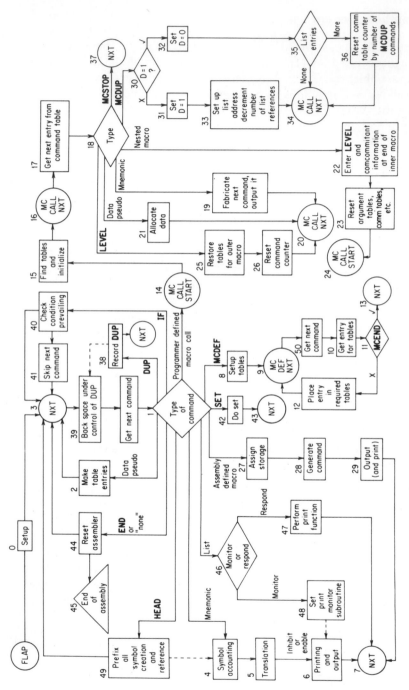

Figure 8.7.2. A crude outline of operations required in a fairly complete assembler. Requirements for both passes are combined.

Overview of Assembler Operation

We have looked at how different portions of the assembler operate. Let us now try to integrate our position and see how the assembler works as a whole. A most inclusive assembler is presented in Fig. 8.7.2. Operations in the figure are shown without regard to where they occur passwise. In fact, assemblers may allocate the pass activity differently. Further, for the single-pass assembler all these jobs must be done in one pass.

Most important is (1) in Fig. 8.7.2 where the command is classified. Depending upon its category, one of the many phases of the assembler is brought in.

DATA PSEUDOS

Data pseudo (1) entries are made in the appropriate tables (2).

MNEMONICS

A mnemonic (1) requires symbol accounting, translating and outputting (4), (5), (6). For the first pass of $\mathscr{FLAP}$, these are shown in Figs. 5.4.2, 5.5.1 and 5.5.2; the second pass is diagrammed in Figs. 5.6.2 and 5.6.3.

MACRO DEFINITIONS

When MCDEF is encountered (1), operations (8) through (12) are performed. Tables are fabricated as outlined in Figs. 6.5.2 and 6.5.3. New prototype commands for the macro definition are procured within the loop (9), (10), (11), (12), until MCEND is detected. This calls for the definition windup and the next source command is typed (1).

PROGRAMMER DEFINED MACRO CALLS

When a macro call is detected (1) we initialize the macro generation sequence (14), (15), (16). Commands are then brought from the applicable macro command table (17) and classified by the associated tag (18). A mnemonic (19) is fabricated immediately and a new entry is obtained from the command table and classified (20), (16), (17), (18).

For a data pseudo, space is allocated (21).

The macro command table is processed until MCSTOP (18). This takes us out of the macro call sequence and brings in the next command to be assembled (37). The diagrams for these functions are found in Figs. 6.4.3 and 6.4.4.

NESTED MACROS—INWARD GOING

When a macro call is encountered in the macro command table (18), nesting initialization is done (22). Level information is entered and new tables are referenced (23), (24), (14), (15). As processing of the inner macro begins, the next entries in the new inner macro command table are examined and typed (16), (17), (18) as illustrated in Fig. 6.6.3.

NESTED MACROS—OUTWARD GOING

When LEVEL is encountered in the macro command table (18) the inner macro is completed and we proceed to the next outer macro in our nest. Tables are restored and examination of the outer macro command table is reinstated (25), (26). The next command is procured in the normal macro generation sequence (20), (16), (17), (18). This was examined in Fig. 6.6.4.

MCDUP

When MCDUP is first encountered (18) we set up the list which is to be used in the commands we are duplicating (30, 31). Commands within the range of the two MCDUP's are processed normally through the chains (18), (19), (20), (16), (17) or (18), (21), (20), (16), (17). When the second MCDUP appears (18) it causes the next entry in the list to be used (30), (32), (35), (36), (34), that is, unless the list has been exhausted. In that case we continue to the next command in the macro command table through the sequence (30), (32), (35), (34), (16), (17), (18).

MNEMONIC DUPLICATIONS

DUP (1), calling for the duplication of a number of steps in the source language program, is recorded (38). An internal monitor subroutine is set up to backspace the input for a command review when *times* steps have been entered into the object language program (39).

ASSEMBLY DEFINED MACROS

When assembly defined macros are encountered we assign storage, generate a set of commands, and output this set (27), (28), (29). The generation for GET was shown in Fig. 7.2.4; that for SAVE, was shown in Fig. 7.3.4. Some assemblers provide many more assembly defined macros for which the generator may be brought in from a library tape during assembly.

SET

The SET command requires that the assembler enter a value into the symbol table (42), (43).

CONDITIONAL ASSEMBLY

When conditional assembly is encountered (1) the assembler checks the prevailing conditions (40) and then either scraps the next command (41) or presents it for assembly (3).

LISTING

When a list pseudo is encountered (1) we determine if this is a command to which the print mechanism responds directly (45), such as a page or line advance, in which case this is performed (47) and the next command examined (7), (3), (1). It may be a monitor function (46) which requires the suppression of output for all or some commands. In that case the monitor is put into effect to inhibit or enable printing (48).

HEAD

When HEAD is detected (1) the head monitor is invoked to prefix all symbols with the heading character (49). Of course, those which are exempted by $ are not so headed.

END

The end of the assembly program is indicated in FLAP by END or by the absence of any further entry cards. In any case the assembler is reset (44), and we determine if another assembly is required (3) or not (45).

An Assembly Listing

For the uninitiated, a sample assembly listing provides a fascinating example of the power of a proven assembler. Bell Telephone Laboratories uses a variant of FAP, which they call BELFAP, for the IBM 7090. The BELFAP† manual contains a splendid printout of the assembler's activity. It is adapted to FLAP and appears as Fig. 8.7.3.

† *BELFAP Manual*. Murray Hill, N.J.: Bell Telephone Labs, 1963. The major portion of this material was prepared by Miss F. L. Bagely.

```
PAGE 1                        ASSEMBLY LISTING EXAMPLE            137653948  05/18/64
SUBROUTINE ENTRY POINTS
       00001   SAMPLE

SUBROUTINE JUMP TABLE
00000  62642512160   SUBRA

              1              NOTE THE SEQUENCE NUMBER TO THE LEFT OF EACH
              2              INSTRUCTION EXCEPT THOSE GENERATED BY THE MACRO
              3              "ADS"
              4
              5              COMMENTS IN THE PROGRAM ARE INSERTED BY USING
              6              "COMMENT" PSEUDO. NOTE THAT "COMMENT" IS DELETED
              7              FROM THE LINE, ADDING SOME ELEGANCE TO THE
              8              COMMENTARY
              9
             10              NOTE THAT THE NEXT TWO CONTROL CARDS, DIRECTIONS
             11              TO THE ASSEMBLER, DO NOT PRODUCE OCTAL INSTRUCTION
             12              WORDS
             13
             14    CNTRLST   PRINT CONTROL CARDS
             15    MCXPND    PRINT GENERATED MACROS
             16
             17              DEFINE A MACRO. NOTE THAT THERE IS NO ASSEMBLY
             18
             19 ADS  MCDEF  ADDR   START OF MACRO DEF TO "ADD TO STORAGE"
             20      ADD    ADDR
             21      XAM    ADDR
             22      MCEND         END OF DEFINITION
             23
             24 SAMPLE  RSRV  0    ENTRY POINT FOR PROGRAM

00001
```

FIGURE 8.7.3. BELFAP assembly printout.

ASSEMBLY LISTING EXAMPLE 13763948 05/18/64

PAGE 2

```
00001  0500 00 0 00016  25        XMA   =1                      NOTE LITERAL DEFINITION AT END OF
00002  0601 00 0 00013  26        XAM   CT                      ASSEMBLY
                        27
                        28                                      NOTE THE SUBROUTINE JUMP TABLE AND CALLING SEQUENCE
00003  0074 00 4 00000  29        GET   SUBRA, ARG1, ARG2 PRODUCED BY THIS "GET" STATEMENT
00004  0000 00 0 00014
00005  0000 00 0 00015
                        30
                        31                                      USE THE MACRO DEFINED EARLIER
00006  0500 00 0 00012  32        XMA   TWO
                        33        ADS   CT                      GENERATES THE NEXT TWO INSTRUCTIONS
00007  0400 00 0 00013            ADD   CT
00010  0601 00 0 00013            XAM   CT
                        34
U  00011  0020 00 0     35        UCJ   UNDEF                   NOTE ERROR FLAG BECAUSE ADDRESS IS
                        36                                      UNDEFINED ANYWHERE IN PROGRAM. A "U" FLAG ALSO CAUSES
                        37                                      THE FATAL COMMENT AT END OF ASSEMBLY. SEE ERROR FLAGS.
                        38
                        39                                      DATA DEFINITION
00012  +00000000002     40  TWO   DEF   2                       DEFINES WORD WHICH IS 2
00013                   41  CT    RSRV  1                       RESERVES ONE WORD FOR SYMBOL. CT
00014  +00000000004     42  ARG1  DEF   4
00015  +00000000006     43  ARG2  DEF   6
00016          00001    44        END                          END THE ASSEMBLY. FIRST PROGRAM STEP 1

LITERALS
00016  +00000000001
00017 IS THE FIRST LOCATION NOT USED BY THIS PROGRAM
ERROR IN ABOVE ASSEMBLY
```

FIGURE 8.7.3. (continued)

The printout is self-explanatory for the most part. However, note that all source cards including commands are numbered in decimal. Information in the left-most column is the relative cell number (starting with 0) of the object program datum. The actual datum in *octal* follows.

The IBM 7090 machine word contains 36 bits which are broken down into 12 octal digits for command printout. What are the four fields used for?

SYMBOLIC REFERENCE TABLE

The table in Fig. 8.7.4 is produced by the assembler at the end of its job.

```
SYMBOLIC REFERENCE TABLE     137653948  05/18/64
      DEFINITION SYMBOL REFERENCES
          13    CT        2,  7,  10,  13
          12    TWO       6,  12
          14    ARG1      4,  14
          15    ARG2      5,  15
           0    SUBRA     3
           1    SAMPLE    1
      REFERENCES TO UNDEFINED SYMBOLS
              UNDEF      11
          FATAL ERROR TABLE
       FLAGS    LOC     PAGE
         U      00011     1
```

FIGURE 8.7.4. Symbolic reference table produced by BELFAP assembler for the problem of Fig. 7.9.3.

PROBLEMS

8.1   Use DUP to store the constants 0 through 3 inclusive at ZERO through ZERO + 3.

8.2   Use DUP to store 1955 through 1965 at THEN through THEN + 10; at NOW − 10 through NOW.

8.3   Write a subprogram with DUP to find the sum of the cubes of the numbers at NUM through NUM + 5 and place it at SIGMA.

8.4   Write a macro SMCUB1 using MCDUP to find the sum of the cubes of six numbers which are itemized in both the call and in MCDUP (exactly six).

8.5   Write a macro SMCUB2 with MCDUP to find the sum of the cubes of a list of numbers. The list is furnished, parenthesized, in the call and called CLIST in MCDUP.

8.6   Flow chart a MCDUP generator that can handle only fixed size lists specified in the prototype.

8.7   Describe a change to make the generator of problem 8.6 usable for variable length lists.

8.8   Using list in macros requires some method to keep track *and* communicate between the GET generator and the MCDUP mechanism. When the GET generator encounters a list, announced by a left parenthesis, it places each list in one cell of the call sequence. Then, when the right parenthesis is met, one more cell of the call sequence is filled with a sentinel (call it SENT for the moment) to inform MCDUP generator that there are no more list elements. Augment the GET flow chart of Fig. 7.2.4 to accommodate MCDUP lists.

8.9   Redo problem 7.4 with the feature of problem 8.8 added.

8.10 Redo problem 7.5 with the feature of problem 8.8 added.

8.11 Flow chart a MCDUP generator using the feature of problem 8.8.

8.12 We wish an SR to find:

$$Y = \sqrt[3]{\sum_{i'=1}^{N} X^3{}_{i'}}$$

We define a macro RMC (root-mean-cube) which includes MCDUP and permits a list of variable length of the X's in the GET for RMC. Use SET within MCDUP to find the list length. Write the macro with an error exit should the sum become excessive (use JOO—jump on overflow).

8.13 Describe the assembly of the RMC of problem 8.12.

8.14 Write a call for RMC applied to a list of seven items starting at location VAR. Describe the action of the generator and the coding produced.

8.15 Consider the general polynomial:

$$W = A_n V^n + A_{n-1} V^{n-1} + \cdots + A_1 V + A_0$$

Rewrite in a nested factor form similar to:

$$(V + B(V + C(V + \cdots$$

Next, write a macro which performs a multiply by the variable V and an addition of the next term, TERM, to the sum so far, SOFAR, returning it to SOFAR; call it CONTINU. Finally, write a subprogram to evaluate a polynomial of power, POWER, where POWER is furnished at assembly time and the subprogram uses conditional assembly statements and the macro, CONTINU.

8.16 Make a complete FLAP program for assembly from COUNT to END for problem 7.12, allowing any macros to be printed.

8.17 How is HEAD incorporated into the assembler? Flow chart the activity for (a) HEAD and UNHEAD (b) when only HEAD is used.

8.18   In a segment headed A how do we address: data headed A called DATA,
       TIME, X; data headed B called DATA, BOY, TIME, ALBERT, X; unheaded
       data called BERRY, ALFRED, X, X3, TIME?

8.19   Repeat problem 8.18 for a segment headed B, for an unheaded (macro)
       segment.

8.20   Explain the need for several kinds of data definition as DEFOCT, DEFDEC,
       etc.

8.21   Write a FLAP sequence (using DUP?) to make the following data definitions:
       (a) Fifty consecutive decimal numbers starting with 158.
       (b) A decreasing sequence of five even decimal numbers starting with 36.
       (c) A decreasing sequence of twenty-five octal numbers starting with 133
           (octal).

8.22   When does one use these commands: MCSYMB, EXT, ENTRY, COUNT?

9

INPUT-OUTPUT CONTROL SYSTEM, IOCS

9.1   ORIENTATION

IOCS with simple commands and subcommands provides elaborate sequences of machine commands to control the activities and buffering of IO devices. This detailed discussion precedes an investigation of subsequent software systems because they rely so heavily on IO communication. If we understand IOCS and its operating principles, then the discussion of the loader, monitor and service routines can assume this comprehension and carry on from there. When *IOCS* is not present these other systems must still perform their functions. They do so by using machine command sequences assembled from many statements supplied by the programmer and which may run more efficiently. Thus *IOCS* provides great writing efficiency for IO segments at the probable cost of running efficiency and a considerable portion of memory.

As we pick up the study of *IOCS*, we should have a firm background in IO devices and the interrelation between IO devices and the computer memory, called buffering. The specific functions of interest to us are:

- device management
- blocking and deblocking
- buffer management
- routine errors and exceptions
- file protection
- rollback

QUESTIONS ABOUT *IOCS*

The concept of *IOCS* may still be somewhat vague. In this section we answer two questions concerning this software. First, where is the *IOCS*? Although it is hard to point to a physical entity which we refer to as the *IOCS*, at least we can say that at such and such a time it is on *this* tape or it is *there* in memory, etc.

Second, how do we talk to *IOCS*? We have to communicate information of several kinds and the reader must wonder whether this is done in the program or through an input device or just how.

Finally, we would like to know how *IOCS* does its job. This will take more than one section, and the rest of the chapter is devoted to answering this question.

Run Time

The question we asked earlier about where *IOCS* is must have a time connected with it because the *IOCS* may be at different places at different times. Let us look at the condition of memory at run time for a system that uses *IOCS*.

Figure 9.1.1 shows a possible commitment of memory cells at run time for a system using *IOCS*. Notice the large area allocated to *IOCS*. This is deliberate. The IBM 7090/94 IOCS occupies between five thousand and six thousand words of storage out of usually 16 K, and occasionally 32 K! Other systems may keep this as low as 1 K or 2 K with some loss in sophistication.

What else is in memory? The *FOREMAN* takes charge of certain errors and exceptions. Sometimes he is included in *IOCS*, other times in the monitor. Our *FOREMAN* is separate and takes charge of other things too, such as detected arithmetic errors, parity defects and so forth.

The supervisor, $\mathscr{SYSTEM}$, is most active between jobs. When a job is completed, control returns to $\mathscr{SYSTEM}$ which then will load in a new job. During the program it takes care of other eventualities and has the power to abort a run.

The loader, $\mathscr{LOAD}$, is shown in memory although very little, if any, may be retained there; it frequently exterminates itself as it does the final load. The loader may be eliminated when it has performed its function and the object program is in control in memory.

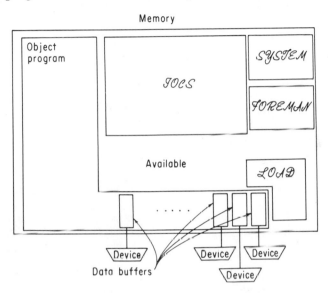

FIGURE 9.1.1. The relation of $\mathscr{IOCS}$ to other software and the object program at run time.

The *object program* is the *raison d'eître* of the whole programming system. Although most of $\mathscr{IOCS}$ is required during an object program run, a portion of each of $\mathscr{FOREMAN}$ and $\mathscr{SYSTEM}$ may suffice to be in memory at run time if memory gets crowded because of a large object program.

Notice that several buffer areas are delineated in the figure. These areas hold information arriving from or departing to IO devices. They may be considered as part of the object program or part of free storage according to the software system design. When dealings take place between memory and a device, $\mathscr{IOCS}$ takes over. $\mathscr{IOCS}$ is a large set of subroutines that performs communication between memory and the devices. When IO data exchange is required, the object program enters an $\mathscr{IOCS}$ subroutine which performs the required service. Return is made to the object program when the IO function is satisfactorily set up by $\mathscr{IOCS}$.

Where Does *IOCS* Come From?

There are several alternatives regarding how *IOCS* gets into memory.

ASSEMBLED INTO OBJECT PROGRAM

Figure 9.1.2 shows one of the most popular alternatives for the source of *IOCS*. This method is used in the Autocoder-IOCS for the IBM 1401, 1410, 7070 and the RCA 301.

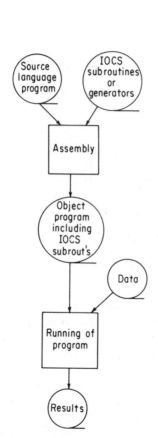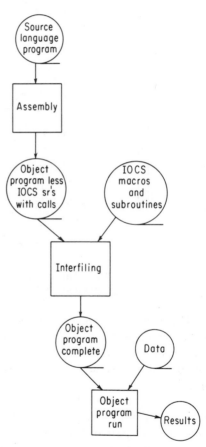

FIGURE 9.1.2. *IOCS* may be incorporated into the object program by the assembler as in the IBM 1401/1410/7070 Autocoder-IOCS *system*.

FIGURE 9.1.3. References to the tasks of *IOCS* in the source language program in the Univac Boss III system for its Univac III. Later subroutines and macros are included using a separate interfiling run as shown above.

The source language input into the assembler makes reference to specific subroutines of $IOCS$. These subroutines are previously defined and are supplied during the assembly phase. They are *assembly defined* SR's. $IOCS$ consists of assembly defined subroutines which are incorporated separately into each object program during assembly.

$IOCS$ subroutines have many parameters associated with them and are variable in length. They are produced by assembly incorporated variable generators. Usually there is insufficient room during assembly time to hold the complete stock of $IOCS$ generators or subroutines. To make the process manageable, these are supplied on some external medium available to the assembler at assembly time, as shown in Fig. 9.1.2.

The output of the assembler is the object program into which are built the $IOCS$ subroutines. This object program is loaded into the computer at run time with the data to produce the results, as shown in the figure.

INTERFILER PASS FOR $IOCS$

Another alternative practiced by the BOSS III for Univac® III is shown in Fig. 9.1.3.

As in the previous system, the source program contains references to $IOCS$ subroutines. The assembler makes note of these as it performs a normal assembly. It makes no attempt to supply the subroutines during assembly since they are not accessible to it. $IOCS$ subroutine incorporation is performed on the next pass. The object program, with references to $IOCS$, is turned over to a new run, called the **interfiler**. During this run the $IOCS$ subroutines are entered into the object program together with the proper calling sequences so that the same $IOCS$ routine may be made available to several portions of the object program.

Subroutines for this $IOCS$ may be nested in depth. The innermost subroutines used by $IOCS$ outer routines are entered only once in the final object program, and links are produced between $IOCS$ routines and the innermost subroutines used by them. The completed object program containing $IOCS$ routines is now loaded and the data is brought in by them as requested by the object program to produce the required results. Although requiring the extra pass, redundant $IOCS$ segments have been eliminated, saving valuable memory.

OMNIPRESENT $IOCS$

In machines with large memory, such as the IBM 7090/94, there is usually enough room to have the full $IOCS$ present at run time. This simplifies matters, especially assembly. Now reference to $IOCS$ is supplied in the source program like calls for library subroutines. Long parameter lists and subcommand sequences may be incorporated in a single call so that $\mathscr{IOCS}$ has a detailed description of the command it is to perform.

The assembler is well-equipped to handle calling sequences and creates the appropriate object program containing them. The operation shown in Fig. 9.1.4 results.

To make the system even more adaptable, file descriptions are entered at run time. This permits the same program to be run with different files by simply adjusting the file descriptions which are supplied when the program is run.

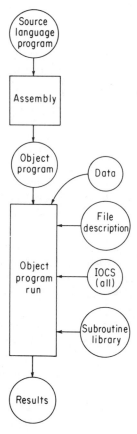

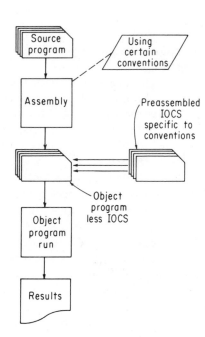

FIGURE 9.1.4. If the $\mathscr{IOCS}$ is normally present in memory during run time as for the IBM 7090, the above method is used. Only short macros are required in the source language program.

FIGURE 9.1.5. Much assembly time can be saved for the assembly incorporated $\mathscr{IOCS}$ as above. Established conventions permit prepackaged $\mathscr{IOCS}$ to be entered with the object program at run time.

Comparison of Entry Methods

DIRECT ASSEMBLY

This method lengthens the assembly time considerably, for all $\mathscr{IOCS}$ routines must be entered into the object program by the assembler. It removes the obligation of loading a separate $\mathscr{IOCS}$ into the memory at run time. However, it lengthens the object program so that loading it takes a little longer.

INTERFILER

Assembly can be performed rapidly. However, a separate pass must be used to enter $\mathscr{IOCS}$ into the object program. As before, a separate $\mathscr{IOCS}$ need not be loaded. But, now the object program is longer, so its load time in turn is longer.

OMNIPRESENT $\mathscr{IOCS}$

This method has the advantage that both the assembly time and the object program length are considerably shorter than in the previous methods. Since $\mathscr{IOCS}$ is almost always contained in memory, we need not load it; hence, total load time is short. The big disadvantage is that so *much* of memory is tied up *most* of the time to hold $\mathscr{IOCS}$.

Preassembled $\mathscr{IOCS}$

In some installations the files handled, the input devices available, the buffer areas used and so forth, are fairly standard. Knowing this, we can simplify the procedure, as shown in Fig. 9.1.5. Establishing conventions in the installation allows us to use a preassembled $\mathscr{IOCS}$. Programs that are submitted for assembly make reference to $\mathscr{IOCS}$; however, the assembler is instructed not to insert the routines into the object program. It produces the object program without the $\mathscr{IOCS}$ routines. These are then edited into the object language either by manual insertion of the deck or with a separate pass. This reduces the assembly time tremendously without changing the effect of the operation.

To make the preassembled $\mathscr{IOCS}$, an assembly pass is made on a proto-type problem *with* $\mathscr{IOCS}$ being entered. The object program produced by this is stripped of the parts which are not $\mathscr{IOCS}$, and what remains is the preassembled $\mathscr{IOCS}$ ready for insertion into later object programs.

Setup

In the remainder of this chapter we discuss how *IOCS* is set up. Since we wish the system to handle information automatically, we must supply full particulars. Setup instructions take two forms:

- Fixed instructions (e.g., file names, size) are incorporated into the program.
- Job-variable instructions (e.g., file assignment to physical unit) are entered with the job, usually by control cards.

The fixed instructions are established by the programmer before he uses the *IOCS* commands. The job-variable instructions on control cards are entered before *IOCS* is activated on the job. Both of these are setup operations to precondition the system to the job.

Simultaneity

IOCS is able to exploit the simultaneity of the computer as long as the feature is available for the IO devices. *IOCS* manages the devices and interrelates with the program; it sees that data is available ahead of time for all files. Once data is available, the program running and devices executing assignments, *IOCS* handles completion and reinitiation of the devices.

IOCS is the liaison between the devices (usually as managed by *FOREMAN*) and the program: it queues up new requests as determined by the needs of the program; it handles completed requests. It is the ability of the *IOCS* to make ready new blocks of data as they arrive, queue processed data for output and, most importantly, get appropriate requests ready for devices that have become idle, which exploits the capability for concurrence.

9.2   ACTIVITY ACCOUNTING

Monitoring IO Activity

Four phases of IO activity are monitored by *IOCS* which is always cognizant of what is taking place in these areas:

- devices
- buffers
- channels
- files

How does it keep track of what is going on in each one of these areas? A record is established for each item in each class: these records are cross-referenced so that any operation referring to more than one item can be accurately followed. Records are named as follows:

- Unit Activity Block (UAB)—one for each device in the system.
- Buffer Activity Block (BAB)—one for each buffer in the system.
- Channel Activity Block (CAB)—one for each channel in the system.
- File Activity Block (FAB)—one for each file in the system.
- Pool Activity Block (PAB)—one for each pool of buffers in the system.

Activity Blocks

All the activity blocks pertinent to a given program are in memory at job run time. Some of these blocks come in with the program; some come in with control information; still others are established within the software at an earlier date.

DEVICES AND CHANNELS

Figure 9.2.1 shows that both the unit activity blocks and the channel activity blocks reside within the supervisor. Least transient within the over-all system is the number of devices and channels available to the system. For each physical unit and for each channel where channels exist in the system, a block is set aside to keep track of activity for this unit or channel.

Assignment of devices can be made by the programmer or it can be made automatically by the supervisor, $\mathscr{SYSTEM}$. In either case all such assignments are cleared through the supervisor to be sure that the units desired are available and/or attached to the system.

The units and channels present in the over-all system are established by the operator within the supervisor. This operation is discussed in Chapter 13 about $\mathscr{SYSTEM}$. Suffice it to say that when one or more units break down and are removed from the system, the supervisor must know about this; contrarily, when a repaired unit is returned, $\mathscr{SYSTEM}$ is notified.

BUFFERS

For the FLAP $\mathscr{IOCS}$ the buffers required for a program are established entirely by the programmer who has full knowledge of the structure of the files used and the structure of the incoming and outgoing information. In other systems such as IBM IBSYS, buffer establishment may be done automatically. Then the jobs examined below are done by the programming system.

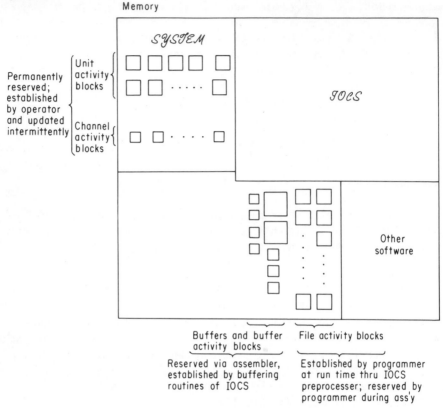

FIGURE 9.2.1. The source and the run time location of the various activity blocks.

For the FLAP $\mathcal{IOCS}$ the programmer performs a number of operations with regard to the buffers:

- reserves space for each buffer
- reserves additional space with each nonpool buffer or pool of buffers for a pool activity block to keep track of buffer assignments
- groups the buffers together in pools
- reserves space and assigns buffer activity blocks

As per his instructions, the assembler provides space for the buffers and their activity blocks.

At run time the buffer activity blocks, reserved by the programmer via the assembler from information supplied by the programmer in his *IOCS* calls, are now set up by the *IOCS* buffering routines in the input-output control system. These direct the buffering system regarding interconnection of pools, their length and all the details about them.

Files

The file description may vary from one job to the next which uses the program; the description may be varied as long as the buffers supplied by the program can accommodate one or more blocks of the file. To provide this flexibility, file information is supplied just before run time. Hence, if a programmer wishes to run a different set of files with his program, he may do so as long as it meets the original buffer restrictions.

Information about the files is supplied by control input to the *IOCS* monitor which sets up file activity blocks (FABs) and enters information about the files there. The monitor is supplied with identification information which includes:

- the file name
- the number of reels
- the expiration date

The file may be assigned to a specific device and, in the case of multireel files, an alternate input or output device may also be indicated. Connection information between a file and a buffer pool is supplied via the program and is processed by the buffering subsystem rather than the monitoring subsystem. This information, however, is stored in the FAB.

Other information stored in the FAB includes:

- use statistics indicating what errors have arisen and how much of the file has been processed
- control information about the file which includes the present attachment status and pointers to devices and buffers or to the pool

Device Designation

An input or output device may be designated in three ways:

- physical
- machine (or algebraic)
- symbolic

The use of these terms is explained in Fig. 9.2.2.

Each unit has a serial number. A different **physical unit** is one with a different serial number. If a unit breaks down and is replaced by a different

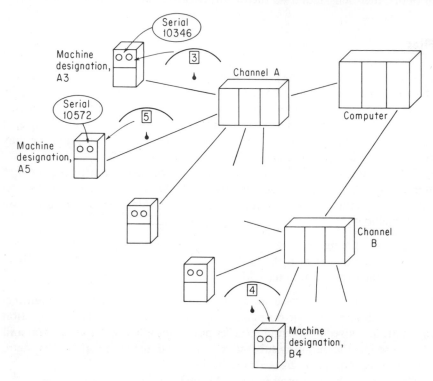

FIGURE 9.2.2. The serial number is the unchangeable physical name of the IO unit. The machine number is manually settable for each IO unit. The symbolic name is independent of these; it is devised by the programmer and assigned by him or by the supervisor.

physical unit, it may be assigned the machine designation and symbolic designation of the unit it replaces. However the physical unit designation is unalterable.

MACHINE DESIGNATION

When a device is referenced in a machine language command or in a control word, the **machine designation**† is used. In most computers a

---

† The *machine designation* of a device is equivalent, in some sources, to *logical designation.* "Logical" does not convey that the labeling is due to the present position occupied by the device or its switch setting, nor does it contrast with *symbolic device* or *symbolic file*; it is eschewed here.

physical unit can be made to correspond with almost any machine designation. For instance, it is possible to relabel some tape units by turning their label knob. The machine in the upper left-hand corner of Fig. 9.2.2 is labeled A3, since it is on channel A and its dial reads 3. Of course, if we label two tape units A3, this will confuse the computer and we hope that its *IOCS* will make it halt until the situation is remedied.

The arrangement shown in Fig. 9.2.2. includes a channel designation where several units report to the same channel, several channels reporting to the computer proper. Some computers do not permit this flexibility: the units report directly to the computer. Still, in this case, we can relabel units with regard to machine reference usually by positioning a knob or interchanging cables.

SYMBOLIC

Symbolic reference to files is common with the assembler or with *IOCS*. Thus in a posting problem, the old master file may be referred to symbolically by such a concoction as OLMASR.

File activity blocks are established by symbolic name. Within the block a reference is made to a device, specific in the machine language sense. Assignment of a machine designation to a symbolic unit is made by control information supplied to the *IOCS* monitor just before run time. If a machine assignment is lacking, this is done by an assignment routine which is contained either in *IOCS* monitor or in *SYSTEM*.

COORDINATION

IOCS coordinates files and devices. Files designated symbolically refer to specific devices. More than one file can refer to the same device provided that only one file corresponding to the device is active at one time. *IOCS* checks that assignments made earlier are carried out at run time.

The Buffering Problem

In Fig. 9.2.3 the heavy lines indicate the flow of information; control activity is in dashed lines. The particular device under consideration in the figure has the machine designation A3. Its activity is reported in the unit activity block which, in turn, is under the control of the file activity block. The file activity block points to a number of things. The pool to which it is attached is recorded by a pointer to the pool activity block. FAB also has a pointer to the buffer being used for the *take* operation by the object program (buffer 1). Another pointer establishes the *fill* buffer (buffer 2).

It is up to the file manager—a routine within *IOCS*—to control the updating of all the activity blocks.

The $\mathcal{IOCS}$ read/write routine communicates with the object program and is called in every time READ or WRITE is found there. When a major change in the buffer pool occurs, this subsystem calls in the file manager to do the list processing, device assignment and buffer connections as required.

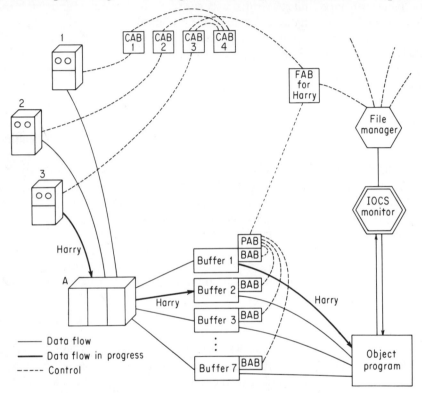

FIGURE 9.2.3. Some intimation of the interrelation of the IO units, the activity blocks, the buffers, the object program and $\mathcal{IOCS}$.

Extent of Activity

We have been describing a rather large $\mathcal{IOCS}$, one in which buffer pools are permitted and encouraged. Smaller $\mathcal{IOCS}$s limit buffering activities to simple rotating buffers or swinging buffers. This certainly reduces buffer management requirements and space needed for $\mathcal{IOCS}$, but the toll is a loss in efficiency of some IO operations.

Further, we have examined a computer system which contains both channels and unit stations. When units report directly to the computer, device management is simplified. Of course, overlap and simultaneity are reduced, but this is the price of simplicity.

9.3 𝒫ℛℰ𝒫ℛ𝒪𝒞ℰ𝒮𝒮𝒪ℛ DESCRIPTION

Relation of 𝒥𝒪𝒞𝒮 to Other Programming Systems

The supervisor, 𝒮𝒴𝒮𝒯ℰ𝑀 has all software reporting to it. As the coordinator, it accepts directions from the programmer's control instructions. After all, everybody has a boss; the final say of the computer activity still resides with the human.

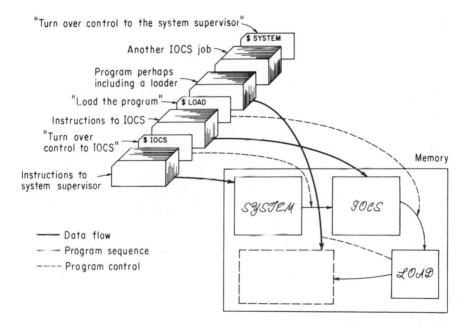

FIGURE 9.3.1. Control information for all the software enters via the control input. Change from one programming subsystem to another is also controlled thus.

Long-term instructions, requests of which the operator is aware in advance, are entered via a preassigned input unit. This unit enters control instructions for the supervisor, the subsystems reporting to the supervisor and, for small programs, may be the input for the object program. This is illustrated in Fig. 9.3.1.

𝒥𝒪𝒞𝒮 reports directly to 𝒮𝒴𝒮𝒯ℰ𝑀 and gets its setup instructions from the control input; it may turn over control to other software subsystems and finally to the object program itself at run time.

Interrelation of the Supervisor and $\mathscr{IOCS}$

Figure 9.3.1 shows the interrelation of $\mathscr{SYSTEM}$ and $\mathscr{IOCS}$. When a task is completed, control is turned over to $\mathscr{SYSTEM}$ which gets information about its next function from the control input. This might consist of the assignment of IO devices, setting of new job priorities, and so forth.

Once new operating conditions are established, a control instruction is given to $\mathscr{SYSTEM}$ to delegate its responsibilities to a subsystem such as $\mathscr{IOCS}$.

Now $\mathscr{IOCS}$ gets details about its operating environment via the control input. When $\mathscr{IOCS}$ is set up, it in turn receives a *delegate* instruction to cause the loading of the object program, which may follow, on the control input unit.

When the object program and all required subroutines are located and loaded, control is turned over to the object program. The object program frequently turns over control (via calls built into the assembler) to $\mathscr{IOCS}$ routines for IO functions. This is temporary and control is returned to the object program when the IO function is completed.

In certain, obviously rare, instances $\mathscr{IOCS}$ turns over control to $\mathscr{SYSTEM}$, $\mathscr{FOREMAN}$ or other software when the system gets into trouble. The object program can also turn control over to $\mathscr{SYSTEM}$ if it should get into trouble, such as with a floating-point multiply underflow.

If the program does not get into trouble and passes to normal completion, it turns over control to $\mathscr{IOCS}$ or $\mathscr{SYSTEM}$. In turn, $\mathscr{IOCS}$ *Preprocessor* reads in new control information. If another job using $\mathscr{IOCS}$ is forthcoming, then $\mathscr{IOCS}$ remains in control.

Control Information

Information for $\mathscr{SYSTEM}$ or a subsystem is entered via the control input, indicated as a number of punchcards in Fig. 9.3.1 and other diagrams which follow. This is for convenience rather than adherence to practice. Control information initially entered through punchcards is transcribed to magnetic tape. Normally, then, control information in large installations is entered by a magnetic tape unit which has this specific assignment. Medium-size installations may actually use a punchcard input. Small installations might use paper tape.

The intermediate translation makes the operator more remote from the system operation. However, when something important arises and he wants to interrupt the present job to change a priority or to remove a faulty tape unit, he does not have to get to magnetic tape to enter control information. If the system has an interrupt function, he can speak directly with the supervisor via the console. Without an interrupt function he can stop the computer with the *stop* button and then make contact with the software system of his choice. These topics get further consideration in Chapter 20.

At present we are interested in instructions for $\mathscr{IOCS}$ and how control can be transferred between $\mathscr{IOCS}$ and other software subsystems; so we examine control instruction format.

FLAP-IOCS Directives

Here, in the IBM 7090 IOCS and in several others, control information for $\mathscr{IOCS}$ bears the prefix $, a label indicating its nature. This symbol, $, alerts $\mathscr{Preprocessor}$ that control information follows.

$$\text{\$IOCS}$$

We indicate to an alien subsystem monitor that we desire to shift control to $\mathscr{IOCS}$ with the control card labeled **$IOCS**, formatted as:

$$\text{\$IOCS} \qquad blank \qquad\qquad (9.3.1)$$

Of course, this card causes no reaction when it is detected by the $\mathscr{IOCS}$ monitor. That would be like telling your wife to go home when you are sitting in the living room.

$$\text{\$ACCT}$$

This requests through $\mathscr{IOCS}$ the accounting routine unique to the installation. Each installation has its own method of charging time for the computer. Allowance is made for this fact by permitting the customer to devise routines that conform with his particular accounting needs.

The accounting card contains information about charges to be made for the forthcoming program. The format of this information again depends upon the user's requirements:

$$\text{\$ACCT} \qquad directions \qquad\qquad (9.3.2)$$

$$\text{\$JOB}$$

This card tells $\mathscr{IOCS}$ the name and number of the job and how many files are involved in the job so that $\mathscr{IOCS}$ knows how much space to allocate for file activity blocks.

For some $\mathscr{IOCS}$ systems this card gives the user a choice of the extent of the system which he wishes: which features he does not need and which ones he wants.

$FILE

Each of the files referred to by the program are described in sufficient detail to set up the file activity block. The ability to use the same program with different file descriptions is another flexibility of $\mathscr{IOCS}$.

The $FILE card furnishes full information for the FAB, the name of the file, the primary unit assigned to the file, the secondary unit assigned to the file and so forth, as described in Section 9.4 and listed in Table 9.4.

$DATE

This is a way of communicating today's date to $\mathscr{IOCS}$.

$LOAD

When all preparations are made, the computer may be turned over to the object program, except when the object is inputted on some other unit. The sole message on $LOAD is its title.

$RESTART

This card communicates to $\mathscr{IOCS}$ that the rollback procedure is to be called into play.

$SYSTEM

A subsystem turns over control to $\mathscr{IOCS}$ with $IOCS. To turn over control to other subsystems, $\mathscr{IOCS}$ calls $\mathscr{SYSTEM}$ with $SYSTEM.

The Run Deck

In Fig. 9.3.2 we see a typical set of control cards. The set is preceded by $IOCS if $\mathscr{SYSTEM}$ is in control.

$ACCT submits to the user's accounting routine the name and description of the job. $ACCT subsumes the function of $JOB so that the latter is not required. A set of $FILE cards follows, one for each file used by $\mathscr{IOCS}$. If the date has not been indicated or if it is changed for this run, $DATE appears. $\mathscr{IOCS}$ should now have all the information it requires, but it must be told this by the $LOAD card. The set of loader cards shown in Fig. 9.3.2 is needed only if a loader is absent from the over-all system.

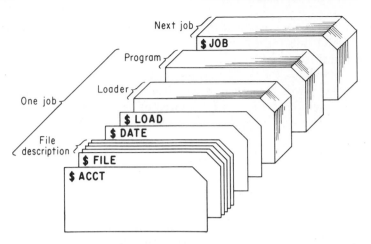

FIGURE 9.3.2. A typical set of control cards for information entry into the 𝒥𝒪𝒞𝒮 preprocessor.

Finally we get to the program. Translation is done before 𝒥𝒪𝒞𝒮 sees the program. When 𝒥𝒪𝒞𝒮 finishes this job successfully, it reads in further control information. Another run deck follows. When the set of runs for 𝒥𝒪𝒞𝒮 is completed, control is turned over to the system using $SYSTEM.

9.4 PREPROCESSOR OPERATION

Setting Up 𝒥𝒪𝒞𝒮

The last section described communicating information to 𝒥𝒪𝒞𝒮. A portion of 𝒥𝒪𝒞𝒮 called 𝒫𝓇𝑒𝓅𝓇𝑜𝒸𝑒𝓈𝓈𝑜𝓇 incorporates the control information and then turns over control to the loader.

FIRST CARD

𝒫𝓇𝑒𝓅𝓇𝑜𝒸𝑒𝓈𝓈𝑜𝓇 gains control at the end of the last run involving 𝒥𝒪𝒞𝒮 when 𝒮𝒴𝒮𝒯𝐸𝑀 encounters a $IOCS card. 𝒫𝓇𝑒𝓅𝓇𝑜𝒸𝑒𝓈𝓈𝑜𝓇 requests the next card, the image of which is entered into an analysis area in memory. Its type is determined as shown in Fig. 9.4.1. Only four types are acceptable as *first cards*: $ACCT, $RESTART, $SYSTEM and $JOB.

$ACCT brings in the user's accounting routine. This card should also contain job information so that when the accounting routine is completed the operations of Fig. 9.4.2 are begun.

When $JOB is encountered the routine *Job* of Fig. 9.4.3 is performed.

$RESTART calls for restart procedure and return to the object program, as shown in the figure.

$SYSTEM allows the system supervisor to take over. All other cards are illegal as first cards. They cause an error message to be printed on the monitor printer but no action is required of the operator. *Preprocessor* reads the next card hoping, this time, to find a *first* card.

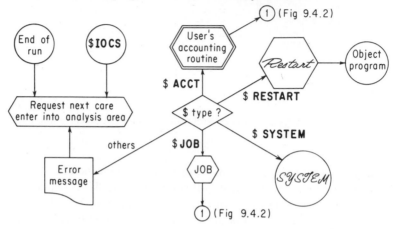

FIGURE 9.4.1. First card of *Preprocessor* series.

FOLLOWING CARDS

Figure 9.4.2 shows what happens to other cards in the preprocessor

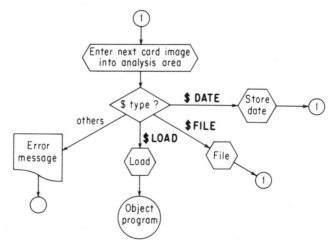

FIGURE 9.4.2. Other cards of *Preprocessor* series.

series. The card image is entered into the analysis area and typed. Three kinds of cards are legal: $DATE, $FILE and $LOAD. All others produce an error message after which *Preprocessor* looks for another card, hopefully a legal one.

$DATE calls forth a simple subroutine which stores the date in a pre-assigned location and returns to *Preprocessor*. $FILE and $LOAD both require extensive subroutines, discussed below.

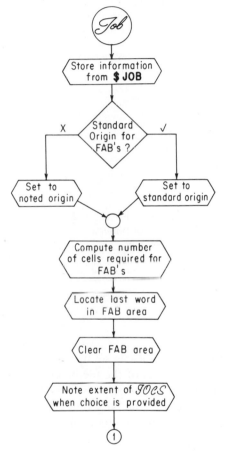

FIGURE 9.4.3. *Job* routine.

$JOB **Processing**

Figure 9.4.3 illustrates *Job*. The card may request another origin for the file activity blocks. The FAB origin is then set either to the standard origin or the noted origin. The number of cells required for the FABs is calculated to locate the last cell in the FAB area. The area is then cleared. The extent of $\mathscr{IOCS}$ required for the run is noted for $\mathscr{IOCS}$s which can be varied in the duties they perform.

TABLE 9.4   Contents of File Activity Block

Type	Data	From $FILE?
Label	Name	Yes
	File number	
	Sequence number (multireel)	
	Retention period	
Assignment	Primary device identification	Yes
	Secondary device identification	
Control	Label standard	Some
	File type	
	File density	
	File mode	
	Check sum	
	Check point	
	Restart	
	End of tape	
	etc.	
Dynamic	Buffer pool	No
	Buffer in use	
	Number of buffers used	
	Number of buffers	
	Wait pointer	
History	Errors found	No
	Erasures performed	
	Block count	

The File Block

Before we see how the file block is set up by $\mathscr{Preprocessor}$ from $FILE cards, let us examine the contents of the file block.

While the format of the file information is variable from one manufacturer to another, the content of the file activity block is generally as displayed in Table 9.4. The table contains three columns for:

- the type of information   • the subtype of information
- whether the source of this information is from the $FILE card

LABEL

The $FILE card describes the file label so that the label routine can verify that the proper file is being used. The label contains a name (or symbolic referent) or a number. For multireel files a sequence number is used to indicate how many reels must be processed before the file is exhausted.

A retention period may be contained in the label.

When an input file is first read, the label information is verified and an error printout is made if it does not agree. For an output file, label information is written in the first block before anything else.

ASSIGNMENT

The programmer may make a *machine designation* for an IO unit for a given file. For multireel files it is advisable to designate a second unit so that reel loading and unloading can take place without halting the machine. If no assignment is made by the programmer, the task is done by an assignment algorithm in $\mathcal{IOCS}$ or $\mathcal{SYSTEM}$.

CONTROL

A number of minutiae about the file and unit assignment is recorded in the control area of FAB. Most of this information comes in on the $FILE card, as indicated in Table 9.4.

DYNAMIC

$\mathcal{IOCS}$ records in FAB decisions it has made, such as:

- buffer pool attachment
- present status—blocks ready for computer, ready to write, etc.
- readout error condition, etc.

This is dynamic information because it changes during the progress of the job. For instance, the buffer pool pointer is set up by $\mathcal{IOCS}$ in an assigned portion of FAB. It points to a location from which the address of the next *empty* buffer can be picked up when $\mathcal{IOCS}$ needs it.

HISTORY

It is a boon to the user to furnish him with information about how well his equipment functions. Errors that occur and are corrected can easily be noted by $\mathcal{IOCS}$ and recorded in FAB. These can be printed out at the end of the run and can help the user forestall trouble.

Recording FAB

When a $FILE card is encountered the routine $\mathcal{File}$ of Fig. 9.4.4 is invoked. It checks to see if the file number is legal and prints an error message if it is not. It further assigns a legal file number so that processing can continue. The address of the file activity block is calculated. The labels are then entered from the card image area as well as the control entries.

The unit assignment is checked. If it is illegal, the assignment is replaced by 0's and an error message printed on the console monitor. A legal assignment is made by the assignment algorithm if possible.

The *Assign* Function

Although $LOAD contains practically nothing, it calls in a large routine, *Assign*. The purpose of *Assign* is to do all the cleanup work and set the object program in motion. All files which do not have unit assignments must have these assignments made during this period.

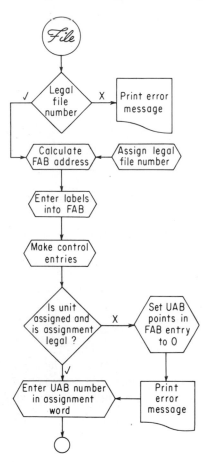

FIGURE 9.4.4. *File* routine.

In Fig. 9.4.5 *Assign* gets the unit assignment from the proper word of the first FAB. If no unit is assigned, it continues through the FAB list (3). To verify an assignment it is necessary to determine if the unit specified is available (4) by examination of an IO device table. This table has been previously set up by *SYSTEM* but is available to *IOCS* for reference. It contains the physical and symbolic device designation, the function assigned to it and the address of the unit activity block for that function. The unit assignment in the FAB is replaced by the absolute address of the unit activity block since this is the only reference required by *IOCS* (5). Should the unit requested be unavailable (4), the FAB address and unit number are entered into a conflict table (6). Then the assignment word is replaced with 0's so that the assignment algorithm can be invoked (7).

Whether a secondary unit is assigned is determined in (8). If it is, the same check (4)–(7) is performed for the secondary unit. With the unit assignment for this block checked out, we continue down the list of FABs, making the same check for each.

When we have examined the whole list (1), we go back over the list again, this time to assign unassigned units. The pointer is reset (9), and we start at the top of the list (10). We get the next FAB (11) and check to see if it is assigned (12). If an assignment was made, we check to see if the unit meets the requirements communicated by the $FILE card (13). The unit

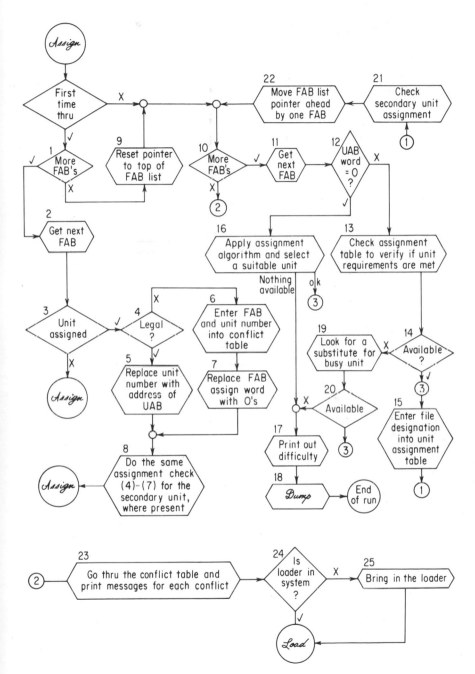

FIGURE 9.4.5. *Assign* routine for $LOAD.

assignment is legal (4) and we check for availability (14). We enter the file designation of an available unit into the unit assignment table (15).

The assignment algorithm is applied to select a suitable unit (16) for an unassigned file (12). When one is found, an entry is made into the unit assignment table (15). If there is no unit available, we are in trouble! This is printed out (17), the dump routine $\mathcal{D}ump$ is called in (18) and the run is aborted.

If the unit assigned is not available (14), we call in a routine to look for a substitute unit (19). If we cannot find one (20), we are in trouble and dump the job. If we do find one, the information is posted (15). We do the same sequence for a secondary assignment if present (21). Then we move the FAB list pointer ahead (22) and see if there are more FABs which have not been checked (10).

When unit assignment has been completed successfully, we supply the operator with information about the conflicts we have arbitrated (23). If the loader $\mathcal{LOAD}$ is in the system, we turn control over to it (24). Otherwise, we bring in the loader using the control input device (25).

Extent of Independence

$\mathcal{IOCS}$ provides for extrication from all kinds of programmer errors, is autonomous, and provides automatic unit assignment. This degree of programmer independence costs something. It may be more economical to depend more on the programmer for unit assignment etc., and thus reduce the extent of the software.

9.5 BUFFER AND FILE ALLOCATION

Requirements

This section investigates:

- allocation of space
- definition of buffers
- interrelation between the buffers and the files

FILES

File space is allocated by the programmer in assembly language before the program is assembled. Space is reserved by use of the RSRV pseudo. The programmer names files and lists them by their uses.

The files are defined specifically by input control information to the $\mathcal{IOCS}$ monitor at run time. This particular method permits variability in the files so that a single program can serve different purposes by redefining the files.

BUFFERS

Space for each buffer, singly or in groups, is reserved by the programmer using RSRV pseudos. When a pool of buffers is needed, he defines this pool by calling upon $\mathcal{IOCS}$ routines in assembly language to make the links. He reserves space for the pool activity block for each pool used by him with the RSRV pseudo.

Buffer Space

To reserve a buffer which is to operate singly—not as part of a pool—a simple pseudo is given:

$$\text{FIRSTBUF} \qquad \text{RSRV} \qquad 0030 \qquad\qquad (9.5.1)$$

This command reserves thirty words for a buffer named FIRSTBUF.

To reserve a pool, all buffers must be the same size. Space must be allocated for each buffer activity block (BAB) and for each pool activity block (PAB). Assume that two words suffice for each of these functions.

We reserve enough words for a buffer plus two more for BAB. Let us call this total buffer size b. Thus for FIRSTBUF we have $b = 30$ for an active area of twenty-eight words, the other two words being for FIRSTBUF's BAB.

For any pool we need two extra words for the PAB. For a pool of n such buffers the total number of words in the pool, p, is given by:

$$p = nb + 2 \qquad\qquad (9.5.2)$$

For example, if we want eight buffers in the pool, each buffer to contain fifty words, then we allocate fifty-two words for each buffer and two words more for PAB. This gives a total of 418. Somewhere in the assembly language program there is reserved a pool of 418 words. If we call the pool FIRSTPOOL, then the following pseudo would perform this function:

$$\text{FIRSTPOOL} \qquad \text{RSRV} \qquad 418 \qquad\qquad (9.5.3)$$

We reserve space for a buffer with RSRV *either* by naming the buffer or by naming the pool, *never both*.

Pool Definition

RSRV allocates space for a pool but does not establish the pool as such. In FLAP we call in $\mathcal{Pool}$ using GET and calling for POOL. We communicate the name of the pool which is under definition, the number of buffers in the pool and the size of each buffer (they are all the same size). We postulate the form of this call as:

$$\text{GET} \qquad \text{POOL, pool name, number of buffers, buffer size} \qquad (9.5.4)$$

As an example, this routine call *establishes* the pool of eight buffers, each of fifty words:

$$\text{GET} \qquad \text{POOL, FIRSTPOOL, 8, 50} \qquad (9.5.5)$$

Noncontiguous pools

It is sometimes inconvenient to establish very large pools because they occupy so much memory. After pools have been

- established by reserving space for them using RSRV
- defined using the *IOCS* routine *Pool*

they may be pasted together using an *IOCS* routine, *Join*. It would be silly to use this routine unless the pools were not adjacent in memory. In order to use this routine we give the call:

$$\text{GET} \qquad \text{JOIN, first pool name, second pool name} \qquad (9.5.6)$$

The new and larger pool has the name that appears *first* in the routine call; if the second pool is ever called or referenced by name, *IOCS* responds to this as an error.

As an example of the use of this call, let us connect two pools thus:

$$\text{GET} \qquad \text{JOIN, BIGPOOL, FIRSTPOOL} \qquad (9.5.7)$$

After this routine is performed, a new and larger pool is performed which is spread over to known adjacent areas, and the name of the pool is BIGPOOL. Theoretically FIRSTPOOL no longer exists. It is legal to join *another* pool to BIGPOOL, but it is illegal to join another pool to FIRSTPOOL.

File Space

Space for the file activity block is reserved in assembly language so that *IOCS* will have a place to put the information from the $FILE card. The number of words required for each FAB depends on the software manufacturer, of course; we allocate twelve words for this purpose by:

$$\text{file name} \qquad \text{RSRV} \qquad 12 \qquad (9.5.8)$$

For example, the FAB for a pay system file named PAYROLL is reserved by:

$$\text{PAYROLL} \qquad \text{RSRV} \qquad 12 \qquad (9.5.9)$$

FILE TYPES

An *IOCS* of some sophistication distinguishes several kinds of files. A **full file** requires one buffer per file. A **reserve file** permits sharing of a pool of buffers among several files. An **internal file** is not connected to any IO device; it is only used for internal purposes and may require fewer buffers for a group of files than there are files in the group.

Attaching Files to a Pool

So far we have buffers completely defined and space reserved for them; we also have files defined on incoming $FILE cards and space reserved for the information on these cards. It remains to interconnect the files to the pool of buffers. This is done by *Attach* called thus:

$$\text{GET} \quad \text{ATTACH, pool name, list name, file count} \quad (9.5.10)$$

All the files that are ever going to be used by the pool must be attached to the pool with this one command—it can be given only once for a given pool. What if we do not want to use a particular file right away? Well, although a file is attached, it is not ready for use until it has been opened. The separate *open* procedure to connect the file to the buffer is discussed in Section 9.7.

The File List

The list of files attached to a pool made in assembly language by the programmer contains sublists, one sublist for each type of file, *full*, *reserve* and *internal*. There may be several sublists for each type if desired. The list serves two purposes: it communicates those files which are to be attached to the pool as required by the call; it also provides a control word for each sublist. This control word keeps track of the number of active files in each sublist, as well as the number of buffers reserved in the pool for that sublist. The prototype form for such a list is given as:

```
list name   NOOP     FULL
            NOOP     file name sublist
            NOOP     RES, maximum number open, number of
                        buffers supplied
            NOOP     file name sublist
            NOOP     INT, maximum number open, number of
                        buffers supplied
            NOOP     file name sublist              (9.5.11)
```

This list is presented to the assembler which does no processing, except for translating the symbols into binary and reformatting for *IOCS*.

9.6 BUFFER DEFINITION ROUTINES

Pool Layout

Pool definition is illustrated using an example. Suppose we define a pool labeled **LITLPOOL**, which consists of four buffers, each of eight words. A

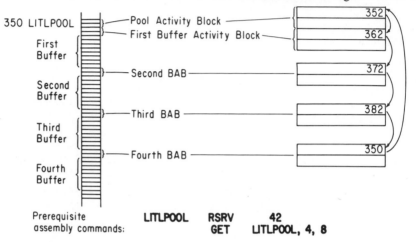

FIGURE 9.6.1. Arrangement of buffers, BABs and the PABs in memory together with pointers for the assembly commands directly above.

buffer activity block of two words is required for each buffer and the pool activity block of two words is required for the pool. The 42 words required for the pool are laid out in memory as shown in Fig. 9.6.1.

Let us suppose that the first word of the pool is finally (after loading) at the absolute location 350. Then the pool consists of the 42 cells from 350 to 391. The first two cells are for the pool activity block. Each successive buffer of eight words is prefixed by a buffer activity block of two words.

The commands required to reserve and define the pool are:

$$\text{LITLPOOL} \quad \text{RSRV} \quad 42,$$

$$\cdots$$

$$\text{GET} \quad \text{POOL, LITLPOOL, 4, 8} \qquad (9.6.1)$$

These two assembly commands need not be given consecutively as long as the former precedes the latter. $\mathscr{P}ool$ cannot divide space not yet allocated.

POOL LIST

The pool is a list structure as shown on the right side of Fig. 9.6.1. The pool activity block contains a pointer to the first buffer activity block; this in turn points to the second BAB; . . . ; the third BAB points to the fourth BAB; the fourth BAB points back to the buffer pool block, to form a circular linked list.

When $\mathcal{P}ool$ is called, an absolute cell number has been assigned to the start of the pool. In the example, the pool and the PAB both start at cell

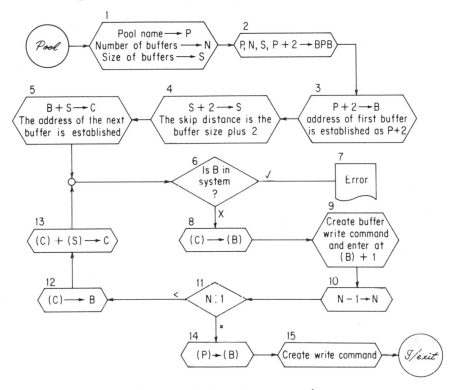

FIGURE 9.6.2. Flow diagram, $\mathcal{P}ool$.

350. The first BAB begins two cells later at 352. The second BAB is ten cells after the first at 362, and so forth. $\mathcal{P}ool$ sets up the pool by linking the PAB and all of the BAB's as in Fig. 9.6.1.

$\mathcal{P}ool$

A flow diagram of $\mathcal{P}ool$ is shown in Fig. 9.6.2. When $\mathcal{P}ool$ is entered, the information from the call is stored in several working cells (1):

- *pool name* is placed in P
- *number of buffers* is placed in N
- *buffer size* is placed in S

Actually P contains the absolute address of the pool name. This translation from name to address is done either in the assembler or, if a dictionary is provided, by the $\mathscr{IOCS}$ buffer routine.

Next the PAB pointer is filled in. A two-word pool activity block is shown in Fig. 9.6.3. This is the form used in the IBM 7090 IOCS. All information for PAB is available. A calculation fills in the terminal pointer for Fig. 9.6.1 which indicates the address of the last BAB starting at 382.

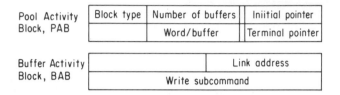

FIGURE 9.6.3. Contents of the activity blocks associated with the buffer pool.

To set up the BABs, two more working cells are required:

- B indicates the address of the buffer being serviced.
- C indicates the address of the next BAB linked to it.

The address of the first BAB begins two cells after the pool address (3). The address of the next BAB depends on how many cells we skip in going from one BAB to the next. The number of cells to skip is just two more than the buffer sizes. Take the number from S and change it to the number of cells to be skipped (4). Now the address of the *next* BAB is obtained when we add S to the address of *this* BAB (5).

SETTING UP THE BABS

Before any buffer is serviced, the block is checked to be sure that it is not already included in the system (6). If the buffer is already in the system, an error printout is made and the system hangs up (7). If the buffer is not presently in the system, we are ready to process the present buffer, B. Into its pointer we place the address of the next BAB which is contained in C (8). To complete the BAB we enter a *write* command in the next word of the BAB (9).

Next we check to see if we are ready to process the last buffer in the pool (10), (11). If the next buffer is not the last buffer, we alter B and C (12), (13) and fill in the next BAB (6)–(11).

When the BAB is the last in the pool, its pointer is set to the address of the pool. The *write* command is entered to completely define the pool (14).

The Join Function

The join process is not commutative: *joining* X to Y is not the same as joining Y to X. We distinguish two participants in the join operation: the pool to which we join is the **joinee**; the pool being joined to the joinee is called the **joiner**. In the routine call the first pool name mentioned is the joinee and the second pool is the joiner. The new pool has the name of the first pool:

$$\text{GET} \qquad \text{JOIN, joinee, joiner} \qquad\qquad (9.6.2)$$

Once a pool is used as a joiner it is no longer eligible to be joined to. In Fig. 9.6.3 there is a joiner bit in the pool activity block which is set to 1 if the pool is a joiner and to 0 for a joinee or if it has not participated in joining. A pool can be either the subject or object of a join only when the joiner bit is 0. It is desirable to require that all pool definitions and join operations are performed before any files are attached to the pool.

The Join Operation

In Fig. 9.6.4 the joinee pointer at the start points to the first buffer in its pool. *Join* makes this pointer point to the first buffer in the *joiner* pool.

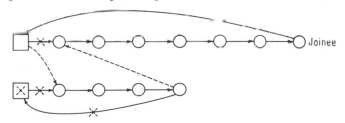

FIGURE 9.6.4. How the routine *Join* operates upon two buffer pools; changes are shown by dashed lines.

The last buffer in the joiner pool is used to point to the joiner pool activity block. *Join* makes it point at the first buffer in the *joinee* pool. The last buffer in the joinee pool points to the joinee PAB which remains unchanged.

The foregoing technique is the one used in the IBM 7090 IOCS. Notice in Fig. 9.6.4 that the joiner PAB points at nothing. Actually, it still points to the first buffer in the joiner buffer pool, but it is disqualified because the joiner bit in the PAB is set to 1.

Join is mainly a list manipulation routine. It has checking functions to perform, but otherwise its main task is resetting pointers in the list.

Join Flow Chart

The flow chart for *Join* is shown in Fig. 9.6.5. First, checks are made to be sure that neither pool is a joiner and that the buffer sizes in both pools are the same (1), (2), (3). If an error is present, it is printed out and processing stops. The rest of the flow chart shows the manipulations required with the pool lists to make a single list structure out of it (5)–(8).

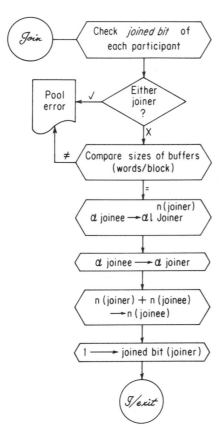

FIGURE 9.6.5. Flow chart of the *Join* routine.

9.7 *Attach* AND *Open*

Purpose

In preceding sections we have separately defined pools and files. This is not sufficient to make a complete picture of the buffering system. Two more routines are required to interconnect the files and the pools of buffers and to make them ready for use by IOCS.

The purpose of *Attach* is to set forth those files which *may* be required to operate with a given pool. A given file may be attached and opened to only one pool at once.

The routine, *Open*, makes a file available to *IOCS*. The routine, *Close*, withdraws a file from use. Each of these requires the subroutine call, thus:

GET	ATTACH, pool name, file name(s) *or* file list, count	(9.7.1)
GET	OPEN, file name(s) *or* file list	(9.7.2)
GET	CLOSE, file name(s) *or* file list	(9.7.3)

ATTACH refers to the pool by *pool name*. One or more files called *file name(s)* may be manipulated with one call. The name of a list may be supplied at *file list* instead.

Here is a list of reserve files:

```
ROBERT      NOOP      RES, 3, 3
            NOOP      RF1
            NOOP      RF2
            NOOP      RF3                    (9.7.4)
```

They all may be opened with:

```
        GET     OPEN, ROBERT                 (9.7.5)
```

When a file is closed more of the pool to which it is attached is available to other files attached to that pool. When a file is opened it is entitled to use any buffer in the pool to which it is attached. File management would be impossible unless we establish that a file may be attached to one and only one pool.

Function of *Attach*

Two activity blocks, PAB and BAB, keep track of the buffers in the pool. File activity is kept track of by a large file activity block, FAB. *Attach* links a given FAB with the PAB and the BAB for the pool. Although attached, the file remains inactive until opened.†

Attach creates a direct link from FAB to PAB, making it possible for the file to use buffers in the pool as required. An available buffer is found by traversing two links.

Queues, described in Chapter 4, are established using the FAB as a pointer and chaining buffers to it. An available buffer found in the pool buffer availability chain is disconnected from the pool and reattached to a chain (e.g., *take* chain, *fill* chain), the pointer for which lies in FAB. The end of such a chain is the location of a blank word. When the chain is void—when no chain has been established or when an existing chain has been destroyed or emptied—then the FAB pointer for that chain points to a blank word. Another job of *Attach* is to initialize the FAB queue pointers.

Attach Flow Chart

Attach, flow charted in Fig. 9.7.1, checks that the pool is not a joiner (1). A joiner PAB is tagged as unavailable. An error printout is made for a *joiner* and the routine is abandoned (2). If the pool checks out, the list

---

† In the IBM 7090 IOCS the *Attach* routine automatically opens certain types of files. This is *not* true here because omission of this feature simplifies the presentation.

entry point for the list of files to be attached is established in absolute terms (3). The list is then reviewed sequentially (4). The word which starts the list [ROBERT in (9.7.4)] is called the **group word**. $\mathscr{IOCS}$, during operation,

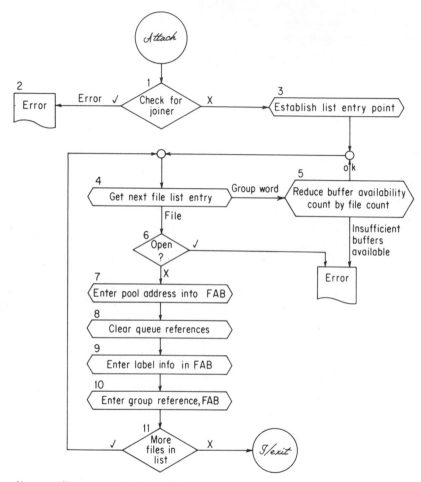

FIGURE 9.7.1. $\mathscr{Attach}$ routine.

uses the *group word* to keep track of activity within the group of files of the same type sharing a portion of the pool. When a group word is found by $\mathscr{Attach}$, reference is made to the PAB to determine the number of available buffers. If insufficient buffers are available (5), an error printout is made. Otherwise the availability count is reduced by the number of buffers that will be withdrawn from this group of files.

Subsequent list entries following the group word refer to files within the group. As files are encountered they are checked to see if they are open. Open files cannot be attached and an error printout is made (6).

If the FAB is acceptable, then the pool address is entered into the FAB (7). References to queues are cleared so that new lists can be established under the control of $\mathcal{IOCS}$ (8). Type information is also entered into FAB (9) as well as the location of the group word (10).

After a file activity block is processed, we see if there are more files in the attachment list (11). If so, we return to (4) and get the next list entry; otherwise the routine is over.

The Function of $\mathcal{Open}$

$\mathcal{Open}$ makes ready for read or write commands. A file may be attached to only one pool but several files may represent the same IO unit. Since different files (representing the same unit) may be attached to different pools, we thus have the ability to attach the same physical unit to different pools at different times. Further, the same unit may be attached as two different files to the same pool. In this way, after opening a file, we can use its unit for reading; then later we close the file and open a different file representing the same IO unit; now we can write onto that unit. One unit attached to a single pool is used to serve different functions.

$\mathcal{Open}$ sets up the file activity block for use with an IO unit by setting up control bits in the block, clearing old history information, establishing the history area for new information and providing any links not heretofore provided. The IO unit must be linked to the file by pointers between the unit activity block and the file activity block.

When a unit is first brought into use, one or several preparatory functions may be required:

- Rewind the tape.
- Check the label.
    * For an input unit this means reading the first block and verifying that the block contains a label and the right label.
    * For an output operation the first block to be written is the label—since the label is presently known, $\mathcal{Open}$ writes the first block containing the label.

$\mathcal{Open}$ interrelates FABs, BABs and UABs. All files must be first attached before being opened.

The OPEN Command

The format of OPEN is:

GET   OPEN, file name list, number of files, options   (9.7.6)

where: *file name list* is a list name or a file name.
> *number of files* is a number indicating the length of list or *blank*
> > for single file.
>
> *options* are REWIND, LABEL or both.

Flow Chart, *Open* Routine

The flow chart for *Open* is shown in Fig. 9.7.2. It begins by checking if the file is already open (1). It is permissible to open a file which is already open. All this does is to clear the history and other monitor operations found in the FAB. If the file is opened, FAB is initialized and we exit from the routine immediately, saving time.

Another possibility is that we try to open a file that has previously been closed and disconnected. This is not permissible and an error is recorded (4).

When the file has not been previously opened (1), (3) we set it to *open* and record that no *end of tape* has occurred (5). Next we check to see if the file is internal or reserve. If either, we must refer to the group word. When we try to open more files in a group than were specified in the group word, we get into trouble. This is checked for in (7), (8). If an error arises, it is recorded and the routine terminated. We continue to (9) and make a check to see if this is an internal file. If it is, we perform a rather large subroutine called *Open Internal File*. The double hexagon shows that this is a sizeable subroutine.†

For external files the routine determines if the reel is mounted (11). If it is not mounted, instructions should be printed for the operator, telling him what reel to mount and where to mount it (12). Processing ceases until the operator performs his task and signals that he is done (13).

With the unit ready for operation, we set the request list pointer and enter auxiliary information, such as density when multiple density tape units are used (14). Next the legality of the file name is checked against the *SYSTEM* assignment table. The unit should not be previously assigned

---

† Major subroutines called forth in a flow chart use double hexagons hereafter. These subroutines are explained elsewhere in the text. Appendix E contains a cross reference of these subroutines.

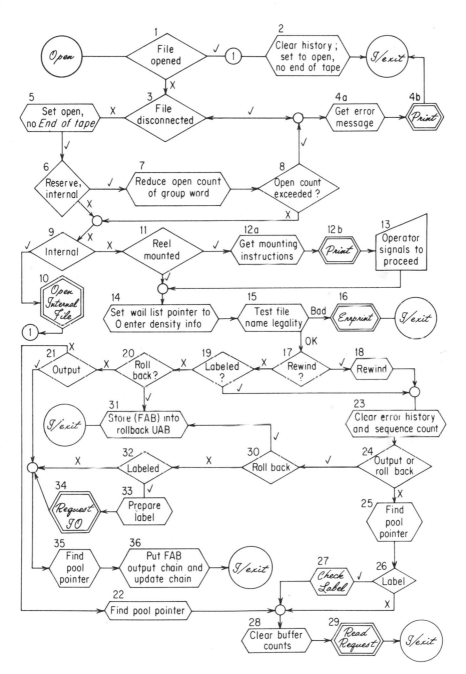

FIGURE 9.7.2. *Open* routine.

for program or system functions (15). An error here calls for a printout and error stop (16). The file is checked to see if rewind is required (17) and, if so, it is performed (18). Label requirements are checked (19). If no label is associated with the file, it may be a rollback file, and this is checked for (20). If it is an unlabeled, unrewound, nonrollback file, we check to see if it is an output file (21). If so, we find the pool pointer (22) and do the cleanup operation discussed later. Labeled or rewound files (18), (19) are cleared of their error history and emptied of their sequence count (23).

If the file is neither output nor rollback (24), then it is an input file. We get the pool pointer (25) and check for labels (26). When the label is used, a major subroutine is called for to read and check the input tape (27). If no label is called for, this is bypassed. The buffer queue assigned to this file block is cleared now (28). The last function for an input operation is to request that the input device read a block. Communication with the unit proper involves *Read Request* (29) discussed in Section 10.6.

The rollback operation (31) can be entered from either (20) or (30) of the flow diagram of Fig. 9.7.2. When the rollback operation is performed the first time, all information about the function being performed is stored on the rollback unit (31). When a labeled output tape is opened (32), the label must be prepared (33). A request must then be made to write the label onto the output unit (34) using *Request IO* discussed in Section 10.5.

Next the pool pointer is found for the write operation (35). This is done after the write request (34) in the case of the labeled file, and after the check for output (21) in the case of the unlabeled file. The only thing that remains to ready the unit for output is to set up the request chains for the write unit (36).

Open Internal File

The overall picture is that first we must determine if this is a read or a write file. We must then set up the file and clear it. In the case of the write file, we have the option of saving information or destroying it.

9.8 CLOSING FILES

Purpose

Close removes or detaches a file or list of files from the buffer pool. All buffers associated with the file or file list are returned to the pool. However, if they have information in them, it would be wise to make some provision for storing the information, writing out the information or otherwise refraining from destroying it.

It is easier to discuss *Close* in several nested steps; hence, our analysis will contain several inner routines, some of which are described here, others being postponed to the next chapter.

Close **Flow Diagram**

THE COMMAND, CLOSE

CLOSE has these parameters associated with it:

- the name of the list
- the number of files in the list
- a choice of options

> GET   CLOSE, file list name, number of files, option   (9.8.1)

File list name is the name of the list or the file.
Number of files is the number of files in the list or *blank* for a single file.
Option is UNLOAD or one, none or both of REWIND and EOF.
There may be a number of control words in the file list but these are ignored when counting the number of files in the list.

FLOW DIAGRAM

Figure 9.8.1 shows a flow chart of the accounting associated with *Close* the buffer and file manipulation is done in *Shut*.

In Fig. 9.8.1 we first set up the routine (1). Next we establish the list entry point and the list count (2), which are passed along as parameters in the routine call.

The accounting process begins when we obtain the next entry from the file list (3). If this is a group word, we record its location (4). To close a group of files, we scan through the entire group. Some of these files may never have been opened. In this case it is unfair to count them as being closed when closing the rest of the group. Hence we cannot post the number of files closed in a given group until we have examined that portion of the list. This is the reason that in (5), if this is the first time a group word is encountered, it is ignored and we continue down the list.

If we have just finished scanning a group of files and we encounter a group word, the previous group has been completely scanned. We have kept track of the number of files actually closed. This count is added to the buffer availability count so that the record of buffers tied up for this group can be eliminated and the buffers freed for other use (6).

When a file word is encountered in the list (3), we augment that file activity block by resetting part of its dynamic control word to indicate that the file is closed (7). We clear the other sense functions in the FAB next (8). We now check to see if the file is already closed tight (cannot be opened) (9). If so, we skip the *Shut* function and continue at (13).

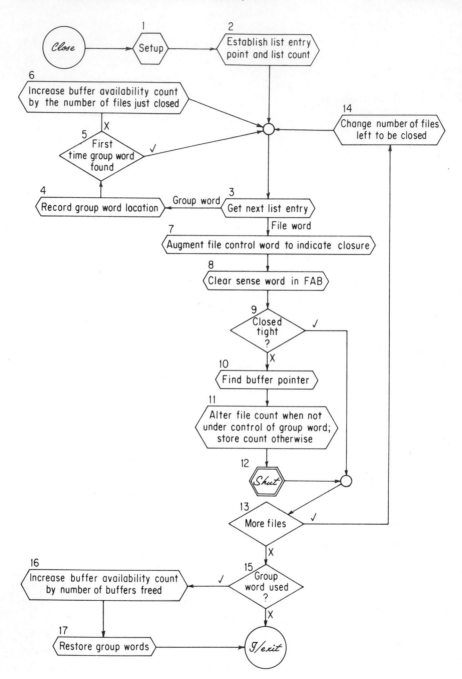

FIGURE 9.8.1. *Close* routine.

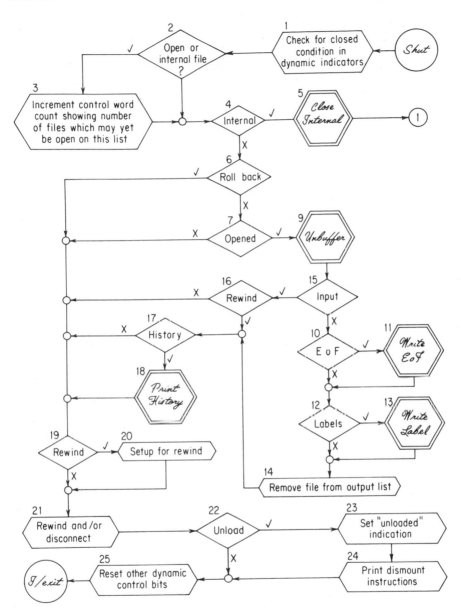

FIGURE 9.8.2. *Shut* routine.

If the file is not closed tight (9), we get the buffer pointer so that buffers may be released (10). If the file was not closed when we encountered it, we alter the file count furnished us as one of the parameters. If the file was part of a group, then we tally up the number we are closing so that later we can release buffers for the group (11). We now perform *Shut* discussed in the next subsection (12). When it is completed, if there are more files to be closed (13), we change the number of files left to be closed (14) and get the next list entry (3).

When there are no more files to be closed (13) we check to see if we have just completed a group of files (15). If so, we must increase the buffer availability count for this group (16) and restore the associated group words so that if this group should require reopening, the proper listing will be found for the group within the file list (17).

Shut

Shut looks for all eventualities which may occur in closing files and treats them as required. In the flow chart in Fig. 9.8.2, we first check for a closed condition in all the dynamic indicators in the file activity block (1).

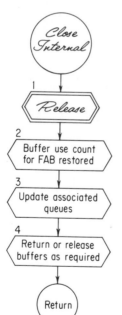

FIGURE 9.8.3. Flow chart, *Close Internal*.

If it is an open or internal file (2), the count for the control word must be tallied to keep track of the number of files being closed (3). For internal files (4) we perform, *Close Internal* (5), discussed later.

We now make a number of checks to determine the kind of file under consideration for an open output file which is not being used for rollback (6),(7),(8).

We unbuffer the output with *Unbuffer* (9). If an end of file block is required (10), this is written by, *Write End of File* (11). If a label is required (12), this is done by *Write Label* (13). The file is then removed from the output list (14), and we continue processing at (17).

If the file is an open input file not used for rollback (6)–(8), then we unbuffer it using the routine, *Unbuffer* (9).

Input files are checked at (16) to see if a rewind is required. Both input and output are checked at (17) to see if a history record should be printed. If so, this is done by the *Print History* routine (18). All files are checked possibly a second time for rewind (19), and if this is to be done, the proper word is set up in the accumulator so that a control command can be given to the unit for rewind (20). A nondata command is given in (21) which performs a rewind or a disconnect or both, if this is required. Next we check to see if this file must be unloaded (22). If so, we set the indications (23) and print dismount instructions to the operator (24). Other appropriate dynamic control bits are reset (25) before exciting.

Close Internal

The flow chart, Fig. 9.8.3, shows the few steps required to perform this action. *Close Internal* relies on *Release* (1) which truncates output buffers and disconnects input buffers, as described in Section 10.7.

All that remains is simple accounting. The count of buffers in use in the file activity block is restored to 0 (2). All queues which this file may have used are updated to eliminate reference to this file (3). Finally, if permissible, the buffers are released to the pool. If not, their information is retained as required (4).

PROBLEMS

9.1   What functions does *IOCS* perform with respect to:
    (a) device management?
    (b) blocking and deblocking?
    (c) buffer management?
    (d) errors and exceptions?
    (e) file protection?
    (f) rollback?

9.2   What choices are there for where and when *IOCS* is supplied to the computer and coordinated with the program?

9.3   *IOCS* needs all these activity blocks: UAB, BAB, CAB, FAB and PAB. What is the purpose of each? How are they related? What programming system establishes each? What is the programmer's role in setting them up? Where are they found?

9.4   What are all the operations the programmer must do to establish a buffer pool?

9.5   Distinguish the three kinds of device designations: physical; machine; symbolic.

9.6   What is the task of *Preprocessor*?

9.7   What information is conveyed by the title of each of these cards; what additional information may or must they contain: $IOCS; $ACCT; $JOB; $FILE; $DATE; $LOAD; $RESTART; $SYSTEM.

9.8   Indicate the order (preferably by a precedence graph) in which $ cards are presented to the *Preprocessor*.

9.9   As in Fig. 9.3.2, show the makeup of a deck using IOCS which requires FLAP translation first but which does not contain any procedure oriented or machine language information.

9.10   What is the purpose of each of the *Preprocessors*: *Job*; *File*; *Assign*?

9.11   Give FLAP and IOCS commands to establish these pools:
(a) POOL1: 8 buffers of 50 words.
(b) POOL2: 10 buffers of 50 words.
(c) POOL3: 12 buffers of 50 words.
(d) POOL4: 15 buffers of 12 words.
(e) POOL5: 20 buffers of 12 words.

9.12   Give commands for the pools of problem 9.11 to make the following (not in same program):
(a) POOL1 of POOL1 and POOL2
(b) POOL2 of POOL1 and POOL2
(c) POOL3 of POOL1, POOL2 and POOL3
(d) POOL4 of POOL4 and POOL5
(e) POOL5 of POOL1 and POOL5

9.13   Characterize the three kinds of files: *full*, *reserve* and *internal*.

9.14   Consider these files:
           full: FRANK, FREDA, FRAN, FANNY
           internal: IDA, IRV, IZZY
           reserve: RITA, RALPH, RICKY, RANDY
(a) Attach FRANK to POOL1.
(b) Attach all the reserve files to POOL2.
(c) Attach all *internal* and reserve files to POOL3.
(d) Attach all files to POOL1.
(e) Attach FRAN, FANNY, IRV, RITA and RALPH to POOL2.
Make lists, name and use them.

9.15   Under what conditions can
(a) pools be *joined*?
(b) buffers be *attached*?

9.16   What linked manipulations are performed to
(a) establish a pool?
(b) *join* two pools?
(c) *attach* buffers?

9.17   What is the total effect accomplished by *Open* and *Close*?

9.18   Why doesn't *Attach* automatically open a file?

9.19   How do these differ: *Close*; *Shut*; *Close Internal*?

10

IOCS OPERATING COMMANDS

10.1   COMMANDS AND SUBCOMMANDS

Compound Commands

The purpose of *IOCS* is to make it simple for the user to request complicated IO processing routines. The basis of this facility is to enable the user to request processing in terms of a record so that his thinking can be application oriented rather than machine oriented.

Further, he can designate separate operations for the different fields that make up the record, not blocks or words, so that he can be application oriented.

Finally, deviations from normal which may occur as his request is being satisfied are automatically handled by the system. The user decides beforehand what measures are to be taken in the case of each eventuality.

In reading or writing a tape, either the *end of tape* or the *end of file* may present itself. We do not want to continue either reading or writing if there is no more tape left. A number of things must be done when this situation is detected. Usually these functions are uniform for all files concerned. They are referred to as an *end of tape* routine.

Usually the operator is notified and a reel is replaced. However, many deviations from such a procedure are possible and, in fact, necessary. When an alternate tape unit is supplied, an automatic transfer to this tape unit should be performed; when the file is known to occupy less than a complete reel of tape, a retry of some kind should be attempted; and so forth. *IOCS* provides different alternatives for different files and with all the flexibility that the user could desire.

Two other conditions for which provisions are made are the *end of buffer* condition and *parity error*. If a buffer is exhausted before processing of a record is completed, automatic exit to a specified routine can be made. Similarly, if a parity check fails, an error routine may rescue us from the situation.

Command Components

In the discussion of compound commands which follows, we refer to the FLAP IOCS system which is modeled after the IBM 7090 IOCS system. It is capable of quite a number of complex functions, many of which are not present in simpler IOCS's. Comprehension of the most extensive case facilitates understanding of the less complex cases.

The format of the compound command found in Fig. 10.1.1 consists of one main part followed by a number of subparts. The main part consists of the subroutine call, GET, with a function, either READ or WRITE and a parameter list. Following the main command is a list of subcommands which designate operations on separate fields of the record.

Function in Fig. 10.1.1 has a number of parameters associated with it. The *function* is either READ or WRITE, operations performed with respect to the outside world. READ inputs information from cards or tape or other input devices; WRITE outputs information to tape or printer or other output devices.

The explanation of the *buffer switch* entry is left for later in this chapter.

The *file end exit* is the name of a subroutine in the user's program. If the *end of file* should occur on either READ or WRITE, $\mathscr{IOCS}$ jumps to the location specified by the symbolic name of this parameter in the parameter list.

The *error exit* is also the name of a subroutine to which $\mathscr{IOCS}$ returns when an error is detected in incoming or reread information.

```
label     GET     function, file name, buffer switch, file end exit, error exit
label     I       subcommand
label     I       subcommand
                  . . .
label     I       tubcommand
```

function:	READ or WRITE
buffer switch:	0 *or* entry name
file and exit:	name
error exit:	name
subcommand:	count option, proceed option, locate option, start address, number of words
count option:	COUNT *or* BLOCK *or* FINISH *or* JUMP
proceed option:	*blank or* END *or* TRUNCATE
locate option:	LOCATE *or blank*
start address:	name
number of words:	number

FIGURE 10.1.1. Format of the compound $\mathscr{IOCS}$ command.

When the last command has been processed, $\mathscr{IOCS}$ returns to the step in the user's program from whence control came.

SUBCOMMANDS

The subcommand contains:

- A *count option* for how or if counting is to be done.
- A *proceed option* indicating if more subcommands follow.
- A *locate option*. This is discussed in detail by example in Section 10.2.
- A *start address* indicating the symbolic address in memory which is a source or destination of information for the subcommand.
- *Number of words* indicates how many words are manipulated.

The COUNT Option

Three possibilities for the *count* option are COUNT *or* BLOCK *or* FINISH. COUNT requests information transmittal between buffer and *number of words* cells starting at *start address*. In Fig. 10.1.2 the subcommand:

$$\text{I} \quad \text{COUNT, , HARRY, 15} \qquad\qquad (10.1.1)$$

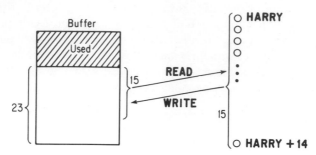

FIGURE 10.1.2. Performance of one of the subcommands:

	I	COUNT, END, , HARRY
or	I	FINISH, END, , HARRY, 15

is given. There are twenty-three words left in the buffer. For READ the next fifteen words are transmitted from the buffer to symbolic locations, HARRY to HARRY + 14. For WRITE fifteen words are transmitted from the cells, HARRY to HARRY + 14, to the fifteen spaces in the buffer. A place marker is advanced so that new subcommands will start in the buffer where *this* subcommand has left off.

If the buffer does not contain enough spaces to satisfy the subcommand, the buffer is used up and we continue with the next buffer in the chain, as illustrated in Fig. 10.1.3. When the subcommand:

$$\text{I} \qquad \text{COUNT, , JOE, 15} \qquad\qquad (10.1.2)$$

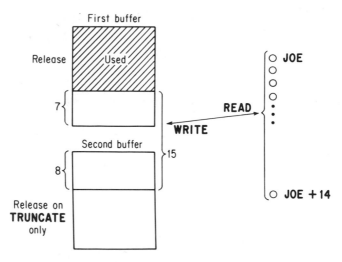

FIGURE 10.1.3. Performance of the subcommand:

I   COUNT, END, , JOE, 15

where the available words in the current buffer is less than *number*.

is given, there are only seven words left in the first buffer. These seven words are used and the buffer is immediately released. Eight words of the next buffer are now used to complete the subcommand. For READ we *take* information; in the case of WRITE we *put* information.

If the number of words requested just completes a buffer, the buffer is used and released, but a new one is not started.

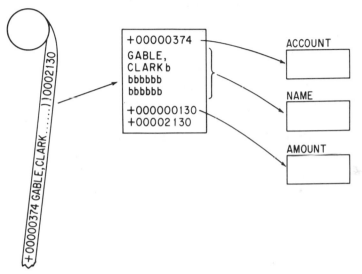

FIGURE 10.1.4. How COUNT gets information from magnetic tape into the proper cells in memory for the program.

Example of COUNT

An incoming file of records named ACTIVE is used for a savings account application where one record indicates each transaction. The record has three fields:

- The account number consists of seven digits (one word).
- Twenty characters are allocated for the name of the individual who holds the account (four words).
- Eight digits and a sign are allotted to indicate the amount deposited or withdrawn (one word).

$\mathscr{IOCS}$ enters an ACTIVE record into a buffer block, as shown in Fig. 10.1.4. From there an IO command together with subcommands distribute the information to the proper words in memory:

- The account number goes to ACCNT.
- The depositor's name goes to NAME.
- The amount deposited or withdrawn goes to AMNT.

NAME has four words associated with it so that it can hold the twenty characters in the name field; the other two locations require a single word each.

One $\mathscr{IOCS}$ command with three subcommands gets the information from the ACTIVE file into the proper locations in memory. This includes all the buffer management, automatic readin and buffering, and automatic call of exception routines. It is done by the sequence:

```
IN      GET     READ, ACTIVE, , WINDUP, MISTAKE
        I       COUNT, , ACCNT, 1
        I       COUNT, , NAME, 4
        I       COUNT, END, AMNT, 1              (10.1.3)
```

Let us dissect the command in (10.1.3):

IN is a label used solely to distinguish the occurrence of this command in the rest of the program.

READ is the function

GET is the subroutine call to IOCS.

ACTIVE is the name of the file.

Blank occurs because the *end of buffer* switch is not set—no change is made in processing procedure when the end of the buffer is reached.

WINDUP is the name of the *file end exit* routine.

MISTAKE is the name of the *error exit* routine.

The subcommands are self-explanatory.

Other Count Options

BLOCK

When *count option* is BLOCK, the remainder of the block is transmitted whether some of the block has been used already or whether it is a fresh block. For BLOCK, *number* is left blank because no reference is made to it. At the completion of the subcommand, the number of words transmitted is found at *number*.

Figure 10.1.5 illustrates the use of this option. The buffer size associated with the figure is apparently 21. This particular block has not been referred to yet. The subcommand illustrated is:

```
I       BLOCK, END, JIM, blank              (10.1.4)
```

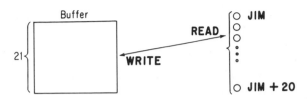

FIGURE 10.1.5. Performance of the subcommand:

| BLOCK, END,   , JIM,

where the present buffer is unused. The subcommand is changed to:

| BLOCK, END,   , JIM, 21

The 21 words of the block are transmitted between the buffer containing them and the locations JIM through JIM + 20. Then the subcommand appears as though it had been assembled from:

$$| \qquad \text{BLOCK, END, } \text{ , JIM, 21} \qquad\qquad (10.1.5)$$

In Fig. 10.1.6 we find a buffer of 21 words, seven of which have been used by a previous subcommand. When we give the subcommand:

$$| \qquad \text{BLOCK, END, } \text{ , KATHY, } \textit{blank} \qquad (10.1.6)$$

the remaining 14 words in the buffer are transmitted to the locations KATHY through KATHY + 13, and the subcommand winds up in memory as though it had been written from:

$$| \qquad \text{BLOCK, END, } \text{ , KATHY, 14} \qquad\qquad (10.1.7)$$

FINISH (READ)

The action of this option depends upon whether the *number of words* is less than or greater than the number of words left in the buffer when the subcommand is examined. As long as there are more words in the buffer than are requested in the subcommand, the action is exactly the same as for the COUNT option illustrated in Fig. 10.1.2.

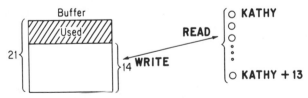

FIGURE 10.1.6. Performance of the subcommand:

| BLOCK, END,   , KATHY,

where the buffer of 21 words has 7 of these used. The subcommand is changed to:

| BLOCK, END,   , KATHY, 14

When more words are requested than remain in the buffer, the situation of Fig. 10.1.7 arises. Here we give the command:

$$\text{I} \quad \text{FINISH, END,} \quad \text{, LOIS, 15} \qquad\qquad (10.1.8)$$

There are only six words left in the buffer. These six words are transmitted to LOIS through LOIS + 5; *number of words* is not changed, for this would alter the subcommand and perform something different the next time the command was used. The buffer which is now exhausted is released. This

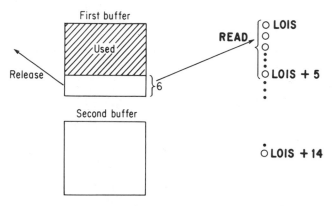

FIGURE 10.1.7. Performance of the subcommand for READ of:
$$\text{I} \quad \text{FINISH, END,} \quad \text{, LOIS, 15}$$
where the first buffer does not have enough unused words left.

implies making another input request of the device assigned to this file. Of course, we would like to know how many words have been transmitted, and this is recorded by means of a history which is kept in the active registers and is discussed in Section 10.2.

FINISH (WRITE)

When the *number of words* is less than those remaining in the buffer, the subcommand is performed, as in Fig. 10.1.2. If there is insufficient space in the buffer, the situation of Fig. 10.1.8 occurs. There is room for six more words in the buffer and the subcommand:

$$\text{I} \quad \text{FINISH, END,} \quad \text{, MARY, 15} \qquad\qquad (10.1.9)$$

is encountered. The old buffer is released since there is not enough room in it. This means that it is passed over to the waiting list for the device assigned to this file to eventually be written out and have the buffer returned to the pool. This subcommand is completed when the information from MARY through MARY + 15 is put into the next free buffer assigned to this file, as shown in the figure.

JUMP

The format of this subcommand is:

| JUMP, name   (10.1.10)

Here *name* refers to the label of another list of subcommands. This is useful when two $\mathcal{JOCS}$ commands refer to the same subcommand list or when

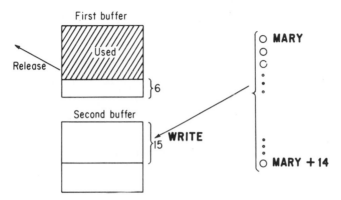

FIGURE 10.1.8. Performance of the subcommand for WRITE of:
| FINISH, END,   , MARY, 15
where the first buffer does not have enough empty space left.

their subcommand list is duplicated in part. JUMP is a communication to $\mathcal{JOCS}$ to get the next subcommand at the location given in *name*. This call:

```
IN        GET    READ, ACTIVE, , WINDUP, MISTAKE
          |      COUNT, , ACCT, 1
          |      COUNT, , NAME, 4
          |      JUMP, NEWSUB
                     . . .
NEWSUB    |      COUNT, END, AMNT, 1              (10.1.11)
```

performs the same job as the $\mathcal{JOCS}$ command associated with Fig. 10.1.4. For some reason we wish to disassociate the last subcommand from the rest of the list.

RECORD

This is *not* a FLAP $\mathcal{JOCS}$ subcommand count option. It would be used in the $\mathcal{JOCS}$ of a variable word length or character oriented computer. For the character oriented computer, words are not of fixed size; their end is usually indicated by a word mark. Therefore, the COUNT option should suffice for this type of computer. Sometimes an *end of record* mark is also available in the character oriented computer. In this case it would be easy to provide a subcommand built around this *end of record* mark. The commands of the $\mathcal{IOCS}$ for the IBM 7070 and for the RCA 301 (called the File Control Processor instead of IOCS) contain a RECORD type of command.

10.2   MORE ABOUT COMMANDS

Proceed Option

The *proceed* option, in Fig. 10.1.1, can be one of three things: *blank*, END, TRUNCATE.

BLANK

This simply indicates that this is *not* the last in a sequence of subcommands.

END

This is the *last* in the sequence of subcommands. The choice of these two options allows the subcommand itself to indicate when the sequence of subcommands terminates. An alternative to this is to have the command incorporate a number telling $\mathcal{IOCS}$ how many subcommands are in the sequence. It could then monitor the sequence and, when the proper number of subcommands have been used, return to the user's program.

The difficulty comes when we incorporate JUMP. This requests that a new list of subcommands be used. This list may be shared by another list. How many commands are there in the combined initial and final lists? It becomes encumbent upon the programmer to know this.

When the *proceed* option is available, the JUMP is included without any difficulty. JUMP requests that we continue examining subcommands in the location indicated by the JUMP. The new subcommand list may in turn refer to another subcommand list using JUMP. When several JUMP's are used, return is made, after a subcommand containing END, to the next command in the user's program following the *first* JUMP, the one in the original sequence. There is no longer a need to specify the number of commands in a sequence.

TRUNCATE

TRUNCATE indicates that this is the last in the subcommand sequence and that the last buffer used is released regardless of the number of words that are still available in it. In the case of READ, any unused words are lost and the buffer is released to the pool. For a WRITE command, as many as have been placed in the buffer are written out, and the buffer is then released to pool.

Let us see how TRUNCATE would work with respect to Figs. 10.1.2 and 10.1.3. We give the command,

$$\text{I} \qquad \text{COUNT, TRUNCATE, HARRY, 15} \qquad\qquad (10.2.1)$$

There are twenty-three words left in the buffer of Fig. 10.1.2, and transmission occurs between the designated cells in memory and the first fifteen of the twenty-three words left in the buffer. Since TRUNCATE is requested, the buffer is released despite the remaining eight unused words. For any other option, this buffer would be retained until it was completely used.

In Fig. 10.1.3 for (10.2.1) fifteen words are transmitted between memory and *two* buffers. There is not enough room in the first buffer! When transmission is complete, the first buffer is released. The second buffer is now also released because TRUNCATE is indicated.

Locate Option

The *locate* option can be either *blank* or LOCATE. For *blank* this is a transmission subcommand and is performed as described earlier. The LOCATE subcommand is used to locate information without transmission. The located information is available for use by the user's program by indirect addressing, or addresses may be entered directly into the user's program by $\mathcal{IOCS}$ when an indirect option is called for in the subcommand, as will be explained.

The function of LOCATE is therefore to:

- find the *actual* address of fields within a buffer
- make these field addresses available to other processing commands
- skip fields where information is not required

LOCATE may be applied to any combination of *count* and *proceed* options regardless of the starting address and number of words involved. Further, indirect addressing may be specified.

COUNT, LOCATE

This subcommand functions similarly for both READ or WRITE. The subcommand inserts the starting address of the next available word in the buffer into *address* of the subcommand and then counts off the number of words specified in *number* in the subcommand to advance the buffer pointer.

Examine the first two subcommands in Fig. 10.2.1; they are:

$$\text{JOE} \quad | \quad \text{COUNT, , LOCATE, , 3} \qquad (10.2.2)$$

$$| \quad \text{COUNT, , LOCATE, , 7} \qquad (10.2.3)$$

Notice in the figure that the buffer starts at some address which we symbolically designate as PAUL. Notice also that the first five words between locations PAUL and PAUL + 4 in the buffer have already been used, and the BAB pointer indicates PAUL + 5. When (10.2.2) is encountered,

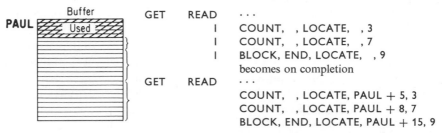

FIGURE 10.2.1. How LOCATE is used to locate information in a buffer and enter its position into the subcommand proper.

PAUL + 5 is entered into its address portion. The pointer is automatically advanced to PAUL + 8. When (10.2.3) is encountered, the new portion of the pointer PAUL + 8 is entered into the address portion of the command word and the pointer again advanced, this time by seven positions. The two subcommands then appear as:

$$\text{JOE} \quad | \quad \text{COUNT, , LOCATE, PAUL + 5, 3} \qquad (10.2.4)$$

$$| \quad \text{COUNT, , LOCATE, PAUL + 8, 7} \qquad (10.2.5)$$

USE

Having the address of located information in the subcommand word makes it immediately available to the program by indirect addressing. To place in the accumulator the first word of the field found in (10.2.5), we use a transfer command which indirectly addresses that subcommand. Thus:

$$\text{XMA,I} \quad \text{JOE + 1:} \quad \text{(PAUL + 8)} \rightarrow \text{A} \qquad (10.2.6)$$

(10.2.6) indirectly addresses JOE + 1 in the address portion of which $\mathscr{IOCS}$ has placed PAUL + 8. The computer does not know and does not care that the cell being addressed is part of $\mathscr{IOCS}$ reference. It simply extracts the address portion of whatever is at JOE + 1 and works with it. It is led to the proper location in the buffer, PAUL + 8, and this word winds up in the accumulator.

According to the design of $\mathscr{JOCS}$, it may or may not be possible to locate with a single command words that lie in two buffers. To reduce the bookkeeping task of our $\mathscr{JOCS}$, we do not require it to locate words in more than one buffer.

The first time we use LOCATE, *address* is blank; after the first use, the subcommand at JOE + 1 contains PAUL + 8. What happens the *next* time we go down the subcommand list? Well, any time the COUNT, LOCATE option is used, *address* is ignored. Hence the next time around we might find at the address portion of JOE + 1, SAM + 3, which has replaced PAUL + 8.

Indirect Locate and Count

Indirect addressing used *within* a subcommand permits us to place the location of the next available word in the buffer within the address portion of a command of our choice. A command of this kind appears as:

$$\text{I,I} \quad \text{COUNT, proceed, LOCATE, address, number} \quad (10.2.7)$$

The result of this command is to place the address of the first available word in the buffer at *address*.

Suppose that the following two subcommands are given in connection with the buffer situation shown in Fig. 10.2.1:

$$\text{JOE} \quad \text{I,I} \quad \text{COUNT, , LOCATE, TOM, 3} \quad (10.2.8)$$

$$\text{I,I} \quad \text{COUNT, , LOCATE, VIC, 7} \quad (10.2.9)$$

After these subcommands are performed, they remain unchanged. Only the destination locations TOM and VIC are changed. Thus suppose that before we encountered the subcommand sequence we had in the user's program the following FLAP commands equivalents:

$$\text{TOM} \quad \text{XMA} \quad \text{ANYONE} \quad (10.2.10)$$
$$\cdots$$
$$\text{VIC} \quad \text{ADD,3} \quad \text{ANYONE} \quad (10.2.11)$$

After (10.2.8) and (10.2.9) are performed, (10.2.10) and (10.2.11) appear as:

$$\text{TOM} \quad \text{XMA} \quad \text{PAUL} + 5 \quad (10.2.12)$$
$$\cdots$$
$$\text{VIC} \quad \text{ADD,3} \quad \text{PAUL} + 8 \quad (10.2.13)$$

After a LOCATE subcommand is performed, even if a buffer is completely used it must be held and not released so that the user's program may have access to the words which have just been located.

BLOCK, LOCATE

This subcommand is used to locate the next available word in the block and determine how many words are left in the block. It has a form:

| BLOCK, proceed, LOCATE   (10.2.14)

Notice that *address* and *number* are absent; these will be filled in when the subcommand is executed.

EXAMPLE

Examine the last subcommand in the sequence of Fig. 10.2.1:

| BLOCK, END, LOCATE   (10.2.15)

Fifteen words in the buffer have been located by previous commands. The address of the next available word is PAUL + 15, which will be entered into *address* in (10.2.15). Since there are just nine unused words left in the block, 9 is placed in *number*. Then (10.2.15) appears as:

| BLOCK, END, LOCATE, PAUL + 15, 9   (10.2.16)

Since this READ command may be entered several times within the program, we expect that *address* and *number* in (10.2.15) have trash left in them from before. This is permissible; the execution of the subcommand writes over this information.

For a LOCATE subcommand the buffer must be held until the next READ or WRITE is given, at which point it is released.

BLOCK, LOCATE with WRITE

For BLOCK, LOCATE in a WRITE command, a number is included in *number*. Two cases arise: there may be more than *number* available words; there may not be enough available words.

When there are enough words left in the buffer, the location of the first available word is entered into *address*, and *number* is left alone. At the next opportunity the buffer will be released for writeout. Thus for the case in Fig. 10.2.1, the subcommand:

| BLOCK, END, LOCATE, , 7   (10.2.17)

when in a list applying to a WRITE command, would be changed to;

| BLOCK, END, LOCATE, PAUL + 15, 7   (10.2.18)

The buffer would be held until the next command, at which point it would be written out. Of course, instead of 24 words written in the block, there would be only 22 words.

Suppose for Fig. 10.2.1 the following subcommand is given;

$$\text{I} \quad \text{BLOCK, END, LOCATE, , 17} \qquad (10.2.19)$$

There are only 9 words left in the buffer. $\mathcal{IOCS}$ enters the location of the first available word, PAUL + 15, into *address* and keeps track of the number of words left in the buffer in the history record, discussed later. Since it is illegal to locate words in more than one buffer with a single subcommand, the *end of buffer* exit is taken and this $\mathcal{IOCS}$ command is terminated.

FINISH and LOCATE

This subcommand takes the form:

$$\text{I} \quad \text{FINISH, proceed, LOCATE, , number} \qquad (10.2.20)$$

It combines the properties of BLOCK and COUNT.

READ

The first available location in the buffer is entered at *address*. We then skip over *number* words. If the end of the buffer is reached before all these words have been skipped, then activity ceases. The number of words scanned is entered into the history record.

WRITE

If the requested number of words is available in the buffer, the address of the first available word in the buffer is entered at *address*. If not, this buffer is truncated and a new buffer is obtained. The address of the first word in the new buffer is entered at *address*. This subcommand is more useful if the available word pointer is not advanced automatically. This must be done by a separate subcommand.

Indirect Addressing

Indirect addressing can be done in two ways. The subcommand in $\mathcal{IOCS}$ can refer to information in the user's program if we make the addressing in the subcommands indirect, **outward indirection**.

On the other hand, it is possible for the user's program to have access to information obtained by $\mathscr{IOCS}$ and deposited in the subcommand sequence, **inward indirection**.

This applies to a subcommand in the form:

   I,I   count, proceed, LOCATE, address, number   (10.2.21)

When (10.2.21) is encountered, the address of the next available word in the buffer is placed at the *location* given by *address* instead of being placed within the subcommand field, *address*.

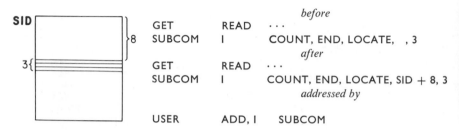

FIGURE 10.2.2. How a READ subcommand is addressed indirectly from without. In this way information found by LOCATE can be used by a source command.

The purpose of a locate command is to find information and make it available to the user through indirection. Suppose this sequence occurs;

SUBCOM   I   COUNT, proceed, LOCATE, address, number
                                                          (10.2.22)

                            · · ·

USER   ADD,I   SUBCOM   (10.2.23)

When $\mathscr{IOCS}$ executes SUBCOM, it leaves the address of the first available word in the buffer at *address*. This is the location desired by the user. Later in the program he gains access to the desired word in the buffer by addressing through *inward indirection* the subcommand where $\mathscr{IOCS}$ has placed the address. This is shown in Fig. 10.2.2. The command at USER addresses indirectly (because of the I following the command mnemonic) the address SUBCOM contained in the $\mathscr{IOCS}$ sequence. In executing USER the computer uses indirection and abstracts the address portion of the word at the cell labeled SUBCOM. This is *address*. The desired location in the buffer is pointed to by *address*. Eventually that quantity will be added to the accumulator.

History

After $\mathcal{IOCS}$ executes a subcommand in the command list, it leaves information about what it has done and for which there is insufficient room in the subcommand word in a convenient location. For the IBM 7090 IOCS, information is left in the accumulator. It could be left at a fixed word location but the accumulator seems a most convenient place to dump it.

This additional information provided by $\mathcal{IOCS}$ is called **history** (it is rather recent history, at most). Besides possible tags, it contains the following significant information:

- The **history address** is usually the address of the *next* available word in the buffer.
- The **history number** usually indicates the number of words remaining in the buffer.

End of Buffer

A provision is made in READ or WRITE for the eventuality that a buffer is exhausted during a subcommand. Space is left in the command for an *end of buffer* field. When this field is empty it calls for truncation of a buffer in transmission commands, as well as automatic transition to the next buffer. When the *end of buffer* contains a nonzero address, it is referred to when an attempt is made to exhaust the buffer during execution of the subcommand. In that case subcommand execution is inhibited and control is transferred to the address found at *end of block*. In other words, a subcommand that would exhaust the buffer is aborted, and a jump is made to *end of buffer*.

Of course, it is permissible to exactly exhaust a buffer for COUNT, since we have not violated the rule of trying to exhaust more than one buffer. In this case we proceed to the next subcommand. We truncate or hold the buffer according to whether a LOCATE subcommand has occurred previously within a subcommand sequence.

Notice the effect of *end of buffer* upon LOCATE: when *end of buffer* is 0, information is skipped; when it is not 0, information is located.

10.3   COMPLETE EXAMPLE

This section integrates the information we have obtained so far about IOCS by presenting an example which calls upon most of its commands. First we review superficially the aspects of IOCS which have been presented so far.

Review

𝒥𝒪𝒞𝒮 is capable of facilitating portions of problems which involve complex input and output manipulations.

COMPONENTS

- *Preprocessor*
- buffer management
- file management
- READ and WRITE commands
- frills (to come)

PREPROCESSOR

Control information is given to IOCS by control cards, specifically:

$IOCS	$DATE
$ACCT	$LOAD
$JOB	$RESTART
$FILE	$SYSTEM

BUFFERS, FILES

Buffers and files are managed by the following subroutine calls incorporated into the user's program:

POOL	OPEN
JOIN	CLOSE
ATTACH	

READ/WRITE

Most user directives to 𝒥𝒪𝒞𝒮 are given by these commands and their information-bearing fields, followed by a subcommand list detailing specific tasks.

Problem

This simple problem gives us a chance to employ the whole 𝒥𝒪𝒞𝒮 system together with some of the assembly procedures. We produce an output tape consisting of a number of predetermined blocks which becomes an input tape to be read back and checked. As each block is read back, it is written onto a new tape.

The first block written consists of numbers from 1 to 50; the second consists of numbers from 2 to 51; and so forth. One hundred blocks are written; the last contains words, each one consisting of a single number starting with 100 and ending with 149. Each block is on the file called INFO; each block contains 50 words.

Setup

To begin our program we set up pools and attach the file, as shown in Fig. 10.3. BEGIN calls for the $\mathscr{IOCS}$ routine $\mathscr{Pool}$. We fabricate PETER (the name of the pool) of 10 blocks of 50 words each. In the assembly program we reserve space for the pool. The collection of 602 words reserved

Label	Command	Addresses	Comments
BEGIN	GET	POOL, PETER, 10, 50,	
	GET	ATTACH, PETER, LISA, 3	
	GET	OPEN, FIRSTOUT	
LISA	NOOP	RES, 2, 3	⎫List of files to be opened
	NOOP	FIRSTOUT	⎬and closed
	NOOP	NEXTIN	⎪
	NOOP	NEXTOUT	⎭
FIRSTOUT	RSRV	12	⎫Blocks reserved for the
NEXTIN	RSRV	12	⎬file activity blocks
NEXTOUT	RSRV	12	⎭
PETER	RSRV	602	For buffers and BABs
	DUP	1, 50	⎧INFO consists of numbers
INFO	DEF	#	⎨from 1 thru 50
	XPN,1	100	⎩Set up to write 100 records
	GET	WRITE, FIRSTOUT, ,	
		MISTAKE, MISTAKE	
	I	BLOCK, END, , INFO, 50	
ALTER	XPN,2	50	⎰Set up to add 1 to each
	XMA,2	INFO	⎱word in the record
	ADD	=1	
	XAM,2	INFO	
	TDN,2	ALTER + 1	End of alteration
	TDN,1	INFO + 2	End of block write operation
	GET	CLOSE, FIRSTOUT, REWIND	End of first tape write
	GET	OPEN, LISA + 2, 2	
	GET	READ, NEXTIN, , WINDUP,	
		MISTAKE	
SUB	I	COUNT, , LOCATE, , 10	
	I	COUNT, , , CHECK + 7, 10	
	I	COUNT, , LOCATE, , 10	
	I	COUNT, , , CHECK + 17, 10	
	I	COUNT, END, LOCATE, , 10	
	ISN,4	CHECK	⎰Go to subroutine to check
			⎱the accuracy of the block
	GET	WRITE, NEXTOUT, ,	
		MISTAKE, MISTAKE	
	I, I	BLOCK, END, , SUB	
	UCJ	SUB − 1	
WINDUP	GET	CLOSE, LISA, 2	
	GET	IOCS	$\mathscr{IOCS}$ "end"

FIGURE 10.3. A FLAP program demonstrating the use of $\mathscr{IOCS}$.

is called PETER. We attach to PETER a list of files which have access to the pool, LISA, consisting of three files using GET   ATTACH at BEGIN + 1. The list called LISA is found at the top of the program and consists of four words. The first word indicates that the files are reserve files, that there are three files on the list, and that a maximum of two of them will be active at once. The names of the files then follow: FIRSTOUT, NEXTIN, NEXTOUT.

First we write the entire tape called FIRSTOUT. We open only FIRSTOUT by the command given at BEGIN + 2. To write the hundred blocks of information, we set up an index at INFO + 1, loop around, and write a block at a time. We then give the main WRITE command. It contains the file name, FIRSTOUT, and indication for error exits called MISTAKE. These exits are not provided in this program segment; we do not expect them to be used.

There is only one subcommand requesting that the block of 50 words called INFO be written. The loop at ALTER to ALTER + 4 adds 1 to each word in the block called INFO. After 100 blocks have been written we pop out of the loop at ALTER + 6. The first task is done, so we close the file called FIRSTOUT and rewind it.

The second task begins when we open the other two files, NEXTIN and NEXTOUT, by referring to LISA at LISA + 2, using GET   OPEN. Although FIRSTOUT and NEXTIN are different files, file cards are entered into 𝒫𝓇𝑒𝒻𝓇𝑜𝒸𝑒𝓈𝓈𝑜𝓇, for these files assigning the same tape unit to both. FIRSTOUT is an output file and NEXTIN is an input file on the same tape unit and, therefore, reads in the tape we have just written.

The command READ for the file NEXTIN, 10 words at a time is at SUB − 1; it contains an *end of file* exit, WINDUP. When NEXTIN has been totally read, 𝒥𝒪𝒞𝒮 goes to WINDUP.

SUBCOMMANDS

There are five subcommands for READ, one for every ten words in a block read. The second and fourth subcommands transfer information respectively to CHECK + 7 and CHECK + 17. These are locations in a check routine. This routine is not included in our program, but an exit to it is found at SUB + 5.

In other words, after locating the five sets of ten words in the block being examined and after transferring two of these sets into the check routine, we perform a return jump to that subroutine. The return from that subroutine is at SUB + 6.

We now write out the tape called NEXTOUT. We know the location of the block to be written out: it is contained at *address* of the subcommand at SUB. By indirectly addressing this subcommand we refer to the beginning of the desired buffer. WRITE at SUB + 6 contains a BLOCK subcommand at SUB + 7 which writes out the entire buffer using indirect addressing.

After writing out a block, we return unconditionally to the READ command at SUB − 1. We will get out of this loop when an *end of file* on the tape takes us to the *end of file* exit, WINDUP.

COMPLETION

We have finished the job except for closing out the program and releasing the computer to the next job. This is done at WINDUP. CLOSE requests $\mathcal{IOCS}$ to close the list of files at LISA. Although there are three file names on that list, only two of the files indicated are open, and this should be communicated to $\mathcal{IOCS}$.

The program is now complete and would normally contain STOP. However, we do not wish the computer to stop; we wish $\mathcal{IOCS}$ to call in the next job. This is done by the subroutine request to get $\mathcal{IOCS}$. This turns control over to the $\mathcal{IOCS}$ $\mathcal{Preprocessor}$ which reads in the next control card. In this way the new job, if there is one, can be loaded in and performance initiated.

Reservations

Let us turn to the reservations shown at the top of the program. Although it could be placed at the end, it is more easily available to the assembler if it is encountered first. The list of files is in the format required by $\mathcal{IOCS}$ and is referred to as LISA. Twelve words are assigned to each file to make up the file activity block. Finally, the pool is named PETER and 602 words are reserved for it.

A DUP pseudo creates the words which make up the record to be transcribed. The main block, called INFO, is made up of words which contain the numbers in order from 1 to 50. DUP requests that the one definition command, DEF, be repeated fifty times. The DEF command has in its address portion the symbol #, which indicates that each time the command is repeated, the next successive integer replaces the symbol #.

10.4   READ/WRITE ACTIVITY

Symbol Convention

This section discusses what happens in a READ or WRITE command when any given subcommand request is made. For brevity a symbology is illustrated in Fig. 10.4.1. Here the buffer associated with the *current* subcommand is displayed as it appears after the previous subcommand is performed. A number of words of this buffer have been used; the buffer pointer has been moved ahead to point to the word, B. Words preceding B in the buffer have either been transmitted, skipped or located. There are a words left in the s word buffer. Hence the beginning of the partially used buffer is at location $B - s + a$.

The buffer activity block contains two words. The first word contains:

- a pointer to the next BAB at $S - 2$
- a pointer to the next available word in this buffer at location B
- the number of available words remaining in the buffer, a.

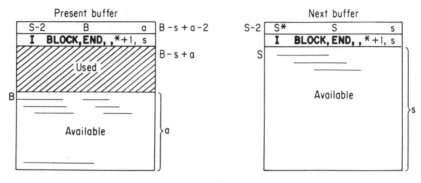

FIGURE 10.4.1. Diagram of the presently attached buffer and the one which will be used next in order to visualize the meaning of the symbols used in describing the history record, etc. The subcommand takes the form:

I   count, proceed, locate, A, n

The second BAB word is an $\mathcal{IOCS}$ subcommand for emptying the buffer.

The useful part of the next buffer starts at location S. It too contains s words. Its buffer activity block starts at $S - 2$. It contains a link address to the next buffer in the chain, $S*$. It also contains the address of the next available word, which is S, and shows that there are s available words (all) since the buffer is totally unused.

For READ, *next* buffer means next on the *take* chain; for WRITE, it is the next buffer to be *filled*. Of course, before it is brought into use, one must be withdrawn from the buffer pool.

The subcommand that we consider contains *address*, which we call A, and *number*, which we call n, to facilitate the forthcoming discussion.

Activity Completion

A subcommand is executed or ignored according to the present buffer condition and the *end of buffer* indication, as well as exception conditions which arise. If there is an *end of buffer* indication in the command, insufficient room in a buffer may cause an *end of buffer* exit to be taken instead of the command executed. If exception conditions arise, the subcommand is not executed at all. This is discussed later under "History."

What is done by the subcommand when it is executed is also dependent upon the condition of the buffer. Some subcommands, upon execution, have new information inserted into *address* and *number*.

Subcommand Performance

Subcommand performance is summarized in the table of Fig. 10.4.2. The rationale for each decision found there is now presented.

WORDS ADVANCED

When FINISH and LOCATE is part of WRITE, the *next word* pointer is not advanced; this is the only such case. The pointer is advanced by the

Variable	*Value*	*Conditions*
words advanced	0	WRITE & FINISH & LOCATE
	a	BLOCK & $n > a$ $\lor$
		FINISH & READ & $n > a$ $\lor$
		LOCATE & EoB $\neq$ 0 & $n > a$ & words adv $\neq$ 0
	n	otherwise
buffers released	both	COUNT & TRUNCATE & $n > a$
	first	COUNT & TRUNCATE & $n \leqslant a$ $\lor$
		BLOCK $\lor$
		WRITE & FINISH & $n > a$ $\lor$
		COUNT & $n > a$
	none	otherwise
release to hold	yes	EoB $\neq$ 0 & *released*
	no	otherwise
conditional hold	yes	*hold* & $\overline{\text{LOCATE}}$
	no	otherwise
EoB exit	jump	COUNT & LOCATE & $n > a$ & EoB $\neq$ 0
	cont.	otherwise
change number		
to $c =$	a	READ & BLOCK
	n	LOCATE & $\overline{\text{READ & BLOCK}}$
	don't	otherwise
change address		
to $C =$	S	COUNT & LOCATE & $n > a$ & EoB $= 0$ $\lor$
		WRITE & FINISH & LOCATE
	B	COUNT & $\overline{\text{S}}$
	don't	otherwise

FIGURE 10.4.2. Values of subcommand and command variables and action for prevailing conditions and captions.

number of available words only when n is greater than a or for the sub-command options in the figure. Usually the pointer is advanced by n.

When COUNT and TRUNCATE are specified and the number of available words is insufficient, both the present and the next buffer are released. In some cases only one buffer is released, as shown in the figure, but usually none is released.

Buffers that are released may be held if the end of buffer switch is nonzero. This means they are available to the main program until the next READ or WRITE, when they will either be returned to the pool or released for output, respectively. Although the present subcommand may not require it, another subcommand such as a hold command in the subcommand list would override the release and require that the buffer be held.

Subcommand Change

The conditions for which the subcommand *address* and *number* are changed are summarized in Fig. 10.4.2. The new *number*, noted as C, is a for a BLOCK subcommand in a READ sequence. It is made to equal n for all LOCATE subcommands except those for which a is entered. Otherwise, no change is made.

The new *address*, noted as C, is S for the subcommands shown. For the skip option when insufficient words are available in the buffer, a new buffer is started and, since the old buffer cannot be referenced any longer, the first word in the new buffer is recorded in the subcommand. This holds for FINISH and LOCATE with WRITE where the address, S, of the new buffer appears in the new subcommand.

For COUNT not covered by the preceding cases, the original starting point, B, is recorded.

Not enough information is available from the subcommand even when a change is made in it by *IOCS*. Sometimes the main program must know more, and further information can be furnished it by a history record. The

IBM 7090 IOCS uses the accumulator and the multiplier registers to store this information for the main program. Normally stored there are the location to which the pointer points after execution of the subcommand and the number of words then available in the buffer.

EXCEPTIONS

Sometimes a normal exit (return to the main program at the next step) is not taken at the end of a subcommand sequence. The most frequent exception is when the end of buffer is encountered and the end of buffer switch within the command is nonzero. This requires that $\mathscr{IOCS}$ return control to the main program at the symbolic address contained in the READ/WRITE command.

In a READ command other eventualities may arise. Most usual is the end of file exit which is encountered at the completion of a run. When the file is exhausted this exception exit is taken. During reading, several checks are made to assure the validity of information presented to the system. The first of these is the **block sequence check**, for which each block read into the system is numbered consecutively. When the expected number does not arrive, a *block sequence error* is indicated. A **check sum** is possible when an extra word is provided in a block wherein each bit is the logical sum of the corresponding bit position contents for all the words in the block. $\mathscr{IOCS}$ makes a similar sum and compares it against the sum that was read in. If they do not agree, a *check sum error* is indicated. Furthermore, the parity error is possible, but this is usually handled by $\mathscr{IOCS}$ before the block is made available to the READ command.

EXCEPTION RECORDING

$\mathscr{IOCS}$ may provide in the history record an indication of the following items when an exception arises:

- location of subcommand during whose execution the error arose
- command location
- error type
- expected next word out from present buffer

Normal History Record

When a subcommand has been executed without an exception exit, the history record contains an address and a number, given by the table in Fig. 10.4.3.

It should prove an interesting exercise to the reader to see if he understands the subcommand structure well enough to determine the values in the figure from the nature of the command and the conditions shown on the right.

Variable	Value	Conditions
history address†	$C + n$	READ & FINISH & n a $\lor$
		WRITE & BLOCK & n $>$ a $\lor$
		COUNT & LOCATE & n $>$ a & EoB $\neq$ 0
	$C + n - a$	COUNT & LOCATE & n $>$ a & EoB $=$ 0
	$C + c$	otherwise
history number	0	BLOCK & READ $\lor$
		WRITE & BLOCK & n $>$ a $\lor$
		READ & FINISH & n $>$ a $\lor$
		COUNT & LOCATE & EoB $\neq$ 0 & n $>$ a
	s	WRITE & FINISH & LOCATE & n $>$ a
	a	WRITE & FINISH & LOCATE & n $\leq$ a
	$s - n$	WRITE & FINISH & n $>$ a
	$s - n - a$	COUNT & n $>$ a & $\bar{0}$
	$a - n$	otherwise

FIGURE 10.4.3. Values of the history number and address for various subcommands and conditions.

† C is the new command address if changed, or else B. c is the new command number.

Assembly of an $\mathscr{IOCS}$ READ/WRITE Command

Figure 10.4.4 shows a typical READ sequence presented to the assembler. At the bottom of the figure the translation provided by the assembler is shown.

We find labels on the left side of the original command for our convenience to keep track of what happens to the command. Notice that the quasi, GET, is used to call in the subroutine. READIN is the name of the subroutine. The other names which follow on the top line are symbolic addresses which will be replaced by the assembler as a calling sequence. The next lines contain subcommands. Each of these subcommands is replaced by the assembler, as discussed later.

FLAP METHOD

Our method is to replace GET by JSN whose address is supplied by the assembler in the SR jump table. This gets us to the READ subroutine using index 4.

For each symbolic address which follows within the subroutine call, a word is provided in the calling sequence. The symbolic address is replaced by the location assigned by the assembler to the symbol. This is shown in Fig. 10.4.4 by the bracketed names corresponding to each parameter in the READ subroutine call.

Our assembler is capable of translating the subcommand. It creates a code which reflects each one of the three options: *count*, *proceed* and *locate*. Only a couple of bits are required for each so that a code field of six bits is sufficient to inform IOCS of the subcommand options.

```
READIN    GET    READ, PAYMASTER, , FILEND, ERR
FIELD1    I      COUNT, PROCEED, , INMASTR, 10
FIELD2    I      COUNT, PROCEED, , INMASTR + 10, , 5
FIELD3    I      BLOCK, END, , , OTHER
```

becomes

```
[READIN]      JSN,   4  [Jump vector for READ]
              0         [PAYMASTER]
              0         0
              0         [FILEND]
              0         [ERR]
[FIELD1]      code      [INMASTER]  10
[FIELD2]      code      [INMASTR + 10]  5
[FIELD3]      code      [OTHER]
```

FIGURE 10.4.4. The assembler takes the $\mathcal{IOCS}$ coding above and converts it into machine language as though it were the source program segment in the lower section of the diagram.

The subcommand symbolic address is looked up in the symbol table and replaced by the assigned numerical address. *Number* in the subcommand is translated into binary (or decimal for some computers). Each assembly language subcommand is thus replaced by one machine language word by FLAP. The labels associated with the subcommands are now associated with their translation.

The IBM 7090 version of IOCS uses a direct jump to the subroutine instead of using its equivalent of the GET quasi. To specify READ it uses JSN,4   READ. (In FAP this turns out to be TSX   READ, 4.) Hence, every time $\mathcal{IOCS}$ is used, a jump vector has to be entered manually by the programmer. He inserts an assembly language equivalence table in his program which contains an entry for READ, such as;

$$\text{READ} \qquad \text{EQU} \qquad \text{IOCS} + 14 \qquad\qquad (10.4.1)$$

10.5   READ/WRITE COMMAND SETUP

READ/WRITE Command Handling

There are a great many things to be done in connection with READ and WRITE, hereafter abbreviated RW. Here is a list:

- setup
- analysis of the command
- performance of the subcommands including saving of buffers and transmitting of information
- counting and accounting
- storing of information in the subcommands
- posting of history information
- completion of subcommand and command activity
- reinitiation of fill and empty activity associated with IO devices
- other buffer manipulation.

PROCEDURE

The procedure of the discussion is to present in the remainder of this section the following routines:

- *RW Command*—this is a setup routine.
- *Request IO*—this is a routine called for by RW command.
- *RW Start*—this routine begins the analysis of the subcommands.

In the next section we continue the discussion of other routines called upon by the RW sequence:

- *RW Analyze* completes the analysis of subcommands and makes up the history record.
- *RW End* does the performance of the subcommand and provides an exit from the RW over-all routine.
- *Request Read* is a subroutine used by *RW End* and also by at least one other routine of *IOCS*.

RW Command

This routine, flow-charted in Fig. 10.5.1, begins by saving register information (1). We then check to determine whether this is READ or WRITE (2) and whether it is legal (3), (4). If there is something wrong with the command or the subcommand, an error exit is taken (5) and return is made to the program (6). For a legal READ the pool pointer is found (7). If a buffer was given up on the last READ (8) and if a buffer is available (9), get

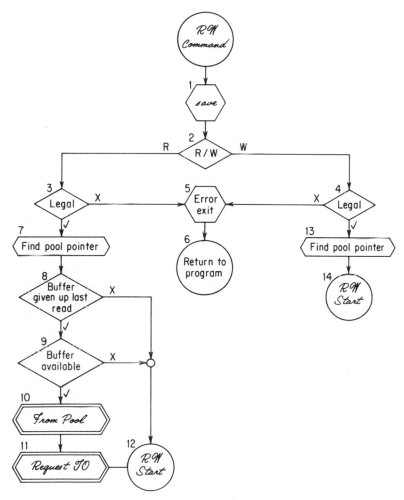

FIGURE 10.5.1. *RW Command* setup.

one from the pool using *From Pool* (10) and tack the buffer on the *request* chain using *Request IO*.

When a buffer is still connected or when there is no buffer connected *and* none available for assignment (9), enter *RW Start* immediately.

For WRITE, find the pool pointer (13) and enter *RW Start*; no buffer manipulation is required.

Request IO

This routine, shown in Fig. 10.5.2, is referred to not only by *RW Command* but also by *Release* (Section 10.7). It may be entered for either **READ** or **WRITE**.

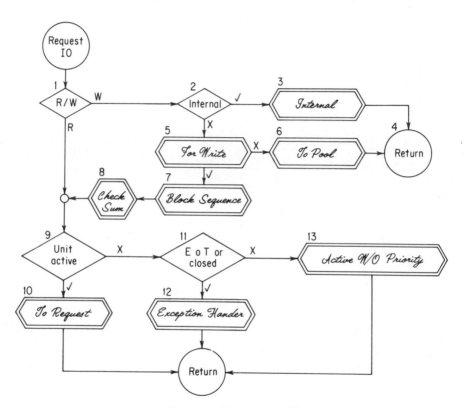

FIGURE 10.5.2. Request *IO*.

For **WRITE**, if an internal file is called for (2), *Write Internal* does this job (3) and a return is made (4). For an external file (2) we check if writing is really to be done (5). If not, the buffer is returned to the pool using the routine *To Pool* (6).

When writing is to be done, as determined by *For Write* (5), we perform block sequencing (7) and make up a check sum (8) when required.

Whether reading or writing is done, we check to see if the unit called for is active (9). If so, we enter this buffer on the *request* chain and set it up for activity with *To Request* (10).

If the unit requested is not active (9), we need not enter the buffer on the *request* chain but can activate immediately. However, first we check to see if an *end of tape* has been given on this channel or if the file is actually closed (11). For either, *Exception Handler* takes over (12) before return. For an open but inactive file (11) we call upon *Activate* (13).

RW Start

The operations required for the start of processing for READ or WRITE are shown in Fig. 10.5.3. The first task is to set the buffer pointer (1). If there are no buffers in use (2) but there are buffers in the *hold* chain (3), they must be released: *put* buffers are to be written; *taken* buffers are released to pool; *Release* (4), discussed in Section 10.7, does either.

With no buffers held, routine housekeeping chores are performed (5). The first (next) subcommand is procured for analysis (6) (each succeeding subcommand requires this phase of examination).

JUMPS

JUMP (7) requires special handling (8). If this is the first JUMP encountered, we store the location of the next subcommand [JUMP] + 1 as the place to which return is made after subcommand processing of the next sequence is terminated. If this is not the first JUMP encountered, this operation is omitted. We always return to the subcommand after the first JUMP. The location of the next subcommand is in the address accompanying JUMP. This is stored in the subcommand counter before return to the loop to get the next subcommand (6).

INDIRECT ADDRESSING

For indirect addressing (9) we set up the target address (10). Only single indirect addressing is possible in this *IOCS* design, so we need never fear a continuing chain. Step (10) establishes the cell into which will be placed the address of the next word in the buffer.

For the subcommand

$$1,1 \quad \ldots \text{FRANK, 17} \quad (10.5.1)$$

enter the address of the first buffer word referenced into the location symbolically referenced as FRANK. How does *IOCS* get the absolute location of FRANK? There is no symbol table available at this time.

During assembly, one job is to replace symbolic references in subcommands by an absolute or relative address. In the latter case, $\mathscr{LOAD}$ relativizes both the program and references to it.

Suppose that the $\mathscr{IOCS}$ subcommand is assembled so that it is assigned the cell 500 and that FRANK is assigned to cell 700. Suppose further that the next word to be addressed in this buffer is at location 305. The result of performance of the subcommand is to insert 305 into the address portion of the word at location 700.

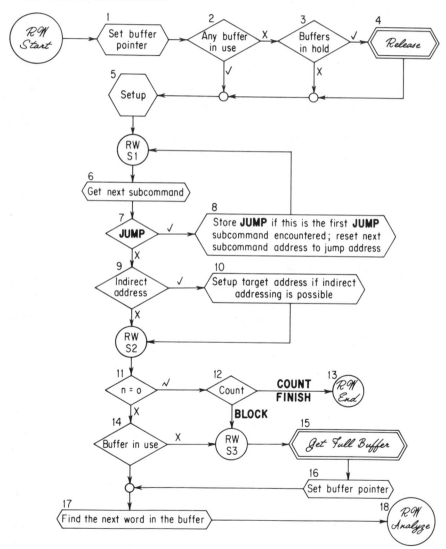

FIGURE 10.5.3. $\mathscr{RW\ Start}$.

If $\mathcal{LOAD}$ has offset the program by 135 cells, the subcommand appears at location 635 and FRANK occupies the absolute location 835. Now performance of the subcommand enters 305 into the address portion of cell 835.

OTHER FORMALITIES

We check the count associated with this subcommand (11). If the count is 0, we check the subcommand *count option* (12). The number is ignored only in the case of BLOCK. Nothing need really be done for the case where the option is COUNT or FINISH (12). When no analysis is required, we exit to $\mathcal{RW}$ $\mathcal{End}$ (Fig. 10.6.2).

Should *number* be nonzero, we check to see if there is a buffer in use. If not, we get a full buffer using $\mathcal{Get\ Full\ Buffer}$ flow-charted in Fig. 10.7.3. When the buffer is obtained (15) we still need to set the buffer pointer (16). We must also determine the address of the next word to be referenced (17). For the new buffer, it is the word at the beginning of the buffer; for a buffer already in use, it is the word after the last one referenced. We continue with the routine $\mathcal{RW}$ $\mathcal{Analyze}$.

10.6 ANALYSIS AND COMPLETION OF
$\mathcal{RW}$ $\mathcal{Subcommand}$

Analysis Phase

The purpose of this phase is:

- determine the intent of each subcommand
- do the accounting associated with each subcommand
    * determine history entries
    * number of words to be transmitted
    * location of words to be transmitted

The flow chart for $\mathcal{RW}$ $\mathcal{Analyze}$ is Fig. 10.6.1. For LOCATE (1), we get the location of the next buffer word (2). We check the *count option*. For COUNT (3) where *number* is 0 (4), we return to $\mathcal{RW}$ $\mathcal{Start}$ at entry point 3. A null count requires no processing.

We continue the analysis whose aim is to determine a number to be entered into the history record. It also sets up a number of words for transmission and locates the beginning of this set of words. For READ (5) the rest of the block is transmitted if *count* is BLOCK. For FINISH the number of words to be processed depends upon *number* and the words that remain in the block; these are compared (7).

For WRITE (5) we set up the file activity block word (8) and then compare *number* with the number of words still available in the block (9). In most cases this will allow us to fill in the history number immediately (14). In the case of FINISH, if there are not enough words left in this buffer, we disconnect it and try to pick up another buffer (11), (12), (13). Two tries at this are permitted. If neither is successful, we abandon further attempts.

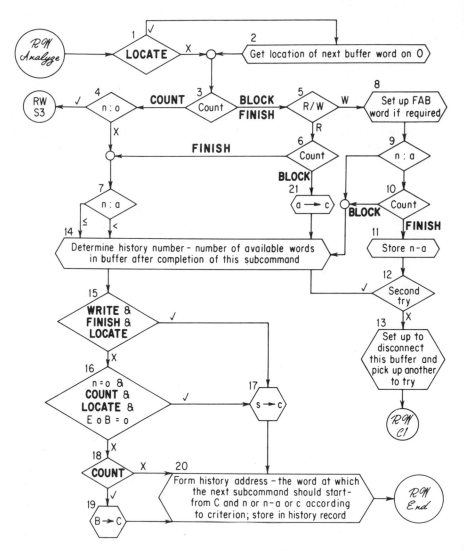

FIGURE 10.6.1. *RW Analyze.*

HISTORY ADDRESS

The address at which the next subcommand is to reference a buffer is to be entered into the history. Further, information about the subcommand in progress in some cases is entered into the subcommand word proper. If this buffer is exhausted (15, 16) we enter the address of the first word in the *next* buffer into the subcommand. Also for COUNT (13), the location of the first word accessed is entered into the subcommand (19). We complete the history record (20) and we enter the next phase, *RW End*.

RW End

TRANSMISSION

The first housekeeping function performed in the *RW End* flow diagram, Fig. 10.6.2, is to revise the availability word of the buffer activity block so that it will be ready for the next subcommand (1). We determine if words are required for transmission (2). If so, we check the destination. For some troublemaking destinations such as *IOCS* or the program (3), we print the error with *Errprint* (5) (see *FOREMAN*). If the destination is safe (3), the subcommand requires no transmission as for LOCATE (4). If the *locate* option is empty (4), a transmission is done with *Transmit*, which takes a word at a time from the buffer, passes it through the accumulator and places it into the proper cell in memory (6).

When we try to locate words in more than one buffer, *end of buffer* exit is called for (7). For LOCATE (8), the buffer should be entered into a *hold* chain rather than released immediately (9). We next check if no disconnect is required:

- if words are still available for use in the buffer
- if the buffer is entered into the *hold* chain

For no disconnect (10), we check if this is the last subcommand in the sequence (18). For more subcommands, we return to Fig. 10.5.3 at *RW S1*.

DISCONNECT

For *disconnect* (10) we call in *Release* (discussed later) whose purpose is to permit a used buffer to be removed from a demand chain and returned either to the pool or to an output chain. If an *end of buffer* exit is actually required as shown by COUNT (12), LOCATE (13) and a positive setting of the *end of buffer* switch (14), this is noted (17).

When an *end of buffer* exit is not required (12), (13), (14), the new word count and address are set up (15) and we return to Fig. 10.5.3 at *RW S2*.

Windup

When the last subcommand has been processed (18), if a hold is required (19), we enter the buffer into the *hold* chain (20). For READ only (21), we request another read operation in order to refresh the buffer chains when required using *Request Read* (22), discussed later.

For READ or WRITE, if the *end of buffer* exit is now required (23), we get exit information (24), prepare the history and store it (25), and then

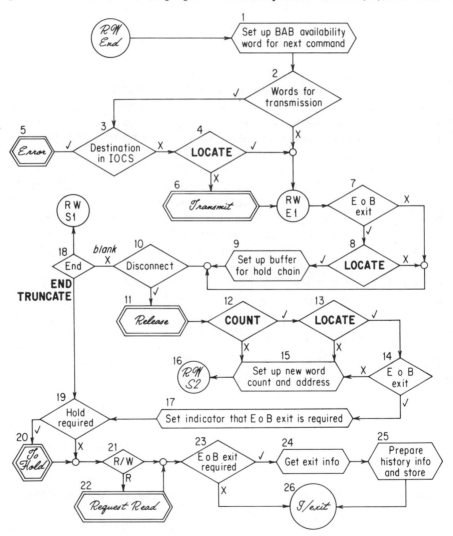

FIGURE 10.6.2. *RW End*.

exit (26). In the case of END and TRUNCATE, return is to the program; for disconnect it may be an EoB exit or a return to some phase of $\mathscr{RW}$.

If no *end of buffer* exit is required, the processing for the command and all its subcommands is complete and we exit (26).

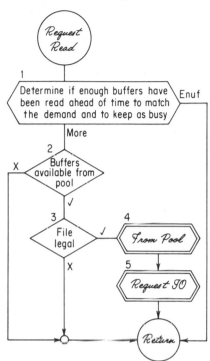

FIGURE 10.6.3. *Request Read*.

Request Read

Request Read determines if enough buffers have been dispatched to keep well ahead of the program so that its needs will be fully met even when the computer is hard at work on the input task. The file activity block contains information about the number of buffers in use and the number of buffers which are presently *full* and waiting to be *taken*.

Request Read, Fig. 10.6.3, first compares the number of buffers ahead with the present potentialities of the chain (1). When a file is attached as a group with but a single member and with a number of buffers assigned to it, the task is simple. At other times the file may be one of several associated together in a group. The group buffer assignment is listed in the group word which, when used for this purpose, is called the group activity block. Dispatching philosophies which use the group activity block are discussed in Section 11.6. Suffice it to say that the routine has recourse to a fixed philosophy for determining if enough buffers have been filled to meet the present needs of $\mathscr{IOCS}$.

When more buffers could be used we check to see if buffers are available from the pool (2). If so and the file is legal (3), we call upon the routine *From Pool* (4) (Chapter 4) to get a buffer. With this buffer in hand we call upon the routine *Request IO* (Fig. 10.5.2) to fill the buffer just obtained.

We exit from *Request Read* under one of the following conditions:

- there were sufficient buffers on hand initially
- there were no buffers available in the pool
- the file referenced was not legal
- another *filled* buffer was required, an empty buffer was obtained, and the *fill* process initiated

10.7   RELEASE, UNBUFFER, GET FULL BUFFER

Three More Routines

This section describes three *IOCS* service routines.

Release

This routine releases buffers in two fashions: those which are no longer needed are returned to the pool; those for which READ or WRITE with *hold* was completed are entered into the hold chain. A buffer is written after *put*; another buffer is readied to read after we have *taken* or *located* in a present buffer.

Unbuffer

This routine is used to get rid of unneeded buffers. Why should we ever have unneeded buffers lying around? Hopefully we don't, but some exceptional cases arise where buffers that we have set up can no longer be used. The simplest example is on the backspace. Suppose that we have just *taken* information and that there is a queue of *full* buffers waiting to be *taken*. Back spaces completely mess up the queues unless we make provision for handling them. The simplest expedient releases all waiting buffers and begins a new queue after the backspace: *Unbuffer* releases the buffers.

Another example of *Unbuffer* is for *Close*. It is natural to close a file at the occurrence of an *end of file* mark. However, the user or the system can close a file anytime. When an input file is closed, all the buffers read previously and now on the *take* queue can be discarded.

When an output file is closed, all the buffers on the request queue or which are otherwise waiting to be written must be written before the file can be considered closed.

Get Full Buffer

This routine obtains a buffer from the *take* queue and presents it for use so that a READ command can address it. There are many tasks associated with this seemingly simple request.

Release

Figure 10.7.1 is the flow chart of *Release*. As usual we have to save register content before we start the routine (1). If there are no buffers presently connected to the pool (2) and none held (3), or if there are buffers connected to the pool now (2) but they are not ready to be disconnected (4), then there are none to be released and we *unsave* (5) and *return* (6).

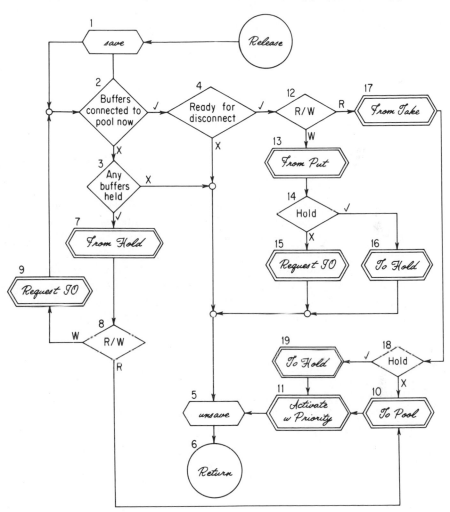

FIGURE 10.7.1. *Release.*

When there are no buffers connected (2) but there are buffers being held (3), we get a buffer from the hold chain (7). For a *write* buffer (8) an output operation is performed when we call *Request IO* (9). If there are several buffers in the *hold* chain to be written, return is made from (9) to (2), and we take the same path (2), (3), (7), (8), (9); thus all buffers in the hold chain are eventually written out.

For buffers connected to the pool (2) which are ready to be disconnected (4), we check if these are read or write buffers (12). For WRITE, *From Put* (13) removes a *put* buffer from the *put* chain. If not *held* (14), this buffer is written with *Request IO* (15). To enter a write buffer into the *hold* chain, we call *To Hold* (16). We then *unsave* and *return* (5), (6).

For a read buffer we have completed a *take* operation and call *From Take* (17) to remove the buffer from its present status. If a *hold* is required (18), we enter it into the *hold* chain with *To Hold* (19); otherwise we release it to the pool with *To Pool* (10). In either case, we want to get another buffer to start filling and, hence, call *Activate with Priority* (11).

Unsave and *return* follow the release activities outlined above.

Unbuffer

This routine, outlined in Fig. 10.7.2, begins with *save* (1) which is followed by *Release* (2). This gets rid of all the buffers in the *hold* chain and the most recent buffer used, which is released to the pool after *taking* or is outputted after *putting*.

For writing we review the request chain (4) to see if there are entries on it which should be written. If so, we call in *Activate with Priority* (5) which requests output activity and waits for it to be performed. Thus we alternate between the actions of (4) and (5) until all the buffers on the request chain have been outputted. We can then *unsave* (6) and check for *end of tape* (7). This condition requires *EoT Handler* (8) not discussed here. When an *end of tape* does not arrive, we return to the main program (9).

The read activity requires that we look at the request chain entries again (10). If there is more than one item on the request chain (11), we pare off these buffers one at a time by calling *From Request* (12) and then *To Pool* (13), finally checking to see if this is the last buffer on the chain.

When there is only one buffer on the chain, it is the one that is being procured. To make sure that we can complete this *Unbuffer* activity, we call in *Activate with Priority* (14). We wait for this activity to be completed (15) and then enter the filled buffer on the *take* chain. We are then ready to investigate it. If there are any entries on the *take* chain [there may be none if we come directly from (10)], then we wish to remove them. To do this we call in *From Take* (17) and then *To Pool* (18), making sure that we keep track of the number of *take* chain buffers we have deleted (19).

The unbuffering activity must correctly associate the file with the proper block on tape. Each buffer that was on the *take* chain got there through a read operation. If we are presently requesting a backspace operation, that operation is with respect to a block just used. To reread that block, we backspace over all the blocks which were read in after that block was read

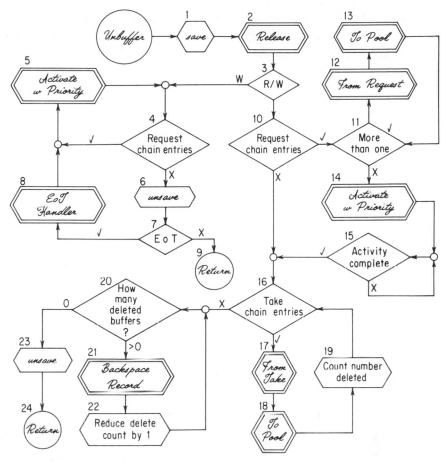

FIGURE 10.7.2. *Unbuffer.*

in. We know how many blocks this is because we have kept track of it (19). We check this number (20) and if we have to, we backspace over a block (21), reduce the delete count (22) and then check the count again (20). We continue this loop until a backspace has occurred for each deleted block. This brings us to the proper point so that we are ready for any activity associated with the unbuffering. We then *unsave* (23) and *return* (24).

Get Full Buffer

The purpose of this routine is to procure a buffer from the *take* chain which, of course, has been previously filled. Further, the routine handles all eventualities that could arise, such as an *end of file*, an *end of tape* or an empty *take* chain.

The routine, flow-charted in Fig. 10.7.3, begins with *save* (1) and *suspend* (2) activities. If there are any buffers in the take chain (3), we get one using the routine *From Take* (4) to see that no *end of file* has been read (5). If this is not an internal file (16) and if there are no buffers ahead, we use *Request Read* (8) to get one. For an internal file (6) or if there are buffers ahead (7), we skip *Request Read* (8).

Now we apply routine checks to the block just obtained. A block sequence check (9) is done with a *Check Block Sequence* (10). If it is correct we see if a check sum is required (11) and, if so, we use *Check Sum* (12). If either of these routines (10), (12) indicates an error, we use *Error* (13). If no checks were required or if the checks were required, performed and proved okay, then we check for parity (14). It too could result in an error which would call for *Error* (13). If all these checks prove satisfactory, then we can *unsave* (15), *restore* (16) and *return* (17).

NO BUFFERS NOW

If there are no buffers available (3), and if an internal buffer has been asked for (18), this is an error and we go to *Error* (19). If this is not an internal buffer, but there is a request in progress (20), we give that request priority with *Activate with Priority* (21). We are stuck until the buffer arrives (22). When it does, we go back to the beginning of *Get Full Buffer* (23), and we should now pass through the chain which allows the buffer that was just received to be processed properly.

For no request in progress (20), we revert to *Request Read* (24). Of course, it is possible that the read request may go unfulfilled because there are no buffers available from the pool. If that is the case, we take the *no buffer* exit from (24), and if this is the first try (25), we request a release of buffers using *Release* (26). This should prove successful and will return us to the *Request Read* (24). However, there are cases when there are no buffers releaseable elsewhere; when we enter the *Request Read* (24) from *Release* (26) and it is not the first try (25), then we can do nothing further and go on to record an error (27). A successful use of *Request Read* (24) should return us back to *Get Full Buffer* via (18), (20), (21), (22), (23).

END OF FILE

When the next block requested contains an *end of file* (5), we enter *Release* (28). If this is not a system unit (29) and if the file uses the standard label procedure (30), we call *Label* (31). For a unireel file (32) we use the *end of file* exit incorporated in READ (33), and we return using this exit (34).

For a multireel file (32) or for a system file (29), we switch from the main tape unit to the auxiliary. This should have been set up by the operator

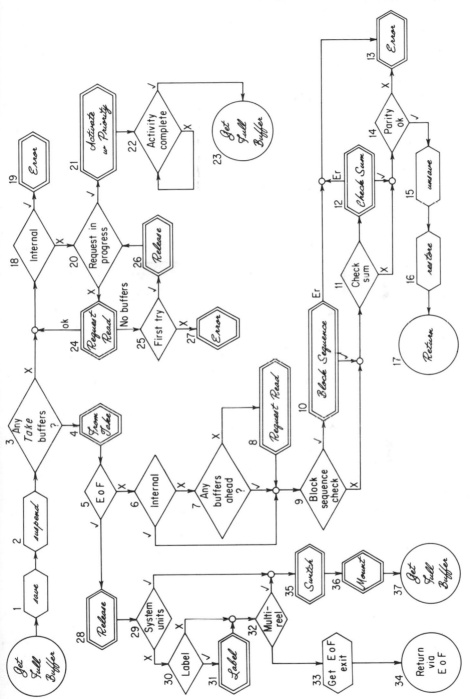

FIGURE 10.7.3. *Get Full Buffer.*

309

when he mounted the original tapes. This task is done by *Switch* (35). The old tape is released and new mounting instructions issued with *Mount* (36).

After doing all this work, we still have not obtained a new record for processing. We reenter *Get Full Block* (37).

10.8   OTHER COMMANDS

This section describes several commands but does not cover them in great detail. It explains what they are and how to use them. From what we have said so far, it should be easy to outline how they are done.

The commands discussed here are:

- COPY—a data command to transfer information from one file to another.
- A number of nondata commands.
- ROLLBACK—enabling us to perform restart procedures.

COPY

Frequently it is required to transfer a bufferful of information from one buffer to another. In most computers, a memory-to-memory transfer requires that each word be transferred from a cell in memory to the accumulator and then back to the destination cell. This is wasteful and time-consuming, especially when the same task could be done if we simply relabel the buffer by the destination name instead of the source name.

That is, in fact, what this command accomplishes. It allows us to take a buffer presently assigned to an input file and rename it as an output file. The same command can be used between an input file and an internal file, or an internal file and an output file, or between two internal files. (*This is contrary to the procedure of the IBM 7090 IOCS which requires a special command,* STASH, *for dealing with internal files.*)

FORMAT

This command is requested by the usual type of call:

GET   COPY, first file, second file   (10.8.1)

First file and *second file* are symbolic names for files that have been previously defined.

OPERATION

To use COPY, we must have already located information in a buffer. To make COPY more powerful, we wish to perform a partial as well as a full copy; we designate which part of the buffer is to be copied. One convention is for COPY to copy information up to and including the last word that was located in the buffer. All words thereafter, whether valid or not, are omitted from the copy.

You can almost see the mechanics for doing this. It is simply a matter of entering the *number of words used so far* into the space provided for *buffer size.*

Caution is used so that information located in the buffer is not released. A released buffer is no longer available for copying, or anything else, for that matter. Obviously, we cannot use a *proceed* option such as TRUNCATE.

Suppose we have an input buffer HARRY and an output buffer ED, each capable of containing 25 words. The following commands show how we might employ COPY to partially duplicate twelve words of HARRY into ED:

GET   READ, HARRY, BUFEXIT, FILEXIT, EREXIT   (10.8.2)

I   COUNT, , , JIM, 3   (10.8.3)

I   COUNT, LOCATE, END, , 9   (10.8.4)

GET   COPY, HARRY, ED   (10.8.5)

The first subcommand (10.8.3) passes the first three words of HARRY over to JIM; (10.8.4) locates nine more words, thus a total of twelve words has been located in HARRY. We cannot tell how many words were stored in this buffer. Once the command COPY is given, the twelve words in HARRY are transferred to ED. We know that this is not a transfer but merely a relabeling. A number of queues must be manipulated and before this is done, the number of words in the buffer is established as twelve by the previous locating commands.

IMPORTANCE

COPY is very useful. We see just how useful it is when we design service routines in Chapter 12.

Nondata Commands

We discuss the operation of the **nondata commands**:

- ENDFILE
- REWIND
- BACKABLOCK

- SKIPABLOCK
- BACKFILE
- SKIPFILE

These are called nondata commands; although they do involve some data, the information they handle is fixed. It is known in advance by the user.

This command has the format:

GET   ENDFILE, file name, exit name   (10.8.6)

The purpose of this command is to write an *end of file* mark or block on *file name*. All buffers previously written for this file and presently on request or hold chains are truncated and outputted. After this is done, a final block which contains the *end of file* mark is written onto the output tape.

Of course, this command cannot be given for an input file or an internal file, for it makes no sense. In these cases it is disregarded as though it were NOOP.

It is possible that while we are writing the truncated buffers or the block with the *end of file* mark, we may reach the *end of tape*. This is the reason for *exit name*. It gives us a means for coping with this rare exception.

This command has the format:

GET   REWIND, file name   (10.8.7)

It simply requests that the tape corresponding with *file name* be rewound. All buffers associated with the file are released.

These commands provide for backing up over a block just read and for skipping a block from which information is not required. Backup procedure is more complicated, requiring that we release all the previously read buffers that are associated with this file. In some cases the skip command can be performed if we drop a buffer from the *take* chain. (SKIP is not implemented in the IBM 7090 IOCS.)

The two commands have the formats:

GET   BACKABLOCK, file name, exit name   (10.8.8)

GET   SKIPABLOCK, file name, exit name   (10.8.9)

We back up or skip a block of *file name*. When we back over the *beginning of tape* or *end of file*, we take the *exit name*. Similarly, if we should skip over an *end of file*, we go to *exit name*.

File Review

Sometimes file marks are used to set off multiblock records. In this case, to go backward over a number of records, we can employ the command BACKFILE, which has the format:

$$\text{GET} \qquad \text{BACKFILE, file name, number} \qquad (10.8.10)$$

The *beginning of tape* causes the operation to be terminated even if *number* has not been reached.

A similar command is available for skipping over files. It has the format;

$$\text{GET} \qquad \text{SKIPFILE, file name, number} \qquad (10.8.11)$$

Rollback

Rollback is the procedure by which the programmer can take the program back to a previous period in time. A programmer with even a small amount of experience knows the need for this procedure. It is certainly handy in debugging programs; but even in supposedly operating programs when difficulties or errors arise, frequently the only way to recover is to go back to a point where we know the program was functioning correctly.

Rollback requires that everything be restored to its condition at a given time slice. This includes:

- registers and indicators
- all of core storage
- the position of all tapes and IO devices associated with the program

MECHANICS

To be able to restore these conditions, we must have a record of them. We assign a special tape to record rollback conditions. It records the three items mentioned before: memory, registers and tape position. Since, to be useful, this must be done at several or many points of the program, we must be able to distinguish among these different points, and also between them and any other program for which rollback information is taken. We should therefore record each time a rollback recording is made:

- program identification
- sequence and restart information

The ability to automatically take rollback information can be built into $\mathscr{IOCS}$. It will then take such information whenever files are open or closed. A program can run for a long time between such intervals. Therefore, we should provide for other checks. It is up to the programmer to do this by means of the call:

$$\text{GET} \qquad \text{ROLLBACK} \qquad\qquad (10.8.12)$$

It is also convenient to be able to take rollback information when errors of various sorts arise. It is hard to determine automatically which errors require rollback information and which do not. Since important errors are presented to the operator for examination through $\mathscr{Pause}$, at this time the operator may request a rollback record by means of console switches.

DEVICE RESERVATION

To use the rollback system, we must provide a rollback tape to record the information. This means that a rollback file must be established by a control card when the program is initially entered. Further, a tape unit must be set up by the operator with blank tape ready for writing.

RESTART

The rollback recording procedure would be in vain if we did not have some means of returning to the desired point in the program. When we get into trouble, it is up to the operator to determine which rollback point to use. Once he has done this he identifies this point with both the program identification and sequence code. This information is put into a $RESTART card which is then entered through the control channel. $\mathscr{IOCS}$ picks up this information and does all the necessary mechanics associated with the rollback procedure.

10.9   VARIABLE-LENGTH RECORDS

Block Length vs. Record Size

Recall from Section 3.1 that the records we deal with can be in three possible forms:

- unirecord block   • multiblock record   • multirecord block

UNIRECORD BLOCK

When the block contains only one record and it is a fixed size, the methods discussed previously are adequate. When the record is of variable size and we wish to keep the unirecord block format, the buffer supplied must allow for the maximum record available. Between the $\mathscr{FOREMAN}$ and $\mathscr{JOCS}$, the READ operation enters the block read from tape and fills up the buffer to the exact size furnished from the tape. This is noted in the buffer activity block so that the user may act accordingly.

Within this format it is possible to have variable fields in either the fixed or variable record. This can be handled by the same procedure discussed later under the heading *Multirecord, Variable Field*.

MULTIBLOCK RECORD

For the completely fixed case of a record of exactly k blocks, previous methods prevail. For the case where there are $k - 1$ blocks of fixed size and the kth block can be of variable size, we handle the fixed blocks. The last block presents no difficulty, for the BLOCK option of *count* can handle this.

A multiblock record can consist of a number of blocks where that number is not previously determined. This is handled by the techniques discussed later.

MULTIRECORD BLOCK

The multirecord block and the multifield record are both discussed later.

Unirecord Block

With respect to the variable record size, we keep track of the number of words of information being processed in the buffer activity block. Thus when a block of r words is read in from tape, as long as this is less than the buffer size, s, we note this in the BAB as demonstrated in Fig. 10.9.1.

READ

When information is taken using READ, BLOCK takes r words from the buffer the first time it is used regardless if r is equal to s or is smaller than s. For COUNT we use u words the first time, say; then the number of available words, a, is given by:

$$a = r - u \qquad (10.9.1)$$

Subsequent COUNTs reduce a by the next value of u until either a BLOCK occurs or until the available words are used up.

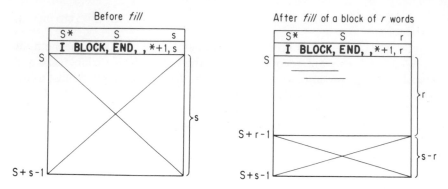

FIGURE 10.9.1. If the block being read from tape to fill the buffer is less than the buffer size, the *full* size of the buffer is recorded as the number of words entered (*r*) instead of the actual buffer size (*s*). This is entered into the buffer activity block.

WRITE

It is easy for the user to write a block of the length he desires, provided that it is smaller than the buffer size. He fills the buffer a little at a time using COUNTs. The last subcommand for the block can exercise the TRUNCATE option. Regardless of how many words have been written into the buffer, they are written out at the end of the subcommand.

Of course, the user can do the same job with LOCATE and then fill the buffer indirectly. Again, he releases the buffer when the block is partially full to the point where he desires it.

Multiblock Record

The multiblock record in Fig. 10.9.2 has *r* words in its last block. BLOCK reads in the last record regardless of its size. How do we identify that this is the last block of the record? One way is to place a special flag as the last word in the record. The alternative is a record prefix which identifies the number of blocks and/or the number of words in the record. This device also solves the inconvenient eventuality that the last block contains exactly *s* words.

FIGURE 10.9.2. A multiblock record consists of several maximum size blocks followed by a final block of a variable length.

Multirecord Block

When we pack several records into a block, as long as the block size is smaller than the buffer size, there are several records in the buffer, as shown in Fig. 10.9.3. How do we know when one record leaves off and the next one begins?

We could have a table of contents at the beginning of each block. We could construct commands from the table of contents, which we would then use. An appealing alternative is to prefix each record with its own loading subcommand. The records then become self-loading.

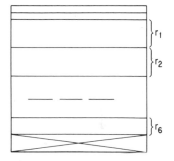

SELF-LOADING RECORDS

Prefix each record with the following sub-command code

| I   COUNT, , LOCATE, , r_i,   (10.9.2)

FIGURE 10.9.3. Several variable size records may occupy the buffer when a multirecord block is read.

where there are r_i words in the record. If there are six records of variable length which may be found in any one block, the user provides the command structure of Fig. 10.9.4 to bring in and locate each successive block.

COUNT at I1 transfers the first word in the first record to the word following COUNT at I1 + 1, the subcommand itself. The first word of the record conforms with our rule and is the prefix word of (10.9.2). A blank has been provided for this in the user's program, as shown in Fig. 10.9.4. After reading all six records in this block, READ appears as in Fig. 10.9.5. The fact that these commands are filled in and then performed in sequence does not affect their nature.

```
          GET     READ, etc.
    I1    I       COUNT, , , * + 1, 1
                    blank
    I2    I       COUNT, , , * + 1, 1
                    blank
                  . . .
    I6    I       COUNT, , , * + 1, 1
                    blank
          I       COUNT, END, LOCATE, , 0
```

FIGURE 10.9.4. An $\mathcal{IOCS}$ program subsequence to locate six variable length records whose maximum size does not exceed the buffer size. Each of the incoming records is properly prefixed as described in the text.

```
            GET    READ, etc
     11  I         COUNT, , , * + 1, 1
         I         COUNT, , LOCATE, ,  r₁
     12  I         COUNT, , , * + 1, 1
         I         COUNT, , LOCATE, ,  r₂
                   . . .
     16  I         COUNT, , , * + 1, 1
         I         COUNT, , LOCATE, ,  r₆
         I         COUNT, END, LOCATE, ,  0
```

FIGURE 10.9.5. After the six records have been located in the input buffer using the $\mathscr{IOCS}$ sequence of Fig. 10.9.4, the sequence appears in the program as though the above had been assembled.

After entering the prefix word of the first record into location $I1 + 1$, $\mathscr{IOCS}$ uses it as the next subcommand to execute. COUNT placed at $I1 + 1$ requests that we locate the r_1 words of the first record.

When this is accomplished $\mathscr{IOCS}$ goes on to COUNT at location $I2$, which loads the prefix word into $I2 + 1$ which is then executed to bring in the r_2 words in the next record.

This continues until we bring in the last record prefix word with COUNT at $I6$ and execute it at $I6 + 1$. The subcommand which is performed could include an END option, but this would make it too specific. Instead, it is a simple matter to enter at $I6 + 2$, the subcommand shown in Fig. 10.9.5. This subcommand provides the END option and requests $\mathscr{IOCS}$ to locate 0 words. This seems strange! But the only purpose of this subcommand is to end the subcommand string—no words need be located.

Variable Number of Records Per Block

The technique previously prescribed is applicable when records are of variable lengths but of a fixed number of records per block. What do we do if not only the record size is variable but also the number of records per block? This is easily handled with a loop structure.

The technique now is to handle one record with each $\mathscr{IOCS}$ command. READ, as shown in Fig. 10.9.6, contains a single subcommand followed by a blank. COUNT brings in the record prefix word and places it in the

```
     I        COUNT, END, LOCATE, ,  rᵢ        Prefix

     GET      READ, etc                        The read command has
     I        COUNT, , , * + 1, 1              only one subcommand.
              blank
```

FIGURE 10.9.6. When there are a variable number of records per block, each is prefixed as above. The read command locates only one record; it is embedded in a loop to find records and use them as they appear.

following cell which is blank or contains trash from the last use. The prefix shown in Fig. 10.9.6 includes END. When the prefix word is performed it locates all the words of the record it prefixes and then terminates READ.

The program now has available all the words of this record which have been properly located for it. After processing, it loops back to READ. This procedure is applicable even for the last record in the block.

The last record uses up all the remaining words in the buffer. When COUNT in the prefix is performed, the buffer is released but held. This means that the information located in the buffer is available to the program until the next READ. Then the saved buffer is returned to the pool and READ operates on a new buffer which it acquires from the *take* chain.

Multirecord Blocks. Variable Field Length

This is a rather complicated situation where we can have a variable number of records per block and, within each record, we can have fields of variable length. The complexity of this technique may be compensated for by its efficiency in packing information. Not only that, we have the machinery for it! The following sentinel words, examples of which appear in Fig. 10.9.7, may facilitate the technique, depending upon the complexity of the situation.

I	COUNT, END, LOCATE, , r_i		Record prefix for the *i*th record
I	COUNT, , LOCATE, , f_{i1}		Field prefix for the first field of the *i*th record
I	COUNT, , LOCATE, , f_{i2}		Field prefix for the second field of the *i*th record
	. . .		
I	COUNT, , LOCATE, , f_{in_i}		Field prefix for the last field of the *i*th record

. . .

YYYYYYYYYYYYYYYYYYYYYYYYYYYYYY   *End of record* flag
ZZZZZZZZZZZZZZZZZZZZZZZZZZZZZZ   *End of block* flag

FIGURE 10.9.7. Prefixes and flags for handling variable records with variable field lengths.

- Record prefix—to self-load the record of variable length.
- Field prefix—the self-load feature may be extended to cover field.
- *End of record* flag—required when multirecord blocks and multi-block records exist simultaneously.
- *End of block* flag—required for combined multirecord blocks and multiblock records.

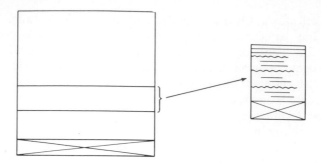

FIGURE 10.9.8. Variable size records with variables size fields can be handled by *IOCS* if a record is copied into an internal file as large as the maximum record to be encountered.

We describe the case when only multirecord blocks are considered—combination with multiblock records is omitted and should serve as a challenge for the reader.

PROCEDURE

We want to pick out a record and then review the information within that record by fields. *IOCS* presently cannot review the information in the buffer more than once. The expedient for a second review is provided by an *internal file* of maximum *record* size.

A record found by LOCATE is copied into an internal file as in Fig. 10.9.8. There it can then be examined by self-loading or self-locating prefixes: the fields are then automatically available to the program.

```
        GET    READ,  MASTR,
        I      COUNT,  ,  , * + 1, 1
                  blank
        GET    COPY,  MASTR,  INTNL
        GET    READ,  INTNL,
FLDI    I      COUNT,  ,  , * + 1, 1
                  blank
FLD2    I      COUNT,  ,  , * + 1, 1
                  blank
                  . . .
LSTFLD  I      COUNT,  ,  , * + 1, 1
                  blank
        I      COUNT,  END,  LOCATE,  ,  0
```

FIGURE 10.9.9. An *IOCS* sequence to bring in a variable record, copy it into an internal file and then locate its fields.

IOCS SUBPROGRAM

The subprogram to do the task is in Fig. 10.9.9. The first READ brings the self-load prefix into the next subcommand space. It is executed and it locates all the information for a record.

This is copied by COPY into an internal file, INTNL. The next READ sequence uses self-load field prefixes for locating fields in INTNL (the record). At FLD1 the first field prefix word is loaded into FLD1 + 1 and then executed. The number of words indicated by the first field prefix word is located.

We continue thus until we have located all the words in the last field. The dummy terminate subcommand at LSTFLD + 2 terminates READ and begins processing. Notice that allowances must always be made for prefixes and flags when counts of buffer size, field size, record size, etc. are taken.

PROBLEMS

10.1   What advantage does the command/subcommand structure for $\mathcal{JOCS}$ have?

10.2   What relation do READ, WRITE and COPY have to the buffer operations *fill, take, transfer, put* and *empty*?

10.3   What purpose is served by the *buffer switch, file end exit* and *error exit* of READ or WRITE?

10.4   Describe the use of COUNT, BLOCK and FINISH for READ and for WRITE.

10.5   Fabricate a READ for the file MASTR to transfer information to the location MASREC
(a) Seventeen words from this and the next block if necessary
(b) Seventeen words or the rest of this block, whichever is less
(c) The rest of this block.

10.6   Fabricate a WRITE for the file MOUT to get information from MREC
(a) Thirteen words onto this and another block, if necessary
(b) Thirteen words or enough to fill this block, whichever is less
(c) Finish this block.

10.7   Indicate the uses of the three *proceed* options.

10.8   LOCATE requires indirection either in the RW subcommand or in the using command. Distinguish these cases and show the advantages and diasdvantages of each.

10.9   Redo the problem explained in Section 10.3 with the following changes: (1) blocks consist of 30 words: the first block contains words A1, A2, A3 . . . A30; the next A3, A4, . . . A32; (2) there are 65 blocks in the file; (3) the generated tape is called ONE; it is called TWO when read back; the final output is called THREE; (4) the pool is called PAPA and the list LILA; (5) the routine CHECK verifies words 9-12, 15-20, 26-29 placed in consecutive cells starting at CHECK + 10.

10.10   Consider a file **MAIN** of records each twenty-five words long with a key in the first word and an *EoF* record terminating the file. Another file, **OTHER**, has the same structure. Flowchart a FLAP $\mathscr{IOCS}$ program to merge these two files into a single file called **FINAL**. Assume both **MAIN** and **OTHER** are in order of ascending keys. Write the program with READs and WRITEs but no COPYs. Use a pool of twelve blocks. Make sure **FINAL** has an *EoF* record.

10.11   Revise the program of Problem 10.10 to include a sequence which checks the order of incoming files and **GET UNSORT** when an out-of-order record is discovered.

10.12   Summarize the purpose of these routines: (1) $\mathscr{RW\ command}$ (2) $\mathscr{Request\ IO}$; (3) $\mathscr{RW\ Start}$; (4) $\mathscr{RW\ Analyze}$; (5) $\mathscr{RW\ End}$.

10.13   To save space we pack variable length records into a file called JIM of twenty-five word blocks. Each record is prefixed. Write a FLAP $\mathscr{IOCS}$ sequence to bring in four records and place them in the four files **INR1**, **INR2**, **INR3** and **INR4**. Consider records of lengths 17, 5, 15, 22, 8, 7, 21, 13. Show how they are blocked and what happens as they are called for and used.

11

THE FOREMAN

11.1 INTRODUCTION

Who Is He?

The $\mathscr{FOREMAN}$ carries out routine clerical tasks associated with input and output. There are other names for $\mathscr{FOREMAN}$ such as IOEX and trap supervisor, but these are not as descriptive. In this chapter we discuss the specific tasks of the $\mathscr{FOREMAN}$, how he does them, and how he knows what to do.

TASKS

Below are listed most of the tasks which $\mathscr{FOREMAN}$ carries out:

- Gives all the *actual* IO commands to the devices or controllers. A command or subcommand in $\mathscr{JOCS}$ is interpreted by $\mathscr{FOREMAN}$ before it gets out as a machine language command coded to the channel controller.
- Receives all the traps. Although traps are performed in hardware, like a subroutine call, they require the computer to jump to a specific location in memory. This location is part of the $\mathscr{FOREMAN}$.

- Reports results to other software in the program. The performance of the IO device is intercepted by the $\mathcal{FOREMAN}$ who reinterprets it so that other software, such as $\mathcal{IOCS}$ or the object program, can best interpret it.
- Keeps track of device activity.
- Furnishes error-recovery machinery. The $\mathcal{FOREMAN}$ detects a parity error, for instance, and automatically rereads the faulty block a specified number of times until, hopefully, it is read error-free. The user does not even know that an error takes place when recovery from it is successful.
- Provides recording and diagnosis of error activity.
- Does conversion from medium language to computer language, and vice versa.
- Provides direct printout of error and exception messages. This facility can also be used by other systems or the main program.

WHO USES THE $\mathcal{FOREMAN}$?

In a complete system the $\mathcal{FOREMAN}$ is indispensable. In a partial system the $\mathcal{FOREMAN}$ is still one of the essential parts that we would not wish to trim away, for we must have a method of handling traps and for doing printouts. So we might eliminate $\mathcal{IOCS}$, but most programmers would choose to keep the $\mathcal{FOREMAN}$.

Interrelation With Other Software

A sketch of the interrelation of the $\mathcal{FOREMAN}$ with other pieces of software is shown in Fig. 11.1.1. The $\mathcal{FOREMAN}$ is shown in the center. Connected to it are the channel controllers, each of which communicates with several IO devices. The $\mathcal{FOREMAN}$ is responsible for initiating each channel and thereby, a device on the channel. It does this by giving machine language commands. When the operation of a device is complete the channel controller, through the hardware, interrupts the computer. Eventually the $\mathcal{FOREMAN}$ gets control and handles the interrupt. It communicates the results of IO activity to either the main program or a programming system.

When the $\mathcal{FOREMAN}$ is not servicing devices it is servicing device requests from other software or from the main program indicated in Fig. 11.1.1 by the multiple hexagons which circumscribe the bottom of the $\mathcal{FOREMAN}$.

The system supervisor ($\mathcal{SYSTEM}$), discussed in Chapter 13, manages the other pieces of software under directions that it receives from humans. The information for $\mathcal{SYSTEM}$ can be supplied through the console but is most easily supplied through a control IO device. This device is mediated by the $\mathcal{FOREMAN}$ who is notified by $\mathcal{SYSTEM}$ when new information is needed, brings in the information, and then turns over control to $\mathcal{SYSTEM}$.

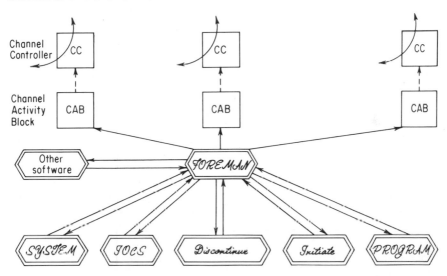

FIGURE 11.1.1. Relation of the $\mathcal{FOREMAN}$ to the rest of the programming system.

$\mathcal{IOCS}$

The main program describes IO demands to $\mathcal{IOCS}$ in terse terms. These are interpreted by routines and subroutines in $\mathcal{IOCS}$, resulting in directions to the $\mathcal{FOREMAN}$. These in turn are interpreted into machine language commands which cause the devices to operate.

As an indication of the coordination required, note that a file is opened by a simple directive from the main program to $\mathcal{IOCS}$, which gives a directive to the $\mathcal{FOREMAN}$ to bring in information at the earliest opportunity when the desired channel is free. The main program merrily rolls along with the assurance that when READ is given, information will already be available to service the request.

When READ does appear in the main program, it is a direction to $\mathcal{IOCS}$ to make available a *filled* buffer. This triggers a chain of events which probably terminates in a request to the $\mathscr{FOREMAN}$ for a new block for this file. The $\mathscr{FOREMAN}$ is monitoring all channels and when the proper one becomes available, it initiates a READ action for the desired file.

Two other users of the $\mathscr{FOREMAN}$ are $\mathscr{LOAD}$ and the translating program, such as the assembler and compiler. They, as everybody else, require information from the outside which is brought in through the IO devices. The $\mathscr{FOREMAN}$ is the sole mediator for these devices, and hence, the software must have recourse to them.

Initiate and Discontinue

Two routines which have most frequent conversation with the $\mathscr{FOREMAN}$ are called $\mathscr{Discontinue}$ and $\mathscr{Initiate}$.

$\mathscr{Discontinue}$

$\mathscr{Discontinue}$ receives the trap analysis furnished by the $\mathscr{FOREMAN}$ after it has done the preliminary processing required to absorb descriptive information about the completion of the IO device's task. $\mathscr{Discontinue}$ examines the results of the activity to determine what should be done next and also posts the information where it is accessible either to the main program or to $\mathscr{IOCS}$. It then returns control to the $\mathscr{FOREMAN}$ as described later.

$\mathscr{Initiate}$

After the $\mathscr{FOREMAN}$ has received an IO request which it has analyzed and for which it seems proper to give an IO command, it then calls in $\mathscr{Initiate}$. $\mathscr{Initiate}$ creates the machine language command for the IO device and furnishes it to $\mathscr{FOREMAN}$ who causes the computer to execute it.

WHERE ARE THEY?

$\mathscr{Discontinue}$ and $\mathscr{Initiate}$ routines are known by other names by other manufacturers. The names used in the IBM 7090 software package for $\mathscr{Discontinue}$ and $\mathscr{Initiate}$ are, respectively, Select — and Select +. The two are incorporated into a single routine which distinguishes them by the sign of the accumulator when the routine is entered. This slender association is ignored here.

Discontinue and *Initiate* should be available in *IOCS* when it is used. However, *IOCS* is not a compulsory item. When *IOCS* is omitted but when the *FOREMAN* is included, *Discontinue* and *Initiate* must be available:

- as part of the object program
- in another portion of software
- in the *FOREMAN*

Normal Trap Events

The most important use of the *FOREMAN* is in connection with interrupts and is presented in Fig. 11.1.2. After the trap has occurred, control passes among routines in the *FOREMAN*, in other software or in the main program.

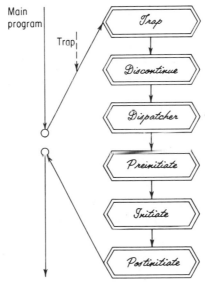

FIGURE 11.1.2. The normal chain of routines called in for *Trap* operation.

At some point in the main program, we know not where, a trap occurs. This causes the hardware to interrupt computer activity at the end of command and jump to some location in memory, presumably part of the *FOREMAN*. The *FOREMAN* takes over with *Trap* which analyzes the causes of the interrupt. Errors may have occurred which require further handling by $\mathcal{T}rap$. Normally, however, it completes its analysis and posting activities and turns control over to $\mathcal{D}iscontinue$.

$\mathcal{D}iscontinue$ makes a further analysis of the interrupt with respect to the program in progress. Some activities may require a unique handling, such as the occurrence of *end of file* while reading. Although this is not an error, it is a major exception of which the main program or $\mathcal{IOCS}$ should be immediately informed.

Where no exceptions occur, $\mathcal{D}ispatcher$ is called upon to investigate the situation. We examine later where $\mathcal{D}ispatcher$ resides. It assigns a new task to the trapped channel. Before return to the main program, we try to make the device active so that it produces useful work while the main program functions.

$\mathcal{D}ispatcher$ turns over control to $\mathcal{P}reinitiate$ in the $\mathcal{FOREMAN}$ which sets up the request with $\mathcal{I}nitiate$. If no assignment was made by $\mathcal{D}ispatcher$, $\mathcal{FOREMAN}$ returns to the program without initiating another device.

$\mathcal{I}nitiate$ fabricates a command for the next slated action of some device on the trapped channel and presents it to $\mathcal{FOREMAN}$ which does the final delegation.

$\mathcal{P}ostinitiate$ of the $\mathcal{FOREMAN}$ gives the command to the IO device. The $\mathcal{FOREMAN}$ may also distinguish other business to which it must attend; otherwise its task is completed and return is made to the main program.

The Presentation

In the sections that follow, the components of the $\mathcal{FOREMAN}$ are discussed and analyzed. The list below serves both to introduce the components and to summarize the remainder of the chapter:

- $\mathcal{T}rap$. The portions of $\mathcal{T}rap$ which reside in the $\mathcal{FOREMAN}$ and introduced in Fig. 11.1.2 are presented in detail in Section 11.2.
- $\mathcal{R}ecover$. When the $\mathcal{FOREMAN}$ detects errors in the block that was just handled by the device which trapped, it can recover from these errors in some instances with $\mathcal{R}ecover$.
- $\mathcal{P}rint$. The $\mathcal{FOREMAN}$ contains a routine, $\mathcal{P}rint$, which it uses and makes available to other software in the main program. $\mathcal{P}rint$ conveys a message to the on-line printer and causes it to print it. $\mathcal{P}rint$ is complicated because it may be called for while a trap is being analyzed and hence, it must also prevent other traps from interfering with its operation.

- Halts. There are times when the computer must stop. This can be done only through the *FOREMAN*. It supervises the cessation of activity to be sure that the program or software is picked up at the proper place when the start button is pressed.
- Errors. We frequently handle errors by combining *Print* with halt routines.
- *Discontinue.*
- *Initiate.* Although both *Discontinue* and *Initiate* are external to the *FOREMAN*, it is appropriate to discuss them here.
- *Dispatch.* The *Dispatcher* may or may not be in the *FORE-MAN*, but obviously it is one of the *trap* tasks that is attacked during a trap.
- *Activate.* This routine handles the communication from an outside system to the *FOREMAN* indicating a request, priority or otherwise, for the activation of a given device.
- *Scan.* A simple dispatcher called *Scan* is incorporated into *FOREMAN*.
- *Preinitiate.* This routine comes between the *Dispatcher* and the *Initiate* routine, as shown in Fig. 11.1.2.
- *Nondata.* Some commands to devices do not require an interruption by the device upon completion of the command. Such commands require a different scheme of initiating.
- Noninterrupt. Some computer systems do not incorporate a facility for interruption. How is the *FOREMAN* going to be constructed to take this into consideration?

11.2 THE TRAP ROUTINE

Flow Chart

The flow chart of *Trap* is Fig. 11.2.1. Two things are done automatically by the hardware:

- program interruption
- cause of interrupt is recorded

Incoming information from the channel controller is stored automatically. One cell is probably allocated to each channel to store information about suspended traps, if these cells are always available to the channel supervisor.

Interruption is automatic, causing a jump to *Trap* after the command in progress is completed. Entry to *Trap* may be multiple with one for each possible channel causing the interruption; or there may be a single entry with recourse to a special cell to determine which is the trapping channel.

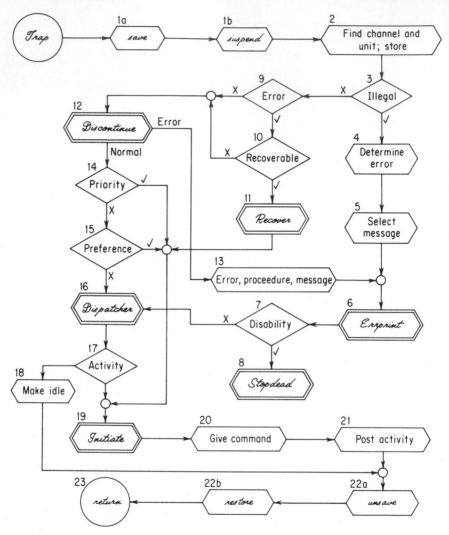

FIGURE 11.2.1. Trap routine.

$\mathcal{Trap}$ uses several routines:

- $\mathcal{Discontinue}$
- $\mathcal{Recover}$
- $\mathcal{Dispatch}$
- $\mathcal{Initiate}$
- $\mathcal{Errprint}$
- $\mathcal{Stopdead}$

Setup

When the trap is first entered, the registers, indicators and other informa-tion as necessary is saved by the subroutine, *save* (1a). Next, traps on all channels are suspended with *suspend* so that the operation of servicing this trap cannot be interrupted (1b).

Trap determines which channel and which unit did the trapping (2). This, together with the indications of how the operation turned out, is stored in a cell available both to the *FOREMAN* and to other software.

Impossible Unit

Theoretically, a unit which is not connected to a channel cannot interrupt us. Similarly, a unit which is connected but has not been made available for use should not interrupt us. Occasionally an error arises in recording the interrupt, indicating an illegal unit has a message for us (3). *Trap* determines the kind of illegality (4), selects a message to inform the operator of the difficulty (5), and causes it to be printed by recourse to the error-printing routine, *Errprint* (6). If this illegality is disabling (7), the computer grinds to a halt using *Stopdead*.

Errors

For a legal trapped unit (3) with an error (9) that is recoverable (10) (most of them are), control passes to *Recover* (11). For nonrecoverable errors, control passes to the user's system through *Discontinue* for him to determine their disposition.

Recover (11) operates generally by making another try at the activity in which the error was discovered. Hence *Trap* circumvents *Discontinue* and *Dispatcher* and simply calls in *Initiate* (18).

Discontinue

A normal return (such as successful completion of an IO activity) (9) or a nonrecoverable error (10) proceeds to *Discontinue* which presents the information to a routine in the user's program or *IOCS*. In the latter routine, the completion of the activity requested is posted and the information made available.

When it finds an error, the user's routine, through *Discontinue*, may choose to ignore it and make the error return. The *FOREMAN* then chooses an error procedure and a matching message (13) which is printed via *Errprint* (6). Since this is no longer a disabling error (7), *Trap* returns to the *Dispatcher* (16).

For normal activity, *Discontinue* returns to the *FOREMAN*. If there is a priority (14) or a preference (15) request on hand, *Trap* continues to *Initiate* (18), for then no dispatching is required.

The *Dispatcher*

Dispatcher may include several philosophies. The best but most involved uses a system of priority. The next unit chosen for activity is based upon the present overall situation, not on the sequence of arrival of the requests. A request for a unit belonging to a file which already has several blocks on hand is postponed in favor of a file with only one or no blocks on hand.

A simpler philosophy is to establish a queue of requests on a channel The first to arrive is serviced first.

Another simple philosophy is that of rotation. After one unit is serviced, the other units are examined in rotation, and the next one with a request is serviced. This may be the first or the last of the requests so far received.

Another simple system combines a simple single priority with rotation, or first come, first served.

Dispatcher (16) uses one of these philosophies of the simple scan described in Section 11.7 and selects the next unit if there are any requests waiting. *Trap* then asks the question (17), "Is there any activity requested?" If not, the channel becomes idle (18).

NEED FOR *Activate*

At this point it should be noted that once a channel becomes idle it will not be trapped and we will not go through this sequence of examinations which includes *Dispatcher*. A request for a unit on an idle channel must have some synthetic method for making the channel active. This is where *Activate* comes in.

Cleanup

When an activity is requested, a command is fabricated using *Initiate* (19) and sent over to the *FOREMAN*. The command is given to the controller (20) and posted in the channel activity block (21).

Whether the channel is active or becomes idle, we *unsave* (22a) and, since this trap has been serviced, we *restore* suspended traps on other channels (22b). Finally, return is made to the main program at the command right after the one that was last performed (23).

Traps During Trap

What happens if another trap should arrive while we are servicing one trap using *Trap*, shown diagrammatically in Fig. 11.2.2.

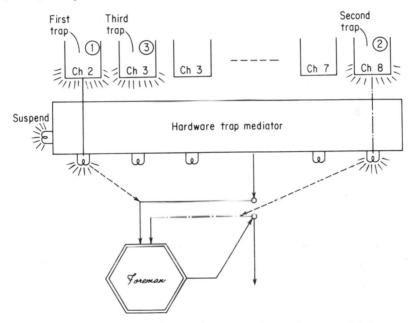

FIGURE 11.2.2. Traps are suspended via the hardware when a trap is being processed by the *FOREMAN*. If another trap should be detected during that period it is held in abeyance. When return is made to the main program it is intercepted by the *FOREMAN*.

Suppose that Channel 2 was first to trap. Hardware caused a jump to *FOREMAN*. The place to which it jumps might be the controlling factor in indicating that Channel 2 was the cause of the trap. In any case, one of the tasks of *FOREMAN* is to suspend further traps. The diagram shows that as *FOREMAN* is working, a trap arrives on Channel 8 and then another one on Channel 3. These cause us no inconvenience because interrupt has been suspended.

When the Channel 2 trap has been serviced, the *FOREMAN unsaves* and *restores*. As *restore* is initiated, one of the waiting traps intercedes.

Which one intercedes depends upon the hardware design. If it is a first-come, first-served design, Channel 8 will interrupt and bring back the 𝓕𝓞𝓡𝓔-𝓜𝓐𝓝 who goes through another complete analysis. If it is a rotational trap discipline, then Channel 3 interrupts next and is serviced before Channel 8.

𝓣𝓻𝓪𝓹 does not return to the main program because the waiting interrupts take effect during 𝓇𝑒𝓈𝓉𝑜𝓇𝑒 and bring the 𝓕𝓞𝓡𝓔𝓜𝓐𝓝 right back in.

11.3   ERRORS AND EXCEPTIONS

Hardware Oriented

Some difficulties which arise in computer operation are communicated to the operator through direct communication: information from the computer to the human appears on some hardware indicator.

CARD EQUIPMENT

As an example of an indicator, when the cardhopper becomes empty the *cardhopper empty* lamp goes on. Possibly an audible signal is also given to the operator to alert him to look for trouble. If the computer needs cards from this particular card unit and there are no cards for it, there is no alternative but for the computer to stop. Some hardware will give an alerting signal before the hopper is absolutely bare so that the operator can get the loading underway before the computer runs out of information.

PRINTER

Many troubles can arise on the printer, but a most natural event is that the printer runs out of paper. We do not want words to come out on a bare platen, so print commands must be rejected when no paper is left. In most cases this will cause the computer to stop.

Again, a warning may be given to the operator that the paper is running out. It is usually necessary for the printer to stop so that a new roll of paper can be fed into it. A warning simply saves time; the operator can have the paper ready and the printer open. When it runs out he can immediately replace the roll.

CARD JAM

Sometimes equipment becomes inoperative. Thus, for a high speed cardreader, cards are speeding by the read station at the rate of twenty or so per second. One may be of poor quality or mutilated and will not pass through the card moving mechanism. It will tear apart and jam. The operator must open up the equipment and remove the card or the pieces of it so that the rest of the deck can be read.

When the jam occurs the reader stops immediately. Unless the computer is multiprogrammed it too will stop. The operator does his utmost to restart the reader.

A further handicap presents itself when the cards are informationally interdependent, i.e., the job being processed requires complete information—information from all cards. If the one that has caused the jam is unusable, it must be reproduced. If the information from the mutilated card is not recoverable, we must go back to the original manuscript. This can take time. It is often better to skip this job and go on to the next so that the computer will not waste its valuable time.

MAGNETIC TAPE

In general, magnetic tape is more self-sufficient than other media because most difficulties that arise can be handled with software. Only direct impairment of the unit or the medium causes a catastrophic breakdown: when magnetic tape breaks it requires splicing; the machine itself can break down, and this happens, but it is usually detected by software.

Software Aided Error Handling

Errors which are normally directly communicated to the operator can also be displayed on the console printer so that, should it be handier to him, he can get the information there. Some hardware may produce program or interrupt indications of impending trouble. These are passed over to the $\mathcal{FOREMAN}$. He in turn sends a message on the console printer to the operator and then the program continues. The operator can now service or prepare to service the predicted difficulty.

Software Handled Errors

READ

Many errors, especially those arising from magnetic tape operations, can be handled automatically by the software. The decision rules which the human would normally apply are incorporated into the software; it then does what the human would do if he encountered the error.

Tape, disk and drum lend themselves most to automatic error-recovery techniques. Since the latter two have been given only superficial coverage in this book, we restrict this discussion of software error handling to magnetic tape.

In reading a block of information from the tape, many kinds of difficulties may arise. One of these is a parity failure (called by some manufacturers a redundancy check failure). A parity bit is associated with each frame in the block. If one bit in the block is incorrectly transmitted from the tape medium to the computer, a parity failure occurs. The number of 1's contained in any frame when the parity bit is included should be odd (in some machines it should be even). When an even number of 1's is counted for a frame, a parity error occurs.

For a block of information received in error, it seems most natural to try to read the block again. If no error occurs this time, the block is accepted. If an error persists, we can try reading a few times more. If the error still persists, we may resort to a manual cleaning technique, wiping any dirt off the heads and blowing the dust off the tape. Finally we may be forced to give up. We acknowledge the impossibility of reading the block correctly and either abort the program or find means of continuing without the block.

This method can be incorporated into the software. Instead of a manual cleaning technique we may cause the tape to go forward and backward several times very rapidly over the spot in question.

WRITE

How can there be errors detected during a write operation? Different machines have different techniques; one of these is called an echo check. The information being written is picked up directly from the heads and verified to see if it matches with what was intended to be put there. Suppose it does not check. We can go back and rewrite the block or we can suspect this particular area of the tape. In that case, we go back and erase this block, skipping the area entirely and writing our block on the next area of the medium.

Suppose we get another error. Do the same thing! This can continue, of course, until we reach the end of tape where we must obviously give up. We can call the operator to get another tape or abort the program.

RECOVERY

Automatic recovery from both types of errors is discussed in the following two subsections. They describe *Recover* included in *FOREMAN*.

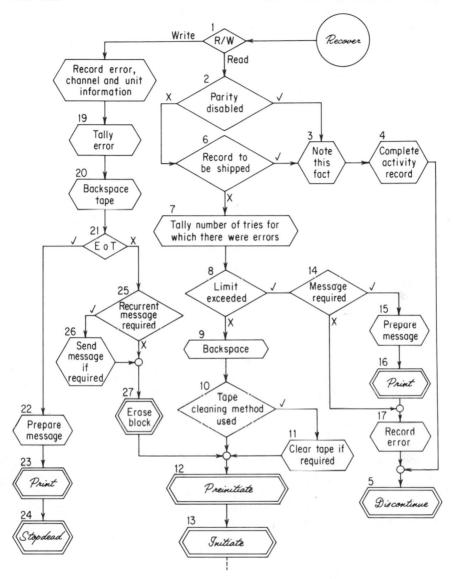

FIGURE 11.3. *Recover*.

Recover, **Read**

For *Recover*, presented in Fig. 11.3, we first determine if the error occurred on a read or write command (1). When it is possible by program to disable the parity-checking equipment entirely, and if this has been done (2), we note that a parity error has occurred (3), complete the activity record

(4) and go on to *Discontinue* (5). For a skipped record (6), we do the same operations (3), (4), (5).

When parity is not disabled or the record is not to be skipped (6), we add 1 to the number of tries that have been made (7) and then check this against a pre-established limit (8). If this limit is exceeded we note this (14), (15), (16), (17) and turn further decision over to other software (5). If the limit has not been exceeded, we backspace the tape (9). If an automatic tape-cleaning method is used (10), we check the cleaning requirements. Usually the operation is repeated only after a fixed number of read operations. If that number has been reached, a tape clean operation is performed (11).

We now continue by initiating another read operation on this unit, calling upon, in sequence, *Preinitiate*, *Initiate* and *Postinitiate*. *Preinitiate* requests a read command from the user. *Initiate* fabricates that command for the *FOREMAN*. The *FOREMAN* gives the command through *Postinitiate* and starts a new cycle.

The sequence of events is best reviewed in Fig. 11.1.2. If a device read request terminates with a parity error, the main program is trapped and processing within the *FOREMAN* begins with *Trap*. The error is discovered by *Trap*, which turns over control to *Recover*. After processing, *Recover* turns over control to *Preinitiate*. Both *Discontinue* and *Dispatcher* are circumvented. The read operation is not posted to the user because the *Discontinue* routine was omitted. A backspace and a new read operation are initiated instead, and return is made to the main program.

If several errors occur, we pass several times through *Recover* and back to the main program after initiating a reread—but the read operation is not posted as completed.

When, hopefully, the block is correctly read, *Trap* detects this and goes on to *Discontinue* instead of *Recover*. An added function within *Trap* is to reset the parity error counter so that it will not read incorrectly should another error occur later on in this program. This is done when *Trap* writes a history record in the unit activity block.

ERROR LIMIT EXCEEDED

If in (8) of Fig. 11.3 the limit to the number of retries has been exceeded, we check to see if a message is required (14). If so, we prepare a message (15) and call upon *Print* (16) for a printout. The error is then recorded (17) and we enter *Discontinue* (5).

Now when *Discontinue* finds that this is an irrecoverable parity error, it refers to its recovery table to see what it should do. It may accept this error and print out a message to the operator or take other action.

Write

The procedure for a write error is on the left side of the flow chart, Fig. 11.3.

After the command in process is distinguished (1), we record the error, channel and unit information (18). We then tally the error (19) and backspace the tape (20). Has an *end of tape* signal been detected (21)?

If an *end of tape* has been received, there is no hope. We prepare an error message (22) and call upon *Print* to produce a message for the operator. We then call on *Stopdead* to halt the computer, telling us, of course, that it has done so.

As long as no *end of tape* is received (21), we check to see if a recurrent message is required (25). If so, we check the number of errors that have occurred since the last error message. If the proper number has occurred, a new message is required. This is determined (26), and a message is prepared there after *Print* sends the message.

In any case, the block just written must be erased (27). This requires a subroutine to give a *backup tape* command and then to give an *erase* command. These operations are done "while we wait." They do not require the use of *Initiate* because we know full particulars about the unit for which the operation is required. The program and other traps are held up while this goes on. Finally we try another write operation with *Preinitiate* and *Initiate*. This gets us back to the main program which continues while another attempt to write is in progress.

11.4 PRINT (OR PUNCH)

The *Print* Routine

Print is used to print information immediately on the on-line printer. The technique is equally applicable for off-line printing and for punching. In other words, if we wish to designate one tape unit as an off-line print tape unit, we would use the same sort of routine to supply information to this tape. Correspondingly, if the information for off-line printing is to be punched into cards through an on-line card punch, the routine is again similar. This being the case, we restrict the discussion to on-line printing; the reader can make the extension.

AVAILABILITY

Print is available to everybody with a *FOREMAN*. The *FOREMAN* itself uses *Print* for error messages that occur during traps which it supervises. We have seen uses for *Print* in the last section. When *JOCS* runs into difficulties or wishes to give the operator instructions about what tape to mount and where to mount it, it uses *Print* for this purpose. The same is true of the supervisor.

Finally, the main program can make use of on-line messages simply by using the subroutine call GET followed by PRINT, as outlined below.

FORMAT

Anybody can request *PRINT* with the following call:

GET   PRINT, number of entries; start, words; start, words; . . . ;
        start, words, ENDLINE; start, words; . . . ; start, words,
        ENDLINE   (11.4.1)

If this call appears in a source program for assembly, it would probably be necessary to include ETC card. This will permit other items in the calling sequence to be strung out as required.

ACTION

The item *number of entries* indicates how many entries consisting of *start, words*; or *start, words,* ENDLINE; are associated with the PRINT command. The intention of the command is to transmit to the printer several lines for it to print on-line. Words that compose the line are indicated within the command. We begin to compose the first line right after *number of entries*; we enter *words* words into the line, starting to take these words from location *start*. We continue to compose the line, entering the next *words* words from the next location *start*. We compose a line until we reach ENDLINE. The rest of the line is filled with 0's and the line is then sent off to be printed.

We are ready to compose a new line; we start with the next entry and send *words* words into the next line beginning with the location *start*.

We print lines in this fashion until all the entries are used up. We know when this is so, for then the number of entries used corresponds with *number of entries*.

OCCURRENCE

The time at which *Print* is requested depends upon who asks for it. If the request is from outside, this should not produce too much trouble. However, the *FOREMAN* may have to use *Print* while he is servicing a trap. Several cases arise, and each of these is discussed below. It is important to note that the following convention is employed for the discussion that follows:

The channel to which the printer is attached is called Channel P.

In our computer a channel has several units attached to it. In this case, Channel P not only has a printer on it, but probably several magnetic tape units.

Normal Print Request

By normal print request we mean any one of the following situations:

- No traps are being serviced.
- A trap is being serviced, but presently Channel P is dormant.
- A trap has occurred on Channel P for which the services of *Print* are required.

In the first instance above the services of *Print* are requested by other software or by the main program, since no interrupts are presently being serviced. In the other two instances, the *FOREMAN* is requesting *Print*, for we notice that a trap is in progress and therefore other software or the main program could not be making a request.

FLOW CHART

To expedite the explanations, we use a sequence flow chart. This is not the actual flow chart of *Print* which will be formulated later.

The operations required for a normal print request, case 1, are shown in Fig. 11.4.1. Notice the simple sequence there:

1. traps on all other channels are suspended
2. the print activity is requested in the proper sequence
3. all traps are restored
4. exit

The exit from this routine requires a return to the requesting routine: in the case of an external request, return is to the main program or other software; in the case of a trap request, the return is to that portion of the *FOREMAN* which requested the printout.

External Requests, Channel P Active

When the program or another software system requests *Print*, we cannot immediately make a print request on Channel P because it is occupied. Printing has priority over computer activity to inform the operator of a situation before the computer continues. We can give a print command only after activity on Channel P has terminated.

Because of the priority of the print activity, information about the incoming trap is not acted upon immediately but is saved until printing is underway as in case 2, Fig. 11.4.2.

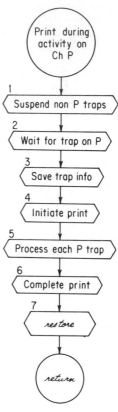

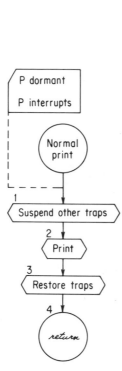

FIGURE 11.4.1. Normal *Print* activity, case 1.

FIGURE 11.4.2. *Print* activity during trap on Channel P, case 2.

DESCRIPTION OF CASE 2 FLOW CHART

We want to get printing started as soon as possible. If other channels terminate before Channel P, we ignore them; if we service another trap, the print operation will be delayed. In (1) we suspend traps on all channels except P and twiddle our fingers until the trap on P arrives (2).

When Channel P terminates we do not process this trap, but we start the print activity first. However, we cannot completely ignore the trapped operation or information about it will be lost. Therefore, we save information about the trap (3) and *then* initiate the print activity (4).

After the print commands are given, we return to the earlier trap and process it (5). We are not done, however; the $\mathscr{FOREMAN}$ is still in control and we should not return to the main program but, rather, to the $\mathscr{FOREMAN}$ itself. The user of $\mathscr{Print}$ is the destination to which $\mathscr{FOREMAN}$ should return. Since this is included in the print routine, return is made from there (6) to the main program or other software (7), (8).

Trap With Channel P Active

This case arises when a trap on some channel other than P which is being serviced must communicate with the operator. Printing is required but Channel P is in use. Case 3, in Fig. 11.4.3, is somewhat similar to case 2 just discussed.

We suspend traps on all channels except P (1) and then wait for the trap to occur on P (2). When it arrives, the information about it must be saved before we continue (3). A print activity is initiated (4).

Now that printing is under way we can go back and finish the servicing of the original trap— the one that was not on Channel P (5). Once it is serviced, we recover the information about the trap occurring on Channel P just before we gave it the print commands. We then process this trap (6). When we finish this processing we take the normal exit for the P-channel trap, which is probably to $\mathscr{Discontinue}$. The exit from this trap includes $\mathscr{restore}$ (7) before exiting (8).

Should the processing of the trap on Channel P require the use of printing, then this comes under case 1, and no difficulty arises.

Interrelation of Print and Trap

The relation between these two routines is illustrated in Fig. 11.4.4. With Channel P dormant and $\mathscr{Print}$ requested by the program or software, $\mathscr{Print}$ is executed without any reference to $\mathscr{Trap}$.

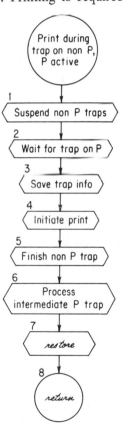

FIGURE 11.4.3. $\mathscr{Print}$ activity resulting from a trap on another channel while channel P is active, case 3.

If Channel P is dormant and an error is detected in $\mathcal{T}rap$, the error exit is taken to $\mathcal{P}rint$. When $\mathcal{P}rint$ is completed, the print exit returns us to $\mathcal{T}rap$. When $\mathcal{T}rap$ in turn is completed, it exits to the main program where the trap occurred.

If the trap being serviced was a Channel P trap, the same path is taken as described in the preceding paragraph.

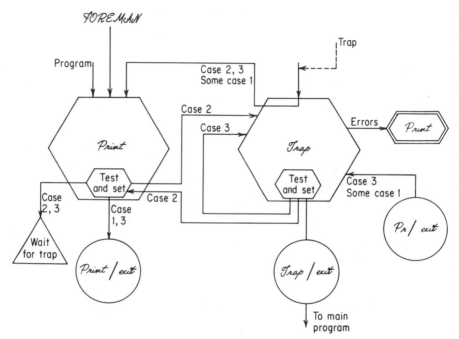

FIGURE 11.4.4. Interaction between the trap and print routines of the $\mathcal{FOREMAN}$.

CASE 2

Here a request for print is made while Channel P is active. The $\mathcal{FORE}$-$\mathcal{MAN}$ is entered directly while no interrupt is taking place. However, $\mathcal{P}rint$ cannot proceed, since Channel P is active. This is determined at the end of $\mathcal{P}rint$. Everything grinds to a halt and we wait for a trap to occur (the triangle directly below $\mathcal{P}rint$).

When the trap occurs it takes us directly to $\mathcal{T}rap$. We do not spend much time there; we just save information about the trap and return directly to $\mathcal{P}rint$. The test at the end of $\mathcal{P}rint$ indicates that there is another channel P waiting to be serviced. This returns us to $\mathcal{T}rap$. At the end of $\mathcal{T}rap$ we determine that part of $\mathcal{P}rint$ remains to be serviced. This returns us to the end of $\mathcal{P}rint$; we finish up and exit.

CASE 3

For this case a print request occurs during *Trap*. This takes us to *Print*. We cannot proceed until Channel P becomes trapped, and hence, we exit to the wait triangle.

When Channel P is trapped we save the information in Trap and go immediately to *Print*. On completion of the print sequence we return to *Trap* where the original error took place. We can now finish servicing the trap on this other (non-P) channel.

At the end of servicing the trap, we check and determine that there is another trap, a Channel-P trap, waiting to be serviced. This returns us to the beginning of *Trap*. After servicing the Channel-P trap, we exit normally to the main program unless some other eventuality should forestall this.

Print-Associated Switches

As you can see from the last subsection, the present state of affairs must be communicated somehow to each of the routines, *Print* and *Trap*. The means for doing this is the setting of cells in memory called **switches**. One or more of these switches is tested each time we pass through one of the routines. They store a record of which case is acted upon and what has transpired so far.

The switches, their use, setting and resetting are summarized in Table 11.4.

TRAPACTIVE

This cell contains the location of the unit activity block for the unit and channel for which a trap is being serviced. This information is stored there only when a trap is in progress *and being serviced*. In other words, when a trap occurs on Channel P which is not acted upon but the information is saved instead, nothing is entered into *trapactive*. When the trap is fully serviced, 0 is entered into this cell.

PWAIT

This cell is set to 1 when printing is required but Channel P is active. This means that printing must wait for a trap on Channel P. It is also the signal to *Trap* that an immediate return to *Print* is required.

PTRAPRETURN

This cell stores a 1 when it is necessary to return to *Trap* to service a previous trap which has occurred on Channel P, but which was ignored because *Print* had to continue.

TABLE 11.4 *Print*-associated switches

Switch name	Meaning	Reset to 0 by *Postinitiate* when	Nonzero setting	Set nonzero by
trapactive	A trap is being processed	Always	Location of UAB for unit for which trap is being processed	*Trap*
pwait	Must wait for trap on Channel P before print continues	Always	1	*Print* when Channel P is active
ptrapreturn	Must return to *Trap* to service Channel-P trap ignored so far	Trap/exit if pwait & twotraps	1	Print/exit & pwait & trapactive
twotraps	A non-P trap being processed and a P-trap yet to start processing	pwait	1	Print/exit & pwait & trapactive & ptrapreturn

TWOTRAPS

This cell is set to 1 when there is a trap being serviced on some channel other than P *and* when there is a trap on Channel P for which processing has not started yet.

Flow Chart for Print

Once we have established the switches outlined in Table 11.4, the series of events that occur during *Print* is a simple matter to analyze. They are summarized in the flow chart in Fig. 11.4.5. Notice that *Print* can be entered from:

- outside
- within the *FOREMAN* from a calling routine such as *Trap*
- the very beginning of *Trap* when the *pwait* switch is 1

In all cases the same steps are followed.

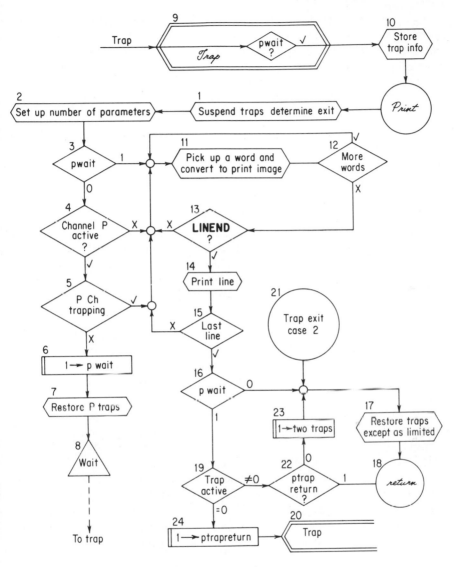

FIGURE 11.4.5. *Print* flow chart.

CASE 1

We enter *Print* from:

1. outside with Channel P dormant
2. inside with Channel P dormant
3. a trap on Channel P

We suspend all traps (1) and determine the exit for the operation. We then set up the number of parameters for the operation (2). We find that *pwait* is 0 (3) and that either Channel P is inactive (4) or Channel P is active and is causing the trap (4), (5). We then enter the print sequence.

PRINT SEQUENCE

We pick up a word from the call sequence and convert it to a print image (11). If there are more words (12), we go and get more (11). Otherwise, we determine if this is the end of the line (13). If not, we have a new starting address and a new number of words; so we pick up more words to make the print image for this line (11).

If this is the end of the line (13), we print the line (14) and then check the number of entries to see if that is the last line (15). If not, we get the next entry and prepare the image for the next line (11), (12), (13).

If this is the last line (15), we examine *pwait* again (16), and since it is 0, we restore all traps (17) and return to the caller (18).

CASE 2

After we enter *Print*, the setup steps are performed (1), (2). We make a few checks and find that *pwait* is 0 (3), Channel P is active (4), but Channel P is not trapping (5). We therefore set *pwait* to 1 (6), restore the traps on Channel P but not on any others (7) and then grind to a halt to await a trap on Channel P (8).

When the trap on Channel P arrives (9) we enter *Trap*. The information from the trap is then stored (10) and we re-enter *Print*. We do the initial steps (1), (2) and then test *pwait* (3) to find that it is set to 1. We then do the print sequence described before (11), (12), (13), (14), (15).

On completion we check *pwait* and find it to be 1. Since *trapactive* was never set (19), we return to *Trap* where the Channel P trap is processed (20). At the end of this trap we enter *Postinitiate*. In this routine we check *pwait* again and, finding that it is set to 1, we return to *Print* at (21) where we restore all traps (17) and return to the user's program (18).

CASE 3

Here Channel P is active and a trap has arrived on some other channel which requires a printout. We enter *Print* and do the setup (1), (2). We find that *pwait* is set to 0 (3). Channel P is active (4), but Channel P is not doing the trapping (5); so we set *pwait* to 1 (6), restore traps on Channel P only (7) and wait (8).

Soon Channel P interrupts and takes us to *Trap*, (9). Since *pwait* is set to 1, we exit and store the trap information as we do so (10). We enter

Print, perform the setup (1), (2) and find *pwait* set to 1 (3). We now do the printing (11), (12), (13), (14), (15).

When we check *pwait* again, we find it is set to 1 (16). Because we had entered *Print* originally during a trap on another channel, *trapactive* contains the address of the trap we are servicing (19). We now test *ptrapreturn* (22). This is set to 1 because we have to service the trap on Channel P which is yet pending. Since there are two traps pending, we set *twotraps* to 1 (23). We are now finished with *Print*, so we can restore traps except as limited originally by *Trap* (17). We then return to *Trap* which originally called *Print*.

At the end of *Trap* a test is made (not shown here) where it is determined that a return should be made to *Trap* to service the awaiting Channel P trap. This is discussed in Section 11.7 with regard to the routine *Preinitiate*.

11.5 HALTS AND ERRORS

Halts

NECESSITY

It is necessary for the computer to stop for one of these reasons:

- to communicate information to the human
- to cause the human to take action
- to have him make a decision
- because there is nothing else to do

WHAT DOES THE COMPUTER SAY?

It is possible for the computer to stop without saying anything to the operator. However, this is not customary and it would worry the operator; he would suspect, and probably rightly, that the computer broke down. Therefore, if the computer stops of its own volition (the volition of the program, of course), then it is obligated (the system programmer is obligated at any rate) to tell the operator why it has done so.

It can provide information in four ways:

- It can print information without stopping.
- It can print, then stop, to be restarted when the operator presses the start button.
- It can stop with an error message, unrestartable by the start button; the operator must use a special restart procedure to get the computer going again.
- It can stop without any message (undesirable).

The IBM 7090 version of FOREMAN provides a printout after 25 unsuccessive tries at writing a block. In such a case it would produce the following message.†

UNIT number   FILE ident   REC ident

25 ERASES DURING WRITE   (11.5.1)

For a multireel file, instructions to the operator are followed by a machine pause. The computer prints out the following:

mounting instruction

OPERATOR ACTION PAUSE   (11.5.2)

machine pause—operator action

ACTION COMPLETED

The printer produces a message of what the operator should do, followed by an indication that it is going to stop and wait for him to take the action. The operator does the job and then presses the start button. The machine acknowledges the operator activity by printing out the final message stating that the action is completed.

When writing retries have continued to the point where all the tape is used up, then IOCS is impotent to continue. The following message appears:

UNIT number   EOT ON ERASE   CANNOT PROCEED

(11.5.3)

There is no way for the operator to have the computer recover normally from this. He must invoke a special procedure such as dumping the program and telling the supervisor to bring in another one. Another less disquieting case arises when the computer runs out of jobs. The supervisor is notified of this by a $STOP card (see Chapter 13). It prints the following remark:

$STOP

END OF JOBS   (11.5.4)

CANNOT PROCEED

No programming system known allows the computer to stop without a message. Should it do so, the operator hunts for an internal difficulty or else calls in the customer engineer.

What May Be Requested of the Operator?

The answer is twofold:

- action
- decision

† *Note:* Items in printout do not appear in sans serif type because they are not part of assembly language.

ACTION

Operator action takes three forms:

- device manipulation
- information entry
- call in other software

The many kinds of device manipulation include such things as placing a specified tape on a specified tape unit or making a given tape unit active. Information entry includes answers to specific questions. When a program comes to an error halt the operator must recover by resorting to another piece of software, such as the dump service routine, recall of the supervisor, or analysis by a debugging routine.

DECISIONS

The computer may ask questions which the operator answers not with facts but with decisions. He may have to gather information that is missing. He may determine whether an error may be tolerated. He may decide if processing can continue with one or more records being omitted.

He may determine whether processing continues altogether or whether it is terminated. If it is terminated, he may decide if a next job in the job list is performed, or if some other job should be taken out of turn, or if other software should or should not be called in.

We now discuss how the FOREMAN implements different kinds of halts.

Nonpause

When a message is produced by the computer for the operator without any cessation of computer activity, the procedure is simple. The originator of the message, whether it is the main program or software, is responsible for assembling the message. It is produced on the output printer by a simple request for *Print*.

The Pause

This activity is typified by (11.5.2). The user, whether it is the main program, *IOCS*, or other software, chooses or fabricates a message for the operator, then makes a request for *Print*. Next, *Pause* is called in to do the following:

- print the message, OPERATOR ACTION PAUSE, or the like
- suspend all computer activity, including trapping, until the *start* button is pressed by the operator
- print the message, ACTION COMPLETED, or the like
- resume normal activity

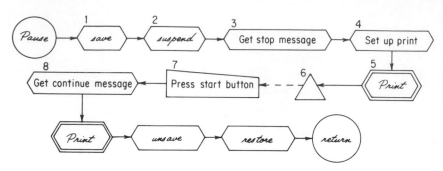

FIGURE 11.5.1. *Pause*.

In Fig. 11.5.1 we find the flow chart for *Pause*. We save register information (1), suspend all traps (2), procure the stop message (3) and set it
up to print (4). *Print* produces the message (5) and stops (6), enabling the
start button to recall *Pause* (7). *Pause* picks up the *continue* message (8)
after the operator has pressed the *start* button and recalls *Print* (9). Finally,
the register information (10) and the suspended traps are restored (11)
before return to the caller (12).

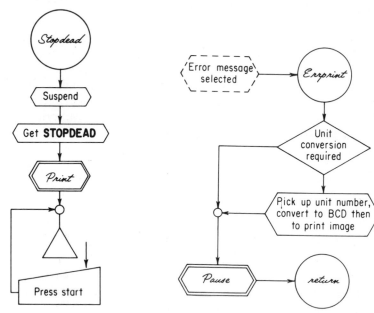

FIGURE 11.5.2. *Stopdead*.   FIGURE 11.5.3. *Errprint*.

Stopdead

When we are in trouble we call in *Stopdead*, flow-charted in Fig. 11.5.2. We suspend interrupts (1), get the *Stopdead* message (2), print it with *Print* (3) and halt (4). When the operator presses the *start* button, the computer goes back to the previous step in the program, which causes another halt (4).

The only way for the operator to stop this vicious circle is to enter new information into the console keyboard to cause the computer to jump to a known location in memory—the start of a dump or debug routine, perhaps.

Errprint

When the message involves the naming of a tape unit or other IO device, the name should be comprehensible to the human. Within the computer memory, reference to IO devices is usually maintained in straight binary form (except for the decimal or alphanumeric computer, of course). We incorporate the conversion from binary to BCD (which precedes the conversion-to-print image) into a routine which includes *Pause*, and call the whole thing *Errprint*. The flow chart for this is presented in Fig. 11.5.3 without explanation.

11.6   DISCONTINUE, INTERNAL DISPATCHER AND INITIATE

Event Sequence

We discuss here three routines which participate in the normal trap operation;

- *Discontinue* (IBM Select −)
- *Dispatcher*
- *Initiate* (IBM Select +)

Normal trap operation is outlined in Fig. 11.1.2, and discussed in connection with *Trap* in Fig. 11.2.1, and summarized below.

Discontinue

This routine is included in the user's program to assimilate the results furnished by the *FOREMAN*. It does collateral processing to furnish information to the *Dispatcher*. It also examines exceptions to determine their dispositions. By a choice of returns, it can ignore the *Dispatcher* and turn over control to other routines for exception processing.

Dispatcher

From information furnished by *Discontinue* or otherwise available, the *Dispatcher* determines which unit on the trapped channel should be given the next command. We examine two kinds of dispatchers: the user-furnished dispatcher may use a sophisticated priority-decision methodology; a simpler routine, *Scan*, is incorporated into *FOREMAN* in Section 11.7.

Preinitiate

This routine takes the information provided by the *Dispatcher* and sets it up for the user's routine, *Initiate*. The user may furnish different initiate routines for different kinds of uses or for channels. *Preinitiate* has recourse to a table to determine the suitable routine, whether it be $Initiate_1$ or $Initiate_2$, etc.

Initiate

This routine supplies a command to be given by *FOREMAN*. It also provides list updating—it does the internal accounting associated with the request being serviced. *Initiate* resides in the user.

Postinitiate

In this routine described in Section 11.7, the actual IO command is given to the channel control unit or actual device.

Discontinue

The routine described here is similar to the one which is incorporated into the IBM 7090 IOCS. It is flow-charted in Fig. 11.6.1 and begins by saving register information (1). We check for a short record (2); for an error (3), its type is noted in the file activity block (4). The buffer attached to the device is now detached therefrom and from the request chain (5). It is simple to check the chain at this point to see if a new request is forthcoming (6). If there is none, the chain is eliminated and the channel activity block,

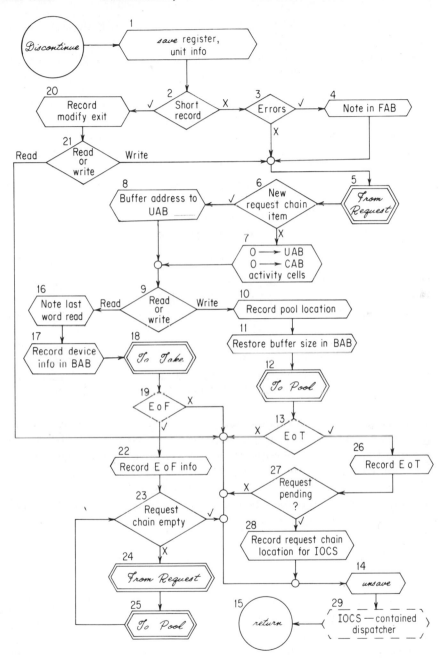

FIGURE 11.6.1. *Discontinue.*

described later, is cleared (7). When further requests exist, the next buffer address is furnished to the unit activity block (8).

The next actions depend upon whether the activity completed is read or write (9). For a write activity we have to get the location of the pool where the buffer was attached (10). The buffer that was just used may have had only part of its contents written. A statement of the portion of the block written is contained in one of the buffer activity block words. This is restored to indicate full buffer size (11), and the buffer is returned to the pool (12). If no *end of tape* was encountered (13), we *unsave* (14) and return to the user (15).

For a READ buffer (9) not completely filled, we record in the BAB how many words have been entered there (16) along with device activity (17). The buffer is then attached to the *take* chain to be made available for future READ commands (18). If no *end of file* is detected (19), we *unsave* (14) and return (15).

A short record (2) requires a modified exit procedure (20). For READ (21) we unsave (14) and return (15). This permits the *Dispatcher* to request another read operation on this channel since the read request was not filled. For WRITE where the short block is permissible, (20), (21) the write procedure is entered at (5).

When an *end of file* is encountered during READ (19), this is recorded (22). No more read requests can be honored for this file since there is no file left. For requests in the request chain (23) we remove the buffer from the chain (24) and return it to the pool (25). We then examine the chain.

When the request chain is empty (23) we *unsave* (14) and *return* (15).

When an *end of tape* is encountered on writing (13), we record it (26) and then check to see if there are further write requests pending (27). If not, we are done. For further write requests, we inform *IOCS* of the location of the request chain, so it can dispose of the matter (28).

Notice in the diagram that a block (29) is provided for a user-furnished *Dispatcher*. If one is not furnished, we simply return to the *FOREMAN* where we have recourse to *Scan*.

Initiate

The *Initiate* routine flow chart is shown in Fig. 11.6.2. This routine is incorporated in the user's program or other software (it is found in the IBM 7090 IOCS as Select +).

We save the register information (1) and then supply the device control information to make up the command (2). Block sequencing information is required when such a procedure is requested (3). Memory accessing information is acquired from the buffer activity block (4). Request chain information can be traced down through the file activity block (5). Enough information should now be on hand to set up the IO command (6). Registers are restored (7), and we return to the $\mathcal{FOREMAN}$ (8).

The Internal Dispatcher

PROBLEM

Between $\mathcal{Discontinue}$ and $\mathcal{In}$-itiate we select the next job for the channel which has become free. The ideal selection philosophy is based upon file requirements, channel activity and present buffer status.

IDEAL PHILOSOPHY

The ideal philosophy has a very simple goal: to keep the computer and its software as busy as possible so as to accomplish the most in the least time. If we assign an IO oper-

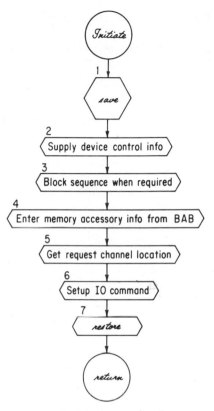

FIGURE 11.6.2. $\mathcal{Initiate}$.

ation to furnish information for a file which will not immediately use it and disregard other files where information is vital, we will slow down the computer. The question is how to determine which activity is most necessary, for once we do so, it is simple to expedite this activity. We explore the interrelation between the file and the device to this end.

FILE-UNIT RELATION

$\mathcal{FOREMAN}$ and $\mathcal{IOCS}$ are kept as separate as possible. The $\mathcal{FOREMAN}$ relates to the devices through the channel activity blocks and unit activity blocks. It has full information about what is happening on all channels and all units of these channels. However, the less it knows about the files the more independently it can operate.

Conversely, $\mathcal{IOCS}$ is aware particularly of files; it would rather not know about the devices or the channels to which they are assigned. This is unrealistic when several units report to a single channel; files cannot be used independently if the units which they reference are on the same channel.

Another complication is that a file may have only one buffer assigned to it, or it may have several buffers, or it may share buffers with other files. This latter problem is most difficult to resolve.

INDIVIDUAL FILE

The individual file is one that does not share buffers with other files. Its importance or priority may be rated according to the number of buffers assigned to it. A multibuffer individual file which is *open* and *attached* and which has none or few buffers full (for read) would have top priority for filling. What happens when almost all the buffers assigned are full? A dispatching discipline can be arranged which sets priority according to the ratio of full to available buffers.

Group File Dispatching

For the group file, several files share a number of buffers. The list which appears in the assembly program indicates several things:

- the number of files included in the group and their names
- the number of buffers reserved for the group
- the maximum number of files which may be opened at any one time

The list which defines the group is also the group activity block (GAB). It is examined each time assignments are made.

EXAMPLE

Suppose we define a group consisting of three files and seven buffers, where any two of the files may be active at once and the files are reserved files. This is done in the source language program by;

```
CLUB    NOOP    RES, 2, 7
        NOOP    BILL
        NOOP    RALPH
        NOOP    JIM              (11.6.1)
```

Suppose at this particular moment the situation which prevails is that diagrammed in Fig. 11.6.3. Notice that the group activity block, CLUB, is associated with the pool activity block PAUL. The files in turn are associated through the FABs to CLUB. Figure 11.6.3 displays that;

- BILL has three buffers presently associated with him.
- JIM has two buffers associated with him.
- RALPH has none (he is inactive).

The dispatcher concludes that if this group is active, JIM should have another buffer activated for him.

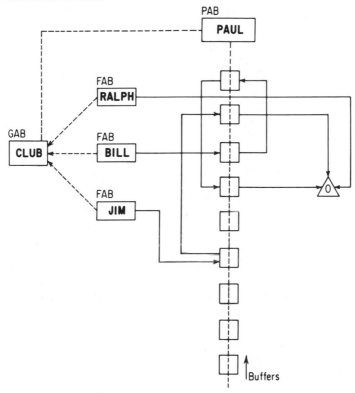

FIGURE 11.6.3. The Group Activity Block (GAB) dictates the maximum and minimum number of buffers available to a file belonging to the group.

However, although this group has needs, we could imagine that a single file which is open and attached and which has only one buffer assigned to it might have that buffer empty and waiting to be read. It would seem preferable to fulfill the needs of the loner before we saturate the group's needs.

The complexity of even an apparently simple situation is shown in Fig.
11.6.4. The activity blocks pertinent to a given program are displayed here.
Notice that the channel activity block points to a chain of unit activity
blocks for units attached to the channel. The UABs in turn point to or are

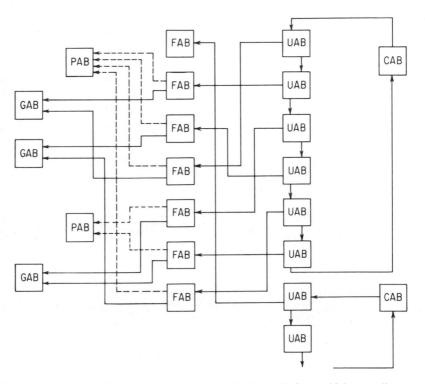

FIGURE 11.6.4. A glimpse of some of the interrelations which prevail
among the Activity Blocks for the Unit, Channel, File, Pool and Group.

pointed to by file activity blocks. These in turn are connected to buffer
pools, but not necessarily the same pool. Two pools are indicated here,
since two pool activity blocks are noted. Further, each file may point to a
group through the group activity block. Omitted from consideration here
are the buffer assignments. Each buffer points to the pool to which it
is assigned and is pointed to by the FAB to which it is momentarily
assigned.

The comprehensive dispatcher should consider the Gestalt—the status of
all activity for the program. This might entail an activity summary table of
some sort. Presently, no comprehensive dispatcher exists.

Simple prevalent dispatchers do not occupy much memory space and are certainly better than no dispatcher at all. What amount of complexity in the dispatcher would cause enough improvement to be worth the additional space in memory and the additional time to operate it?

11.7 INITIATE-ASSOCIATED ROUTINES

The routines discussed in this section all bear on *Initiate*.

- *Activate* provides a synthetic activation of an inactive channel.
- *Preinitiate* sets up information for *Initiate* and selects the proper *Initiate*.
- *Scan* is the internal dispatcher provided in *FOREMAN*.
- *Postinitiate* finishes off trap processing and permits return either to the program or to another trap waiting to be processed.

Activate

The normal sequence of initiating a unit on a channel is to call in *Dispatcher* as part of the processing associated with *Trap*. When a channel is idle no traps occur on it. How does one start up the channel again? *Activate* does this.

USERS

The program refers to *Activate* by using the call described below. *SYSTEM* frequently calls upon *Activate* to bring in information for its own use to call in other routines or other pieces of software. *LOAD* uses *Activate* to start up a unit for bringing in a program or a subroutine. *IOCS* needs *Activate* whenever a file is opened with *Open*. The tasks which this routine performs are:

- It checks a request using *Test*.
- If the channel is idle, it immediately starts it up.
- If the channel is busy and no priority is given to this request, the request is recorded so that it will be the next task performed.
- If this request has priority, we wait for the present business to be finished and then start the unit on this task.

CALL

We call *Activate* with:

$$\text{GET} \quad \text{ACTIVE, priority, channel/unit number} \qquad (11.7.1)$$

Here *priority* is a single bit which is 1 for priority and 0 otherwise. The *channel/unit number* provides identification of the desired unit and depends upon the manufacturer for which $\mathscr{FOREMAN}$ is designed.

Activate Flow Chart

The flow chart for $\mathscr{Activate}$ is in Fig. 11.7.1.

TEST

The first seven boxes are designated $\mathscr{Test}$. An illegal unit designation incapacitates the routine. To determine this, we first $\mathscr{save}$ the registers (1) and $\mathscr{suspend}$ the traps (2). An error occurs if the unit activity block address is not in the proper area in $\mathscr{FOREMAN}$ (3) or if the unit designated is illegal (4). In this case we get an error message (5), request an $\mathscr{Errprint}$ (6) and come to a $\mathscr{Stopdead}$ (7).

LEGAL REQUEST

If the channel is not in use (8), we get the address of $\mathscr{Initiate}$ from the unit activity block (9) where it was put by the user. If he has failed to put it there, $\mathscr{Activate}$ is powerless (10) and must $\mathscr{restore}$ (11), $\mathscr{unsave}$ (12) and $\mathscr{return}$ to the user (13). If a proper address is found (10), the unit activity block is set up for the request (14), and the proper word of the channel activity block is posted (see below) to indicate the activity of this unit (15).

$\mathscr{Initiate}$ is now called upon (16) with a subroutine call so that a return is made to $\mathscr{Activate}$ when $\mathscr{Initiate}$ is finished. $\mathscr{Initiate}$ has two returns, one which is normal and the other for errors detected. The housekeeping activity required is performed on return from $\mathscr{Initiate}$ (17), (18). If Activate is used during trap time, the traps are not restored, but the registers are unsaved (12) before return (13). At nontrap time (19) both $\mathscr{restore}$ (11) and $\mathscr{unsave}$ (12) are done before $\mathscr{return}$ (13).

CHANNEL IN USE

When the channel is in use (8) but if the request has no priority (20), we post the request in the channel activity block preference word (21) (discussed later), and exit.

When priority is indicated we post the priority cell of the channel activity block (22), $\mathscr{unsave}$ (23) but do not $\mathscr{restore}$. During trap time (24), we return to $\mathscr{FOREMAN}$ for further processing (25). For nontrap time (24), we restore the traps on this channel only (25) and wait for a trap to terminate the activity on the channel (26), at which time we $\mathscr{restore}, \mathscr{unsave}$ (27) and $\mathscr{return}$ (25). $\mathscr{Return}$ eventually enables the trap to be processed and the priority request to initiate action on the desired unit.

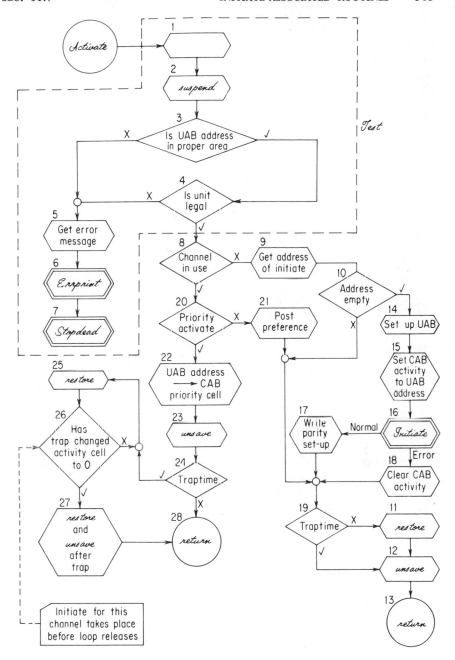

FIGURE 11.7.1. *Activate.*

The Scan Discipline

The channel activity block for $\mathscr{Scan}$, the sample dispatcher of $\mathscr{FORE}$-$\mathscr{MAN}$, is found in Fig. 11.7.2. It contains three cells to indicate the preference status of activity on this channel. The activity cell is either empty or contains the address of the unit activity block belonging to an

Channel Activity Block	0 *or* active UAB	Activity Cell
	0 *or* priority UAB	Priority Cell
	0 *or* preference UAB	Preference Cell
	Number of devices *and* UAB address	UAB Locator
	0 *or* non-0	Parity Inhibit
	Number recoveries *and* number of permanent errors	Recovery History

FIGURE 11.7.2. Contents of the channel activity block.

active (running) unit. The priority cell indicates the unit activity block which must be initiated next on this channel. It may be blank. The preference cell contains UAB address for the unit which should be initiated if no priority is present.

The UAB locator is used during scan of the units presently attached to the channel. The address of the first UAB in the chain appears in this cell, as does the number of devices attached. The parity inhibit cell and the recovery history cell serve obvious purposes.

The priority hierarchy is as follows:

- If the priority cell is not empty, the unit it indicates must be serviced next.
- If the priority cell is empty, then the unit indicated by the preference cell is serviced next if that cell is not empty.
- If the priority and preference cells are empty but the activity cell is not, the unit which is presently active is checked next; if the corresponding UAB for the unit which just completed the activity contains an $\mathscr{Initiate}$ address, the same unit is reactivated.

- If the active unit becomes dormant, the UAB's of all the other units attached are examined; if an unempty one is found, it is activated.
- If the three CAB cells are empty, as well as all the UAB cells, the channel becomes idle.

CAB cells can be set by *Activate*. *Discontinue* can also enter information into these cells or clear them (see Fig. 11.6.1).

Preinitiate

Preinitiate, flow-charted in Fig. 11.7.3, first checks the priority cell (1). If it is nonvoid, get the UAB address from it (2). If it is empty, but the preference cell (3) is nonvoid, get the UAB address from there (4). From either (2) or (4) initiate a new unit: save the registers (5) and get the *Initiate*

CAB SETTINGS

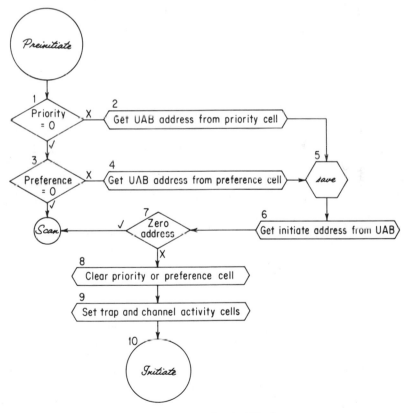

FIGURE 11.7.3. *Preinitiate*.

address from the UAB (6). If this word of the UAB is empty (7) (if it has not been set by some routine in 𝓕𝓞𝓡𝓔𝓜𝓐𝓝 or 𝓘𝓞𝓒𝓢), return to 𝓢𝒸𝒶𝓃.

Clear the priority or preference cell, whichever brought us here (8), when the 𝓘𝓃𝒾𝓉𝒾𝒶𝓉𝑒 address is obtained. Set trap and channel activity cells (9) and call in 𝓘𝓃𝒾𝓉𝒾𝒶𝓉𝑒 (10).

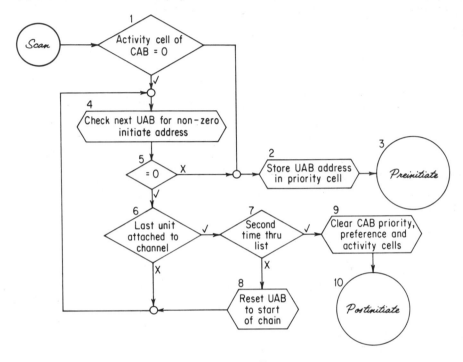

FIGURE 11.7.4. 𝓢𝒸𝒶𝓃.

If both the priority and preference cells were empty (13), or if the 𝓘𝓃𝒾𝓉𝒾𝒶𝓉𝑒 word of UAB is empty (7), go to 𝓢𝒸𝒶𝓃.

𝓢𝒸𝒶𝓃

For 𝓢𝒸𝒶𝓃 in Fig. 11.7.4, if the activity cell of the channel activity block has not been cleared to 0, it is an indication that further activity for this unit is required (1). In this case we store the UAB address in the priority cell (2) and return to the routine 𝓟𝓇𝑒𝒾𝓃𝒾𝓉𝒾𝒶𝓉𝑒 (3).

If the activity cell is empty (1), we go on to the next UAB in the chain. The first time this sequence is performed we have no marker. We therefore go to the channel activity block and obtain from the unit activity block locator the address of the first UAB in the chain. An alternative is to use the address of the last UAB activity if this was preserved somewhere in a previous routine.

After obtaining this address (4) we go to the unit activity block and examine the *Initiate* word to see if it contains an *Initiate* address which is nonzero. If this is the case (5), we store that address in the CAB priority cell (2) and return to *Preinitiate*.

If this UAB contains a void *Initiate* word, we obtain the next UAB in the chain from the pointer in this UAB provided that we have not examined all the UABs in the chain (6).

This routine entitles us to another review of the chain if we have examined all the unit activity blocks once (6), (7). For the first time through, we reset the starting address of the UAB chain (8) and make another trip through. After two trips through the chain (7), it is pretty clear that there are no units for which activity is desired. We therefore make sure that the priority, preference and activity cells for this channel have been cleared (9) and go to *Postinitiate* (10).

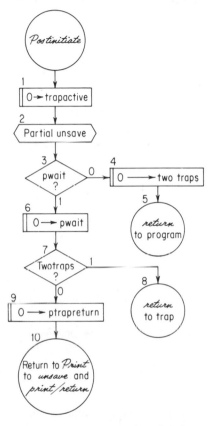

FIGURE 11.7.5. *Postinitiate.*

Postinitiate

This routine, shown in Fig. 11.7.5, is entered on return from the *Initiate* routine or when *Scan* has permitted this channel to go idle. The purpose of this routine is to determine what to do next when two traps are in progress. The first task is to clear the *trapactive* cell, since trap servicing is complete (1). We now may restore some of the register functions (2). We then check *pwait* to see if another trap is waiting (3). If not, then *twotraps* can be reset also (4) and trap time is over; we return to the user's program (5).

If there is another Channel P trap waiting (3), we are now going to service it; so we reset the indicator *pwait* to 0 (6) and then check the other indicator, *twotraps* (7). If it is 1, we have to return to *Trap* (8). If it is 0, the *Print* routine has not been completed. Before we leave to service the *Print* routine, we reset *ptrapreturn* (9) and then return to *Print* (10).

11.8   NONDATA

Requests That Do Not Involve Data

Here is a list of operations which do not involve a transfer of data:

- density change
- rewind
- rewind and unload
- backspace a record
- backspace a file
- write an end of file mark
- NOOP (for generality)

NEED FOR A DIFFERENT PROCEDURE

We distinguish data and nondata commands for both hardware and software needs. The computer hardware may provide different facilities for nondata commands:

- A different instruction register; the command must be presented to the channel controller at a different location.
- The trap activities for nondata commands may be different or no trap may be provided for them.
- A sequence of nondata commands is not provided, whereas a sequence of data-accessing commands may be referenced automatically by a controller.

The nondata command may differ from the data command with respect to:

- format procedure for fabrication
- nondata *Initiate*

SOFTWARE APPROACH

A routine similar to *Activate*, called *Nondata*, activates a channel for a nondata request. *ND Initiate* fabricates the proper command. We could have a separate *ND Initiate* for each command or a single *ND Initiate* could determine and fabricate a command according to computer specification. We choose the second course, although the details of routine are not examined.

Nondata Flow Chart

Nondata, found in Fig. 11.8, begins with *Test* (1) (refer to *Activate*, Fig. 11.7.1). We *suspend* traps, *save* registers (2), (3) and set up the exit address (4). We then make tests to see which of the following conditions prevails:

- an external command with the unit and channel inactive
- an external command with the unit inactive but the channel active
- an external command with the unit active
- a command from *FOREMAN* with another unit active
- a command from *FOREMAN* with the required unit active

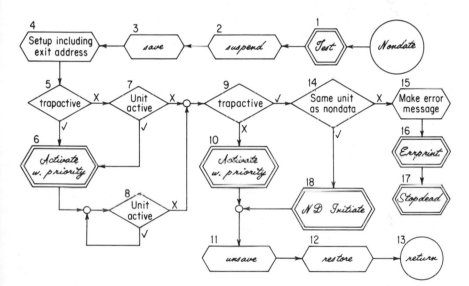

FIGURE 11.8. *Nondata.*

For an active channel (5), we enter the post-*Test* portion of *Activate* indicating a priority (6). In any case we must wait for the unit to become inactive (7, 8). If the request did not arise from a trap (9), the post-*Test* portion of *Activate* is now called in (10) and, after *unsaving* (11) and *restoring* (12), we return (13).

If this request arises because of a trap (9) on an unrequested unit (14) something is wrong. We create an error message (15), print it (16) and *Stopdead*. For a trap on the requested unit (14), we call in *ND Initiate* (18) and return (11), (12), (13).

N D Initiate

This routine:

- fabricates the nondata command
- monitors the special command, WRITE END OF FILE.

It fabricates the command by a table lookup of the request.

The WRITE END OF FILE command needs special attention because it is a WRITE command requiring an echo check after writing. When trouble is detected we must backspace and rewrite the block. If this procedure does not work out, we may have to erase this block and advance to a new area of tape to write the block. Finally, we may get into an end of tape area where we cannot write an end of file successfully. We print an error message and terminate the procedure.

11.9 ATTENTION REQUESTS: NONINTERRUPT

A Problem of Extremes

At the present time any unit on a channel which has been assigned an activity by the *FOREMAN* can interrupt when it is done. We want to remove the restriction that the *FOREMAN* must have made the assignment. Devices, such as telephone lines, then, are capable of interrupting us without a pre-existing work assignment. This is a rather *laissez-faire* environment and could easily lead to trouble unless we provide an option to the programmer to suspend traps on channels which might disturb him.

Why would we wish to be so permissive? We can give overriding interrupt privileges to the operator, for he may have need to transmit top-priority information via the console; communication lines must be serviced immediately for the information is volatile.

The other side of the coin is the complete lack of interrupt. Let's face it, all the old computers were built this way. To use modern software, we must make some synthetic provision for them.

The discussion to follow describes unexpected internal interrupts first, then external interrupts are discussed, followed by a definition of mechanics to handle them. Finally, the no-interrupt case is examined.

Unexpected Internal Interrupts

These interrupts are predictable but rare:

- parity error during memory transmission
- arithmetic errors
- timer
- memory protect infringement

What remedies are possible when these interrupts occur?

- ignore
- return to $\mathcal{SYSTEM}$
- correct

An error is most easily ignored if we suspend its ability to interrupt should it occur. For instance, we can suspend memory transmission parity interference.

A return to $\mathcal{SYSTEM}$ usually means that the difficulty is catastrophic and we wish to abandon the job. $\mathcal{SYSTEM}$ may have its own capability for making a decision built into it; however, if this is not the case, it merely moves in the next job, dumps information from this job and informs the operator.

Correction procedures require sufficient programming to explore the eventualities. For instance, a floating point overflow or underflow may require entire rescaling of a problem. This may be built into a program so that it is supplied with enough versatility to do its own rescaling.

TIMER

One of the purposes of the timer is to provide a limit in running time for the program. The timer interrupts to indicate the expiration of a single interval. The number of intervals so far is compared with the limit supplied to the program. If further intervals are left, the program is set on its way; otherwise it is terminated. The simple routine to do this checking may be built into the program or into $\mathcal{SYSTEM}$.

MEMORY PROTECT

This feature permits several programs to reside in memory without mutual interference. It is a multiprogramming feature. We are quite accustomed by now to the coexistence of several programs, namely, software and the main program. The memory protect feature can prevent clobbering of software by a running program.

The remedy for a memory protect violator is only to dump him and bring in another job. No *on the spot* patching is possible.

Spontaneous External Interrupts

Certain devices are privileged to interrupt without previous assignment:

- communication lines from outside the computer center
- console entry
- communication with another computer or computer memory

Each spontaneous interrupt has its own trap program. Device trapping causes this program to take over the computer until the trap is serviced. The special program independent of the running program may be contained in *SYSTEM* or *FOREMAN*. Authority is delegated to this program through the *FOREMAN*, to which it returns control when it is done. *FOREMAN* remits authority to the main program.

Mechanics of Spontaneous Trap Processing

The first question we ask is where the trap arose; theoretically, there are three choices for this:

- an inactive channel
- an active channel and from the selected unit
- an active channel but from a different unit from that to which an assignment is made

An attention request arising on an idle channel poses no problem. A request arriving from a unit which has had a previous assignment seems to be a contradiction in terms. It is hard to think of a reason why the interrupt would be unexpected.

An attention request from an inactive unit on an active channel is handled very much like the *Print* situation discussed earlier. We must suspend traps on this and other channels and service the unexpected interrupt. The suspension permits the assigned unit to report without being immediately observed.

Servicing of the spontaneous interrupt should be done without the requirement for other IO devices if this is possible. When other devices must be resorted to, pending traps for them must be received first and information about them stored for later processing. Then these units are available for use associated with the spontaneous interrupt.

The sequence of restoring traps must be such as to honor the original channel first and then other channels that were pressed into service for this special call. Above all, we must not issue an *Initiate* on a channel that is working on a previous *Initiate*.

No Interrupt

Supplying software to a system which has no interrupt is justified only when at least simultaneous IO activity is possible. If all processing is sequential, the situation falls apart. To properly implement *FOREMAN* activity, all the channels must be reviewed at optimum intervals: if the interval is too long, channels become idle and productivity is low; if the interval is too short, nothing has happened and the activity review time has been wasted.

Let us call the routine to review channel activity, *Sweep*. How do we call in *Sweep*? Remember, nothing from the outside is going to tell us when a channel's job is completed. Can we leave it to one of the programming systems? We do not know if it will be called in frequently enough to provide adequate service.

The problem is tough to solve. It is usually left to the programmer to spot calls of *Sweep* at sufficient intervals in his program to approach the optimum. What else can we do?

PROBLEMS

11.1   Distinguish the functions of *FOREMAN* from those of *IOCS*.

11.2   What routines of *FOREMAN* are directly available to other programs?

11.3   When does READ or WRITE in *IOCS* result immediately in device activation by *FOREMAN*, and when not?

11.4   What happens if the computer is *trapped* when (a) *IOCS*, (b) *SYSTEM*, (c) *LOAD*, (d) *FOREMAN* (e) the program, is in control?

11.5   Explain the normal sequence of *FOREMAN* routines displayed in Fig. 11.1.2 and their functions.

11.6   Why is *Initiate* not in *FOREMAN*?

11.7   For *Trap* (a) what checks are required; (b) when is *Discontinue* entered; (c) when is *Dispatcher* required; (d) in general what does *Dispatcher* do; (e) what clean-up is required?

11.8   How is a *trap* handled during a *trap*? During *Trap*?

11.9   Explain the *read* recovery procedure; *write* recovery.

11.10   How do the three cases differ when PRINT is requested? Contrast.

11.11   Discuss the use of the four program-contained print switches, *trapactive*, *pwait*, *twotraps* and *ptrapreturn*. Why are all four necessary? When is each *set* and *reset*?

11.12   On what occasions does the computer stop? What messages are printed at those times?

11.13   What is the difference between *Pause* and *Stopdead*?

11.14   What considerations go into the design of a *Dispatcher*?

11.15   What priorities may exist for unit use? What is the role of the *priority* cell and the *preference* cell in setting priorities?

11.16   Explain *Scan*.

11.17   Why are separate routines required for *nondata* commands?

11.18   What are *unscheduled* traps? How does *FOREMAN* contend with them?

11.19   Discuss traps originating from:
(a) the console;
(b) another computer;
(c) the clock;
(d) telephone lines;
(e) floating point underflow.

11.20   How does *FOREMAN* work for a computer without interrupts? Flow-chart *Sweep*.

12

SERVICE SYSTEMS

12.1 INTRODUCTION

Our Purpose

This chapter serves a twofold purpose:

- study service systems
- get practice with $\mathscr{IOCS}$ commands developed in Chapters 9 and 10

We design *simple* service routines, oversimplified because they do not provide the versatility that most good service routines take for granted.

Orientation

Service systems are designed for:

- user servicing
- system servicing

The principles are the same; the details may diverge considerably. Thus, an editor for manipulating systems tapes may be standardized in different respects from an editor for user's programs.

375

The Nature of Service Systems

If their orientation is neglected, service systems can be characterized by:

- the subroutines they contain
- the tasks they perform
- where they are found and how they are called upon

SUBROUTINES

Here the word *subroutine* is used particularly loosely. Probably a more appropriate term would be *subtasks*. An incomplete list of the subtasks which may be performed within a service system is:

- duplication   • deleting
- finding   • code conversion
- appending   • verifying

TASKS

A service routine is often titled according to its task. Thus an editor does editing. Some service routines perform several tasks. This is often a good policy, since subroutines can then be shared. We have as examples of tasks:

- copying   • editing   • collating

A task involves two or more of the subroutines discussed before. Thus copying, to be at all useful besides duplicating information, should verify its operation.

WHERE IS IT?

The service routine may be classified more on a continuous scale by its relative dependence or independence of other software. Along the scale we notice three benchmarks:

- It is a separate entity.
    * The RCA 501 service routines are an example of this.
- It may be a separate system subservient to another piece of software.
    * IBEDIT is a subsystem of the IBM 7090 IBSYS System.
- It can be integral with the system.
    * The system loader is part of IBM 7090 IBSYS.
    * Merge and collate routines are integral with most SORTs.

Data Being Processed

The data upon which the service system works can be characterized in two ways:

- its nature—its function
- its physical or logical characteristics

NATURE

The service routine may work on one or more of the following:

- program
- subroutine
- data for program
- programming library
- system library

Some service routines can work with only one type of information; others can work on several types of information if they are instructed about what they are dealing with.

BLOCK SIZE

As discussed in Section 3.4, our records may be organized in one of these modes:

- multirecord blocks
- unirecord blocks
- multiblock records

The service system has more or less versatility built into it, depending upon how many categories of block type it can handle. The easiest to cope with and the one for which we make our initial design is the unirecord block of fixed size. It is so simple that we would hardly require a service routine to cope with just this type of information.

VARIABILITY

Granted that we have one or more of the block sizes mentioned, we can categorize the format further as to whether the record size is

- fixed   - variable

It is easy to deal with records of fixed size. It is also easy to deal with records of variable size if our elaborate $\mathscr{IOCS}$ is available to the service routine. The techniques of Section 10.9 are invoked.

Service routines are most useful when they can adjust to the widest range of information. As always, when considering the adoption of software, we must match the capability with the requirement. An installation which always deals with fixed record size in unirecord blocks has a modest requirement and would find it wasteful to use a service system with large capability.

On the other hand, some business installations deal with a wide variety of data and programs and require a versatile service system. How can we implement this? Do we expect the system to adjust itself? Self-adaptability is a characteristic that programming systems can acquire only at great expense. To make service systems efficient we supply them with control information about the data they are to handle. This means the independent service system must have a monitor built into it. The integrated service system can use the monitor of the over-all system of which it is a part.

Design of Service Routines

In the rest of the chapter we simply refer to our act of service routines as $\mathscr{SERVICE}$. For the design of routines for $\mathscr{SERVICE}$, we consider the following:

- data organization
- data format
- independence of other software
- presence of $\mathscr{IOCS}$
- versatility of the routine

We have already mentioned considerations about data.

$\mathscr{SERVICE}$ includes facilities for control management and other functions if it is independent. When $\mathscr{SERVICE}$ is part of a larger system these functions can be fulfilled by that system. We postpone examination of control functions until the end of this chapter.

We assume that $\mathscr{IOCS}$ is available to $\mathscr{SERVICE}$ to facilitate our design and to make it possible to present simple designs. In many cases it is undesirable to expect $\mathcal{IOCS}$ to be available and especially an $\mathcal{IOCS}$ as extensive as the one we have described. In fact, when independence is a necessity, $\mathcal{IOCS}$ is proscribed.

Simple service functions, even with variable data structure, can be performed with a good service routine and a $\mathcal{FOREMAN}$ without any $\mathcal{IOCS}$. However, our system does have $\mathcal{IOCS}$ available.

VERSATILITY

Versatility applies not only to the data format, but to its nature and coding. The many kinds of numbers, characters, letters, etc., were mentioned earlier.

The variability that might be required of a routine in $\mathcal{SERVICE}$ can be seen from the following partial list:

- block size
- variable or fixed record
- identification field location
- identification field size
- records of interest
- presence or absence of code conversion
- internal record format
- symbolic printouts
- exceptions

Procedure Within the Chapter

The chapter proceeds by investigating the fabrication of service routines to perform specific functions. These routines are investigated from the point of view of need, and a specific problem is presented for each one. The routines are pictorially described, flow-charted and finally programmed using $\mathcal{IOCS}$.

√ making a copy from a master
√ making a copy from an original with errors
√ finding desired records
√ assembling a new list of records as prescribed
√ editing uniblock records
√ editing multirecord blocks
√ editing variable-length records in multirecord blocks
√ conversion
√ miscellaneous routines
√ service system

12.2   *COPY*

Aim

Copy is a routine which makes an exact duplicate of a reel. *Copy* could be combined with data and format conversion routines to enable us to perform a medium conversion, such as card-to-tape or tape-to-printer. We now concern ourselves solely with the function of making an exact copy without regard to intermediate functions.

We wish an exact duplicate of a reel of information if we find a fault in the medium itself: a block that is difficult or impossible to read. But how can we copy a reel with a fault in it? Do we want a duplicate that also has a fault in it? Of course not. Our original assumption is partially incorrect—we don't want an *exact* copy of a faulty reel. We want to:

- copy a master
- copy with provisions for editing

COPYING A MASTER

In the case of programming systems and libraries of programs, it would be foolhardy to have only a single source of information, the working copy of the system. Most installations have a master copy of systems or libraries from which they make copies when needed.

A copy of the original is made when a fault is found in the present working edition of the system. In this case, *Copy* makes an exact duplicate of the master. We do not expect the routine to encounter bad blocks when it reads the master.

COPYING A FAULTY REEL

Sometimes we have a reel of data or job programs with faults in occasional blocks and no accurate copy of the reel is available. To get a good copy requires human intervention. A service routine detects errors, prints the location of erroneous blocks and leaves it to the operator to remedy the errors and provide a faultless copy.

Our version of *Copy* takes account of this requirement and provides for special handling of detected errors.

Philosophy of *Copy*

The philosophy of *Copy* is portrayed in Fig. 12.2.1. The original tape to be copied is called ORIG. From it we are going to make a first copy called COPY1.

A block read correctly from ORIG is written exactly onto COPY1. For a block that cannot be read correctly, a substitute block is written onto COPY1, together with an identification and an indication that the block is bad. At the same time, the bad block is duplicated, naturally with any error it contains, onto another file called BAD.

MERGE RUN

Copy has not achieved its purpose in simply producing COPY1. This output is *not* an accurate copy. It must be modified.

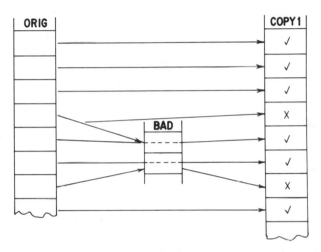

FIGURE 12.2.1. The program *Copy* copies good records from ORIG onto COPY1; those with errors are noted and copied onto BAD.

An accurate copy is obtained only through the intervention of the human and the application of another routine, *Merge*, outlined in Fig. 12.2.2.

The information on BAD is printed out and supplied to the human who determines where the error lies. He may be able to determine this by examining the printout: the error may simply be a misspelling, or it may be in the parity detection scheme itself—the block may be okay.

Printout of BAD is a function of the type of information and format of ORIG. We probably need another service routine to properly print and format BAD.

Once we determine the errors in BAD, we correct them and produce another small reel of corrected blocks which, to be consistent, we call GOOD. We might be able to use a service routine to copy the good portions of BAD and insert corrections to get a good block for GOOD. In any case, for every block on BAD, there is a corrected block on GOOD in the same order and properly identified.

The function of *Merge* is to take COPY1 and GOOD and produce the accurate copy called COPY2. Each unidentified block (and therefore corrected block) is copied from COPY1 to COPY2. When an error block is observed on COPY1 it is skipped and the next block from GOOD is entered onto COPY2. However, the bad block on COPY1 and the good block on GOOD must have the same identification. (What if the identification portion of the block on ORIG was in error?)

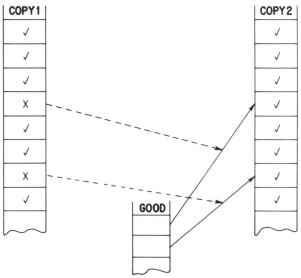

FIGURE 12.2.2. The program *MERGE* takes a corrected record called GOOD and replaces a bad record on COPY1 with a corresponding good record. The final merged copy is called COPY2.

Merge of Fig. 12.2.2 is not discussed here; it is left as an exercise for the reader.

Flow Chart for *COPY*

The flow chart for *Copy* is found in Fig. 12.2.3. First we perform the setup. In the FLAP assembler using *IOCS* we must provide a number of commands for file and pool manipulations (1).

Next we read ORIG (2) and if correct, make a copy of this block on COPY1 (3). We then return and read another block from ORIG (2).

When we take an error exit from READ (2), we write the information into BAD (4). Our routine also makes provision for tallying and keeping track of the errors (5). After we have handled the bad block, we go back and read another block from ORIG.

Another exit from READ when an *end of tape* is encountered signals that out task is done; we close all the files and print either the number of errors or an identifying list of the blocks in which we have found errors (6).

An *end of buffer* exit is possible from the READ and both WRITE commands. They should never be used, but we provide for them with *Print* (7) and *Stopdead* (8).

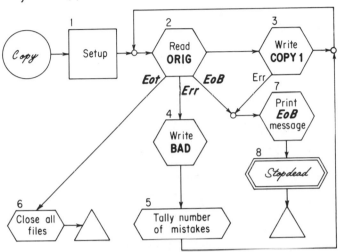

FIGURE 12.2.3. Flow chart for the routine *COPY*.

Program

The first four commands of *Copy* in Fig. 12.2.4 reserve space for the file activity blocks and the pool, PAUL, of ten buffers. The block that we write on COPY1 to replace the bad block begins with a word that contains the ordinal number of the bad block. The other 39 words are blank or could contain a message if we so desire.

The list of files to be attached is found in FILIST. The three calls which follow the list define the pool, attach the files and open them.

The program proper begins at BEGIN. We read a block from ORIG, using the BLOCK subcommand with the LOCATE option. If an error arises, instead of continuing we jump to the point in the program distinguished as MISTAKE. If no error arises, we continue to BEGIN + 2. This is the *IOCS* command COPY, which writes the located block onto the output file, COPY1. We then return to BEGIN to read in the next block.

When an error arises we enter the sequence labeled MISTAKE. This takes the word BADBLK and adds 1 to it to keep a tally of how many bad blocks we have encountered. We then make a copy of the block just read from ORIG, and we place it onto BAD.

We enter an annotated block onto COPY1 at MISTAKE + 4 using WRITE with TRUNCATE which writes 40 words starting from location BADBLK. Having finished handling the error block, we return to BEGIN.

PAUL	RSRV	422
ORIG	RSRV	12
COPY1	RSRV	12
BAD	RSRV	12
BADBLK	RSRV	40
BADBLK	DEF	0
		} message
FILIST	NOOP	RES, 3, 10
	NOOP	ORIG
	NOOP	COPY1
	NOOP	BAD
	GET	POOL, PAUL, 10, 40
	GET	ATTACH, PAUL, FILIST, 3
	GET	OPEN, FILIST, 3
BEGIN	GET	READ, ORIG, NOBUF, DESIST, MISTAKE
	I	BLOCK, END, LOCATE
	GET	COPY, ORIG COPY1
	UCJ	BEGIN
DESIST	GET	CLOSE, ORIG, UNLOAD
	GET	CLOSE, COPYI, EOF, REWIND
	GET	PRINT, 2; MESS, 3; BADBLK, 1, ENDLINE
	UCJ	SYSTEM
MISTAKE	XMA	BADBLK
	ADD	=1
	XAM	BADBLK
	GET	COPY, ORIG, BAD
	GET	WRITE, COPY1, NOBUF
	I	COUNT, TRUNCATE, , BADBLK, 40
	UCJ	BEGIN

FIGURE 12.2.4. Program for *Copy* using *IOCS*.

An *end of tape* at READ at BEGIN causes a jump to the sequence at DESIST. Three *IOCS* commands close the three files. *Print* informs the human of the number of bad blocks that have been encountered. This is especially useful when the copying has occurred without any errors.

We end the program at DESIST + 3 with an unconditional jump to *SYSTEM* to return control to the supervisor, which can now bring in the next job.

12.3   FINDING

Importance

Finding records is important in service systems and in other software. The complexity of the routine concerned with finding depends mainly on the record structure.

WHERE?

We need at least three routines which include finding sequences:

- $\mathscr{S}/\mathscr{L}oad$—the system loader finds the next system.
- $\mathscr{P}/\mathscr{L}oad$—the program or job loader finds subroutines.
- $\mathscr{E}ditor$—it finds the records to be edited.

HOW?

We have two methods of finding the required information:

- counting   • searching

System loader design is simplified greatly if we number each block in the system file. We deal with a few multiblock records. The loader finds the proper record by knowing the number of blocks from the beginning at which the record starts and the number of blocks it contains. All it has to do is to count to find the proper record.

Search (without counting) requires a key for identifying the record. The desired key is compared with the key of the present record; when the two keys coincide we have found our record. Of importance to the search procedure is the size of the key and its location. The more versatile editor permits format information to be furnished by the user.

WHAT?

The format of the data determines the design of the routine. The more versatility we wish in handling different kinds of data, the more complicated becomes the routine. The following choices face us:

- Record variability
    * fixed size   * variable record length
- Relative size
    * multiblock record   * unirecord block   * multirecord block

Design Problem

To see the principles of constructing a *find* routine, we design and write a program called *Build* with the following specifications:

Given:
- a master list containing a number of records
- a list of names of desired records

Do:
- find the named records
- copy these records in proper order onto an output file

Data:
- a known maximum block size
- records may be uniblock or multiblock
- no maximum number of blocks per record
- each block contains its name (key)
- the key is in a fixed position (first word)
- the key is a fixed length (one word long)

Pictorial Presentation of the Problem

In Fig. 12.3.1 we see a representation of how the processing takes place. The files have symbolic names:

- LIBRY—the master list of records.
- RQST—the list of the names of the desired records.
- NEW—the list of desired records.

ASSUMPTIONS

We make several simplifying assumptions:

- Both input lists, LIBRY and RQST, are in ascending order with respect to their keys.
- Any record name in RQST will be found in LIBRY.
- Errors will not occur in reading and writing.

Assumptions such as these should *not* be made by the systems programmer. He must be prepared for all eventualities no matter how unrealistic they seem. None of these assumptions is really necessary except for pedagogic simplicity. For instance, neither of the input lists need be ordered. For each name on RQST we would simply have to scan LIBRY from the very beginning. This is inefficient and a good system would not be so designed. When the system design requires ordered lists, an out-of-order record may inadvertently slip in. The routine must protect us against this and cause an error printout in this case.

Next, although he is not supposed to, a user may request a record not on LIBRY. Again, a simple subroutine can give us protection against this. Finally, errors are easily disposed of by appropriate subroutines.

PROCEDURE

In Fig. 12.3.1 we acquire the name of the first desired record from RQST. When we encounter a record in LIBRY with the same key, we transfer all

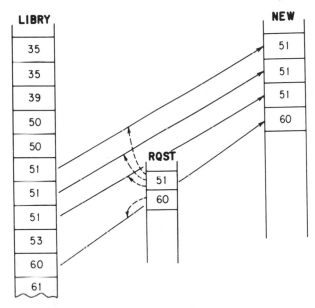

FIGURE 12.3.1. The problem for *Build* is to get *all* the blocks from LIBRY which belong to the record whose key was found on RQST and place them on NEW.

the blocks that comprise this record onto NEW. Then the next name is procured from RQST and LIBRY is advanced until a corresponding record is found and transferred to NEW. We continue thus until no more requests are left and then close up shop.

Uniblock Flow Chart

The flow chart for the procedure when *Build* only has to deal with records consisting of exactly one block appears as Fig. 12.3.2. We read a block from RQST (1), assimilate the information, and then read a block from LIBRY (2). We match the keys (3). If they do not match, we continue by reading another block from LIBRY (2). If they match (3), we copy the block from LIBRY to NEW (4). After copying, we know that the request is fulfilled, so we get another request by reading a new block from RQST (5). Should there be no more blocks left (5), we close all the files and our activity is done.

The logic of this routine is truly simple. It becomes just a little bit more complicated when we deal with multiblock records.

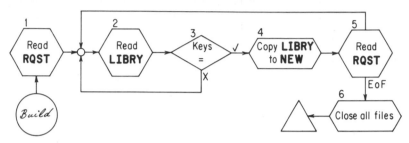

FIGURE 12.3.2. Flow chart for $\mathscr{B}uild$ for unirecord blocks.

Flow Chart for $\mathscr{B}uild$ Operating Upon Multirecord Blocks

The activities required here are just about the same as before. The difference arises when we begin to copy the record we have just found. When do we stop copying? We will get hopelessly confused unless we recognize that the blocks which make up a record are treated as records by $\mathscr{IOCS}$. To clarify the issue, let us make one further assumption:

> Each subrecord of the record from LIBRY contains its name (key) in the same place; the name is the same size as for the initial subrecord of the record.

To determine when a record is completely copied, we must examine the key in each subrecord. As long as this key is that of RQST, the subrecord belongs to the same record; when we find a new key in a subrecord, we do not copy it but terminate our copying procedure. This method adds a complication: the reading of LIBRY gets one subrecord ahead of the reading of RQST. This was not the case in the uniblock problem. It means that we must read a record from RQST and compare it with the last subrecord read from LIBRY before returning to the former procedure.

To determine which phase of operation is in progress, we use a memory cell symbolically labeled simply F for *found*. This is set to 1 when we have found a record and have begun copying it.

In Fig. 12.3.3, first we read a record from RQST (1) and then we read a subrecord from LIBRY (2). We compare the keys (3). If they are unequal, we see if we are operating in *found* phase and, if not (4), we return to read another subrecord from LIBRY (2). The first time around we will be operating in *unfound* phase.

When we find the desired record the keys will match (3). We indicate now that we are in the *found* phase (5) and copy this subrecord (6). As long as the key of subrecords coming from LIBRY match the desired key, we continue to copy them (2), (3), (5), (6). When the LIBRY subrecord key does

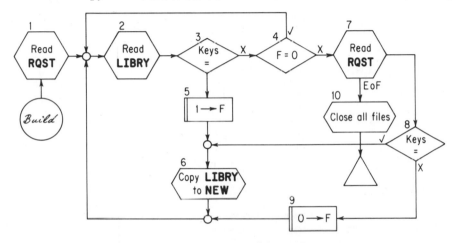

FIGURE 12.3.3. Flow chart for *Build* for multiblock records.

not match, we have gotten a subrecord ahead on this file. We determine the mismatch (3) and note that we are in *found* phase (4). We must now read in the next request (7) and match the keys (8). Notice that if they match, we start another copying sequence which begins by copying this subrecord (6) and then copying all succeeding subrecords that match (2), (3), (5), (6).

When the check at (8) reveals that the LIBRY subrecord and the RQST subrecord are not matched, we go back to *unfound* phase. When the next RQST record is an *end of file*, we terminate (10) by closing the files.

The Program

The program for the FLAP multiblock *Build* begins at START in Fig. 12.3.4. It is correlated with Fig. 12.3.3 by the parenthesized numbers in the description below. The first subcommand of READ enters the RQST block key into the cell RKEY (1). The next subcommand transfers the rest of the block to cells following RKEY. The next pair of commands sets up the *unfound* phase.

We read a block from LIBRY at MORLIB (2). The key of the block is entered into LKEY and the rest of the block is located.

We now compare the keys at CHECK1 (3). If the keys match, we go to FOUND. If the keys do not match and we are not in the *found* phase (4), we bring in a new block from LIBRY by jumping to MORLIB (2). In the *found* phase (4), we continue to IN which follows (7).

```
START     GET     READ, RQST, WRONG, BAD
          I       COUNT, , , RKEY, 1
          XMA     =0
          XAM     F
MORLIB    GET     READ, LIBRY, WRONG, BAD
          I       COUNT, , , LKEY, 1
          I       BLOCK, END, LOCATE
CHECK1    XMA     RKEY
          CMP     LKEY
          JOE     FOUND
          XMA     F
          CMP     =1
          JOG     MORLIB
          JOL     ORLIB
IN        GET     READ, RQST, DONE, BAD
          I       COUNT, , , RKEY, 1
          I       BLOCK, END, , RKEY + 1
          XMA     RKEY
          CMP     LKEY
          JOE     FOUND + 2
          XMA     =0
          XAM     F
          UCJ     MORLIB
FOUND     XMA     =1
          XAM     F
          GET     COPY, LIBRY, NEW
          UCJ     MORLIB

DONE      GET     CLOSE, FILIST, 3
          GET     IOCS
```

FIGURE 12.3.4. Program for *Build* using *JOCS*.

In IN, we bring in the next request from RQST (7), store the key and make a comparison (8). If we have the proper LIBRY subrecord in memory, we jump to FOUND + 2 (6), skipping the phase determination subsequent. If we do not have the proper subrecord, we change the phase to *unfound* (9) and jump to MORLIB (2) to get a new subrecord from LIBRY.

In FOUND we indicate that we are in the *found* phase by setting F to 1 (15). We then copy the subrecord using the *JOCS* COPY (6) and get the next subrecord from LIBRY (2).

Notice that READ at IN, which brings in the next record from RQST, has an *end of file* exit, DONE. The subsegment of the program labeled DONE closes all the appropriate files (10).

The *end of buffer* exits, WRONG, and the *error* exits, BAD, should not occur and no provision is made for them in *our* program. However, the systems programmer must provide for such occurrences, as noted earlier, and it is his duty to write subsequences corresponding to these improbable events.

12.4 SINGLE-BLOCK EDIT—S/EDIT

Editing Files

The job of an editor (the software routine, at any rate) is to make changes:

- to change the information *within* a record
- to remove or replace records *within* a file

The editing process must have its boundaries delimited. What is the smallest unit affected by the editing process? This could be a bit, a character, a word or even a record. The other element of limitation is in regard to the outer boundary. For instance, if this boundary is a file, we can change records in the file, or words in the records of a file, or characters in a word of a record of a file, and so forth. The intrarecord editor changes words within a record.

IMPORTANCE

Editors are so important because programming is dynamic and demands the ability to make rapid changes with either the user or the system in mind. Thus, the user–programmer, after writing a program, determines the errors that exist in it and employs an editor to rework his source language program. After eliminating one kind of error, another kind may show up. He has recourse to an editor several times before he gets a proper operating program.

Against the outcry of the cautious administrator, the user–programmer may decide to alter his program at the machine language level. There are editors which can find and alter any word or set of words of object language program. This procedure is contra indicated because it defies documentation. And an improperly documented program imperils installation management when programmer turnover is at its present high rate.

Programming systems (software) have the unpleasant habit of changing at all too frequent intervals. The manufacturer turns up bugs that were previously unknown or makes improvements of his own initiation or at the request of the user. Each time a software change is issued, the installation must bring its package up to date. When it does not, we find the coexistence of several versions of the same software in the computing community. This is a deplorable but common state of affairs. It is encumbent upon the manufacturer to make his system editor as simple as possible to discourage this coexistence problem.

Extensiveness and Versatility of the Editor

The areas of variability for editor design are:

* Record-block relation
  • multiblock record   • uniblock record   • multirecord block
* Domain of alterability
  • file   • record   • word   • character   • bit
* Key
  • size   • location
* Adaptability—how many of the above are subject to change?

To introduce editor design, we build *𝒮|ℰdit* which edits uniblock records.

𝒮|ℰdit Description

We construct *𝒮|ℰdit* using *𝒥𝒪𝒞𝒮*.

FILES

𝒮|ℰdit manipulates three files:

• MSTR—the information to be edited.
• CHANGE—describes the changes required and includes blocks of information to be added.
• COPY1—the resulting edited output.

The structure of the records in each file is displayed in Fig. 12.4.1. It is emphasized that this is a unirecord block editor. The block size in all three files is 15 words.

CHANGE

The first word of the CHANGE record is ignored by the editor. It can be used for numbering the records in the CHANGE file or any other file bookkeeping procedure. The second word is *named* CHECK. It is used to verify that this particular record is a control record. The contents of the word *named* CHECK *is* the word EDIT. If a record does not contain EDIT in its second word, then it is not a control word.

The third and fourth words contain the edit key—the name of the record at which editing begins. The symbolic name of the location which contains this key is EKEY. It can be a symbol or a number, depending upon the nature of the key prescribed in the file description. We now demonstrate searching for a two-word key.

Record	Word	Name	Use	Contains
Control	1		internal bookkeeping	
	2	CHECK	checking	EDIT
	3, 4	EKEY	edit record key	symbol
	5	DNMBR	number of records to be deleted	number
	6	ANMBR	number of records to be appended	number
	7–15		ignored	anything
Add	1–13		record proper	anything
Master	14, 15	RKEY	key for this record	symbol

FIGURE 12.4.1. Contents of the records on the various files used by the routine $\mathcal{S}/\mathcal{E}dit$.

The fifth word, DNMBER contains the number of records to be deleted. The sixth word, ANMBR contains the number of records to be added. This is the number of records, by the way, which will follow on CHANGE and, of course, must be in the same format as for MSTR, described next.

MSTR, COPY1

Each record in the MSTR and COPY1 files is formatted as shown at the bottom of Fig. 12.4.1. The records of CHANGE which are to be added during editing are also of this format. The first 13 words of the record contain any information and part of the record proper. The next two words are named RKEY. This is the two-word record key. It can be any symbol combination prescribed in the file description.

USE

$\mathcal{S}/\mathcal{E}dit$ could edit a source program in FLAP or ALGOL. Here the first 13 words contain *label, command, address* and possibly comments; the last two words are reserved for an identification number to preserve the sequence of the instructions. $\mathcal{S}/\mathcal{E}dit$ alters the source program by deleting commands and adding new ones. In this case we should have the ability to renumber the commands so that the sequence number is maintained in order.

Actually, it is inefficient to record a source program in unirecord blocks. It is much more sensible to pack several records to a block. This is what we will do when we design *Editor* in Section 12.5.

S|Edit Task

Both MSTR and CHANGE are in order. In Fig. 12.4.2, the CHANGE file contains a control record followed by records to be added. In the

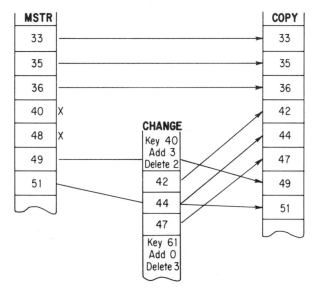

FIGURE 12.4.2. How the single block edit routine, *S|Edit*, works.

diagram, the record at which editing is begun has a key of 40. *S|Edit* reviews MSTR, searching for 40. Records with keys 33, 35 and 36 are encountered and transferred to COPY1 because their keys are less than 40.

When the record with key 40 is encountered, the control record of CHANGE says that two records are to be deleted: hence records 40 and 48 are eliminated. From the control file, three records are to be added with keys 42, 44 and 47; they follow on the CHANGE file and are transferred to COPY1.

The next control record indicates a MSTR record with key 61. The next two records on MSTR contain keys 49 and 51, respectively; these are transferred directly to COPY1 and the search continues. The routine terminates when an empty record is encountered on CHANGE.

Flow Chart

In the flow chart for $\mathscr{S}/\mathscr{E}dit$ in Fig. 12.4.3, we first read a record from CHANGE (1) to guide the reading of MSTR, and we check for a control block (2). We read in a record from MSTR (3) and compare its key with the desired one (4). If they are unequal, we copy this record (5) and read another one (3). When the keys match and the number of blocks to be deleted is

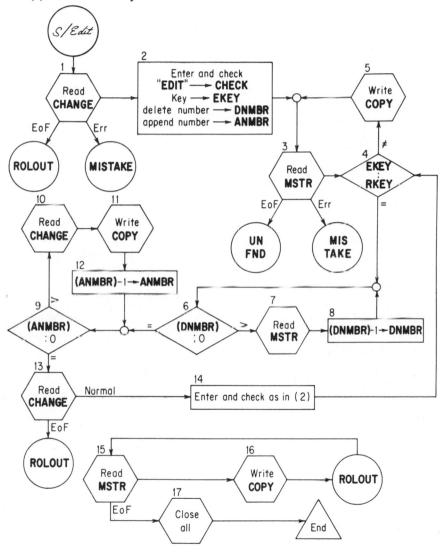

FIGURE 12.4.3. Flow diagram for $\mathscr{S}/\mathscr{E}dit$.

not equal to 0 it is possible to specify that no blocks are to be deleted—that blocks are to be added only. We read another block from MSTR (7) and reduce the delete number by 1 (8). We continue this sequence (6), (7), (8) until the delete number is reduced to 0. At this point we check the add number.

If the add number is nonzero (9) (the number of blocks to be added may be 0 initially), we read a block from CHANGE (10), write it immediately on COPY1 (11), reduce the add number (12) and check it again to see if it has reached 0 (9).

When the add number has reached 0 (9), we read another block from CHANGE (13) and perform an enter-and-check operation on it (14). If it is a valid request, we return to the comparison step (4). We copy blocks from MSTR until the next desired record is found (5), (3), (4).

When an *end of file* is detected on CHANGE (14), we may still have a number of records on MSTR. All these are copied onto COPY1. We take the *end of file* exit to *rollout* the MSTR file, reading a MSTR record and passing it over to COPY1. The end of MSTR is indicated by an *end of file* which takes us to the subsequence that closes out all the files.

$\mathcal{S}/\mathcal{E}dit$ Program

A program for $\mathcal{S}/\mathcal{E}dit$ in Fig. 12.4.4 begins at ENTER where the first control record is read, checked and entered. The next MSTR record is read at READIN and following this, the two key words are checked to see if a match exists. If so, we jump to FOUND; otherwise, we copy the record and return to READIN.

At FOUND we check the delete number. If it is 0, we jump to the add procedure, DOADDS. If there are records to be deleted, this only requires that we continue to read in records from MSTR, disposing of the record we have on hand. The disposal is done automatically because $\mathcal{IOCS}$ advances from record to record automatically and releases a used buffer once a new READ command is given on that file.

When the proper number of blocks is deleted we advance automatically to DOADDS. We COPY each record to be added, checking it. When all blocks have been added, (N2) = 0, we proceed to ADVNCE. As long as there are records to be added, we read the record from CHANGE, copy it onto COPY1, reduce the index and test it.

At ADVNCE we read in the next CHANGE record. The information from the record is to be distributed just as it was in ENTER. The CHECK field is verified after reading (ADVNCE + 3). It would seem, then, that the sequence starting at ENTER could be used in its entirety. However, here is this difficulty: the READ command at this point should have a different *end of file* exit than at ENTER.

```
ENTER      GET      READ, CHANGE, , MISTAKE2, MISTAKE1
           I        COUNT, , LOCATE, , 1
           I        COUNT, , , CHECK, 1
           I        COUNT, , , EKEY, 2
           I        COUNT, , , DNMBR, 1
           I        COUNT, , , ANMBR, 1
           I        BLOCK, END, LOCATE
           XMA      CHECK
           CMP      =EDIT
           JOE      *+2
           UCJ      BADCARD
READIN     GET      MSTR, , UNFIND, MISTAKE1
           I        COUNT, , LOCATE, , 13
           I        COUNT, END, , MKEY, 2
           XMA      EKEY
           CMP      MKEY
           JOE      *+2
           UCJ      OUT
           XMA      EKEY + 1
           CMP      MKEY + 1
           JOE      FOUND
OUT        GET      COPY, MSTR, COPY1
           UCJ      READIN
FOUND      XMN,2    DNMBR
           JNZ,2    DOADDS
           GET      READ, MSTR, , UNFIND, MISTAKE1
           I        BLOCK, END, LOCATE
           TDN,2    FOUND + 2
DOADDS     XMN,2    ANMBR
           JNZ,2    ADVNCE
           GET      READ, CHANGE, , MISTAKE3, MISTAKE1
           I        BLOCK, END, LOCATE
           GET      COPY, CHANGE, COPY1
           TDN,2    DOADDS + 2
ADVNCE     GET      READ, CHANGE, , ROLOUT, MISTAKE1
           I        JUMP, ENTER + 1
           XMA      CHECK
           CMP      =EDIT
           JOE      READIN + 3
           UCJ      BADCARD
ROLOUT     GET      COPY, MSTR, COPY1
           GET      READ, MSTR, , DESIST, MISTAKE1
           I        BLOCK, END, LOCATE
           UCJ      ROLOUT
DESIST     GET      CLOSE, MSTR, UNLOAD
           GET      CLOSE, CHANGE, UNLOAD
           GET      CLOSE, COPY1, EOF, REWIND
           GET      IOCS
```

FIGURE 12.4.4. A program for $\mathcal{S}/\mathcal{E}dit$ using $\mathcal{IOCS}$.

If the first time we read in a CHANGE record we get an *end of file* signal, this is a mistake. However, if we get an *end of file* while reading CHANGE for ADVNCE, this means that we are finished our processing: it is a proper signal and results in an *end of file* exit to the termination processing called ROLOUT.

Another difference between ENTER and ADVNCE is that the former is always followed by the reading of a new MSTR record. This is not necessary for ADVNCE, since one was read in for the last comparison.

The technique is to use the JUMP subcommand to take advantage of the subcommand sequence already written for ENTER. The sequence at ADVNCE contains first a READ command with an *end of file* exit to ROLOUT. The next step is a JUMP to the subcommand sequence at ENTER + 1. $\mathscr{IOCS}$ uses the subcommands at ENTER until it has used the last one, which includes an END option. At that point, instead of continuing to the command following the last subcommand, it returns to ADVNCE + 2. We verify if EDIT appears in the CHECK field with the next two commands. When this is alright we jump to READIN but at a point where the MSTR record is already available, READIN + 3.

The ROLOUT sequence is used after all requested changes have been made. It copies the information left on the MSTR by reading a record at a time from MSTR and then using COPY to place it on COPY1. The COPY command precedes the READ command because as we enter the subsequence we already have a MSTR record available for copying.

We jump out of this loop when an *end of file* signal appears on the READ command. This takes us to DESIST where the files are closed out.

12.5   MULTIRECORD EDITOR

We now investigate a routine, $\mathscr{Editor}$, to edit multirecord blocks. $\mathscr{S/Edit}$, works with only single-block records, but it is more efficient to pack several records into a block. Recall that a tape unit can read information from a block at very high speed, but in starting a new block it may have to stop and start up again.

A temporary restriction is that records for $\mathscr{Editor}$ are of fixed length. The second limitation hardly bothers us: blocks are of fixed size. This means that the maximum number of records in the block is known.

Other improvements we could make (but do not here) are:

- Permit several files of records for editing on the same input reel.
- Permit several editing jobs to be performed sequentially.
- Provide renumbering so that no gaps occur when records are deleted or added.

The last item is practically a necessity for an editor, but it is a simple programming job which is left to the reader.

Files for the *Editor*

We rename our files so as not to confuse them with those used for the last example. The names of the files should be self-explanatory;

SOURCE   ALTER   RESULT

Here are some facts we should know about each of the files:

- The numbering of the records is sequential within the file.
- There is only one file on a reel.
- No renumbering of records is required.
- The blocks on SOURCE and RESULT are composed thus:
    * There are 8 records per block.
    * There are 15 words per record.
    * There is one key word, the 15th word.
    * For SOURCE, the key word is designated as SKEY.
- The ALTER file contains two kinds of records:
    * The control record indicates the next job for the *Editor* to do; it contains the following single-word fields. Starting with the first word, we have:
        CHECK, contains the single word EDIT.
        AKEY, the key of the record we are searching for.
        DNMBR, the number of records to be deleted.
        ANMBR, the number of records to be added.
    Blanks or other words, of which there are 11, are ignored by *Editor*.
    * Records to be appended; these are described:
        They follow the control record.
        They have the same block structure as SOURCE and RESULT blocks.
        As many records should follow the previous control record as indicated in ANMBR of that record.

Editor activity is discussed below with regard to several cases that can arise.

Simple Cases

CASE 1, NO CHANGES

When a full block of SOURCE records contains no key identical with AKEY, we have to copy the SOURCE block onto the RESULT file, as shown in Fig. 12.5.1.

CASE 2, DELETES ONLY

In Fig. 12.5.2, in reviewing SOURCE, we find a desired record. It and some of the others which follow are to be deleted. In the figure no match exists for the first two records; hence, they are copied from SOURCE into the first two record areas of RESULT. The next three records of SOURCE are to be deleted since DNMBR is 3; hence they are ignored. For this case

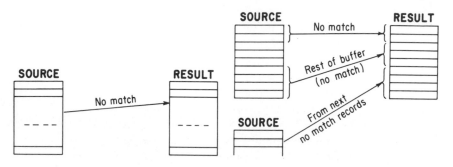

FIGURE 12.5.1. When there is no match for a set of SOURCE records, the complete set may be copied onto RESULT.

FIGURE 12.5.2. When some of the set of records from SOURCE are to be deleted, those that precede from the first part of a set to be written. The rest come from the remainder of the set from SOURCE and part of a new SOURCE set perhaps.

ANMBR is 0—no records are to be added. Therefore, the remainder of the SOURCE block is copied into RESULT. This leaves a void in RESULT which is filled from the remainder of the SOURCE block.

We now read in another SOURCE block and pass records from it to RESULT until the RESULT block is full when it is released for writing. Here, after deleting records from SOURCE, we must get another control record from ALTER before we examine further records from SOURCE. If we encounter a match in SOURCE before RESULT is full, then the operation is repeated: records are deleted and we continue copying records as long as another match is not encountered. Of course, this is when no additions are specified.

CASE 3, DELETES AND ADDITIONS

In Fig. 12.5.3 we begin with an *empty* RESULT block. The first two records of SOURCE do not match the control record key of ALTER and, hence, they are copied directly into RESULT. There is a match on the third record.

We now note the number of records to be deleted and skip over them. The number of records to be added is nonzero. The records to be added are in ALTER following the control record and are entered into the RESULT block. When appending is finished we fill up the RESULT block unless it becomes full during appending, in which case we release it and start a new block.

In Fig. 12.5.3 four records have been appended from ALTER. This leaves room for two more records in RESULT. We get the next key from the control record in ALTER before we can proceed.

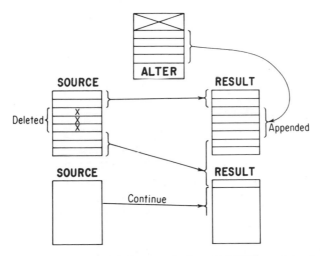

FIGURE 12.5.3. The case where records from SOURCE are deleted and records from ALTER are appended before a set for RESULT is obtained.

We examine the remaining SOURCE records in the block against the ALTER key. The example shows no match for any of these records. Two of them are used to fill the RESULT block, which is then released. The remaining SOURCE records form the start of a new RESULT block, which is filled from another SOURCE block when that becomes available.

Deletes and Adds with Blocks Out of Phase

When one of the blocks of SOURCE, ALTER or RESULT is used up but the others are only partially used, the blocks are said to be *used out of phase*. This does not change the philosophy as seen in Fig. 12.5.4. Here the RESULT file is unused; the SOURCE and ALTER files have been partially used. In the situation represented, two SOURCE records are passed over before a match is found. These are transferred to RESULT. One record from SOURCE is deleted and five remaining records from ALTER are entered into RESULT. Apparently the number of records to be added, indicated in the ALTER control record, is 8. After the first ALTER block is released, we pick up a new block to get the remaining three records to be appended. The first of these is entered into RESULT, at which time it becomes full. It is released and the next two records from ALTER are entered into a new block for RESULT.

This completes the present ALTER task. To find the next one, we must read in the next ALTER block which must be a control block. When this is

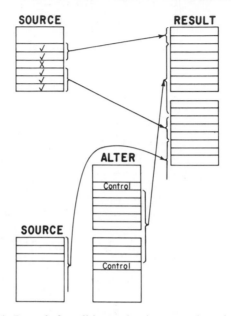

FIGURE 12.5.4. Records for editing and writeout need not be at the start of such sets of records.

done we examine SOURCE records again. Since none of the remaining SOURCE records match, they are all transmitted to RESULT and the SOURCE block is released. There remains an empty space in RESULT, and the control block is not matched yet; so we must get another SOURCE block. Processing continues thus.

Flow Chart

The flow chart for *Editor* in Fig. 12.5.5 uses several indexes: a for ALTER, s for SOURCE and r for RESULT. Further, to show when a match is found between the key in ALTER and that in SOURCE, we use a word denoted by f: f is 1 when we have found a match and are working on

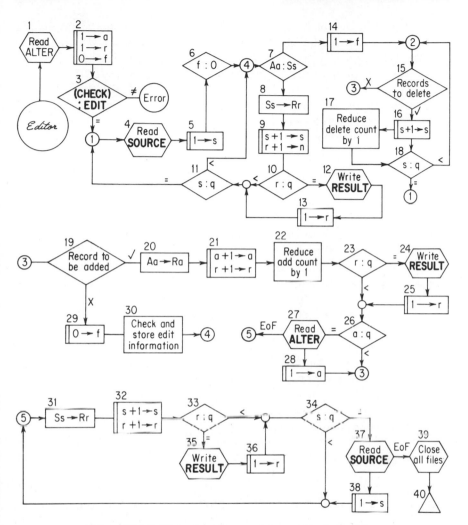

FIGURE 12.5.5. Flow chart for a multirecord block *Editor*.

it; f is 0 otherwise. We begin *Editor* by reading a control block from
ALTER (1), setting a and r to 1 and f to 0 (2), and verifying that we have a
control block (3). We read a SOURCE block (4) and set s to 1 (5). Since
we have set f to 0, it remains so (6).

If the keys of SOURCE and ALTER do not match (7), we copy a record
from SOURCE to RESULT (8), advance the indexes (9) and check if the
RESULT block is full (10). If not, and if the SOURCE block is not empty
(11), we check the key of the next SOURCE record and continue (7), (8), (9),
(10).

When a RESULT block is full (10) we write it (12), reset the corresponding index (13) and check the SOURCE block (11). When the SOURCE block is empty (11) we go to ①, read another SOURCE block (4), reset the SOURCE index (5) and continue as previously (6), (7).

When a match is found (7), we note this (14) and then check to see if there are records to delete (15). If so, we advance the SOURCE index (18) and reduce the delete count by 1 (17). If the SOURCE block is empty (18) we must read another block through ①. This, by the way, will take us through the chain (4), (5), (6) over to ② and thence to (15) again.

If there are records left in the block (18), we also proceed to ②. We delete SOURCE records thus until there are none left to delete (delete count is 0). This brings us out at ③.

If the records are to be appended (19), we copy a record from ALTER to RESULT (20), increase the indexes corresponding to both files (21) and reduce the count of records to be added by 1 (22). When RESULT is full (23) we write it (24) and reset its index (25). When ALTER is empty (26) we read another block (27) and reset the index (28).

In any case we return via ③ to (19) to check if there are more records to be appended. When there are none left we set f to 0 and store and check the information from the next ALTER record. We then return via 4 to check the next SOURCE record for a match (7).

The task is almost finished when we read an *end of file* in an ALTER block (27). When we check and store the information (30) we may also find no more ALTER records left in the block. Either of these eventualities takes us to the rollout procedure ⑤. We transfer one record at a time from SOURCE to RESULT (31). The mechanics of this are (32–38).

When we find that there are no more blocks left on the SOURCE file (37), as evidenced by an *end of file*, then we close all the files (39) and consider the job complete (40).

An interesting challenge to the reader is to implement the flow diagram of Fig. 12.5.5 with subprograms, before seeing how we do it in the next section.

12.6 PROGRAM FOR EDITOR

Programming *Editor* with *JOCS* imposes little additional complexity. The whole point of *JOCS* is to provide automatic block management, removing it from the responsibility of the programmer and letting him deal with the program strictly on the record level. Experience in the last section provides a practical realization of the usefulness of *JOCS* which especially simplifies the task as shown in this section.

We dispense with the indexes a, s and r, and handle information a record at a time; *JOCS* manages the blocks and their release. Thus in

Fig. 12.6.1, one READ command handles record 6; when we give the next READ command for SOURCE, it automatically advances us to record 7.

Similarly, the command READ ALTER advances us to the end of its block. The last record is held while a WRITE or COPY command is issued to place that record onto RESULT. The record is saved until the next READ command for ALTER which requests a new record; the last ALTER block can then be released. Further, when RESULT is full it is released and written without any further ado, and a new block is made available for *filling* at the next WRITE command.

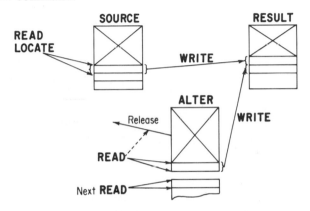

FIGURE 12.6.1. In *JOCS* a READ command causes an automatic advance to the next record in a buffer. When all the records in a buffer have been referred, the buffer is automatically released and another made ready

The Program

The flow chart for *Editor* is identical with that of *S/Edit*, Figure 12.4.3. Since we handle a record at a time, the programmer need only be conscious of the record and not the block and the logic does not change.

JOCS acts automatically because proper information is supplied it through program and control information to establish files and blocks. The programmer uses the technique discussed in Chapter 9.

Although the logic for the program is the same, there are some changes in the steps themselves, and we examine the resulting program here. Because we process a record, not a block, COPY cannot be used. The reader should be sure he understands why this limitation exists. Let us now plunge into the program illustrated in Fig. 12.6.2.

HEADING

The first few commands of the program (not shown) provide the heading wherein we establish file blocks and pool blocks and connect them to the pool.

```
START       GET     READ,  ALTER
            I       COUNT,  ,  LOCATE,  ,  1
            I       COUNT,  ,  ,  CHECK,  1
            I       COUNT,  ,  ,  AKEY,  1
            I       COUNT,  ,  ,  DLETE,  1
            I       COUNT,  ,  ,  APND,  1
            I       COUNT,  END,  LOCATE,  ,  10
            XMA     CHECK
            CMP     =EDIT
            JOE     * + 2
            UCJ     BADCARD
READIN      GET     READ,  SOURCE
            I       COUNT,  ,  LOCATE,  ,  14
            I       COUNT,  END,  ,  SKEY,  1
COMPARE     XMA     SKEY
            CMP     AKEY
            JOE     FOUND
            GET     WRITE,  RESULT
            I,I     COUNT,  END,  ,  READIN + 1,  15
            UCJ     READIN
FOUND       XMN,2   DELETE
            JNZ,2   DOADDS
            GET     READ,  SOURCE
            I       JUMP,  READIN + 1
            TDN,2   FOUND + 2
DOADDS      XMN,3   APND
            JNZ,3   ADVNCE
            GET     READ,  ALTER
            I       COUNT,  END,  LOCATE,  ,  15
            GET     WRITE,  RESULT
            I,I     COUNT,  END,  ,  DOADDS + 3,  15
            TDN     DOADDS + 2
ADVNCE      GET     READ,  ALTER,  ROLOUT
            I       JUMP,  START + 1
            XMA     CHECK
            CMP     =EDIT
            JOE     COMPARE
            UCJ     BADCARD
ROLOUT      GET     WRITE,  RESULT,  DESIST
            I,I     COUNT,  END,  ,  READIN + 1,  15
            GET     READ,  SOURCE,  DESIST
            I       JUMP,  READIN + 1
            UCJ     ROLOUT
DESIST      GET     CLOSE,  LIST,  UNLOAD
            GET     IOCS
```

FIGURE 12.6.2. Program for *Editor* for multirecord blocks of fixed length using *IOCS*.

START

READ for the ALTER file contains five subcommands to enter the control information in cells for easy reference. The record size is up to the programmer. The sixth subcommand establishes the end of the record and terminates the subcommand sequence. The next four commands verify that we are examining a control record.

READIN

READ brings in the next SOURCE record. The entire record is *located* with COUNT and the key is put in SKEY.

COMPARE

We examine the SOURCE record just procured by comparing SKEY with AKEY. If equal, we jump to FOUND; otherwise we write out the SOURCE record using WRITE, for the file RESULT.

How do we distinguish where the record is to be found? The start of the record was determined by the subcommand at READIN + 1. On the completion of this subcommand, the cell address of the beginning of the buffer area for the record was entered into the command word itself. Indirectly addressing this command word makes the record available to us. The number of words to be transferred (our record length is 15) is specified in the subcommand.

This completes the copying activity; the buffer will be held or released according to whether it is full or not. Since we deal with fixed record sizes the buffer either fills up exactly or has room for more records.

After copying is done, we return to READIN to get another SOURCE record for comparison.

FOUND

When a match occurs we jump out of the COMPARE sequence at COMPARE + 2. We fill index 2 immediately with the number of records to be deleted. We may perform either several or no deletes: for an empty (0) index we skip the delete sequence and go immediately to DOADDS.

Deletion uses the FOUND loop. After one record is deleted we advance to another SOURCE record with the READ command. We should now repeat at FOUND + 3 the same two subcommands that appear at READIN + 1, for this is the task to be done by READ. But then the record location for the SOURCE record would be posted in *this* subcommand sequence. Thus the SOURCE record location appears in either of *two* subcommands, and we would have trouble determining which contains the latest information. The solution is to keep the location in only *one* subcommand. JUMP enables us to use the same command sequence for two different READ commands. We use JUMP at FOUND + 3 so that the location of the latest SOURCE record is always at READIN + 1.

Now that the SOURCE record is read we may have to delete it. This depends upon how many blocks were to be deleted originally. We tally down index 2 containing this number in FOUND + 4 and return to FOUND + 2 should it not be reduced to 0. When index 2 is reduced to 0 we have deleted all the blocks required and go on to the next subsequence, DOADDS.

DOADDS

First we enter the number of blocks to be appended into index 3. It is conceivable that we may be adding no blocks, and we skip to ADVNCE. If there are blocks to be added, they appear on ALTER. READ brings in the next record. Since no processing of this block is required, we merely locate the record. The record must contain no control information to be a proper entry for RESULT.

We write the record, with WRITE, with an indirectly addressed COUNT subcommand referencing the LOCATE command applying to READ: it indirectly addresses DOADDS + 3.

We determine if enough records have been added by tallying down index 3. If there are more, it jumps back to the READ command at DOADDS + 2. Otherwise, we continue to ADVNCE.

ADVNCE

We get to ADVNCE after deleting and/or appending for a given control record on ALTER. We get another control record from ALTER with READ at ADVNCE being careful to store all pertinent information in the proper cells. Since this is the same task done by the subcommand string beginning at START + 1, we use JUMP at ADVNCE + 1 to acquire that subsequence; it returns us to ADVNCE + 2 when the subcommand sequence is completed.

The next task to be done is a key comparison; we do *not* perform a READ of SOURCE as at READIN. The four steps at ADVNCE + 2 take us to COMPARE when the control record has been verified or BADCARD entered otherwise.

ROLOUT

When we complete the editing proper, the remaining records on SOURCE are copied onto RESULT by a sequence of READs of SOURCE, followed by WRITE's of RESULT at ROLOUT. An *end of file* causes us to enter DESIST, which simply closes the list of files.

12.7   VARIABLE RECORD LENGTH

We have extrapolated from unirecord blocks to multirecord blocks; we can be optimistic about handling records of variable length because our $\mathcal{IOCS}$ is really so versatile. We establish a few conventions:

- We have buffers of fixed size, therefore requiring that records be less than some maximum length.

- Each record is prefixed by a self-loading word so that the number of words it contains is conveyed to $\mathcal{IOCS}$.
- The control record is of fixed length.
- The key is placed at the front of the record (right after the prefix) to permit easy locating.

The prefix for each record is

$$| \quad \text{FINISH, END, LOCATE, , number of words} \qquad (12.7.1)$$

Number of words is the length of the record which follows. FINISH facilitates writing, as seen later.

AUTOMATIC READ

In the $\mathcal{IOCS}$ procedure in Fig. 12.7.1, the self-loading prefix permits any four READs of SOURCE to procure variable length records from SOURCE as they reside in the buffer shown. A fifth record could not fit in the SOURCE buffer as pictured; hence, the buffer space following the fourth record is blank (contains trash). When the buffer was *filled* from input, the number of words loaded there—those contained in the four records—was entered into the buffer activity block. Therefore $\mathcal{IOCS}$ cannot misidentify the words which follow the fourth record in the buffer as something of value.

On the fifth READ all the useful words in the upper buffer—four records worth—have been used up. Since the buffer has been exhausted, it is released. Another buffer is procured from the *take* chain and the first record of this buffer is made available by its self-loading prefix.

WRITING

To write variable length blocks, $\mathcal{IOCS}$ is addressed with the FINISH option. As long as there is room in an output buffer for a RESULT record, it is transmitted there by WRITE with FINISH. Figure 12.7.2 shows what happens when the output buffer is *almost* full. When the $(i + 1)$th WRITE command is given, the number of words to be written is compared with the number of words available in the buffer. There is not enough room so the FINISH option releases this buffer and writes it onto the RESULT file. A new buffer is procured from the pool and placed on the *fill* chain. The record is written from ALTER into this new buffer assigned to RESULT.

Program

The program of $\mathcal{Editor}$ for variable length records again uses the logic of Fig. 12.4.3. The program steps are found in Fig. 12.7.3. The reader should be familiar with the heading information.

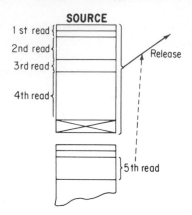

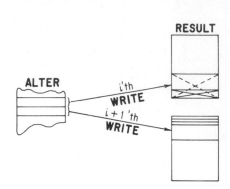

FIGURE 12.7.1. An automatic progression to new records also occurs with self-loading, variable length records. When the last word of the last record of a buffer is used, the next *READ* skips over whatever other trash is left and goes on to another buffer.

FIGURE 12.7.2. For WRITE, using the FINISH option, a buffer is released if there is not enough room for the set of words for which writing is desired. Instead, a new buffer is chosen, the old one being released, and the complete set is entered into this new buffer.

	heading	
START	GET	READ, ALTER
	I	COUNT, , LOCATE, , 1
	I	COUNT, , , CHECK, 1
	I	COUNT, , , AKEY, 1
	I	COUNT, , , DLETE, 1
	I	COUNT, , , APND, 1
	I	COUNT, END, LOCATE, , 11
	XMA	CHECK
	CMP	=EDIT
	JOE	* + 2
	UCJ	BADCARD
READIN	GET	READ, SOURCE
	I	COUNT, , , * + 1, 1
	I	FINISH, END, LOCATE, , number
	XMA,I	READIN + 2
	XAM	SKEY
COMPARE	XMA	SKEY
	CMP	AKEY
	JOE	FOUND
	XMN,1	READIN + 2
	XNM,1	* + 3
	GET	WRITE, INSIDE

FIGURE 12.7.3. An *IOCS* program for *Editor* where self-loading, variable length records are used.

```
COMPARE      I        COUNT,  ,  ,  READIN + 2,  1
             I,I      COUNT,  END,  ,  READIN + 2,    [ blank ]
             JSN,6    WRITRSL
             UCJ      READIN
FOUND        XMN,2    DLETE
             JNZ,2    DOADDS
             GET      READ,  SOURCE
FOUND + 3    I        JUMP,  READIN + 1
             XMA,1    READIN + 2
             XAM      SKEY
             XMN,1    READIN + 2
             XNM,1    COMPARE + 7
             TDN,2    FOUND + 2
DOADDS       XMN,3    APND
             JNZ,3    ADVNCE
             GET      READ,  ALTER
             I        COUNT,  ,  , * + 1, 1

             I        FINISH,  END,  LOCATE,  ,  number

             XMN,1    DOADDS + 4
             XNM,1    * + 1
             GET      WRITE,  INSIDE
             I        COUNT,  ,  ,  DOADDS + 4,  1
             I,I      COUNT,  END,  ,  DOADDS + 4,  blank
             JSN,6    WRITRSL
             TDN,3    DOADDS + 2
ADVNCE       GET      READ,  ALTER,  ROLOUT
             I        JUMP,  START + 1
             XMA      CHECK
             CMP      =EDIT
             JOE      COMPARE
             UCJ      BADCARD
WRITRSL      GET      READ,  INSIDE
             I        BLOCK,  END,  LOCATE
             TUN,1    * + 1
             XNM,1    * + 2
             GET      WRITE,  RESULT
             I,I      FINISH,  END,  ,  WRITRSL + 1,   [ blank ]
             UCJ,6    I
ROLOUT       XMN,1    READIN + 2
             XNM,1    COMPARE + 7
             GET      WRITE,  INSIDE
             I        JUMP,  COMPARE + 7
             JSN,6    WRITRSL
             GET      READ,  SOURCE,  DESIST
             I        JUMP,  READIN + 1
             UCJ      ROLOUT
DESIST       GET      CLOSE,  FILIST,  UNLOAD
             GET      IOCS
```

FIGURE 12.7.3. (*Cont.*)

Start of Program

In Fig. 12.7.3 after the heading (omitted) we bring in the first block from ALTER, storing important portions of it in different cells in memory. We then read in a variable length block from SOURCE at READIN. COUNT at READIN + 1 enters the block prefix into READIN + 2. The command at READIN + 2 has a rectangle around it. This shows that it is not actually in the program but is brought in with the variable length record.

The (prefix) subcommand, LOCATE at READIN + 2 now fills into *address* of its own command the absolute location of the body of *this* subrecord. From the first word of the body of the subrecord we procure the key of the subrecord, entering it into the accumulator by indirection at READIN + 3. This key is placed at SKEY by the command at READIN + 4.

Troublemaking Prefix

The prefix prohibits us from copying or writing the variable length block directly onto output. If we did, the output subrecord would be missing the prefix, which is essential for later processing.

Programmers may be ingenious about the ways they get around this difficulty. Our method is straightforward but requires the use of an internal file called INSIDE. Our plan is this: using INSIDE, we fabricate the new subrecord for the output file which includes,

- a prefix • the body

The technique for copying the complete subrecord is illustrated in Fig. 12.7.4. The first section of the program, labeled A in the figure, brings in the prefix and then locates the remainder of the information. This has been done for *Editor* at READIN. Next we write the file labeled INSIDE by copying the prefix now in the program proper at A + 2 into the first word of INSIDE.

Next we transfer the located input information to INSIDE in B using COUNT, which contains the number of words to be transferred. This information is abstracted from the prefix and entered into the subcommand by a sequence not shown. As illustrated, COUNT contains the subrecord word length, 21, in a rectangle, indicating that this number was entered from an outside subsequence.

At C we locate the full subrecord contained in INSIDE, including the prefix by means of BLOCK. At D we transfer the information located by the sequence at C into the output file, using FINISH and a count of 22. The subrecord length, 22, is obtained when we increment the length of the body of the subrecord, 21, and insert it in the subcommand of subsequence D.

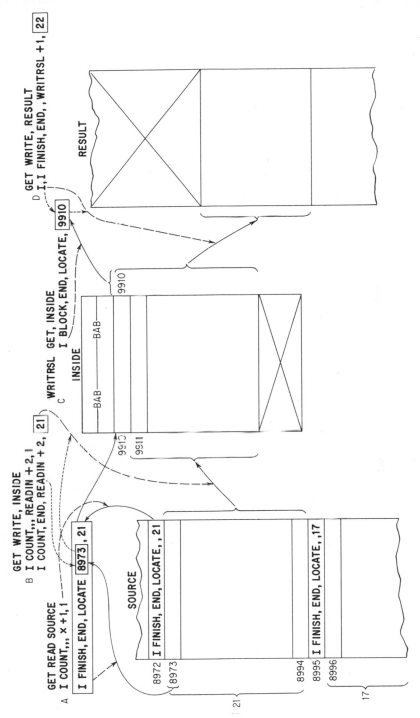

GET WRITE, RESULT
D I, I FINISH, END., WRITRSL + 1, [22]

RESULT

GET WRITE, INSIDE
B I COUNT,,, READIN + 2, I
   I COUNT, END, READIN + 2, [21]

WRITRSL GET, INSIDE
C   I BLOCK, END, LOCATE, [9910]

INSIDE

BAB ——— BAB

9910
9911

GET READ SOURCE
A I COUNT,,, x + 1, 1
   I FINISH, END, LOCATE [8973] [21]

SOURCE

8972 | I FINISH, END, LOCATE, , 21
(8973

8994
8995 | I FINISH, END, LOCATE, ,17
8996

21

17

FIGURE 12.7.4. How the internal buffer, INSIDE, is used to ensure the writing of a complete output record including the self-loading prefix.

413

COMPARE

At COMPARE in Fig. 12.7.3 we look for the desired subrecord from SOURCE by comparing SKEY with AKEY. We jump to FOUND when they are equal. Otherwise we continue COMPARE to copy the subrecord onto the output. At COMPARE + 3 we bring the number of words in the body of the subrecord from the prefix which is READIN + 2 to index 1; *number* is passed from there to the rectangle at COMPARE + 7 by XNM at COM-PARE + 4.

XMN and XNM at COMPARE + 3 correspond with the preparation of subsequence B of Fig. 12.7.4. We now write the internal file, INSIDE; COUNT at COMPARE + 6 writes the prefix; the next COUNT writes the body. INSIDE is written by using the subroutine WRITRSL, which we go to with JSN at COMPARE + 8.

FOUND

When a SOURCE subrecord is found we may wish to delete it for a nonzero delete number, DLETE, which is checked at FOUND. When there are subrecords to be deleted we use READ at FOUND + 2 and the subcommand sequence of READIN + 1. Here JUMP permits the prefix always to be at a known spot in a subcommand string. The rest of FOUND brings in SKEY and jumps us to FOUND + 2 if there are more blocks to be deleted.

DOADDS

When there are subrecords to be appended (determined in DOADDS), we bring in the next subrecord from ALTER, setting it up in the same fashion as the subrecord from SOURCE. It is transferred to INSIDE in the same fashion, and WRITRSL is called on to write out the information.

ADVNCE

When an editing subtask is complete and there are no further blocks to be deleted or appended, we bring in another ALTER record, using the subsequence of START + 1 and checking for validity.

Write Result Routine

This routine performs the task of C and D of Fig. 12.7.4. We locate the block of information in INSIDE at WRITRSL + 1. The number of words in the body is placed in index 1. The whole subrecord contains exactly one more word. The value of the index is incremented using the command TUN. Since it is not used in an incremental sense, its address is * + 1. The number in index 1 is now the size of the block. This must be entered into the WRITE subcommand at WRITRSL + 5 and is done with the XNM command at WRITRSL + 3. The WRITE command at WRITRSL + 4, together with the proper subcommand, writes out the subrecord if there is room in the buffer for it. Automatic termination and acquisition of a new buffer is incorporated in FINISH.

When the routine is finished, the return jump brings us back to the main program where we left off. The remainder of the program should be easy to follow.

12.8　CONVERSION; SERVICE SYSTEMS

Conversion

Service routines consist mainly of two types: editing and conversion. By conversion we mean copying of information from one medium to another. The need for this was discussed earlier:

- speed step-up or speed step-down;
- present vs. desired form of information.

Conversion involves three variables:

- media　　• codes　　• format

The number of different media conversion possibilities is almost the square of the number of different media when we consider that a medium usually can be used for both input or output. Probably the only exception is the high-speed printer which can, so far, serve only as an output device. We might consider the following media:

- punch card
- paper tape
- magnetic tape
- magnetic cards
- memory
- disk
- drum
- printer
- communication lines

Information on one of these media might be in any one of the following codes—only a partial list, of course:

- Hollerith   • alphanumeric
- numeric   • printer

Format applies to one of three possible information packages:

        * word   * record   * file

The way in which bits or characters are assembled into a word is subject to much variation. We summarize briefly, formatting problems thus:

* word
  - multifield words
  - multiword fields
  - fixed-point numbers
  - floating-point numbers
  - double-precision numbers
* record—field locations
* file—record locations

Conversion Components

A conversion routine consists of several or all of the following components:

- control processor (preprocessor or control card reader)
- IO subroutines
- code conversion
- field finding
- field editing
- field formatting

The use of each of these components is evident. A control processor is not necessary for a fixed routine, but then that routine will not be versatile. The more versatile the routine, the more useful it can be to the general programmer. The manufacturer provides routines of versatility so that he will have to write fewer of them. On the other hand, the more versatile the routine, the more extra duty it must perform. From a general routine it must incorporate the parameters given by the user to make itself into a specific program. This self-alteration task can be avoided if the general routine is replaced by a single specific routine. But then we need one routine for each special task we must perform.

The Service Routine with Variable Parameters

To see how many different things can vary when setting up a service routine, let us take a specific example from the RCA 301 service library. This is a punchcard-to-magnetic-tape conversion routine. We only look at the variable information that can be supplied by control cards.

1. *Automatic translation vs. special routine.* Normally the user relies upon the translation subroutine incorporated in the service routine. If he has special requirements he can supply his own routine here.

2. *System characteristics.* System configurations cover a wide range. The routine must know the extent of the computer system on which it is going to be used. This includes such specifics as memory size, tape density, etc.

3. *Record length.* Batching the record length is often an essential. This routine permits batching of records so that another specification can apply to a new batch.

4. *Sequence check.* It would be embarrassing to go through a complete conversion routine on a deck of cards only to find (or maybe even not to find) that cards dropped on the floor had been put back in the wrong order before the conversion. A sequence check terminates the routine for out-of-sequence cards.

5. *Record format.* Format information may be supplied on several control cards to dictate which card fields are assembled at each position on the tape. For the RCA 301 routine, each control card carries the following information for each field:

   • the starting column
   • the ending card column
   • the ordinal number of the characters from the beginning of the tape record at which the field is to start

6. *Extra characters.* The routine permits us to add characters absent from the card at any place in the tape record.

7. *Multipunch.* A punchcard column can contain several punches. It is possible to split this information and enter it as separate characters in a tape field. It is also possible to determine the maximum value of a punch in a given column and use that for a specific character in a field of the tape record.

8. *User-supplied subroutine.* The user may supply his own subroutines for specific or unannounced purposes. One specific purpose is a label check. He may enter subroutines of his choosing at different points of the card analysis, at the end of a batch, or at the end of a run.

9. *Terminal message.* When conversion is complete, the user may specify a terminal message transmitted to the operator.

10. End of file *generation.* At the end of a conversion run, an *end of file* block may be entered as the last block on the magnetic tape.

11. *Label generation message.* When the routine generates labels between batches or runs, a message may also be produced to indicate whenever this is performed.

This itemization conveys some idea of the variability it is possible and sometimes desirable to build into a generalized routine.

Other Service Routines

The two principal kinds of service routines are conversion and editing. Debugging routines, dumps and traces are included in some service systems. The simulation routine is another candidate. Here we try to reproduce the operation of another computer or of a physical system by use of the digital computer. The sorting routine is in a category all by itself. Some manufacturers, however, include it in their service system.

Advantages of a Combined Service System

When one tends toward generalization rather than specificity, the service system seems appealing. From the discussion of the RCA 301 conversion routine, it is obvious that a general routine requires a lot of control information. A preprocessor is a necessity for a generalized routine. This preprocessor can be shared by other routines; hence, only one preprocessor need be written. There are other subroutines which are identical for various uses. Thus we have code conversion, field finding and so forth. Many of these can serve without any alteration for several service routines.

A service system will be rather large, but still, since there are so many shared parts, it will be much smaller than a simple assemblage of service routines.

The service system may be easier to use. A standard control-card format can be designed to serve all the routines. Further, since all subroutines are present, tasks which would formerly overlap two service routines may be done more simply with a service system.

Service systems are furnished by some manufacturers, as exemplified by the Univac I Omnibus and the IBM 7090 IBEDT.

Multiprogramming

When a computer is capable of multiprogramming, we find an excellent solution for doing service routines. An interrupt facility is one of the tools for providing multiprogramming, and we have examined that area. We need a few further tools, which we do not explore here.

The technique is to supply a main program for which activity proceeds at the highest priority. However, when we get stuck because of the slowness of IO activity, instead of the main frame becoming idle, we provide it with another task to do. This task may be one of medium conversion, for instance, which requires some effort by the main frame; although for the most part it involves IO, which can take place simultaneously with other computer activities. When computer activity for a conversion subtask is completed, the computer returns to the main program so that, with little or no waste of time, it keeps two complete and independent activities going.

This is the scheme used by the Univac III UTMOST package with the BOSS III executive routine. The so-called main program is augmented by service routines which are referred to by Univac as *symbionts*.

PROBLEMS

12.1 Why is the routine $\mathcal{M}erge$ of Section 12.2 different from that of problem 10.10? Flowchart $\mathcal{M}erge$.

12.2 Write a FLAP $\mathcal{IOCS}$ program for $\mathcal{M}erge$.

12.3 Flowchart a routine $\mathcal{F}ind$ to find in LIB records named in ASK, and copy them in order onto FOUND much like $\mathcal{B}uild$. However, besides containing the record name in ASK, there is also a count from the beginning of LIB so that LIB may be rapidly advanced by a *nondata* request. The ASK record contains: RKEY in the first word; BLKS, the number of blocks from the start of tape in word two; NUMB, the number of blocks in the record in word three. Requests on ASK are in order. Flowchart $\mathcal{F}ind1$ which finds single block records.

12.4 Program problem 12.3.

12.5 Flowchart and program $\mathcal{F}ind2$ as for $\mathcal{F}ind1$ but where the number of blocks/record is variable.

12.6 Flowchart and program $\mathcal{F}ind3$ as $\mathcal{F}ind2$ but where the requests on ASK are not in order.

12.7 Incorporate checks in $\mathcal{F}ind$: (a) assume only the first subrecord contains LKEY; add an exit should identity be lacking or incorrect; (b) check each subrecord transferred to: (1) ascertain it contains no LKEY, (2) exit if it does, (3) check the next block after the last required block to see that it does contain an LKEY; (c) if the count in ASK brings LIB into an *end of file*, and *error* exit is taken. Flowchart and program.

12.8   Alter the flow chart for $\mathcal{S}|\mathcal{E}dit$, Fig. 12.4.3, to include a sequence check of records in both CHANGE and MSTR and error exit for *out of sequence* records.

12.9   Implement problem 12.8 by reprogramming $\mathcal{S}|\mathcal{E}dit$. The sequence error exit should print (using $\mathcal{FOREMAN}$) a message, "CHANGE (or MSTR) OUT OF SEQUENCE."

12.10   Add a renumbering feature to $\mathcal{S}|\mathcal{E}dit$ of problem 12.8 to get $\mathcal{S}|\mathcal{E}dit2$. Make a new flow chart and program. Now records on COPY2 are in increasing numerical order. Assume the second word of EKEY and RKEY are simple integers for record sequence within the file.

12.11   Add these features to $\mathcal{E}ditor$ (call it then $\mathcal{E}ditor2$):
        (a) a sequence check
        (b) error messages
        (c) renumbering
        and flowchart.

12.12   Write a FLAP IOCS program for problem 12.11.

12.13   Make a flow chart for a sorting merge pass† $\mathcal{S}mrge1$. There are two input files, IN1 and IN2, each containing 15 word record blocks with KEY in the first word. Each file contains strings of records in order of ascending keys. It is required to merge one record from each of IN1 and IN2 to make a new string to go on OUT1. The next merged string goes on OUT2.

12.14   Program problem 12.13.

12.15   Flowchart problem 12.13 for variable length records in blocks of 100 words (or less), with a self-loading prefix in word 1 and KEY in word 2 (call this $\mathcal{S}mrge2$).

12.16   Program problem 12.15.

12.17   A complete sorting merge for unirecord blocks is called $\mathcal{S}mrge3$. It uses four files called AYE, BEE, SEA and DEE with the original unsorted information on AYE. Sorted strings are alternately transferred to SEA and DEE. Input and output files are switched, and SEA and DEE are merged onto AYE and BEE, similar to $\mathcal{S}mrge1$. Switching and merging continue until all the output is one file (How can we tell?)—it is in sequence then! Make a flow chart for files with 15-word unirecord blocks with KEY as word 1.

12.18   Program problem 12.17.

12.19   Add a sequence to problem 12.18 to print a message stating which file contains the output.

12.20   Flowchart problem 12.17 as $\mathcal{S}mrge4$ for multirecord blocks of 100 words (maximum); records are prefixed, and KEY is in the next word. Include the feature of problem 12.19.

† See *Computer Programming*, Section 9.5.

12.21 Program problem 12.20.

12.22 Flowchart and program $\mathscr{S}mrge5$ as for problem 12.17 for unirecord blocks, where the length of the block is found in the first word of the next control card on CNTRL. Include the feature of problem 12.19.

12.23 Flowchart a three-way merge $\mathscr{S}mrge6$ using six files, QUE, ARE, ESS, TEE, YOU and VEE, with input on QUE and triple alternation of merged strings, but otherwise as described in problem 12.17 including the feature of problem 12.19.

12.24 Program problem 12.23.

12.25 Flowchart a word edit program $\mathscr{W}\mathscr{E}dit1$ to alter single words of the unirecord block file, ONE, with 15-word blocks according to the directions on the 16-word unirecord block file DRCT, which contains DKEY, W1, WORD1, W2, WORD2, etc. The key of ONE, OKEY, is in the first word. When OKEY = DKEY, replace the W1th word of the block with WORD1, the W2th word of the block with WORD2, etc. Files are in key sequence. If Wi is 0 . . . 0, no further editing of this block is required.

12.26 Program problem 12.25.

12.27 Flowchart $\mathscr{W}\mathscr{E}dit2$ for variable length prefixed records in multirecord blocks of 100 words—otherwise specified as in problem 12.25.

12.28 Add a feature to problem 12.27 to make an *error* exit and printout if the word specified (Wi) is greater than the record length.

12.29 Program problem 12.28.

12.30 Repeat problem 12.25 for $\mathscr{W}\mathscr{E}dit3$ where fields are replaced. OKEY is followed by WA, which contains the location of the field in the record, WAS and the number of words in the field, WAN. The new field follows at locations called WORDA1, WORDA2, etc.; the next field specified, WB, follows.

12.31 Program problem 12.30.

12.32 Flow chart $\mathscr{W}\mathscr{E}dit4$, a field edit of multirecord blocks combining the specifications of problems 12.27, 12.28, and 12.30.

12.33 Program problem 12.32.

13

SUPERVISORS

13.1 THE SUPERVISOR AND THE JOB

$\mathscr{SYSTEM}$

$\mathscr{SYSTEM}$ is the software that does the supervision. It has the following functions:

- Manager—it directs the other software.
- Mediator—it helps transmit information between the human and other software.
- Watchdog—it keeps other software in line.
- Rejuvenator—it is responsible for keeping itself young (intact).
- Comptroller—it may do the accounting and the billing.
- Communications chief—it makes sure that messages go back and forth between the software.

Figure 13.1.1 shows how $\mathscr{SYSTEM}$ does some of these tasks. The first job requires an $\mathscr{ALGOL}$ translation. The job and its instructions are entered into $\mathscr{SYSTEM}$ at (1–0). It is passed over to the $\mathscr{ALGOL}$ compiler (1–1). When compilation is completed, the system is notified and instructions given to $\mathscr{FLAP}$ to assemble the compilation (1–2). $\mathscr{FLAP}$ reports to $\mathscr{SYSTEM}$ that a satisfactory assembly is completed. Now $\mathscr{SYSTEM}$

turns over the job to $\mathscr{JOCS}$, since this control system is required for the object program (1–3). $\mathscr{JOCS}$ in turn sees that loading is required and calls in $\mathscr{LOAD}$ (1–4).

After bringing in the compiled and assembled program, $\mathscr{LOAD}$ turns control over to the program (1–5). After completion of the program, control returns to $\mathscr{JOCS}$ (1–6) and thence to $\mathscr{SYSTEM}$ (1–7).

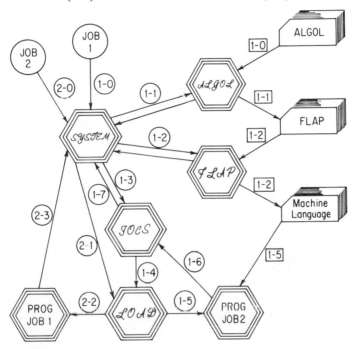

FIGURE 13.1.1. How $\mathscr{SYSTEM}$ interrelates with some of the other subsystems.

$\mathscr{SYSTEM}$ is now ready for Job 2. It appears that this is a pre-assembled program not requiring $\mathscr{JOCS}$. Therefore, $\mathscr{SYSTEM}$ calls in $\mathscr{LOAD}$ (2–1), which in turn brings in the second program (2–2). Upon completion, it returns control to $\mathscr{SYSTEM}$ (2–3).

The Job

There are many ways we can define a job. To make our discussion meaningful, we must pick a definition which, although not satisfying all, at least establishes a point of reference for the discussion. We use **job** as a program-centered term: the servicing of a single program, regardless of how many subsystems are involved, is considered a job.

The first job for $\mathscr{SYSTEM}$ in Fig. 13.1.1 contacts five separate software systems:

- $\mathscr{SYSTEM}$ • $\mathscr{ALGOL}$ • $\mathscr{FLAP}$ • $\mathscr{IOCS}$ • $\mathscr{LOAD}$

Six separate functions were involved;

- monitoring   • assembling   • loading
- compiling   • IO functions   • running

All these functions and subsystems are associated with a single job.

To contrast this term, we introduce two others. The **subsystem run** consists of several jobs for the same subsystem and usually when control is not relinquished to any other intermediary subsystem. For instance, a subsystem run for the loader consists of several jobs to be loaded and run. After the first job is loaded and completed and the results printed or otherwise outputted, control returns to the loader which then brings in the next job. This is another program to be loaded, run and completed.

The **data run** is defined when a program is *executed* for a single set of data. A job may consist of several data runs. Thus a matrix program may be requested to invert five matrices. Each inversion task comprises a data run; the five together comprise a job.

It is reiterated that standard terminology does not exist in these areas. Further, an overlap may exist in the definitions provided. However, at least this is a jumping-off point for discussion.

WHAT IS SUPPLIED IN A JOB?

The job may consist of as many as three parts:

- program   • data   • task description

The program must be present, for it constitutes the instructions to the computer. It may be sufficient to supply a name or a location where the program can be found as far as the software subsystem servicing the program is concerned. A task description is necessary for the subsystem to know the particulars of the task it is supervising. Data may be present if the object program is to be run. If the totality of the job is simply compiling, for instance, then no data is required; the program constitutes the data for the compiler.

Job Information, Short Program

The method by which a job is entered depends upon its extensiveness and how many IO devices are involved. The simplest way to enter small jobs is by means of punchcards as depicted in Fig. 13.1.2. The job subdeck consists of three files. The first file, control information for $\mathscr{SYSTEM}$, indicates to $\mathscr{SYSTEM}$ what subsystems are required and what is to be done. We shall see variations in placement of control information later. The control information also indicates that the program and data follow in the same subdeck. The program which follows may be for compilation, assembly or immediate use. Let us examine just the latter case.

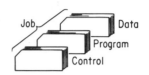

$\mathscr{SYSTEM}$ turns over control to $\mathscr{LOAD}$, which finds out that the program to be run is coming in on the control IO device. It loads the program from there into the computer memory.

FIGURE 13.1.2. All job information may enter on the control IO.

Control is turned over to the program which has built into it the knowledge that incoming data appears on the control IO device.

The difficulty with this scheme is that both the program and the loader must distinguish among incoming cards:

- The loader must know when it has read the last program card so that it does not mistake program for data or control information.
- The program immediately has available data cards, so it seems to have no problem; yet there is one: it must be sure that cards which *follow* the data are not mistaken for data.

Both of these problems may be handled with characteristic punches in specific columns of the cards. The ability to distinguish them must be built into the program and the loader.

The description of Fig. 13.1.2 is applicable even if an intermediate medium conversion is an installation convention. In this case, each card of the job subdeck is converted into a card image and properly formatted by a conversion routine before it is presented to the supervisor. The control input is, hence, in the form of magnetic tape rather than punch cards. This may be a boon rather than a hazard, since blocking and formatting may solve, at least to some extent, the problem of distinguishing between program and data control.

Job Information, Longer Programs

Programs for execution may be so long that it is desirable to have them transcribed earlier and placed on other input devices. Another alternative stores such programs either in job libraries or program libraries (these two cases are distinguished in Section 13.4). One situation is pictured in

Fig. 13.1.3. Control information is presented to $\mathscr{SYSTEM}$ on the control input unit by cards or card images, as discussed earlier. One of these in-

FIGURE 13.1.3. The program may enter from the job library, JOBLIB.

structions is to the system or sub-system where program information is to be found. Since program information is found elsewhere, we do not find a program file in the job subdeck.

The input data for the program immediately follows the control in-formation. Note that it is still encumbent upon the program to distinguish between its data and forthcoming control information for the next job.

Large EDP Jobs

For EDP applications with several inputs and/or outputs, a different organization is preferable. In Fig. 13.1.4 we see the multiple inputs and outputs to the over-all system. Again control information comes in on a control input device. This gives full information to $\mathscr{SYSTEM}$ and the subsystems regarding device assignments. These assignments are in symbolic form, although they may also include the physical correlates for the symbolic devices named.

In the situation pictured, the control cards tell $\mathscr{SYSTEM}$ that the program for the job is found in the job library, giving a location or at least a name. Three input units are needed for the problem and two output

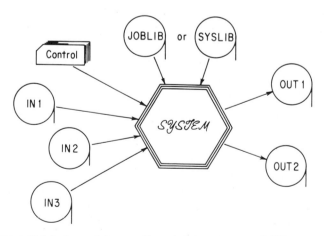

FIGURE 13.1.4. Large jobs may have separate noncontrol IO sources for program, input data and output results.

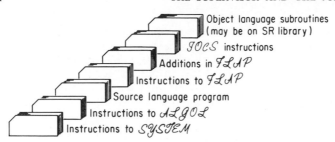

Object language subroutines
(may be on SR library)
$\mathscr{IOCS}$ instructions
Additions in $\mathscr{FLAP}$
Instructions to $\mathscr{FLAP}$
Source language program
Instructions to $\mathscr{ALGOL}$
Instructions to $\mathscr{SYSTEM}$

FIGURE 13.1.5. A large job involving $\mathscr{ALGOL}$ and $\mathscr{FLAP}$ may require many subdecks to describe it.

units are necessary. Label and control information is necessary so that the operator can be instructed to load the proper tapes, and so that the computer can verify if the operator has done what is required.

MULTITRANSLATION JOBS

Figure 13.1.5 shows the card input to $\mathscr{SYSTEM}$ when one or more translations are to be done. We see in the figure, in order, subdecks which

1. talk to $\mathscr{SYSTEM}$ giving it translating details
2. talk to the compiler, $\mathscr{ALGOL}$, about its task
3. convey the $\mathscr{POL}$ program to $\mathscr{ALGOL}$
4. talk to the assembler, $\mathscr{FLAP}$, about its job
5. provide additional assembly commands to be added to source program translated by $\mathscr{ALGOL}$
6. talk to $\mathscr{IOCS}$ giving its initialization
7. provide already translated, machine language subroutine for the rest of the program

Depending on the job items 5 and 7 above may be omitted.

Subsystem Alternation

In Fig. 13.1.1 we saw how a job might require that $\mathscr{SYSTEM}$ delegate a task to $\mathscr{IOCS}$. This task is subcontracted to another subsystem, $\mathscr{LOAD}$. At the bottom of the chain we find the job program. The question is whether a line or staff hierarchy should exist. For line organization, delegation proceeds from the top down to the bottom, and each person reports up to his superior with no line of command skipped. The other alternative is to have someone with complete over-all authority to whom each subsystem reports. This is done in some software systems. In this case, $\mathscr{IOCS}$ could not delegate a job to $\mathscr{LOAD}$. It would return control to $\mathscr{SYSTEM}$, which in turn would delegate that job to $\mathscr{LOAD}$. There are merits and demerits to both concepts.

Remainder of the Chapter

The rest of the chapter is devoted to a discussion of the components of *SYSTEM*. One of the most important features of *SYSTEM* is the directory and the tables it maintains. We should know about the use and updating of each one of these tables.

The *Preprocessor* brings in all the control information for *SYSTEM*. It also interprets this information and turns over control to the proper subroutine of *SYSTEM* in order to incorporate the information for future use. One important kind of information incorporated into the tables is that of unit allocation.

The interaction function of *SYSTEM* is that of delegating tasks to subsystems. Hereafter a subsystem, not any one in particular, will be distinguished by the inclusive name, *SUBSYS*. Then *SYSTEM* must delegate a task to *SUBSYS*. When *SUBSYS* is done with its task it usually returns control to *SYSTEM*. We have already noted the case where several jobs are lined up for *SUBSYS*. In this case, when one job is done the next one is initiated without informing *SYSTEM* until we are all done.

Besides the actual delegation of a task, we are faced with the need for bringing *SUBSYS* into memory and turning over control to it. This is a function for the system loader, *SLoad*. You can see that the principle for loading a subsystem can be much simpler than that for loading a program.

The conditions by which we continue a job, or stop it in the middle, are examined. When we decide to break off a job we must also determine to whom control is given. We also investigate the natural and normal ways to terminate jobs.

Finally, we must examine methods for bringing in *SYSTEM* after some destructive event has destroyed part of it. A simpler but as important eventuality is to bring in and set up *SYSTEM* when the computer is first installed and the memory is blank or has trash in it.

13.2   THE CONTENTS OF *SYSTEM*

What is in *SYSTEM*?

Most importantly, *SYSTEM* contains two things:

• tables   • routines

Tables are necessary to store the present state of everything knowable. Everything to be reported on should be stored in summary form in the system tables. These should be readily accessible to

• *SYSTEM*   • *SUBSYS*

The tables are referenceable because the starting point of each is known both to *SYSTEM* and to *SUBSYS*. In fact, a summarization of the tables is available in most *SYSTEM*s. This is a table of contents or, more precisely, a table of tables. It is even possible to have several directories each of which is listed in a master directory.

The tables meet the two qualifications of being compact and accessible. They should be as extensive as possible within the two previous requirements.

Table Talk

To describe the tables which are so important to *SYSTEM*, we should have a good terminology, one which does not make our references ambiguous. This, by the way, is where most manufacturer's descriptions fall down.

Four features of the table should be kept in mind:

- the name of the table
- the location of the table
- the name of the location of the table
- the name of the pointer to the table

To keep these four features distinct, we write them in different type style.

An explanation of these four features can be made at the same time two of the tables so necessary to *SYSTEM* are described:

- The master directory is used to find the other tables.
- The availability table references IO devices of the system by their symbolic assignment.

Features

Figure 13.2.1 illustrates the table features explained below.

NAME

The name is how we, the humans, refer to the table:

- The name of a table appears in the text type face using upper-case letters.
- Tables in *SYSTEM* are prefixed by "S-".
- Example: S-DIRECT is the system directory.
            S-ASSIGN is the assignment table.

START

The starting point of a table is indicated symbolically rather than absolutely, as noted:

- The starting location of a table is the same as the table name.
- It appears in Gothic type.
- Example: S-DIRECT is the location of S-DIRECT.
  S-ASSIGN is the location of S-ASSIGN.

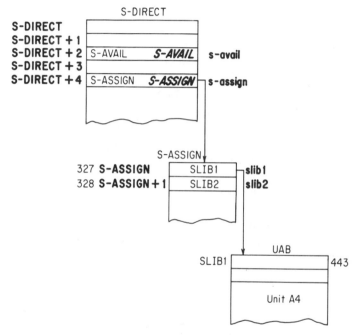

FIGURE 13.2.1. How the directory, DIRECT, points to the system assignment table, S-ASSIGN, with the pointer, S-ASSIGN, located at s-assign. The first system library tape pointer at slib1 is in S-ASSIGN and points to SLIB1

In Fig. 13.2.1 the starting point of S-ASSIGN is the location 327. The name for location 327 is S-ASSIGN.

POINTER NAME

The directory contains pointers to the various tables that it lists. We give names to these pointers:

- The pointer is the same as the table name.
- The pointer is in lower-case Gothic.
- Example: the name of the pointer to S-ASSIGN is s-assign.

In Fig. 13.2.1 the first entry in the directory is s-assign. Another name for this location in the table is S-DIRECT.

NAME FOR LOCATION VALUE

It may seem like splitting hairs to give the value of the location a special name. However, notice that the entry at s-assign is the absolute address of the beginning of the table. We want to refer to this particular value in talking about it. Hence, we use a special form for it:

- The location value has the same form as the table name.
- It appears in upper-case Gothic italics.

S-DIRECT

We now have enough information to review Fig. 13.2.1. The directory contains the locations and maybe the names of each of the tables in *SYSTEM*. It also contains other one-word pieces of information which are summarized in Table 13.2. We are now interested in the table location aspect of the directory.

TABLE 13.2   Contents of the Directory, S-DIRECT

Location name	Use	Location
s-assign	unit-function assignment table	DIRECT
s-uab	UAB location by channel	DIRECT + 1
s-avail	start of availability chain by channel	etc
s-foreman	locations of routines and tables for *FOREMAN*	
s-subsys	locations of each subsystem	
sdate	date	
skeys	key and switch positions for *Coldstart*	
sunits	start of UABs and total number of cells	
sjumps	jumps to various *SYSTEM* routines	
sdump	jump to the routine *Dump*	
sinter	jump to the interrupt routine, *Inter*	
setc	etc.	
ssname	name of current subsystem in control	
ssloc	location of the presently desired subsystem in *SYSLIB*	
ssjump	jump command to the subsystem, when loaded	
sreturn	entry point to *SYSTEM* from a subsystem	
serrtrn	entry to *SYSTEM* when an error has occurred in *SUBSYS*	

One of the tables referred to is the assignment table. This is the fifth entry in S-DIRECT and is at the symbolic location S-DIRECT + 4, otherwise called s-assign. At this location we find the actual absolute address of the table in question, *S-ASSIGN*. The name of the table, S-ASSIGN, may also appear at s-assign. It is now simple to reach *S-ASSIGN* which begins at S-ASSIGN.

The assignment table indicates the physical devices assigned a given symbolic function. The first function listed in the table is the library tape unit. There may be several such tape units, and the first one in our table is the first library tape unit named SLIB1. The name is prefixed by S to indicate that this is $\mathcal{SYSTEM}$ information. It is not hyphenated because it is not a table.

The availability table makes assignments by entering at the corresponding location the address of the unit activity block of the unit assigned this function. We see from the figure that unit A4 has been assigned to the function SLIB1. The name of the pointer for this function is slib1. This is the first slot of S-ASSIGN. This slot is known by the other name, S-ASSIGN, and it is indicated in the figure as having the absolute value 327. The pointer to the UAB is *SLIB1* and it stands for the value 443 in the figure. The symbolic name for 443 is SLIB1. Note that it is possible to change the unit assignments for a given symbolic function. To make this change we alter the cell slib1, entering there the address of a different UAB. The UAB at 443 for unit A4 is no longer assigned to the function SLIB1 and, therefore, the label slib1 does not apply to it. In fact, this location remains unlabeled as long as unit A4 is not reassigned.

No matter how confusing this explanation may seem, imagine how much more complicated it would be if we had not made any distinctions about the names of objects.

The Directory

The contents of the directory is shown in Table 13.2. Entries there are the location, location name and function of each directory item. The directory lists the location of six different tables. Next there is a number of one-word information cells for items such as the date and the start of the unit activity blocks. The table also contains the starting points of the key routines of $\mathcal{SYSTEM}$. These points may be indirectly addressed through these cells in the table.

Another set of cells permits subsystem–system communication. These are prefixed by ss because they deal with the subsystem. The cell *sreturn* contains the return to $\mathcal{SYSTEM}$. It is accessed by $\mathcal{SUBSYS}$ when it has finished its task. The table may also supply an error return for the *subsystem*, such as serrtrn.

Unit Assignment Tables

A diagrammatic view of the interaction of several important tables of $\mathscr{SYSTEM}$ and the unit activity blocks is shown in Fig. 13.2.2.

The most important aspect of an IO device from the point of view of $\mathscr{SYSTEM}$ is its functional assignment. The parallel exists in $\mathscr{IOCS}$ where the physical unit designation gives way to the file assignment which takes precedence. What are the possible functional assignments so far as $\mathscr{SYSTEM}$ is concerned?

* library   * rollback
• system reader   * alternates
• system punch   * utility
• system printer   * etc.

Several functional units may be supplied for those functions which have asterisks.

The assignment table, S-ASSIGN, contains one entry for each possible function and in corresponding multiplicity. Thus, if four library units may be made available, their positions in S-ASSIGN are symbolized as slib1 through slib4.

Each entry in S-ASSIGN contains the absolute location of the UAB for the unit which has been assigned that function. Additionally, for some systems (such as the IBM 7040/44 IBSYS), the location of the file activity block is also found in this word.

In Fig. 13.2.2 some functions may not have units assigned to them. In this case the pointers in the table point to a standard location where 0 is stored (a triangle containing 0).

AVAILABILITY TABLE

To make functional assignments we should know which units are available. It would be rather slow to examine each unit activity block in turn, searching for a free one. Instead, the table S-AVAIL lists the beginning of an availability chain of unit activity blocks—one for each channel. In S-AVAIL, sa is the system pointer for the availability for channel A. In the figure it points to the UAB for unit A1. This UAB in turn points to the UAB for unit A3. The UAB for A3 points to a location containing 0. It can be concluded that for channel A, units 1 and 3 are available. A routine which seeks to obtain an available unit uses a list-manipulation subroutine with which it obtains a UAB for unit A1 and hooks up the availability pointer to point to the UAB for A3.

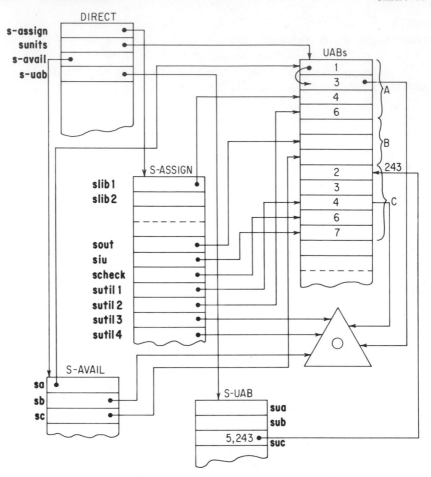

FIGURE 13.2.2. Interrelation of the tables internal to $\mathscr{SYSTEM}$ for keeping track of IO operations and assignments.

THE UAB TABLE

The table, S-UAB stores the absolute starting address of the first UAB for each channel and the number of units available in the configuration for this channel. This information is needed by $\mathscr{FOREMAN}$ for doing dispatching. It is used by the routine $\mathscr{Scan}$.

COMPLETENESS

Notice that all units presently assigned are accounted for in the S-ASSIGN table; all those which are not assigned but are available are accounted for in the availability chain whose start is found in S-AVAIL. There seem to be some unit activity blocks unaccounted for; how so? Some units may be neither assigned nor available. When a unit is down for repair it is not available for any assignment, and the UAB for it should note this fact. However, it is not worthwhile to remove the UAB from the set of UAB's.

The various statuses of IO devices are discussed in more detail in the next section.

13.3 PREPROCESSOR; UNIT ALLOCATION

The Relation of the Preprocessor

The *Preprocessor* is one of the subroutines of *SYSTEM*. It is the mediator between the control information and the other subroutines

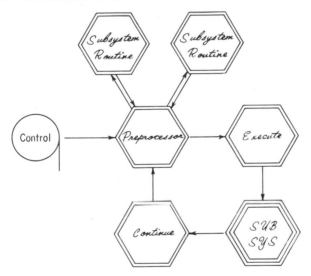

FIGURE 13.3.1. Some routines of *SYSTEM*.

of *SYSTEM*. These subroutines perform the setup services and, in general, carry out the requests entered through the control system. One of these requests is to delegate control to another subsystem. The subroutine to do this is called *Execute*.

Subsystem delegation occurs when a $EXECUTE card is encountered in the control input. The *Preprocessor* recognizes this and turns over control to *Execute* which finds the subsystem requested and turns over control to it. This procedure is illustrated in Fig. 13.3.1.

Return of control follows a reverse path in the subsystem. However, instead of returning to *Execute*, we return to *Continue* where *SYSTEM* determines the disposition of this phase of activity.

After a successful delegation to a subsystem, return is made to the *Preprocessor* where further control information is investigated.

CONTROL INFORMATION

There are four types of information that can enter via the control input to be recognized by the *Preprocessor*. These are classified as:

- operational
- tape manipulation
- miscellaneous
- unit assignment

Although the control entries are referred to here and hereafter as cards, they may be card images which have been transcribed onto magnetic tape by a medium conversion routine. This does not change their nature or philosophy of use.

Operational Requests

This type of request either turns control over to a subsystem or makes a reflexive request of *SYSTEM*. We have the following operational requests:

$$\begin{array}{ll} \text{\$EXECUTE} & \text{\$RESTORE} \\ \text{\$PAUSE} & \text{\$STOP} \\ \text{\$CONTROL} & \text{\$SYSTEM} \end{array}$$

$EXECUTE

This card has the format:

$$\text{\$EXECUTE} \quad \text{subsystem name} \qquad (13.3.1)$$

It requests that control be delegated to *subsystem name*. This request is referred to the subroutine *Execute* (Section 13.4).

$PAUSE

This request has the format:

$$\text{\$PAUSE} \quad \text{operator instructions} \qquad (13.3.2)$$

It causes the computer to stop and print out the operator instructions, indicating that when the operator has fulfilled the instructions he should press the start button, at which time the computer starts again. This request depends upon the routine *Pause*, which is part of *FOREMAN* (Section 11.5).

$CONTROL

This request has the format:

$CONTROL   source of new control instructions   (13.3.3)

This request makes possible a change in the source of control instructions. Thus, if we are reading information from the card input device but wish new instructions to come from a given tape, we enter the symbolic name of this tape unit in *source of new control instructions*. This request affects the *Preprocessor* and, as we would expect, the switchover is performed entirely by the *Preprocessor*.

$RESTORE

This request has the format:

$RESTORE   *blank*   (13.3.4)

It resets the internal tables of *SYSTEM* to a known standard, enabling a programmer who is unaware of the activities preceding his acquisition of the machine to reset the system and then modify it to his own needs. This is done by the routine *Restore* (Section 13.5).

$STOP

This request appears when no further information is forthcoming on the control unit—when all the jobs for the computer have been completed. It has the format:

$STOP   *blank*   (13.3.5)

It calls into play the routine *Stop* of *FOREMAN* (Section 11.5).

$SYSTEM

The purpose of this request is to turn over control to *SYSTEM* when *some other system* is in control. This request is submitted to *SUBSYS* to be recognized by the preprocessor for *SUBSYS*.

This request is very similar in effect to one we have seen already in connection with *IOCS*. After a program has been set up using *IOCS* and it is running, it should not be terminated by the command STOP. Instead, we should make a call to the subsystem *IOCS* using:

GET   IOCS   (13.3.6)

The format for a request for $SYSTEM is:

$SYSTEM   *blank*   (13.3.7)

When this is encountered by the $\mathscr{IOCS}$ preprocessor (for instance, when it reads in the next control card), it will turn over control to $\mathscr{SYSTEM}$. This topic is discussed a little further under, $\mathscr{System}$, Section 13.5.

Tape Requests

There are three possible tape requests. These are formatted as follows:

$EOF	functional unit name	(13.3.8)
$REWIND	functional unit name	(13.3.9)
$REMOVE	functional unit name	(13.3.10)

The purpose of these commands seems evident. They require the issuance of nondata requests to the physical unit corresponding to *functional unit name*. This requires a possible translation, lockup procedure in the S-ASSIGN, and the entry of a nondata select using $\mathscr{FOREMAN}$.

Miscellaneous

$DATE

This furnishes today's date via the entry sdate in S-DIRECT by a subroutine in $\mathscr{Preprocessor}$.

$PRINT MESSAGE

This is a request for the *message* to be printed with $\mathscr{Print}$ of $\mathscr{FOREMAN}$ (Section 11.4).

$UNITS

This is a request to print a list of the functional units and the physical units which have been assigned to these functions. It requires a small subroutine to reinterpret S-ASSIGN using $\mathscr{Print}$ of $\mathscr{FOREMAN}$ (Section 11.4).

$LIST

This card has the format:

$LIST   ON *or* OFF   (13.3.11)

It is similar in function to the LIST and UNLIST commands associated with FLAP and discussed in Section 8.3. It simply requests that the control cards be listed (ON) or that we stop listing these cards (OFF). Listing uses $\mathscr{Print}$ of $\mathscr{FOREMAN}$, of course.

$ACCNT

This request contains no address field:

$ACCNT   *blank*   (13.3.12)

It calls for the system accounting routine to analyze the job just performed.

Unit Assignment

Before we can investigate the unit assignment requests, it is important to understand how the unit assignment and status is recorded and in what status a unit can exist.

UNIT STATUS

We define statuses available to a unit as:

- **referable:** a unit has been defined as existing for the system. A system with 12 magnetic tape units would indicate as referable, 12 or maybe even 14 units, to be on the safe side. For each unit, a unit activity block is established. The UAB is maintained within *SYSTEM* even when the unit is mechanically detached from the system.
- **detached:** a referable unit, disconnected, perhaps for repair.
- **attached:** a physically connected but symbolically disconnected unit.
- **available:** no assignment has been made but the unit is *available* for assignment.
- **assigned:** a functional assignment has been made in one of these general categories:

  * system * job * utility

RECORDED STATUS

Granted that these various statuses exist, how do we know what status a unit presently occupies?

- A unit is referable if a UAB for it has been established in *SYSTEM*.
- Bits in the UAB indicate whether the unit is detached, attached or assigned.
- An attached unit may be made available if we link it to the availability chain for that channel.
- A unit is assigned to a function if we list it in the corresponding entry in S-ASSIGN.

A unit may be assigned a functional task in one of two fashions:

- The programmer gives it a specific assignment through control messages to $\mathcal{SYSTEM}$.
- An assignment is made by $\mathcal{SUBSYS}$.

We have seen how $\mathcal{Assign}$ in $\mathcal{IOCS}$ will make functional assignments if permitted (see Section 9.4).

Unit Assignments through Control Cards

A number of control requests make possible assignment and reassignment of units, as given below.

$ATTACH

Two commands are available to indicate when a physically disconnected unit has become connected and when a connected unit has been disconnected through incapacity or any other reason. These requests have the format:

$$\$ATTACH \qquad \text{physical unit} \qquad\qquad (13.3.13)$$

$$\$DETACH \qquad \text{physical unit} \qquad\qquad (13.3.14)$$

We accomplish this request by changing bits in the corresponding unit activity block. The routines for doing this are described later.

$AS

When the $AS request follows the $ATTACH card, it indicates that the physical unit mentioned on the $ATTACH card should be assigned the function described on the $AS card, which is formatted as:

$$\$AS \qquad \text{functional unit name} \qquad\qquad (13.3.15)$$

$RELEASE

This request has the format:

$$\$RELEASE \qquad \text{functional unit name} \qquad\qquad (13.3.16)$$

It requests that the physical unit assigned to *functional unit name* be released from that function and placed in the availability chain.

$SWITCH

This request has the format:

$SWITCH functional unit name, functional unit name (13.3.17)

It is desired here to interchange the units assigned to the two *functional unit names*. The physical unit assigned the first function is now assigned the second function, and vice versa.

Routines

There are two classes of assignment requests, and we indicate two routines to take care of these classes: $\mathscr{PUnit}$ and $\mathscr{SUnit}$.

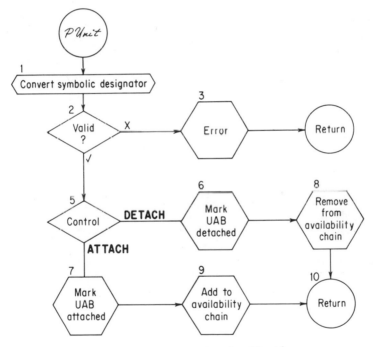

FIGURE 13.3.2. Flow chart for $\mathscr{PUnit}$.

$\mathscr{PUnit}$

The simple routine to handle the requests $ATTACH and $DETACH is illustrated in Fig. 13.3.2. First the symbolic designation found on the card is converted to its BCD equivalent, for that is the way it must appear in order to be found in the proper tables (1). We check to see if this unit is valid—if it is referable (2). If not, there is an error (3).

Next we find the unit activity block by going to S-DIRECT and entering it at location s-uab. This takes us to the table S-UAB. We now look down the list at the cell corresponding to the channel of the designated unit. For instance, if the unit being attached or detached is C4, we look at location suc in the table S-UAB. This location contains the absolute address of the first UAB which is referable on Channel C, as well as the number of UAB's referable for that channel.

We can see more vividly the process outlined so far by referring to Fig. 13.2.2. The cell suc contains the numbers 5 and 243. There are 5 units referable on Channel C; the first UAB, the one for unit C2, appears at absolute location 243 in memory.

The next task is to examine UAB's, beginning at location 243, to check their number. This provides the validity check also: the unit is invalid if it is not found in the unit activity block chain.

When the unit activity block is found (4) we check to see if we wish to detach or attach the unit. We set the bits in the unit activity block accordingly (5), (6), (7). Attaching an already attached unit or detaching an already detached unit has the effect of a NOOP.

Now a detached unit is removed from the availability chain (8) or an attached unit is added to the availability chain (9). This completes the task and we return to the *Preprocessor* (10).

S Unit

The symbolic unit assignments are made by the routine *S Unit*, which is not illustrated. When $AS is encountered, first we find S-ASSIGN and look therein for *functional unit name*. We enter there the *physical unit* dealt with on the previous card. We now go back and find the unit activity block for that physical unit and change its status from attached to assigned.

$RELEASE is handled in the reverse fashion. For $SWITCH we need not tamper with the unit activity blocks. All we have to do is reverse the entries for the two *functional unit names* in S-ASSIGN.

Preprocessor

The *Preprocessor* for *SYSTEM* does not require much discussion because we have already examined a preprocessor for *IOCS* (Section 9.4). Recall that the preprocessor supervises the reading of a control card, entering the information into an analysis cell. The card title is locked up in a card-title table. If there is no match, an error is indicated.

The entry in the card (title table) indicates the routine to which the *Preprocessor* turns over control. This routine takes over and performs the control function.

13.4   THE SYSTEM LIBRARY

What Is the System Library?

The system library, abbreviated as SYSLIB, contains a copy of all the important systems and subsystems. The library is best discussed by enumeration; it contains:

- *SYSTEM*—an original copy of the supervisor including both the nucleus and the operating portion.
- *FLAP*—our assembler is in *our* SYSLIB
- *ALGOL* ⎫ one copy of each compiler
- *COBOL* ⎬ called for by *SYSTEM* must
- *FORTRAN* ⎭ reside in SYSLIB.
- *LOAD*
- *JOES*
- important programs coded in absolute machine language from a subset of SYSLIB which we call PROLIB.

Notice that in this itemization *SYSLIB* and *PROLIB* appear in the text type face. This is because a library is not a software—it is a collection of software. Further, the program library is a collection of programs, not software. Recall our distinction between software and other kinds of programs: programs are used to solve problems directly; software has to deal with the problems created by programs and is not usually meant to solve external problems directly.

The contents of SYSLIB are constructed so that they are:

- easily locatable   • easily loadable   • easily usable

To make them easily locatable the library may be preceded by a table of contents wherein is listed each of the subsystems and programs. Each entry includes how far from the beginning of the tape the program may be found and of how many records it consists.

To make subsystems easily loadable, we usually write them in absolute binary. This means that the absolute location of a word is associated with it on the tape. All the system loader *SLoad* has to do is to enter the word in the prescribed cell.

To make the programs more easily usable, they are written in the library in machine code.

Kinds of Programs

At this point it is well to emphasize the distinction among various sets of object programs. We distinguish three such sets:

PROLIB   JOBLIB   SRLIB

PROLIB

PROLIB is a subset of SYSLIB with frequently referred-to programs which have been debugged and are in good running condition. They are not relocatable, and hence cannot be easily called for by other programs. They are complete entities which are immediately available to be run. For an EDP installation we find the payroll program in PROLIB. In the scientific installation a complete stress design problem might be found in PROLIB.

JOBLIB

At the other extreme, we find the programs coming in on today's job tape. These may include object language programs which are infrequently run and are required today by some particular user. Object programs are in relocatable form and may call upon other programs which either follow on JOBLIB, are brought in on some other unit or are referred to from SRLIB.

Object language programs on JOBLIB may be mixed in with a number of other entities. We find there, of course, source language programs for compiling or assembling.

SRLIB

Programs in SRLIB must be relocatable because they are referred to by other programs and cannot occupy the same space that the calling program does. Further, they must be in a standard subroutine format for the installation.

It is possible to contain SRLIB within SYSLIB. However, this is a bad policy because programs from SRLIB are loaded by $\mathcal{LOAD}$, whereas $\mathcal{SUBSYS}$s are loaded by $\mathcal{SLoad}$. For our system, SRLIB is a set completely separate from SYSLIB.

Getting to SYSLIB

Any subsystem or program stored on SYSLIB is available to $\mathcal{SYSTEM}$ with a $EXECUTE control card. This includes:

- $\mathcal{SUBSYS}$s   • PROLIB

The $EXECUTE request calls in *SLoad*. It is now necessary to reference the subsystem table, S-SUBSYS. We might expect that this table is available in memory at this time, but it is too large and would occupy expensive space. Hence it is usually placed at the beginning of SYSLIB. *SLoad* loads S-SUBSYS into memory and looks up *name* from $EXECUTE to find the location of the desired subsystems or program. S-SUBSYS also gives the number of records that makes up the subsystem.

Bringing in the Subsystem

SLoad now has enough information to locate the desired subsystem. The information obtained from s-subsys was placed directly into two locations of S-DIRECT, namely, ssname and ssloc. The latter cell contains the number of records counting from the beginning of SYSLIB, and also the length of *SUBSYS* in number of records.

Now *SLoad* gives a number of successive read commands as nondata initiates through *FOREMAN*. In this way, SYSLIB is advanced to the beginning of the desired subsystem.

With SYSLIB properly positioned we read *SUBSYS* into the memory using initiate commands directly through *FOREMAN*. The record format for SYSLIB is dependent upon the manufacturer and the installation. Usually it has these characteristics:

- It is headed by a directory.
- It is in absolute binary.
- It is of variable record length.

For computers where variable record length does not have an upper limit, the complete subsystem can be loaded by one read command.

Since *SUBSYS* is normally in absolute binary, it is not relocatable. In fact, starting-point information is included with the record to indicate to *SLoad* where the first word is to be entered. This must jibe with the design of *SYSTEM*. In S-DIRECT under the heading ssjump is the starting point of any *SUBSYS*. If this is not identical with the load point inherent in the *SUBSYS* record, then *SUBSYS* will not be entered properly.

SYSLIB access is designed with simplicity in mind. Therefore, *SUBSYS* should be loaded into memory without much trouble. When *SLoad* has determined that *SUBSYS* is safely in memory, it turns over control to it. The load point is known to *SLoad* through ssjump, which is indirectly addressed through an unconditional jump to release control to *SUBSYS*.

PROLIB Job Programs

We have noted that frequently run programs may be incorporated into PROLIB which is a subdivision of SYSLIB. To be placed therein, these programs should:

- be properly debugged
- include all subroutines
- be written in absolute binary

Once a programmer has loaded and run a relocatable program satisfactorily and he feels it has enough importance to be included in PROLIB, then he may request an absolute binary program dump. At some later date the formerly relocatable program in this form can be reloaded as though it were just another $\mathscr{SUBSYS}$. One precaution that must be exercised is that the beginning of this program must be the same as that indicated by ssjump.

Using $\mathscr{SEdit}$, we enter the absolute binary program that was just dumped into PROLIB.

To rerun this program the operator uses a $EXECUTE card containing the subsystem name (it must have one). When $\mathscr{SEdit}$ enters the program into PROLIB, it must also update the SYSLIB table of contents, S-SUBSYS, so that $\mathscr{SLoad}$ may find the desired program without an interminable search.

Note that changes in $\mathscr{SYSTEM}$ may require relocation of all the programs in SYSLIB if the change advances or retards the location indicated by ssjump.

13.5   INTERPLAY OF $\mathscr{SYSTEM}$ AND $\mathscr{SUBSYS}$

Completeness of Delegation

Let us see the picture right now. $\mathscr{SYSTEM}$ has received a $EXECUTE card containing a system name. $\mathscr{SLoad}$ has entered $\mathscr{SUBSYS}$ into memory. Then it turned over control to $\mathscr{SUBSYS}$. What is the extent of control exercised by $\mathscr{SYSTEM}$ at this moment? Probably either:

- none   • partial and indirect

The extent of control depends upon the computer and the software design.

INDEPENDENT SUBSYSTEM

The subsystem is completely independent of $\mathscr{SYSTEM}$ when:

- there is no real-time clock or interrupt system
- this feature is available but has been suspended

In this case $\mathscr{SUBSYS}$ will grind on until one of the following occurs:

- the operator intervenes
- the task is completed
- a catastrophic error occurs
- an error return is made

RETURN FROM AN INDEPENDENT SUBSYSTEM

No program is allowed to be assembled so that it ends with STOP. The assembler substitutes a return to $\mathscr{SYSTEM}$. This is the normal return and permits $\mathscr{SYSTEM}$ to take over, inform the operator of its success, and permit new jobs to be sequenced. When error returns are included they act in a similar way; however, they inform $\mathscr{SYSTEM}$ of a failure and permit it to pass this information to the operator.

A catastrophic error, by definition, means that the program goes wild and gets out of control. This needs no elaboration.

All systems permit operator intervention. This may be facilitated by software, but hardware intervention is by the simple expedient of pressing the stop button. The operator may restart through software or may enter a jump into the instruction register, which takes the computer to the desired entry to $\mathscr{SYSTEM}$ or $\mathscr{SUBSYS}$.

PARTIAL INDEPENDENCE

When a real-time clock is in the system, it can cause the termination of a program which tries to run into overtime. This may be done through a special timing routine or that routine may be contained in $\mathscr{SYSTEM}$.

When there is a $\mathscr{FOREMAN}$ in the system he monitors IO errors. When a disabling error turns up, the $\mathscr{FOREMAN}$ may not return control to the subsystem but may, instead, pass it over to $\mathscr{SYSTEM}$. Normal and error returns to $\mathscr{SYSTEM}$ still prevail in a $\mathscr{SUBSYS}$ with partial control.

Returns to $\mathscr{SYSTEM}$

FROM PROLIB

A simple program in PROLIB usually only has two choices:

- normal   - error

Trouble is not expected and when it occurs, it is usually catastrophic, causing the program to go berserk and possibly clobbering $\mathscr{SYSTEM}$.

BONA FIDE $\mathscr{SUBSYS}$

For a complicated subsystem which has its own preprocessor and monitor, there is more flexibility provided. For instance, for a compiler like $\mathscr{ALGOL}$ or an assembler like $\mathscr{FLAP}$, its job is to perform a translation. It gets its instruction from control information. It is common to request several translation jobs at once. The assembler may produce a successful translation. It so indicates and goes on to the next job. *It does not return control to* $\mathscr{SYSTEM}$ *if more jobs are waiting.*

The same is true if an *error in translation* is detected. $\mathscr{SUBSYS}$ may terminate the translation process for this job, indicating the error condition; but it does not return control to $\mathscr{SYSTEM}$ if there are other $\mathscr{SUBSYS}$ jobs waiting.

Note that it has successfully completed its subtask, although the subtask presented insurmountable difficulties. When this $\mathscr{SUBSYS}$ has no more jobs to do, it returns control to $\mathscr{SYSTEM}$, provided that it is told to do so by a control card.

It is possible for $\mathscr{SUBSYS}$ to get into trouble due to itself and not to the data or programs with which it is working. In this case it may very well return control to $\mathscr{SYSTEM}$ without being so requested by control information. For instance, suppose it is told that programs for translation will be found on SUTIL1. When it looks there for the programs it finds this functional unit unassigned. It is helpless and must return to $\mathscr{SYSTEM}$ with such an indication.

Of course, it is possible to make a mistake when transcribing $\mathscr{SUBSYS}$ into memory, and $\mathscr{SUBSYS}$ may go wild and get out of hand. This usually calls for operator intervention.

$\mathscr{SUBSYS}$ **Control**

The major subsystem maintains control in advancing from one job to another by using instructions that it receives from its own preprocessor.

The question now arises regarding *SUBSYS*'s powers of delegation. In other words, during the operation of one subsystem, is it possible for that subsystem to request the intervention of another subsystem? If so, how completely is control relinquished?

We have seen an example of this in Section 9.3 with respect to *IOCS*. Here the subsystem *IOCS* is called in. It establishes the operating condition by use of $FILE cards and through the object program. Eventually the object program must be loaded through the use of a $JOB or $LOAD card. In either case *LOAD* is called in to enter the program into the memory.

After the object program gets control of the computer, the question arises: To whom does the object program report—especially when it gets into trouble? It could report to *JOAD* or *LOCS* or *SYSTEM*. Any one of these alternatives is alright, provided this is the way we have planned it.

In some software systems, just as in some businesses, there is a sole authority through which all delegations must take place. In such systems *IOCS* cannot delegate the loading task to *LOAD*; it returns control to *SYSTEM*, which must read in a $1LOAD card and then turn over control to *LOAD*. This is more or less the technique used in the IBM 7040 supervisor IBSYS. This eliminates all hierarchical problems and makes the source of power unambiguous.

Because of the constant alternation of control, there may be a diminution of efficiency. With a more complex set of rules it is not difficult to establish, for instance, that an object program, loaded by *LOAD*, under the direction of *IOCS*, reports to *IOCS* when an error occurs.

Subsystem Transitions

We review the kinds of jobs a subsystem may encounter.

SUBSYSTEM RUN

When several jobs are presented to a subsystem, it maintains control and performs the transition from one job to another. Thus, several FORTRAN translations without assembly are done by *FORTRAN* as it maintains control.

MULTISUBSYSTEM JOB

An ALGOL job for translation and running is a multisubsystem job. If *ALGOL* should detect an error, it indicates this to *SYSTEM*, which prevents either *FLAP* or *LOAD* from being called in. Similarly, if *FLAP* detects an error, it prevents *LOAD* from being called in.

For a multisubsystem job, control usually passes from *ALGOL* to *SYSTEM* and from *SYSTEM* to *FLAP*, for instance, rather than from *ALGOL* to *FLAP*. In this way *SYSTEM* can use the information presented by *ALGOL*, to determine if *FLAP* should be called in or if the job should be aborted.

MULTIDATA PROGRAM

The multidata program is much like the multijob run. Here the same program is to be run with several sets of data. The means of transition between data sets depends upon the program design as well as upon *SYSTEM*. For instance, a multidata program using *IOCS* looks to *SYSTEM* like any other program. Sequencing through the sets of data is done automatically with a READ command wherein an end of file exit is specified. This exit causes the program to wind up and exit to the controlling *SUBSYS* or *SYSTEM*.

On the other hand, small scientific programs often have their data presented through the control input device. In this case the program must return to a preprocessor either in *LOAD* or *SYSTEM* to read in the next set of data.

13.6   COLDSTART: REJUVENATION

What Is a Coldstart?

Loading *SYSTEM* into memory when it is absent therefrom and transferring control to *SYSTEM* is known as a **coldstart**. One might expect that situations where a coldstart is required would be rare. Here is a list of them:

- when the computer system is first installed
- when *SYSTEM* is clobbered by a wild program
- after diagnostics
- after repair
- after alterations in *SYSTEM*

HOW?

How can we make a coldstart easy for the operator? Certainly after one of the listed situations, we wish to get the computer back on the air as soon as possible. Loading of *SYSTEM* requires the intervention of the operator, but we can simplify matters for him. We do this by making sure that *SYSTEM* is the first item to be stored on SYSLIB.

How Does the Operator Use Coldstart?

First, the operator must be sure that SYSLIB is on the proper tape unit, properly mounted and rewound. Next he must bootstrap the records of $\mathcal{SYSTEM}$ from SYSLIB. The procedure for doing this depends upon the computer. One possibility is now described.

A computer such as the IBM 7090 has a special load-tape key. This can be used to read one record of magnetic tape directly into memory, starting at location 0. The operator presses this button, also indicating the tape unit on which SYSLIB is stored. The load point for the record is the bottom of storage, location 0. The load tape button may cause an automatic jump to location 0, or the operator may have to press the computer's start button, depending on the computer design.

For variable length records, all of $\mathcal{SYSTEM}$ may now be in storage. For fixed length records, only a segment of $\mathcal{SYSTEM}$ is in storage; when control goes to this segment it supervises the loading of the other segments. Eventually, the routine which puts $\mathcal{SYSTEM}$ back into memory control goes to $\mathcal{Coldstart}$. It initializes and sets up $\mathcal{SYSTEM}$ and turns over control to it.

Tasks of $\mathcal{Coldstart}$

Copies of all the important tables for $\mathcal{SYSTEM}$ are contained in the upper end of memory all the time. The main task of $\mathcal{Coldstart}$ is to transcribe these tables into the proper portion of memory. It must also set up all the internal switch settings as well as the internal registers of the computer. The unit activity blocks have yet to be written, but this is done by $\mathcal{Restore}$.

$\mathcal{Restore}$

When $\mathcal{Coldstart}$ is done, it turns over control to $\mathcal{Restore}$. This routine may be used separately. Its purpose is to reset the tables having to do with IO equipment which may have been changed by a previous command. To do this it transcribes a copy of a standard set of such tables which is stored in upper memory. Thus a standardized assignment is entered into the tables.

We have seen how the physical and functional assignments of units can be changed by control cards. The vulnerability of this method is apparent when the system is taken over by another programmer. He sets up tasks of his own and wishes to make specific new physical and functional assignments and retain some old standard assignments. However, he cannot be sure how the previous user has left the system. He cannot assume that it is in the standard state, but he can restore it to the standard state by using a $RESTORE card before he makes his own alterations. This card turns over control to *Restore*, transcribing the standard table. Now when the user submits his changes, he knows that these changes, if any, will be entered from a standard state.

Although it takes a bit of time to restate the standard conditions, this appears to be better than the two other alternatives:

- The user states *all* the assignments which prevail during his use.
- The software always resets the system.

The trouble with the latter scheme is telling *SYSTEM* when to reset itself. If we wish it to decide when resetting is necessary, then criteria for this decision must be incorporated in *SYSTEM*. This is far more difficult than using $RESTORE.

PROBLEMS

13.1   Rank the functions of a supervisor on page 422 from most important to least.

13.2   Distinguish among *job*, *data run* and *subsystem run*.

13.3   What alternatives are there for supplying the program to the computer? Rank in order of popularity for (a) scientific and (b) EDP.

13.4   Different type faces distinguish these: S-TABLE; s-table; *S-TABLE*; S-TABLE; why? Define each.

13.5   Discuss the need and use of the tables associated with *SYSTEM*.

13.6   Where in the program does one use the following *SYSTEM* directives: $EXECUTE; $PAUSE; $CONTROL; $RESTORE; $STOP; $SYSTEM $DATE; $PRINT; $UNITS; $LIST; $ACCNT. Who uses them?

13.7   What are the possible unit statuses? How is a status changed?

13.8   What is a *functional* assignment? Give examples. How are functional assignments changed?

13.9   Flowchart a *Preprocessor* for *SYSTEM*.

13.10   Distinguish the need and use of these libraries: PROLIB; JOBLIB; SRLIB; SYSLIB.

13.11   Flowchart *SLoad* to be jumped to from *Preprocessor* which finds *SUBSYS* in the library, loads it and turns control over to it (*SUBSYS* is in *absolute*).

13.12 Program $\mathcal{SLoad}$ with FLAP IOCS.

13.13 Flowchart and program $\mathcal{PLoad}$ to acquire and use *absolute* programs in PROLIB.

13.14 Design $\mathcal{PEdit}$ to handle editing of PROLIB. Work up specs, a flow chart and a program.

13.15 Describe alternatives for $\mathcal{SYSTEM}$-$\mathcal{SUBSYS}$ interaction.

13.16 Describe the need and function of $\mathcal{Coldstart}$ and $\mathcal{Restore}$.

13.17 Flowchart and program $\mathcal{Coldstart}$ with IOCS; without IOCS. Why is the latter required?

13.18 What happens when $\mathcal{Coldstart}$ is clobbered? Describe in detail a "start from scratch."

13.19 Design and program $\mathcal{Restore}$ using $\mathcal{IOCS}$.

14

THE LOADER AND ALLOCATOR—LOAD

14.1 THE LOADER

Discussion

The needs of the assembler with respect to the loader were mentioned in Chapters 5 through 8. We noted in Chapter 13 how $\mathscr{SYSTEM}$ interrelated with $\mathscr{LOAD}$. The simple tasks of the loader are:

- bring in the program and the subprograms
- relocate these as required
- find all subroutines called for in the program and subprograms
- allocate space for the subroutines
- bring in the subroutines and place them properly
- link the subroutines and the subprograms together

Program entities to be loaded into memory can enter through several possible sources:

- control IO device
- utility IO device
- the subroutine library

Short programs are presented to $\mathscr{LOAD}$ through the control IO device preceded by a $LOAD card. Short data sequences of data cards may follow.

A program can be loaded from another input device so long as its location, functional or symbolic, is provided to $\mathscr{LOAD}$ through $LOAD. An alternate source is the job library where longer relocatable programs reside.

Tested and debugged programs for problem solution exist on SYSLIB in absolute binary. They are loaded directly through $\mathscr{SYSTEM}$ using $\mathscr{SLoad}$. $\mathscr{LOAD}$ is used only to enter relocatable programs.

The other source of program information is SRLIB from whence only portions of programs are entered. It is just about impossible to treat an entity from SRLIB as a program, for each subroutine contained therein usually requires a parameter list. It is possible to run a single subroutine by imbedding it in a very simple program.

EXPANDED LOADER FUNCTION

Loaders produced by different software manufacturers differ in the extent of the functions they perform. Some of them are so simple that they are little more than a bootstrap. Others include functions which we have allotted to other software. Some of the functions provided in a single expanded loader are:

- handle and maintain symbolic dictionaries
- provide a program edit function to operate through control entries
- manage pools and files for $\mathscr{IOCS}$
- manage COMMON for the assembler
- produce memory maps
- handle program overflow

All these functions are excluded from our loader.

What Makes Life Complicated for *ℒ𝒪𝒜𝒟*?

Our loader performs the simple tasks enumerated at the beginning of this section. What difficulties does it face?

- Maintain a complete cross-reference between the program, sub-programs and subroutines.
- Keep track of multiple entry points to subprograms and subroutines.
- Keep COMMON under control.
- Organize and cross-reference external references.

It is certainly a simple job to load a single program (without subprograms) which contains no subroutine references. A single main program with several subroutine library references presents few obstacles. The problem gets difficult when there is a number of program entities which communicate with each other. There are many variations on this theme:

- One subprogram may call in another subprogram.
- One subroutine may call in another subroutine.
- A subprogram may request a subroutine.
- A subroutine requested by a subprogram may reference another subroutine.
- It is even conceivable that a subroutine may call upon a subprogram.

Still, none of these requests seems difficult to manage. The rub comes in keeping duplicates of either subprograms or subroutines out of the memory: we want only *one of each* in the memory. Each request must be checked against a list of the subprograms and subroutines presently contained in memory. This is further complicated by segments with multiple entries.

Multiple Entries

Some program segments perform a single function: each time we request a subroutine it starts from the beginning and does only one job. However, longer and more versatile sequences can do several jobs. Such subroutines are efficient because they share large subsequences. For instance, the subroutine to find the sine of an angle can also be used to find the cosine. All that is required is a simple adjustment in the angle. The few steps to do this adjustment are either included or omitted, according to which function is desired. As we have seen in Section 8.6, we can assemble subroutines with multiple entry points. We use the pseudo ENTRY to establish these points during assembly.

Suppose that one subprogram of our program requires the sine subroutine and another subprogram requires the cosine. The loader places the sine/cosine subroutine into memory when the request of the first subprogram is detected. It need not re-enter the subroutine when the request for the cosine is detected: the subroutine is already there—the loader must detect that it has two entry points.

The same philosophy prevails about subprograms. These too may have multiple entry points which are recognized by $\mathscr{LOAD}$. Management of multiple entries requires recourse to a directory described later.

COMMON

COMMON is used to facilitate intercommunication among subprograms and the main program. Information defined as residing in this area is always kept in memory and, hence, is always available to the main program, subprograms and subroutines.

In most systems all information destined for COMMON must be defined and distinguished in the *main program*. Subsequences which have access to portions of COMMON must distinguish data that is accessed and as belonging to COMMON within those subsequences.

When this rule is abided by, no trouble arises; a special section of memory is designated as COMMON storage. Complications may arise when COMMON definitions appear in subsegments that are absent from the main program. Depending upon the sophistication employed, the loader may reject such programs or may have incorporated some means for coping with incomplete COMMON definitions.

External References

During assembly of a subprogram, references outside the subprogram are handled in two ways. GET is used to communicate with subroutines. It establishes an entry in the subroutine jump table and also provides a calling sequence, as described in Section 7.2.

Referencing one subprogram by another, we must refer to labels within the alien subprogram which are not defined in this subprogram. The pseudo EXT indicates that a symbol not defined in this subprogram is defined elsewhere. EXT establishes an entry in the subroutine jump table. It is up to $\mathscr{LOAD}$ to complete this cross reference. Then the local subprogram accesses the alien subprogram indirectly via the subroutine jump table using the reference substituted there by $\mathscr{LOAD}$.

14.2 SEQUENCE OF OPERATIONS

Order of Jobs to Be Done

We present in outline form and in the order of performance the tasks to be done by the loader. Most of these tasks are required by all but the most elementary loaders.

1. Bring in the loader.
2. Clear and reset unoccupied cells in memory.
3. Record the information from the $LOAD card.
4. Record the information from the main program card.
5. Make a directory of COMMON.
6. Enter the main program segment into memory.
7. Establish the required tables:

   * L-ENTRY   * L-REQUEST   * L-PRESENT

Repeated for each subprogram
8. Record the next subprogram card information.
9. Check COMMON entry for this subprogram.
10. Enter the subprogram into memory.
11. Update the tables as required.
12. Make a new table of subroutines which are needed there and not present.
13. Check this against the master subroutine table of contents.

Repeated for each subroutine
14. Record the subroutine header information.
15. Enter the subroutine into memory.
16. Update all tables.
17. Review each subroutine jump table, entering cross references.
18. Destroy the tables and most of the loader.
19. Turn over control to the main program.

It is emphasized that this is not the only sequence but that most of the steps in the sequence are required for most loaders.

What Does Each Program Segment Tell Us?

Each program segment, whether it is the main program, a subprogram or a subroutine, gives information to $\mathcal{LOAD}$:

- The number of cells required for the program.
- The number of subroutines and subprograms that this segment used.
- Erasable storage requirements (not covered here).
- Names by which this segment is known.

- The entry points relative to the beginning of the segment to which these names apply.
- A subroutine jump table.

From the number of cells required for the segment, it is immediately known whether this segment will overflow the present bounds of the program memory. Names and entry points for a segment are required to establish a directory to prevent duplicate segments in memory.

Memory After Loading

Using the sequence of events outlined at the beginning of this section, a map of memory might appear as in Fig. 14.2.1. A different map would result from either

- a different task sequence
- different software allocation
- different sequencing of the available space

At the bottom of memory are the tables and residual portion of 𝒮𝒴𝒮𝒯ℰℳ. Other required software, such as parts of 𝒥𝒪𝒞𝒮 are also found here. Right above this residual software is the **base load point**, the place where the first step of the main program is inserted. This is probably the first entry in the main program subroutine jump table.

The main program extends from the base load point. The next free space after the main segment is loaded is called the **main program break**. The first subprogram is loaded beginning at this point.

Each subprogram and subroutine has a **load point**, the absolute location where the first step in the program or subroutine jump table is placed. The absolute location of the next available cell after the subsegment ends is called the **subprogram break** or the **subroutine break**. The constituents of a subsegment are shown in Fig. 14.2.2.

After the last subroutine in memory, there is some room where trash appears—nothing has been loaded there for the present program, nor is it occupied by software. The top of memory may contain software. Below this software, if any, is a COMMON region for intercommunication between subsegments.

Empty Memory

The section of memory in Fig. 14.2.1 which was said to contain trash (X'ed) was probably used to hold 𝓛𝓞𝓐𝓓 while it was performing its function. Also, the various tables and directories may have been stored in this

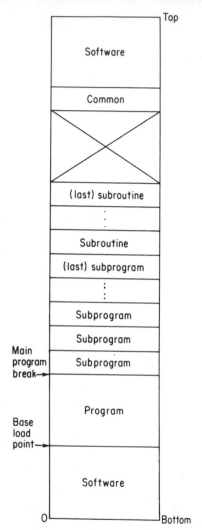

FIGURE 14.2.1. A map of memory at run time, after loading, showing the main program, subprograms, subroutines and software.

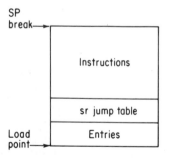

FIGURE 14.2.2. The constituents of a subsegment of a program at run time.

area. Some loaders may simply leave this trash where it is when the object program takes over. A more effective way to deal with this area is to place unconditional jumps to an error routine contained in $\mathscr{SYSTEM}$. In this way, should the program go wild and jump to one of these trash locations, another jump will take it to $\mathscr{SYSTEM}$ for curative action. It is a simple task requiring very little time to write UCIs in the trash area providing this simple precautionary device.

Load Tables

An accumulation of information must be placed at the disposal of
$\mathscr{LOAD}$ in order for it to fulfill its purpose:

- entry points and their names for each subsegment
- the subsegments required at this moment
- the names of subsegments present at this moment
- the names of subsegments absent at this moment
- a directory of COMMON
- the starting point of each subsegment
- the location and length of subroutine jump tables for final review

This information can be compressed into five tables. The names of these
tables are prefixed by L-:

L-PRESENT   L-RQD   L-ABSENT   L-COMMON   L-START

Not all of these tables are present at once, as we see by examining their
functions.

The tables required by LOAD are summarized in Table 14.2.

TABLE 14.2   Tables Constructed by $\mathscr{LOAD}$

Name	Entries
L-PRESENT	begin/enter; name; location; SRJT length; (one for each entry point)
L-RQD	found; name; location
L-ABSENT	name
L-COMMON	symbol name; location
L-START	starting point of SR jump table for those subsegments which have them; length of SR jump table.

L-PRESENT

Each time a subsegment is brought in, one or more entries is made in
L-PRESENT. Each table entry contains the name by which an entry point
is known, together with its absolute location in memory. To make an entry
more useful, it may be tagged to indicate whether this is the beginning of the
subsegment (a main entry point) or whether it is a secondary entry point.
For the main entry point it is useful to have the length of the subroutine
jump table for later review.

The name of a subsegment, so long as it is referred to by any other sub-segment, is found in this table regardless of whether it is present in memory. The table is a list of names. Each entry is tagged to indicate whether the subsegment was found and entered in memory. If so, its location is supplied with the entry.

L-ABSENT

Any subsegment which is required but is not present appears in L-ABSENT. As we shall see, this table is prepared after subprograms are loaded but before subroutines are loaded.

L-COMMON

This table is absent in loaders which rely on the programmer to keep track of his own COMMON. $\mathscr{LOAD}$ keeps track of COMMON, through L-COMMON.

L-START

A later task is a review and cross referencing of subroutine jump tables. L-START is prepared for this purpose.

14.3   PROGRAM LOADING

Memory Reset

When $\mathscr{LOAD}$ takes over it resets memory when this is part of its func-tion. It knows the extent of memory available to the program which, from Fig. 14.2.1, extends from the base load point to the top of COMMON. The reset function is simply the re-establishing of these pointers for some loaders. Into every cell not otherwise occupied is placed a UCJ to a $\mathscr{SYSTEM}$ error point, which we designate simply as SYSERR.

$LOAD

Control is passed over to $\mathscr{LOAD}$ through the $LOAD control card:

$$\text{\$LOAD, deck name, source} \qquad (14.3.1)$$

Source indicates to $\mathscr{LOAD}$ the IO device from where the program in-formation emanates. When the program information is entered on the control IO device, *LOAD* must be able to distinguish the program and subprograms from the data and from other upcoming programs. To do this we enter at proper intervals one of the appropriate cards:

$LOAD $DATA $JOB

Each subprogram is prefixed by a $LOAD card. The data set is preceded by $DATA. A new program is preceded by $JOB.

PROGRAM DECK

Each program and subprogram deck contains:

- a program card bearing the title *deck name*
- the subroutine jump table
- the subprogram proper

PROGRAM CARD

We take as an example of a program card the one used for BELFAP, the Bell Telephone Laboratories' version of the FORTRAN Assembly Program. The following items are contained in the card. When a program has several entry points, the "program card" may consist of several physical punchcards.

- name—this should be equivalent to *deck name* of $LOAD
- length of the subroutine jump table
- number of program steps
- length of *COMMON*
- one pair for each entry point
         * entry name   * step number

LOAD Preprocessor

The *LOAD Preprocessor* first examines information coming into it on the control IO unit. From this unit it enters information on the $LOAD card. The *Preprocessor*, in addition to recording the information, pays attention to it. That is, it notes *source* and thereby determines where it will next find control information.

Next the *Preprocessor* reads information from *source*. The first card is customarily the program card, and we assume that it contains the information itemized earlier. Before examining another card, the *Preprocessor* incorporates the program card information.

PROGRAM LENGTH

If the program or subprogram to be loaded exceeds available memory, we should stop right now. To check this, the number of subprogram steps is added to the present load point setting. This is checked against the maximum break point. Another cell should store this quantity which indicates the upper limit of available storage. We keep track of this upper limit by counting down from the lowest cell storing software in the upper limits of memory. The area below the software is reserved for COMMON, as shown in Fig. 14.2.1. The maximum load point is hence one less than the lowest COMMON cell.

Another precaution observed is that the $\mathcal{LOAD}$ tables are not obliterated by subprogram or subroutine loading. This reduces the maximum load point further.

COMMON

For most systems COMMON only requires handling for the main program, for only there may COMMON definitions be made. Occasionally systems permit extension of COMMON by subprograms. COMMON assignments are handled by moving the maximum break point downward according to the length supplied in the program card.

SR JUMP TABLE

The technique described here loads each subprogram and each subroutine before setting up the cross references required in the SR jump table. To facilitate a review of each subprogram, an entry is made in L-START, indicating the starting point of the main program and each subprogram or subroutine, together with the number of entries in the SR jump table as described in Section 14.5.

ENTRY POINTS

Since the subprogram being entered may be known by several names, all these must be posted into L-PRESENT. $\mathcal{LOAD}$ may then know that another subprogram which references this subprogram by one of its other names already has its need met.

Subprogram Load

Having finished handling the information from the program card, we begin loading. The first thing encountered is the subroutine jump table. SRJ entries are placed in cells starting at the load point which is advanced by 1 for each entry.

The need for the subroutine whose entry we have just loaded is posted into L-RQD regardless of whether the request is for a subprogram already loaded or for a subroutine yet to be loaded. The entry in L-RQD is tagged to indicate whether this entry arose from a SRJ or from the assembly of EXT.

In the technique we are describing, it is not necessary that the location of the SR jump table entry be placed in L-RQD. This information may facilitate later review if another scheme for review is employed. As each SR jump table entry is processed, the number of entries to be processed is decremented. This indicates when all the entries are processed and allows us to proceed to the program proper.

Each step that follows is entered at the cell indicated by the load point, and this point is then advanced by 1. Loading continues regardless of whether items loaded are commands or data reservations. Whenever a COMMON definition is encountered, it is checked with the COMMON table for consistency.

Loading continues until a $LOAD, $DATA or $JOB entry is encountered. The $LOAD card indicates that another subprogram follows directly. A $DATA or $JOB card indicates that all subprograms have been loaded and subroutines may now be brought in.

Subprogram Postload

It is now possible to verify if the number of steps in the program was correctly recorded on the program card. If this does not check, an error can be printed out; but it is not a fatal error as long as available memory is not exceeded and loading may continue.

The *Preprocessor* is now re-established to bring in the next subprogram. When either $DATA or $JOB indicates no more subprograms, subroutine loading begins.

14.4 SUBROUTINE LOADING

Presubroutine Load

The presubroutine load phase begins after we note a $DATA card, a $JOB card or an *end of file* record when entry is made by magnetic tape. We cannot start loading subroutines until we know which ones are needed. These are enumerated in a table called L-ABSENT. To fabricate it requires two operations:

- sorting   - matching

The subprograms currently in memory are all listed in L-PRESENT regardless of whether they are needed by other subprograms. All subsequences that are referred to by those subprograms present are listed in L-RQD. Not all entries in L-PRESENT may be required because of the multiple naming convention. Thus a subprogram may have entry points called EDNA, ETHEL and JUDY. It may be referenced by a subprogram of this job only by EDNA; ETHEL and JUDY are never called upon.

A Venn diagram logically showing the makeup of the tables is found in Fig. 14.4.1. Notice that there are some subprograms present and not required, as ETHEL and JUDY in our example; there are some which are present and required, such as EDNA in our example; there are some which are not present but required, such as SIN. It is this last set which is of interest to us at the moment. We need a tabulation, called L-ABSENT, of all subroutines

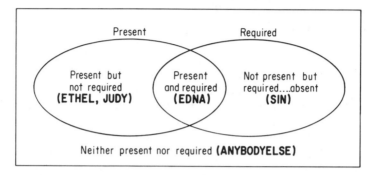

FIGURE 14.4.1. The subsegments; absent is the portion of those required which does not intersect with those present.

required but not present. The diagram shows that we obtain this tabulation by finding all entries in L-RQD for which a corresponding entry is not found in L-PRESENT.

L-ABSENT can be established if we examine entries from L-RQD one at a time. For each entry we must check out *every* entry in L-PRESENT. This is a lot of work; the procedure can be simplified by sorting. With an ordered list for L-PRESENT and L-RQD and a collating operation, it is simple to determine for L-ABSENT all items in L-RQD absent from L-PRESENT.

Check for Absent Subroutines

It would be sad if we started loading subroutines from the list furnished in L-ABSENT only to discover near the end that one of the subroutines could not be found. The job would then have to be terminated after wasting much time loading subroutines.

This waste can be avoided if the subroutine library SRLIB is preceded by a sorted table of contents. The next step is to enter this table of contents into memory for lookup. Our operation is simplified because L-ABSENT is sorted. The entire table of contents for SRLIB need not be present at once; it may be brought in in blocks to be compared with L-ABSENT.

Every subroutine noted in L-ABSENT must be found in the table of contents of SRLIB. In addition, the table of contents may contain information regarding acquisition of the subroutine. The loader may store this information for use when loading each SR listed in L-ABSENT.

When SRLIB does not contain the total complement of SR's listed in L-ABSENT, loading terminates.

Loading the Subroutines

LOAD must now gain access to SRLIB if it has not already done so. Such would be the case when the table of contents for SRLIB is stored separately from SRLIB for quicker access.

The procedure for loading each subroutine depends upon the methodology built into the system. Suppose, for our explanation, that the methodology is to keep SRLIB sorted and to find an SR through a search procedure.

LOAD calls in a search subroutine, such as *Search*, and furnishes it with the next entry in L-ABSENT. *Search* advances records in SRLIB, comparing keys with the name of the desired SR. Because of the initial lookup the subroutine should be present in the library. When it is found, control is returned to *LOAD*.

Each subroutine is headed by a program card identical with that preceding the subprogram:

- name
- SR jump table length
- entry points
- number of program steps
- length of COMMON

Name was used to find the subroutine. The SR jump table length is hopefully 0—then no other subroutines are referenced. When it is nonzero we handle these references by establishing the number of SR jump entries to be reviewed. Before the review we check the number of program steps with the load point to see if enough memory is available.

For SR jump entries we make provision for obtaining the required subroutines if they are not presently in memory. This may be done now or at the end of the load cycle. To do it now we check each SR jump table entry against L-PRESENT. If it is there, well and good; if it is absent, it is entered in L-ABSENT. Since L-ABSENT is sorted, entering the new request requires refabrication of the table if the request is to be placed in its proper position. An alternative is to place the new request at the end of L-ABSENT, making sure that we communicate to the loader where the unsorted segment of L-ABSENT begins.

Each entry in the SR jump table is entered in memory as part of the program, followed by each of the commands of the subroutine, including all data reservations. The load point is advanced as each step is entered. $\mathcal{LOAD}$ knows when the SR has been loaded by comparing the number of steps loaded with the number indicated in the program card. An alternative is to watch for a sentinel, such as all Zs, in the command being loaded.

SR Load Termination

When the sorted part of L-ABSENT has been loaded, the unsorted part must be examined. It may be sorted, checked against the SRLIB table of contents, and the whole procedure reinitiated. The SR load phase is completed when there are no longer entries in L-ABSENT.

Once it has been established that the original SRs required are in SRLIB, loading should continue to completion for two reasons:

- All SRs nested within SRs present in SRLIB should also be present in SRLIB.
- The length in the program card of an SR in SRLIB should be the total length, including any nested SRs, so that the original memory allotment is final and does not depend upon forthcoming inner SRs.

When SRLIB is not set up on this basis it is possible, of course, that space has not been allocated for inner SRs, that late in the SR loading procedure more space may be required than is actually available, and the program must be terminated.

14.5   FINALE

At Present

If we have reached this stage, it is because we have determined that the program, subprogram and all subroutines could fit into memory, and subsequently we have loaded them into memory. If loading would obliterate any of our important tables or the loader itself, we terminate the process. Some loaders provide for an overflow of magnetic tape output. This is not the same as segmentation and does not work nearly as well. We do not discuss this method.

The two tables, L-RQD and L-ABSENT, are now exhausted because the subroutines for all the previous entries in these tables have now been loaded. Every entry point in every subprogram and subroutine now in memory is loaded in L-PRESENT regardless of whether it is referred to at all. The SR jump table for each subroutine and subprogram has been loaded but is not yet cross referenced. To facilitate cross referencing, L-PRESENT is now sorted if this was not already done.

Subroutine Jump Tables

We now refer to L-START which contains the starting point of each subsequence and the length of the SR jump table. For each subsequence, in turn, we perform the cross referencing operation.

We go to the SR jump table for this subsequence and get the first entry. It contains the name of another sequence we have already loaded. We look up the name of this subsequence in L-PRESENT and find the absolute location where it was loaded. This replaces the name of the subsequence in the SR jump table.

The remaining entries in the SR jump table are handled in the same manner. Each jump table for each subsequence is cross referenced thus.

Recall how each subsequence references another. A subroutine call is replaced by the command:

$$\text{JSN,4} \qquad \text{sr jump table entry} \qquad\qquad (14.5.1)$$

We have just replaced the entry in the SR jump table by:

$$\text{UCJ} \qquad \text{sr entry point} \qquad\qquad (14.5.2)$$

In this way, the subsequence gets over to the subroutine through two jumps. Return is no problem since the task is done using the contents of standard index 4.

Reference to data or a subprogram, which has been declared by the pseudo EXT, is done through indirect addressing. Adding a datum from a foreign subprogram is done with;

$$\text{ADD} \qquad \text{data name} \qquad\qquad (14.5.3)$$

Because of a previous pseudo:

$$\text{EXT} \qquad \text{data name} \qquad\qquad (14.5.4)$$

the assembler replaces the command of (14.5.3) by:

$$\text{ADD,I} \qquad \text{sr jump table entry} \qquad\qquad (14.5.5)$$

Finally, the data name appearing in the SR jump table is replaced by $\mathcal{LOAD}$, with the absolute address found in L-PRESENT. This need not be prefixed by UCJ since indirect addressing is used. However, the presence of UCJ in the SR jump table will not affect the process and may be used to standardize the procedure.

Extinguish Phase

The program is now completely loaded and cross referenced. It remains to turn control over to it. This could be done immediately, leaving the loader and the tables that it has fabricated in memory. If the program is properly debugged, it will ignore all this trash and either write over it or have no recourse to it.

However, since not all programs are properly debugged, a precautionary measure is to write over all trash with an unconditional jump to *SYSTEM*, noting a particular rescue location, SYSJMP. This is written over all tables and the loader itself; so nothing remains of the loader except a final transfer to the object program, which begins just past the main subroutine jump table which starts at the main load point. That is the last job of *LOAD* before it drops dead.

PROBLEMS

14.1   How do the duties of the system loader and *LOAD* differ?

14.2   *LOAD* requires a preprocessor *LPrep* to enter control information from $LOAD cards and go to one of *LMain* or *LBring* (see below). Flowchart and program a simple *LPrep*.

14.3   When *LPrep* finds a new program subsegment is to be loaded, *LMain* is called. Flowchart its tasks and program it in FLAP with IOCS.

14.4   When *LPrep* finds no more program subsegments are required, it turns over to *LBring* to get the SRs. Flowchart and program *LBring*.

14.5   *LBring* uses *LSRSearch* to find SRs. Describe, flowchart and program *LSRSearch*.

14.6   Explain the use and preparation of the tables: L-RQD; L-PRESENT; L-ABSENT; L-START.

14.7   *LBring* uses *LReview* to prepare L-ABSENT as it starts and each time L-ABSENT becomes exhausted. Flowchart and program *LReview*.

14.8   Flowchart and program *LExit* which is the transitional routine between *LBring* and the loaded program.

APPENDIX A

REFERENCES

This list is not intended to be exhaustive but rather to guide the reader who feels he needs additional information. The references are divided into three types: *before*, *during*, and *after*.

Before

1. Flores, Ivan, *Computer Programming*. Englewood Cliffs, New Jersey: Prentice-Hall, 1966.

   This book was designed to precede *Computer Software*. It is a generalized approach to the programming of digital computers. It emphasizes the basic principles and does not particularize to one machine. It uses graph theory to present the principles of organization of the program. The mnemonics for FLAP are developed here. There is also a chapter on character oriented machines particularly pertinent to the IBM 360, the RCA Spectra 70 and the Honeywell 200 series. Much of the information required for *Computer Software* and presented in *Computer Programming* is summarized here in the first three chapters. However, additional material and a much more thorough treatment on the following topics are found: arranging data and using them in loops; organizing data in lists and using list structures, including threaded lists; ordered lists and sorting and merging in order to produce them; specification of input and output processes; buffering; an introduction to software; a comparison of assemblers and compilers.

2. Sherman, Philip M., *Programming and Coding for Digital Computers*. New York: John Wiley, 1963. 444 pp.

   This is about the best introduction to programming I know of. It includes quite a bit on assembly language programming, using the IBM 7090 FAP as a sample language. It is especially useful because of the thoroughness with which many topics are presented. Information on

471

storage allocation and error analysis is available. Introductory remarks on ALGOL and FORTRAN are found here. Pseudos and macros are discussed and an introduction to how the assembler operates is given.

3. McCracken, D. D., *Digital Computer Programming*. New York: John Wiley, 1957. 253 pp.

4. Jeenel, Joacain, *Programming for Digital Computers*. New York: McGraw-Hill, 1959. 517 pp.

5. Ledley, R. S., *Programming and Utilizing Digital Computers*. New York: McGraw-Hill, 1962. 567 pp.

The three books above are also useful to introduce programming and as references.

During

6. Mealy, George, *Operating Systems*. Santa Monica, California: Rand Corporation, 1962. 92 pp.

This document was generated as part of the notes for the University of Michigan Summer Engineering Conference for June, 1962. It is rather hard to get hold of. It contains an excellent description of IOCS and buffering. It has the advantage of discussing such systems in general and at the same time remaining specific about features found in actual systems. The second half of the article is devoted to supervisory systems which are also discussed generally with specific allusions to working systems.

7. Wegner, Peter, *An Introduction to Symbolic Programming*. London: Charles Griffin & Co., 1962. 219 pp.

This is an excellent introduction to FAP for the IBM 7090. In fact, I would say the title is highly misleading despite the value of the book. After an introduction to data, formatting and inputting, the first forty pages discuss the 7090 mnemonics. Examples are presented which are very helpful to understanding. The next section introduces pseudos and shows their use together with mnemonics in making up program segments. The next section is devoted to macros, nested macros and conditional assembly. The emphasis is on the use of these devices and many examples are presented. The final two sections discuss FORTRAN.

The book is especially useful in the application of assembly programming for programming problems; the book does not discuss the operation of the assembler. However, we must understand the use of assembly language before we attempt to construct an assembler.

8. Chorafas, D. N., *Programming Systems for Electronic Computers*. London: Butterworth, 1962. 188 pp.

This is a rather superficial and casual introduction to programming systems. It is narrative in nature and therefore easy to follow. For this reason it serves a useful purpose in introducing the subject, especially when we consider the welter of detail presented in *Computer Software* and elsewhere.

9. Fisher, F. Peter and Swindle, George F., *Computer Programming Systems*. New York: Holt, Rinehart & Winston, 1964. 643 pp.

Here is a detailed discussion of programming systems for several IBM computers. Emphasis is on the IBM 1401 and therefore, since the language is the same, the entire 1400 series is covered. Some information is also presented on the 7074 and the 7094. Much detail is presented about auto coders, macros and IOCSs. The emphasis is on use but there is quite a bit about how the assembler and other programming systems are designed and operate. The main difficulty here, I believe, is that so much information is presented in such a concentrated form that it is hard to note general principles.

10. Corbató, F. J., Poduska, J. W., and Saltzer, J. H., *Advanced Computer Programming*. Cambridge, Massachusetts: MIT Press, 1963. 170 pp.

This book was originally written for a programming class as a problem to the class for writing an assembler called CAP, Classroom Assembly Program. The first forty-five pages of the book discuss the features of the assembler and how they are implemented. To this extent the book is valuable. The rest of the book, over one hundred and twenty pages, is devoted to a printout of the assembler. With patience, this may be of some benefit to the reader.

11. Noble, A. S., Jr., Talmadge, R. B., Hedberg, R., Larner, R. and Dorrance, R. T., "Design of an Integrated Programming and Operating System," *IBM System Journal*. Vol. 2, June 1963, pp. 152–179; Vol. 2, September 1963, pp. 297–327.

These articles discuss the design of a very large programming system which includes an assembler and two compilers as well as a supervisor, loader and IOCS. They are well written and especially useful in conveying the difficult job of integration of programming systems.

12. IBM Manuals. Below is a list of IBM manuals which should be useful to the reader in connection with the text. They are identified only by the title and form number. They may be obtained through a cooperative IBM salesman.

a. IBM 7094 Principles of Operation   A22-6705
b. IBM 7094 FORTRAN II Assembly Program (FAP)   C28-6235
c. IBM 7094 IBSYS Operating System, IBJOB   C28-6275
d. IBM 7094 IBSYS Operating System
       Systems Monitor (IBSYS)   C28-6248

e.	IBM 7094 FORTRAN Operating System	C28-6066
f.	IBM 7094 IBSYS Operating System, IOCS	C28-6345
g.	IBM 7094 Programming System MAP (Macro Assembly Program)	C28-6311
h.	IBM 7094 IOCS Program Systems Analysis Guide	C28-6773
i.	IBM 7094 IBSYS-IOEX Program Systems Analysis Guide	C28-6299
j.	IBM 7040-44 Principles of Operation	A22-6649
k.	IBM 7040-44 Operating System IOCS	C28-6309
l.	IBM 7040-44 Operating System Macro Assembly Program	C28-6335
m.	IBM 7040-44 Operating System Programmer's Guide	C28-6318
n.	IBM 7040-44 Operating System System Programmer's Guide	C28-6339
o.	IBM 7040-44 Data Processing System Student Text	C22-6732

Items *a* through *g* discuss the computer programming systems from the user's point of view. They contain all the information that a programmer needs in communicating to the system and using it properly. Besides this, of course, the programmer needs practice and a general understanding of where the programming systems fit in with his program.

Items *h* and *i* discuss the construction of IOCS, the supervisor and the foreman. They give detailed flow charts.

Items *k* through *n* are the manuals for the 7044 system. They are organized in a different way. The Programmer's Guide (*n*) gives a general overview of the programming systems. The Systems Programmer's Guide assumes knowledge of the Programmer's Guide and gives what details of the programming systems are required for a proficient systems programmer to alter the system to the installation's need. Item *o* is a student text which gives a simplified view of the computer and the programming systems associated with it.

13. Bauer, Gloria N. and Gigliello, M. A., *IBM* 7094 *Systems Manual for IBSYS, IOEX, IOCS*, IBM Publication 7090-PRG-35, 1962.

This is a step-by-step explanation of the flow charts in the programming systems analysis guides. It is hard to come by for it was written to be given for a course in programming systems at the Eastern Regional Office.

After

14. Wegner, Peter, Editor, *Introduction to System Programming*. New York: Academic Press, 1964. 316 pp.

15. International Computation Center, Rome, *Symbolic Languages in Data Processing*. New York: Gordon and Breach, 1962. 849 pp.

These two volumes are collections of articles on programming systems. Over 90% of them deal with procedure oriented languages and their translators-compilers.

16. Halstead, Maurice H., *Machine-Independent Computer Program*. Washington, D.C.: Spartan Books, 1962. 267 pp.

This volume discusses the construction of a specific compiler for a specific language, NELIAC, which is a version of ALGOL. Since many of the principles set forth here are general in nature and clearly presented, this is a valuable book for anyone who finds it necessary to write a compiler.

APPENDIX B

FLAP DIRECTIVES

(FLores Assembly Program)

Command	Meaning	Section
	Simple Pseudos (sp)	
ORG	Set object program origin to address	5.3
RGN	Define region of *address* items	5.3
DEF	Define symbol as *address*	5.3
END	END of program	5.3
EQL	Set *label* and *address* as equal	5.3
RSRV	Reserve a block called *label* starting at *address*	5.3
CMNT	Comment	5.3
NRSRV	Change number cells reserved for *label* from *address 1* to *address 2*	5.3
	Programmer defined Macro Pseudos (pdm)	
MCDEF	Begin macro definition	6.2
MCEND	End macro definition	6.2
MCSTOP	End sequence of nested macros	6.6
LEVEL	Inner macro assembly complete	6.6
	Assembly defined macros (am)	
GET	Insert calling sequence	7.2
SAVE	Insert index and indicator saving sequence	7.2
ERROR	Insert error sequence	7.3
	Repeats (rpt)	
DUP	Duplicate following source statements	8.1
MCDUP	Duplicate macro defined sequence	8.1
	Processing within assembly (pwa)	
IFTRU	Conditional assembly, following command	8.2
IFALS	Conditional assembly, following command	8.2
SET	Assign *address* to *label*	8.2

476

List (list)

UNLIST	Stop listing	8.3
LIST	Begin listing assembled commands	8.3
LINE	Skip line, printout	8.3
PAGE	List next step on next page	8.3
CNTRLST	List "list" pseudos	8.3
CNTRLOFF	Stop listing pseudos	8.3
MCXPND	List all steps in macro call	8.3
MCNTRCT	Stop listing steps in macro call	8.3
ABS	Perform absolute assembly	8.3

Segmentation (seg)

COMMON	Data for common pool	8.4
HEAD	Prefix all labels with address	8.4

Data Definition (def)

ETC	Continuation of information from previous card	8.5
DEFOCT	Define octal data	8.5
DEFDEC	Define decimal data	8.5

Miscellaneous (misc)

MBS	Perform absolute assembly	8.3
MCSYMB	Prefix created symbol with *character*	8.6
ENTRY	Subroutine entry at *address*	8.6
EXT	External symbol not otherwise defined	8.6
COUNT	There are *number* cards in the SL program	8.6

APPENDIX C

FLAP DIRECTIVES (alphabetic)

Command	Meaning	Type	Section
ABS	Perform absolute assembly	misc	8.6
CMNT	Print out *comment*	simple	5.3
COMMON	Data for common pool follows	segment	8.4
CNTRLOFF	Stop listing pseudos	list	8.6
CNTRLST	List *list* pseudos	list	8.6
COUNT	*Address* is number of source steps in program	misc	8.6
DEF	Define *label* as *address*	simple	5.3
DEFDEC	Define decimal data	simple	8.5
DEFOCT	Define octal data	simple	8.5
DUP	Duplicate following source statements	repeat	8.1
END	End of source program for assembly	simple	5.3
ENTRY	Subroutine entry at *address*	misc	8.6
EQL	Set *label* and *address* as equivalent symbols	simple	5.3
ERROR	Insert error sequence in object program	assy	7.4
ETC	Previous command fields are continued at *addresses*	misc	8.5
EXT	External symbol not defined in source program segment	misc	8.6
GET	Insert calling sequence	assy	7.2
HEAD	Prefix all labels and addresses with *address*	segment	8.4
IFALS	Assemble next command if *relation* is false	process	8.2
IFTRU	Assemble next command if *relation* is true	process	8.2
LEVEL	Internal indication that inner macro assembly is complete	macro	6.6
LINE	Skip a line in the printout	list	8.3
LIST	Begin listing assembled commands	list	8.3
MCDEF	Begin macro prototype definition	macro	6.2
MCDUP	Duplicate the defined sequence within the macro	macro	8.1
MCEND	End the macro prototype definition	macro	6.2
MCNTRCT	Stop listing the steps with a macro call	list	8.3

MCSTOP	End sequence of nested macros	list	6.6
MCSYMB	Prefix assembler created symbols with *address*	misc	8.6
MCEXPND	List all steps within a macro call	list	8.3
NRSRV	Change the number of cells reserved for *label* from *address 1* to *address 2*	simple	5.3
ORG	Set the origin of the object program to *address*	simple	5.3
PAGE	List next step of the assembled program on the next page	list	8.3
RGN	Define region	simple	5.3
RSRV	Reserve a block called *label* of *address* cells	simple	5.3
SAVE	Insert index and indicator saving sequence in object program	assy	7.3
SET	Assign *address* to *label*	process	8.2
UNLIST	Stop listing the assembled commands	list	8.3

APPENDIX D

CROSS REFERENCE ROUTINES BY FUNCTION

$IOCS$ Routines

Name	Figure	Uses	Used By
Assign	9.4.5		
Attach	9.7.1		
Backspace			Unbuffer
Block Sequence			Request IO
Check Label			Open
Check Sum			Request IO
			Get Full Buffer
Close	9.3.1	Shut	
		I|Exit	
Close Internal	9.8.3	Release	Shut
For Write			Request IO
From Hold			Release
From Pool			RW Command
			RW End
			Request Read
From Put			Release
From Request			Unbuffer
			From Request
From Take			Release
			Unbuffer
			Get Full Buffer
EoF Handler			Unbuffer
Exception			Request IO
Get Full Buffer	10.7.3	From Take	RW Start
		Read Request	RW End
		Check Sum	
		Errprint	
		Activate	
		Release	
		Label	
		Mount	
		Switch	

I|Exit			Open
			Close
			Shut
Job	9.4.3		
Join	9.6.5		
Label			Get Full Buffer
Mount			Get Full Buffer
Open	9.7.2	Read Request	
		Print	
		I|Exit	
		Open Internal	
		Errprint	
		Check Label	
		Request IO	
Open Internal			Open
Pool	9.6.2		
Preprocessor	9.4.1,2		
Print History			Shut
Read, Check Label			
Release	10.7.1	Request IO	Close Internal
		From Take	RW Start
		From Put	RW End
		To Hold	Unbuffer
		From Hold	Get Full Buffer
		Activate	
Request IO	9.5.2	Check Sum	Open
		Exception	RW Command
		Write Internal	Request Read
		To Pool	Release
		Block Sequence	
		For Write	
Request Read	10.6.3	From Pool	Open
		Request IO	RW End
			Get Full Buffer
RW Analyze	10.6.1	RW End	RW Start
RW Command	10.5.1	From Pool	
		Request IO	
		RW Start	
RW End	10.6.2	Read Request	
		Transmit	
		Release	
		To Hold	
		Errprint	
RW Start	10.5.3	Get Full Buffer	RW Command
		Release	
		RW Analyze	

Shut	9.8.2	Close Internal	Close
		Unbuffer	
		Write EoF	
		Write Label	
		Print History	
		I|Exit	
Switch			Get Full Buffer
To Hold			RW End
			Release
To Pool			Request IO
			Unbuffer
			Discontinue
To Request			
To Take			Discontinue
Transmit			RW End
Unbuffer	10.7.2	Release	Shut
		Activate	
		EoF Handler	
		From Request	
		To Pool	
		From Take	
		Backspace	
Write EoF			Shut
Write Internal			Request IO
Write Label			Shut

FOREMAN Routines

Name	Figure	Uses	Used By
Activate	11.7.1	Errprint	Request IO
		Stopdead	Release
		Initiate	Unbuffer
			Get Full Buffer
			Nondata
Dispatch			
Discontinue	11.6.1	From Request	Trap
		To Pool	
		To Take	
Erase Block			Recover
Errprint	11.5.3	Pause	Open
			RW End
			Get Full Buffer
			Trap
			Activate
			Nondata
Initiate	11.6.2		Trap
			Recover
			Activate

INDEX

Pages on which definitions appear are noted in boldface.

Command	Type	Reference	Meaning
XNA	mnem	22	Put contents of index n into a portion of the accumulator
XNM	mnem	21	Put contents of index n into a portion of M
XOM	mnem	4	Fill M with 0's
XPN	mnem	23	Put M directly into index n
Xrs	mnem	1–4	Put the contents of register r into register s
$ACCT	*IOCS*	9.3	Call in the accounting routine giving it *whatever* instruction
$ALGOL	*SYSTEM*	13.1	Turn over to the ALGOL compiler with *directions*
$AS	*SYSTEM*	13.3	*Unit* of previous $ATTACH is labeled *name*
$ATTACH	*SYSTEM*	13.3	Indicate in UAB that *unit* is attached
$COBOL	*SYSTEM*	13.3	Turn over control to the COBOL compiler with *directions*
$CONTROL	*SYSTEM*	13.3	Get new instructions from *source*
$DATA	*LOADER*	14.3	Data follows
$DATE	*IOCS*	9.3	Incorporate the date which is *date*
$DETACH	*SYSTEM*	13.3	Indicate in UAB that *unit* is detached
$EOF	*SYSTEM*	13.3	Write *EoF* on *name*
$EXECUTE	*SYSTEM*	13.3	Turn over control to *name* with *directions*
$FILE	*IOCS*	9.3	The file description occupies *addresses*
$FLAP	*SYSTEM*	13.1	Turn over control to *FLAP* (assembler) with *directions*
$IOCS	*IOCS*	9.3	Return control to the *IOCS Preprocessor*
$JOB	*IOCS*	9.3	Specifications of the job are conveyed
$LIST	*SYSTEM*	13.3	List control cards for on = ON; stop listing for on = OFF
$LOAD	*LOADER*	9.3	Call *LOAD* and provide *option*
$PAUSE	*SYSTEM*	13.3	Stop and print *instructions*; resume when start button is pressed
$PRINT	*SYSTEM*	13.3	Print *message* but don't stop
$RELEASE	*SYSTEM*	13.3	Release unit assigned to *function*
$REMOVE	*SYSTEM*	13.3	Remove from activity the unit, *name*
$RESTART	*SYSTEM*	9.3	Call in *Restart* routine to rollback to proper point
$RESTORE	*SYSTEM*	13.3	Restore *SYSTEM* tables to established standard
$REWIND	*SYSTEM*	13.3	Rewind *name*
$STOP	*SYSTEM*	13.3	Stop!
$SWITCH	*SYSTEM*	13.3	Interchange units assigned to *function 1* and *function 2*
$SYSTEM	*IOCS*	9.3	Return control to *SYSTEM* supervisor *Preprocessor*
$UNITS	*SYSTEM*	13.3	Print out unit assignments by function

ALPHABETIC LIST OF ROUTINES

Name	System	Figure or section
Activate	*FOREMAN*	11.7.1
Assign	*IOCS*	9.4.5
Attach	*IOCS*	9.7.1
Backspace	*IOCS*	10.7
Block Sequence	*IOCS*	10.5
Build	*SERVICE*	12.3.3
Check Label	*IOCS*	9.7
Checksum	*IOCS*	10.5
Close	*IOCS*	9.8.1
Close Internal	*IOCS*	9.8.3
Cold start	*SYSTEM*	13.6
Copy	*SERVICE*	12.2.2
Discontinue	*FOREMAN*	11.6.1
Dispatch	*FOREMAN*	11.2
Editor	*SERVICE*	12.5.5
EoT Handler	*IOCS*	10.7
Erase Block	*FOREMAN*	11.3